Conviction WITHOUT Compromise

NORMAN GEISLER
RON RHODES

HARVEST HOUSE PUBLISHERS
EUGENE, OREGON

Cover by Koechel Peterson & Associates, Inc., Minneapolis, Minnesota

Cover photo © Tschon / iStockphoto

CONVICTION WITHOUT COMPROMISE

Published by Harvest House Publishers
Eugene, Oregon 97402

ISBN-13: 978-0-7394-9548-3

Printed in the United States of America

Contents

Part One: In Essentials, *Unity*

1 —An Overview 7
2 —God's Unity 21
3 —God's Tri-unity 33
4 —Christ's Deity 47
5 —Christ's Humanity 61
6 —Human Depravity 71
7 —Christ's Virgin Birth 79
8 —Christ's Sinlessness 91
9 —Christ's Atoning Death 99
10 —The Bodily Resurrection of Christ 109
11 —The Necessity of Grace 121
12 —The Necessity of Faith 131
13 —The Bodily Ascension of Christ 145
14 —Christ's Priestly Intercession 157
15 —Christ's Bodily Second Coming 167
16 —The Inspiration of Scripture 179
17 —The Literal Interpretation of Scripture 195

Part Two: In Nonessentials, *Liberty*

18 —The Procession of the Holy Spirit 211
19 —Forms of Church Government 219
20 —Grace, Faith, and Works 227
21 —The Extent of Salvation 235
22 —The Candidate, Mode, and Efficacy of Baptism 255

23 —The Nature and Function of Communion 267
24 —The Nature of Sanctification 279
25 —The Use of Musical Instruments in Worship 289
26 —The Nature of Spiritual Gifts 299
27 —The Day of Worship 311
28 —The Order of Second-Coming Events 319
29 —The Role of Women 335

Part Three: In All Things, *Charity*

30 —Lessons from the Past 351
31 —Loving in the Present 359

Bibliography 367
Notes 375

Part One:

In Essentials, *Unity*

In this section we deal with the first third of the dictum, ***In essentials, unity;*** *in nonessentials, liberty; and in all things, charity.* The great essentials of the Faith held in common by all major branches of Christianity are set forth. It is these that we should hold with conviction without compromise. It is these great essentials of the Faith about which it can be said that it is better to be divided by truth than united by error.

1
An Overview

IT IS NOT DIFFICULT TO GET agreement on the venerable dictum, *In essentials unity; in nonessentials, liberty; and in all things, charity.* Disagreements surface quickly, however, when one asks: What *are* the essentials? Because the essential Christian doctrines are the basis for our Christian unity, it is crucial that we be able to identify what these essential truths of the Christian Faith* actually are.

What Makes a Doctrine Essential?

Judging by the doctrines pronounced essential by the historic Christian church, an essential doctrine is one connected with our salvation. For it is these doctrines that are embedded in the great early creeds of Christendom. This definition is confirmed theologically as well, for it is the gospel—defined theologically in Scripture (1 Corinthians 15:1-8; see also Romans 1:16)—that is essential to our salvation. Moreover, there are a number of doctrines that theologically undergird this gospel that saves. The apostle Paul, for example, specifically spelled out three aspects of salvation in Romans 1–8. After discussing our condemnation (chapters 1–3a), he set forth the gospel in three stages: justification (3b–5), sanctification (6–7), and glorification (8). Justification is defined as saving us

* In this book we have chosen to capitalize *Faith* to draw attention to the scriptural use of the term "the faith" to refer to the apostolic teaching and preaching which was regulative upon the church (see Acts 6:7; Galatians 1:23; 1 Timothy 4:1; Jude 3). In the Greek text of Jude 3, where we are told to "contend for the faith," the definite article ("the") preceding "faith" points to the *one and only* faith; there is no other. It is critical that Christians understand the essential doctrines embodied in the Faith.

from the *past penalty* of sin. Sanctification is salvation from the *present power* of sin. Glorification is salvation from the *future presence* of sin.

Now, if an essential doctrine is one that is connected with the gospel, and there are three stages of salvation in the gospel, then the essential doctrines will be those that make these three stages of salvation possible.

How Many Essential Salvation Doctrines Are There?

As we will demonstrate in chapters 2 through 15, the list of essential Christian doctrines for making salvation possible includes the following, chapter by chapter:

2. God's unity
3. God's Tri-unity
4. Christ's deity
5. Christ's humanity
6. Human depravity
7. Christ's virgin birth
8. Christ's sinlessness
9. Christ's atoning death
10. Christ's bodily resurrection
11. The necessity of grace
12. The necessity of faith
13. Christ's bodily ascension
14. Christ's priestly intercession
15. Christ's bodily second coming

Without these being true, there would be no possibility of salvation in the broad, three-stage sense of the word. Just how each is essential to salvation will be detailed in the chapters that follow.

Three Kinds of Essentials

Of course, there are other kinds of essentials than those necessary for salvation. For clarity, at least three kinds of essentials should be distinguished: *salvation* essentials, a *revelation* essential (the inspiration of the Bible), and an *interpretation* essential (the historical-grammatical method of interpreting Scripture).* Let us briefly consider these.

Salvation Essentials

Salvation (or salvific) essentials are those doctrines that make salvation possible. Fourteen of these have just been listed (chapters 2 through 15). Because there are three stages of salvation—justification, sanctification, and glorification—those essentials connected with each particular stage can be delineated.

Salvation from the Penalty of Sin (Justification). Eleven of the salvation doctrines, found in their respective chapters, constitute the basis for God declaring us righteous before Him:

2. God's unity
3. God's Tri-unity
4. Christ's deity
5. Christ's humanity
6. Human depravity
7. Christ's virgin birth
8. Christ's sinlessness
9. Christ's atoning death
10. Christ's bodily resurrection
11. The necessity of grace
12. The necessity of faith

Unless all of these are true, we cannot be delivered from the wrath of an angry God. (We will demonstrate why this is so in each respective chapter.)

---

* To this one might add *moral* essentials (such as the absolute moral nature of God) and even a *preconditional* essential (the doctrine of creation), which is implied in our finitude and fallibility. For the purposes of this chapter, however, we need not discuss these.

Salvation from the Power of Sin (Sanctification). Two salvation doctrines are associated with salvation from the power of sin in our lives (sanctification):

13. Christ's bodily ascension
14. Christ's priestly intercession

Why are these two facts necessary for sanctification? Because Jesus said of His ascension, "It is to your advantage that I go away; for if I do not go away, the Helper [the Holy Spirit] will not come to you; but if I depart, I will send Him to you" (John 16:7 NKJV). The Holy Spirit, of course, plays a central role in our sanctification (2 Thessalonians 2:13; 1 Peter 1:2; see also Romans 8:13).

Moreover, Jesus' ascension to the Father constituted an official completion of His earthly mission of salvation and signaled the beginning of His high priestly ministry on behalf of our sanctification. Indeed, it was by virtue of His blood that He entered heaven on our behalf (Hebrews 9:11-13). And now, at the right hand of the Father, He ever lives to make intercession for us (Romans 8:34; Hebrews 7:25). As the accuser of the brethren, Satan, charges us with our sins before God (Revelation 12:10), Christ our advocate (1 John 2:1) pleads the efficacy of His atoning blood before the Father.

Salvation from the Presence of Sin (Glorification). Chapter 15, "Christ's Bodily Second Coming," is associated with the final stage of salvation. When Christ ascended, the angels foretold His return, saying, "This same Jesus, who has been taken from you into heaven, will come back in the same way you have seen him go into heaven" (Acts 1:11). Christ's second coming signals the final defeat of death, sin, and suffering (1 Corinthians 15:24-26,51-55; Hebrews 2:14; Revelation 21:4). Paul reminds us that presently "the whole creation groans...waiting for the adoption, the redemption of our body" (Romans 8:22-23 NKJV). At the second coming, we will be saved from the very presence of sin: "We shall be like him, for we shall see him as he is" (1 John 3:2). Christ "will transform our lowly body that it may be conformed to His glorious body, according to the working by which He is able even to subdue all things to Himself" (Philippians 3:21 NKJV).

From early times the creeds and confessions of the Faith have made it clear, as Scripture does, that Christ's second coming and subsequent reign will include the separation of the saved from the lost (Matthew 25), the resurrection of the just and unjust (John 5:28-29; Revelation 20:4-6), and ultimately the eternal states of heaven (Revelation 21–22) and hell (Revelation 20). Christ Himself will judge the living and the dead. The Athanasian Creed affirms that at Christ's coming, "all men shall rise again with their bodies; and shall give account of their works. And they that have done good shall go into life everlasting: and they that have done evil, into everlasting fire." Thus, conscious everlasting bliss for the redeemed and conscious everlasting punishment of the unredeemed is part of this essential of the Faith.

Is It Necessary to Believe All the Essential Doctrines in Order to Be Saved? An important distinction must be made at this juncture. There is a difference between a doctrine necessary to make salvation *possible* and one that is necessary to *believe* in order to be saved. All the essential doctrines listed above (contained in chapters 2–15) are necessary to *provide* salvation, but not all are necessary for an individual to *obtain* salvation. More specifically:

- The doctrines in chapters 2 through 12 are necessary for the first stage of salvation to be possible: *justification.*
- The doctrines in chapters 13 and 14 are necessary for the second stage of salvation: *sanctification.*
- The doctrine in chapter 15 is necessary for the final stage of salvation: *glorification.*

It is not necessary, however, to *believe* all of these essentials to be saved (or justified). To clarify, to be saved, it is necessary to believe in one God, that Christ is His Son, that we are sinners in need of God's grace, and that Christ died and rose from the dead for our sins. The other doctrines are *implicit* (implied, though not directly expressed) but not necessarily *explicit* (fully and clearly understood) in what we must believe to be saved.

A Revelational Essential

There is another kind of essential—one that deals with *the source* of knowledge that makes us aware of these fundamentals by which we are saved (chapter 16). This doctrine is not, as such, necessary to believe in order to be saved. But it is the necessary God-ordained source for our knowing about the salvation essentials one must believe to be saved. This revelation essential is the inspiration of Scripture. Since it is the source of the other fundamentals, it has been called *the fundamental of the fundamentals*. Hence, based on the teachings of the church fathers and the Reformers, Old Princetonians such as B. B. Warfield, Charles Hodge, and J. Gresham Machen listed it among the essential doctrines of the Christian Faith.

While one can be saved without believing in the inspiration and (consequent) inerrancy of the Bible,* nonetheless, an infallible and inerrant Bible is the necessary foundation for our Faith. People were saved before there was a Bible, and people are saved through reading errant copies of the Bible, but if there were no original inerrant Bible to begin with, we would not have any sure knowledge about this salvation.†

Thus, while inspiration and inerrancy are not part of the plan of salvation one must believe to be saved, they are part of the foundation that makes that divine plan of salvation *knowable*. Put another way, while inspiration is not a *salvation* (salvific) fundamental, it is nonetheless an *epistemological*‡ (revelational) fundamental. As Thomas Aquinas put it, "in order that salvation might the easier be brought to man and be more certain, it was necessary that men be instructed concerning divine matters through divine revelation."[1] John Calvin added, "Our faith in doctrine is not established until we have a perfect conviction that God is the author [of Scripture]."[2]

It can be demonstrated that belief in the infallibility and inerrancy of the Bible has been the standard view of orthodox Christians down through the centuries.[3] The largest group of evangelical scholars in America, gathered under the umbrella of the Evangelical Theological Society,

---

* We will demonstrate in chapter 16 that inerrancy follows logically from divine inspiration. For if the Bible is the Word of God, and God cannot err, then it follows logically that the Bible cannot err in anything it affirms (or denies).

† Theoretically, God could have used oral tradition to pass on these truths, but He did not because it is less reliable and less certain. A look at biblical history reveals that it was always God's will for His revelations to be written down and preserved for coming generations (see Exodus 24:4; Joshua 24:25-26; 1 Samuel 10:25; Isaiah 8:1; 30:8).

‡ *Epistemology* deals with how we know something is true.

has adopted The Chicago Statement on Inerrancy (1978) as a normative affirmation of their belief.

An Interpretation Essential

Finally, a third kind of essential is presupposed in this whole discussion: an *interpretative* (hermeneutical) essential. For all the essential doctrines relating to our salvation are based on a literal, historical-grammatical interpretation of Scripture. Without this there can be no Christian orthodoxy. Many cults specialize in denying this literal method of interpreting Scripture in part or in whole (see chapter 17). This is how they can so easily twist Scripture to their own heretical advantage.[4] Examples of such Scripture-twisting are presented throughout the chapters in Part One of this book.

The very doctrine of *sola Scriptura* (the Bible alone) is itself based on a literal interpretation* of the Bible.[5] So, the literal hermeneutic is the *essential method* that makes all the *doctrinal essentials* possible. Allegorical and symbolical interpretations of Scripture do not—indeed, *cannot*—yield the orthodox fundamentals. Historically and logically, they lead to heresy and unorthodoxy.

Historical Approaches to the Essentials of the Faith

Throughout church history, a number of important creeds—formal confessions of belief based on Scripture—have been formulated as statements of orthodoxy.† What is significant is that the essential doctrines listed in this chapter also appear in these early creeds of the Christian church. Thus, we have historical confirmation of the theological process by which we have come to the same conclusions.[6] Inserting our chapter numbers‡ (representing their respective essential doctrines) into the earliest creeds confirms this point:

---

* Of course, the literal method of interpretation does not mean there can be no figures of speech. This method states that the whole Bible is *literally true*, just as the author intended it, even though not everything in it is *true literally*. There are parables, metaphors, and many figures of speech in the Bible, all of which convey a literal truth.

† Creeds are not inspired as Scripture is inspired. Neither are they authoritative as Scripture is authoritative. But insofar as they accurately reflect what Scripture teaches, they are helpful "measuring sticks" for orthodoxy.

‡ 2. God's Unity; 3. God's Tri-unity; 4. Christ's Deity; 5. Christ's Humanity; 6. Human Depravity; 7. Christ's Virgin Birth; 8. Christ's Sinlessness; 9. Christ's Atoning Death; 10. Christ's Bodily Resurrection; 11. The Necessity of Grace; 12. The Necessity of Faith; 13. Christ's Bodily Ascension; 14. Christ's Priestly Intercession; and 15. Christ's Bodily Second Coming.

The Apostles' Creed

The roots of the Apostle's Creed began in the second century, and additions have been made in the centuries that followed. All the essential doctrines are found therein:

> I believe [12] in God [2], the Father Almighty, the Creator of heaven and earth, and in Jesus Christ, His only Son, our Lord [3, 4]: Who was conceived of the Holy Spirit [7, 8], born of the Virgin Mary [7, 8], suffered [5, 9] under Pontius Pilate, was crucified, died [5, 9], and was buried. [He descended into hell.]* The third day He arose again from the dead [10]. He ascended into heaven [13] and sits at the right hand of God the Father [14] Almighty, whence He shall come to judge the living and the dead [15]. I believe in the Holy Spirit [3], the holy catholic [universal] church, the communion of saints, the forgiveness [9] of sins [6], the resurrection of the flesh,† and life everlasting [11, 14]. Amen.

It is noteworthy that all 14 salvation doctrines are contained in this earliest of the patristic creeds. Further, the revelational essential (15) is listed as well.

The Nicene Creed (A.D. *325*)

The Nicene Creed likewise contains all 14 essential salvation doctrines:

> We believe in one Lord, Jesus Christ [3, 4], the only Son of God (4), eternally begotten of the Father, God from God, light from light, true God from true God, begotten, not made [4], of one Being [3] with the Father; through him all things were made. For us and for our salvation [11] he came down

* This phrase is not in the earliest forms of the creed, but was added in the fourth century.

† Not until modern times was the word "flesh" gnosticized into "body," a softer word that can more easily be understood in less than a material sense. This is contrary to the whole history of the creed up to and through the Reformation. More importantly, it is contrary to the New Testament (Luke 24:39; Acts 2:31; see also 1 John 4:2; 2 John 7). See N.L. Geisler, *The Battle for the Resurrection* (Nashville: Thomas Nelson, 1989), chapter 6. The neo-orthodox theologian Emil Brunner emphatically declared, "Resurrection of the body, yes: Resurrection of the flesh, no!" (See *The Christian Doctrine of Creation and Redemption: Dogmatics*, vol. 2. [Philadelphia: Westminster Press, 1952], p. 372.) Many neoevangelicals followed suit (see George Ladd, *I Believe in the Resurrection* [Grand Rapids: Eerdmans, 1975] and Murray Harris, *Raised Immortal* [Grand Rapids: Eerdmans, 1985]).

> from heaven, was incarnate of the Holy Spirit [5] and the Virgin Mary [7, 8] and became truly human [5]. For our sake he was crucified [9] under Pontius Pilate; he suffered death [5] and was buried. On the third day he rose again [10] in accordance with the Scriptures [15]; he ascended into heaven [13] and is seated at the right hand of the Father [14]. He will come again in glory to judge the living and the dead, and his kingdom will have no end [15]. We believe [12] in the Holy Spirit, the Lord, the giver of life [3], who proceeds from the Father [and the Son], who with the Father and the Son is worshiped and glorified [3], who has spoken through the prophets [15]. We believe [12] in one holy catholic and apostolic Church. We acknowledge one baptism for the forgiveness [6, 11] of sins [5]. We look for the resurrection of the dead, and the life of the world to come [15]. Amen.

Notice that in addition to the 14 essential salvation doctrines, this creed makes reference to its teaching being "according to the Scriptures" (15) (a revelational essential) as the basis for the salvation doctrines mentioned in the creed.* As well, many of its phrases are taken directly from Scripture, thereby showing its obvious dependence on Scripture.

The Creed of Chalcedon (A.D. *451*)

The Creed of Chalcedon embraces all the essentials of the preceding creeds and adds further definition to the unfolding theological essentials. It stresses the triune Godhead, the virgin birth of Christ, His humanity and deity, as well as the hypostatic unity of His two natures in one person, without separation or confusion. Moreover, the perfection and completion of both natures is emphasized, along with the eternality of the Son, before all time. Also, in accentuating the union of the two natures, the creed calls Mary "the God-bearer" (Greek: *theotokos*) because the person she gave birth to, with regard to His human nature, was also God with regard to His divine nature. The creed also speaks of the revelational essential of Scripture, affirming, "the prophets from the beginning [have

* Various updated translations of this creed have been adopted by different groups, but the general content remains the same.

declared] concerning Him, and the Lord Jesus Christ Himself taught us." Moreover, only by a literal interpretation of Scripture (chapter 17) could the Fathers have arrived at these conclusions.

The Athanasian Creed (After A.D. 451)[7]

The Athanasian Creed affirms the foregoing doctrines (chapters 2 through 15), placing strong emphasis on the deity of Christ (chapter 4). In addition to affirming the essential doctrines of the previous creeds, it emphasizes the Trinity and the incarnation of Christ. Further, it was directed against many heresies. Against Tritheism, it affirms "there are not three Gods: but one God." Against monophysitism (which merged the divine and human natures of Christ) it asserts that there is no "confusion" or commingling of the two natures of Christ. Against the Nestorians (who taught there were two natures and two persons in Christ) it declares there is a "unity" of the two natures in one person. Against Arianism (which denied the absolute deity of Christ), the Son is declared "coequal" in "substance" with the Father, and was not "made" but was "uncreated" and "eternal."

Of course, this also eliminates the heresy of adoptionism, which argued that Jesus was merely a man adopted into the Godhead as Son. Moreover, Apollinarianism, which argued that Jesus was not fully human (having a human body and soul, but lacking a true human spirit), is excluded because it refers to the Son being fully human, a "perfect Man, of a reasonable soul and human flesh subsisting," not partially human.

Finally, this is the first of the creeds to explicitly address the nature of the final judgment after Christ's second coming as leading to everlasting life (heaven) for the saved and everlasting fire (hell) for the lost, thus rejecting both universalism and annihilationism (chapter 15). Once more, the divine authority of Scripture (chapter 16) and its literal interpretation (chapter 17) lie at the basis of these doctrines.

How This Book Is Organized

In this introductory chapter, we have gone to great lengths to define and clarify the essentials of the Christian Faith. Having done this, we now want to give you the basic game plan of our book. Briefly put, the book breaks neatly into three sections, corresponding to the dictum, In essentials unity; in nonessentials, liberty; and in all things, charity. Here's the big picture:

In Essentials, Unity

Part One, which includes chapters 1 through 17, deals with the essentials on which all orthodox Christians have agreed down through the centuries. It is in these essential teachings that the church finds its true doctrinal unity. Indeed, to date every major section of Christendom has assented to these teachings.* It has been correctly noted that what all orthodox Christians have in common is one Bible, two Testaments, three confessions,† four councils, and five centuries. Beyond this, as Part Two of this book observes, there is in nonessentials, liberty.

In Nonessentials, Liberty

Part Two, which includes chapters 18 through 29, is about theological diversity, which, as such, need be no more divisive than ethnic diversity. However, like ethnic superiority, when theological diversity turns to dogmatism in nonessentials, it becomes divisive. So, with the major exception of liberalism, which denies essential doctrines, the problem of true doctrinal unity among all major sections of Christianity has not pertained to the first third of the famous dictum, In essentials, unity. The problem has invariably pertained to the last two parts. The failure to recognize liberty to differ in nonessentials has been one of the great problems plaguing orthodoxy. Indeed, Fundamentalism has constructed nonessentials into essentials, just as surely as liberalism has made nonessentials out of essentials. Both have been divisive.

Historically, for example, the church divided into East and West (A.D. 1054) over the nonessential doctrine of whether the Holy Spirit proceeds from both the Father and Son (West) or from the Father alone (East) (see chapter 18). The doctrine of church government is another nonessential over which many churches have divided. More specifically, the early

---

* The doctrinal essentials have been accepted explicitly by all, and the other two essentials have been either expressed (*revelation*) or implied (*interpretation*) in their teachings as well.

† We refer here to the three early confessions. The fourth, the Athanasian Confession, is omitted.

postapostolic period witnessed the emergence of competing Presbyterian (rule by elders) and Episcopal (bishop over elders) forms of church government. Premedieval times witnessed the emergence of regional bishops over area churches.

This was followed in the medieval church by one bishop of Rome over all churches. By the time of the Reformation and following, all three basic forms of *Episcopal* government (Roman Catholic, Eastern Orthodox, Anglican, and some Lutherans), *Presbyterian* government (Reformed and Presbyterian), and *Congregational* government (Anabaptist) were in full swing (see chapter 19).

The number and nature of the sacraments emerged as a divisive issue during the early Middle Ages and came to a head in A.D. 1215 when the Fourth Lateran Council of the Roman Catholic Church definitively pronounced both seven sacraments and the doctrine of transubstantiation. The division on this issue became apparent when a diversity of views surfaced at the Reformation (chapter 23). Another area of conflict involved the relation of grace and works in salvation. This was the main focus of the Reformation, with Luther insisting that salvation was by *grace alone* through *faith alone,** and the Roman Catholic Church responding that works were a necessary condition of salvation as well (chapter 20). At the same time, Protestants split over whether Christ died only for the elect (Strong Calvinists) or for all men (Moderate Calvinists and Arminians) (see chapter 21). The division over baptism occurred during the Reformation when Anabaptists insisted on adult baptism rather than infant baptism. The practice of baptismal regeneration was also challenged (see chapter 22).

In the late eighteenth century, the traditional doctrine of sanctification was challenged by John and Charles Wesley's concept of Christian perfectionism (see chapter 24). The rise of liberalism in the late nineteenth century drew attention to the importance of fundamental doctrines when radical pietism and antisupernaturalism invaded the church, leading to a denial of the importance and need for fundamental doctrines of the Faith. The restoration movement of Alexander Campbell of the late nineteenth century brought the issue of musical instruments in worship to the fore

---

* Two essential doctrines of Christianity are the necessity of grace (chapter 11) and the necessity of faith (chapter 12).

(chapter 25). This was followed in the early twentieth century by the Pentecostal movement's emphasis on the charismatic gifts (chapter 26). Then Adventists stressed worship on Saturday instead of the traditional Lord's day (chapter 27). This was followed by the controversy over the order of second coming events (chapter 28), and the issue over the role of women in the ministry (chapter 29).

Unfortunately, many throughout church history have not taken these issues as the nonessentials they are, and have therefore failed to show liberty and charity toward those who disagree. Diversity has often turned into divisiveness and dogmatism on issues not essential to the Faith.

In All Things, Charity

As noted above, there has been, in many of these controversies, a tendency by many to forget that these are not essential doctrines of the Christian Faith. Hence, many have ignored the second third of the dictum, in nonessentials, *liberty*. Thus, wise principles such as unity within diversity, diversity without divisiveness, and cooperation without compromise have often been neglected. On the one extreme, orthodoxy has often been expressed without charity. On the other hand, some have shown a propensity to sacrifice orthodoxy for the sake of unity, or they have sacrificed orthodoxy in the name of charity. Still other ecumenically minded proponents have confused uniformity with unity, or diversity with divisiveness.

In all of this there are many lessons to be learned from the history of the church—lessons that can help us overcome these extremes and practice more perfectly the dictum, In essentials, unity; in nonessentials, liberty; and in all things, charity. May the God of truth, love, and peace help us all to learn from church history (chapter 30) and to find this balance (chapter 31). It is to this end that this book has been written.

2

God's Unity

THE DOCTRINE OF GOD IS FUNDAMENTAL to all other doctrines, and the oneness of God is fundamental to the doctrine of God. There are not many gods. Only one God exists. The oneness of God is the consistent testimony of Scripture from Genesis to Revelation. It is a thread that runs through every page of the Bible.

*Monotheism** is basic to all else in theology. It is the heart of the great *Shema* (confession of faith) of Judaism: "Hear O Israel: The LORD our God, the LORD is one!" (Deuteronomy 6:4 NKJV). The Jews of biblical times made a habit of reciting this affirmation twice daily—once in the morning, once in the evening. The importance of the *Shema* is reflected in the Hebrew practice of requiring children to memorize it at a very early age. This same confession was repeated by Christ in the New Testament (Mark 12:29).

The Biblical Basis for God's Unity

The Meaning of God's Unity

Unity literally means "oneness." God is one Being in contrast to many beings. There is one and only one God (monotheism) in contrast to many gods (polytheism). This is one reason the *Shema* was so meaningful to the ancient Israelites. In a world where false gods and idols were worshiped on a daily basis by surrounding pagan nations, the Israelites confessed there was only one true God.

---

* Belief in one God.

Three related words should be kept in mind as we proceed in our study:

1. *Unity*—There are not two or more gods
2. *Simplicity*—There are not two or more parts in God (God is one essence)
3. *Tri-unity*—There are three and only three persons in the one God

Keeping these distinctions in mind contributes to right thinking about the nature of God.

Biblical Texts on God's Unity

The Scriptures affirm God's absolute unity from beginning to end. In the very first verse of the Bible, we are informed, "In the beginning God [not gods] created the heavens and the earth" (Genesis 1:1, insert added). The Hebrew confession, the *Shema,* confirms this oneness (Deuteronomy 6:4). In Exodus 20:3 God thus commands, "You shall have no other gods before me."

God positively affirmed through Isaiah the prophet, "This is what the Lord says—Israel's King and Redeemer, the Lord Almighty: I am the first and I am the last; apart from me there is no God" (Isaiah 44:6). God also said, "I am the Lord, and there is no other" (45:18), and "I am God, and there is no other; I am God, and there is none like me" (46:9).

Jesus affirmed that the most important command is, "Hear, O Israel, the Lord our God, the Lord is one" (Mark 12:29). In 1 Corinthians 8:4, the apostle Paul asserted that "an idol is nothing at all in the world and that there is no God but one." He makes reference to "one God and Father of all, who is over all and through all and in all" (Ephesians 4:6). He affirmed that "there is one God and one mediator between God and men, the man Christ Jesus" (1 Timothy 2:5). James 2:19 likewise says, "You believe that there is one God. Good! Even the demons believe that—and shudder" (see also John 5:44; 17:3; Romans 3:29-30; 16:27; Galatians 3:20).

Answering Objections to Biblical Monotheism

References to God in the Plural

Most biblical objections to monotheism are based on references to God in the plural. It is claimed, for example, that the term "God" itself is plural in form, and God sometimes speaks in the plural, using terms such as "us" or "our" (see Genesis 1:26). It is also claimed that the Hebrew word for "one" (*echad*) can mean "many" (so that "*one* God" can really mean "*many* gods").

In response, it is true that the Hebrew word for God in the Old Testament (*Elohim*) is plural in form (the *im* ending). The term can even be translated "gods" in certain contexts (see Psalm 82:6). However, in those contexts relating to the one true God (which is the majority of cases), *Elohim* is a plural *grammatically,* but not *ontologically* (in being). That is, it is plural in *literary form* but not in *actual reality.* When the term is used of the one true God, it is classified as a "plural of majesty"—pointing to the majesty, dignity, and greatness of God. The plural form gives a fuller, more majestic sense to God's name. Queen Victoria once used a plural of majesty when referring only to herself when she commented, "We are not amused."

The many Old Testament verses that use the term *Elohim* yet declare that God is absolutely one are proof that this plural form is not intended to indicate a plurality in the being of God. For example, the *Shema* uses the term *Elohim:* "Hear, O Israel: The Lord our God [*Elohim*], the Lord is one." The verse points to one and *only* one God.

What about plural pronouns such as "us" or "our" being used of God? We see this in Genesis 1:26, where God says, "Let us make man in our image." Hebrew grammarians tell us that the plural pronouns in the passage are a grammatical necessity. The plural pronoun "us" is required by the plural ending of *Elohim:* "Then God [*Elohim,* plural] said, 'Let us [plural] make man in our [plural] image.'" In other words, the plural pronoun "us" corresponds grammatically with the plural form of the Hebrew word *Elohim.* One demands the other.

Notice the words we've italicized in Genesis 1:26-27: "Then God said, 'Let us make man in *our image,* in *our likeness,* and let them rule over the fish of the sea and the birds of the air, over the livestock, over all the earth, and over all the creatures that move along the ground.' So God created man in *his own image*, in the *image of God* he created him; male and female he created them." The phrases "our image" and "our likeness" in verse 26 are explained in verse 27 as "the image of God" and "in his own image." This supports the idea that even though plural pronouns are used in reference to God, only one God is meant.

As for the Hebrew word for "one" (*echad*), the term can carry the nuance "many in one." For example, in Genesis 2:24 the term is used in reference to male and female being "one" (*echad*) flesh. When used in reference to God, however, the term is best understood as an implication of the Trinity, not as an affirmation of polytheism (the belief that there is more than one God, which is clearly condemned in Scripture—Isaiah 44:7-8; 45:21). More specifically, the "many in one" idea is compatible with the Trinitarian view of three persons within the *one being* of God. So, while not opposing monotheism, the term *echad* does favor Trinitarianism.

The Command Not to Have Other Gods

Some claim the Bible implies there are many gods by the very command not to worship them: "You shall have no other gods before me" (Exodus 20:3). Contextually, however, it is best to take the "other gods" as imaginary beings—namely, gods created by human beings and thus are not genuine. Or, they could be understood as the demons behind these false gods (see 1 Corinthians 10:19), and they are not to be worshiped. The apostle Paul summed it up well:

> We know that an idol is *nothing at all in the world* and that there is *no God but one*. For even if there are *so-called gods*, whether in heaven or on earth (as indeed there are many "gods" and many "lords"), yet for us there is but *one God*, the Father, from whom all things came and for whom we live (1 Corinthians 8:4-6, emphasis added).

References of One Person of the Godhead Talking to Another

There are a number of places in Scripture where one person who is

God speaks to another person who is also God. For example, David wrote, "The Lord says to my Lord, 'Sit at my right hand, until I make your enemies a footstool for your feet'" (Psalm 110:1). Sometimes the Lord (who is God) speaks to the messenger (or Angel) of the Lord (Zechariah 1:12), who is also God (Exodus 3:2,5,14).[1] In the New Testament we see the Father speaking to the Son (Matthew 3:17), and the Son speaking to the Father (Matthew 26:39).

Such verses are easily understood within a Trinitarian framework. According to Trinitarianism, there are three persons in the one and only God (persons who can engage in personal relationships and communicate with others), but there are not three gods (Tritheism). Just as one triangle has three sides but is only one triangle, even so God has three persons but there is one and only one God. God is a *tri-personal* Being, but He is only *one* Being. (We will explore this in greater detail in chapter 3, which deals with the Trinity.)

The Christian Doctrine of God's Simplicity

Early creeds and the teachings of the orthodox Christian fathers insisted on the simplicity of God. By this they meant that God is *absolutely one* in His being, with no parts, poles, or particles. He is *one essence*. So, positing three persons in God seems to be contradictory to His simplicity.

This, however, is a confusion of *persons* and *parts*. Each of the persons are of the very (same) essence of God. They are not separate or separable parts, like three slices of a pie. Just as one and the same stick has two different ends, and yet the ends are of the essence of the stick, even so God has three persons who are of the very essence of God. Yet they differ from each other, just as the different ends of a stick do.

The Theological Importance of God's Unity

The doctrinal importance of the unity or oneness of God cannot be overemphasized. Monotheism is fundamental to everything else in the Bible. There are several reasons for this.

First, monotheism distinguishes God from the false view of polytheism. Religions in the ancient world were predominantly polytheistic. Typically, it was believed that there were a variety of gods and goddesses that were behind the world of nature, controlling rainfall, sunshine, and various events such as military battles. Hence, people went to great efforts to give offerings—sometimes even human sacrifices—to these gods in hopes of placating them. Over against this is the biblical view that there is only one true God who is sovereign over all. The Bible not only consistently sets forth the truth that there is only one God, it also consistently condemns all forms of polytheism.

Second, monotheism distinguishes God from Tritheism, or the view that there are three separate beings (gods) in the Godhead. Monotheism asserts that there is only one Being who is God, not three beings. This one Being is eternally manifest in three co-equal and co-eternal persons who are *equal in substance* (the divine nature) but *distinct in subsistence* (personhood). Hence, God's unity stands against the error of Tritheism.

Third, the unity of God stands against all forms of idolatry. If one and only one Being in the universe is God, then only this Being is worthy of worship. Nothing other than the Ultimate is worthy of an ultimate commitment. To worship more than this one God is idolatry.

Finally, God's unity not only shows His singleness, simplicity, and supremacy of essence, but it is fundamental to virtually all other doctrines in the Bible. For example, when we speak of Christ as the Son of God and the Bible as the Word of God, it is not just *any* god but the *one and only true* God of which we speak. Likewise, when we refer to the virgin birth and resurrection as miracles or acts of God, it is the one and only monotheistic God of which these are said to be special acts. In like manner, virtually every other doctrine has something to do with God, and the unity of God defines specifically and uniquely which God this is.

The Early Creeds on God's Unity

Most of the early creeds were occasioned by denials of some particular biblical teaching. Hence, the history of *orthodoxy* was occasioned by the history of *heresy*. The Apostles' Creed affirms one "God, the Father Almighty, the Creator of heaven and earth." The Nicene Creed explicitly affirms, "We believe in one God, the Father Almighty, maker of heaven and earth." The Creed of Chalcedon agrees, noting they were "following, then, the holy fathers" in this teaching. Although these creeds stressed the deity of the Son, they spoke repeatedly of one "God" in the singular. The Athanasian Creed makes it clear that this teaching is essential to salvation, declaring, "Whoever will be saved, before all things it is necessary that he hold the catholic [universal] faith: which faith except every one do keep whole and undefiled, without doubt he shall perish everlastingly." This, of course, included believing "that we worship one God in Trinity, and Trinity in Unity."

Unorthodox Denials of God's Unity

In each chapter in Part One of this book, we close with a section about unorthodox denials, in which we include a representative sampling* of errant viewpoints on the particular doctrine in question. Our goal is to demonstrate that in view of the tremendous importance the Bible assigns to a given doctrine, modern-day denials of that doctrine are especially heinous and are, in the end, detrimental to those who teach and believe them. As you consider these denials, our prayer is that you—like us—would maintain an attitude of *conviction without compromise* on the essentials of the Christian Faith. And, ultimately, our desire is that you would stand with a long history of orthodox Christians in contending for the Faith that was once for all delivered to the saints (Jude 3).

Certainly the unity of God is an essential for which we must contend, for America's religious landscape is heavily peppered with denials of God's unity.[2] For example, the Jehovah's Witnesses believe in both an almighty God, Jehovah, and a mighty God (a lesser God), Jesus, who was allegedly created by Jehovah billions of years ago.[3] We are told, "Not only is Almighty God, Jehovah, a personality separate from Jesus but He is at all times his superior."[4]

Among the verses Jehovah's Witnesses appeal to is Isaiah 9:6, which speaks prophetically of Jesus as a "Mighty God," apparently not realizing that Jehovah Himself is also called a "Mighty God" in the very next chapter (Isaiah 10:21), thereby demonstrating the equality of Jesus with Jehovah, subsequently lending support to the doctrine of the Trinity. In any event, because Jehovah's Witnesses believe in *two* gods, they have clearly crossed the line outside of Christian orthodoxy.

---

* Space limitations prohibit a comprehensive discussion of *all* deviant viewpoints.

Biblically, of course, Jesus is *eternal* God (John 1:1; 8:58; compare with Exodus 3:14) and has the same divine nature as the Father (John 5:18; 10:30; Hebrews 1:3) (see chapter 4). Indeed, a comparison of the Old and New Testaments clearly equates Jesus with Jehovah (compare Isaiah 43:11 with Titus 2:13; Isaiah 44:24 with Colossians 1:16; Isaiah 6:1-5 with John 12:41).

Another cult that even more blatantly denies the unity of God is the Church of Jesus Christ of Latter-day Saints, also known as the Mormons. Traditional Mormonism teaches that the Father was once a man who, through eternal progression, eventually achieved godhood, as other humans can. Mormonism also teaches that the persons of the Trinity are not three persons in one Being, as historic Christianity has always taught, but rather are three separate beings. In other words, the Father, Son, and Holy Spirit are three separate gods. They are "one" only in their common purpose and in their attributes of perfection.

According to Mormonism, there are innumerable other gods as well. Mormon apostle Orson Pratt once commented, "If we should take a million of worlds like this and number their particles, we should find that there are more Gods than there are particles of matter in those worlds."[5]

Spencer W. Kimball, former president of the Mormon church, likewise made the following remark in a priesthood meeting:

> Brethren 225,000 of you are here tonight. I suppose 225,000 of you may become gods. There seems to be plenty of space out there in the universe. And the Lord has proved that he knows how to do it. I think he could make, or probably have us help make, worlds for all of us, for every one of us 225,000.[6]

In Mormon theology, just as Jesus has a Father, so the Father allegedly has a Father, and the Father of Jesus' Father has a Father. This endless succession of Fathers goes on and on, up the hierarchy of exalted beings in the universe. Joseph Fielding Smith said, "If Jesus Christ was the Son of God, and John discovered that God the Father of Jesus Christ had a Father, you may suppose that he had a Father also."[7] In Mormonism, there is a Father of the Father of the Father of the Father, *ad infinitum*.

Not only are there numerous Father-gods, there is also a heavenly wife (or wives) for each. In 1853, Orson Pratt explained:

> Each God, through his wife or wives, raises up a numerous family of sons and daughters....As soon as each God has begotten many millions of male and female spirits...he, in connection with his sons, organizes a new world, after a similar order to the one which we now inhabit, where he sends both the male and female spirits to inhabit tabernacles of flesh and bones....The inhabitants of each world are required to reverence, adore, and worship their own personal father who dwells in the Heaven which they formerly inhabited.[8]

Of course, a huge philosophical problem for Mormon theology is the claim that each heavenly Father had a Father before him. Such a view sets into motion an infinite regress of finite gods (men who became gods) in eternity past. It is impossible that every heavenly Father has a Father before him, for this view cannot account for a *first* Father that got it all started:

> You can't go on explaining how this finite thing causes this finite thing, which causes this other finite thing, and on and on, because that really just puts off the explanation indefinitely....No matter how many finite causes you line up, eventually you will have one that would be both causing its own existence and be an effect of that cause at the same moment. That is nonsense.[9]

If Mormons based their beliefs *solely* on the Bible as the Word of God (see chapter 16), instead of other books such as the Book of Mormon, and then interpreted the Bible according to the historical-grammatical method (see chapter 17), they wouldn't come up with such absurd doctrines that place them squarely outside of orthodoxy. They would see that the Bible affirms the oneness and unity of God (Isaiah 44:6; 45:18; 46:9; 1 Corinthians 8:4; James 2:19) and condemns polytheism in the strongest possible terms (demonstrated throughout Isaiah 40–55). Note especially Isaiah 43:10, where the one true God affirms, "*Before me* no god was formed, nor will there be one *after me*" (emphasis added). Because there were no gods *before* the God of the Bible, this means God had no Father-gods or Grandfather-gods before Him. And because no gods will come *after* God, this means none of His children will become gods. Such verses make the Mormon viewpoint impossible.

Yet another denial of God's unity may be found in those who advocate both a father god and a mother god. For example, popular modern-day psychic Sylvia Browne—who claims her psychic ability is a gift of the Holy Spirit, and says she does all to the glory of God, and even warns people against the false prophets of which Jesus spoke—espouses both a father god and a mother god (Azna). She says Azna "is the counterpart of the Father, worshipped as His equal and His complement for more than twenty thousand years." The father god is said to be characterized by intellect, whereas the mother god is characterized by emotion.[10] Browne clearly denies the unity of God, even under a Christian guise. Of course we would not expect Browne to hold an orthodox view of God because her entire worldview is engulfed in occultism, which God condemns (Leviticus 19:26; Deuteronomy 18:9-12).

Browne's view is not unlike the neopagan male horned god and mother goddess that are prominent in Wicca. However, most Wiccans add into the mix a vast pantheon of other gods and goddesses. Some Wiccans believe the pantheistic "One" (universal Life Force) is polarized by the female and male deities—the mother goddess (often called Diana, Aphrodite, or Isis) and the male horned god (often called Pan, Adonis, or Apollo). These are dualistic manifestations of the "One."

Amazingly, there is currently a movement emerging known as Christian paganism—aka pagan Christianity—in which individuals participate at some level within the Christian church, but at the same time are practicing pagans who are open to both a God and a goddess. As the one true God has said, however, "I am God, and there is no other; I am God, and there is none like me" (Isaiah 46:9), and, "I am the first and I am the last; apart from me there is no God" (Isaiah 44:6).

We noted earlier that the doctrine of God is fundamental to all other doctrines, and the oneness of God is fundamental to the doctrine of God.

In view of this, we conclude that groups that deny the oneness of God are fundamentally flawed in their entire system of theology.

THEOLOGICAL QUICK-REVIEW

Chapter 2 Main Idea: There is only one God who is *absolutely one* in His being, with no separate or separable parts.

Importance: A correct view of God is foundational to all other theology.

Unorthodox Viewpoints: Groups that subscribe to any form of polytheism or to dualistic Mother/Father gods are outside of Christian orthodoxy.

Course of Action: On the doctrine of God's unity, there must be conviction without compromise.

3

God's Tri-unity

NOT ONLY IS GOD'S UNITY (chapter 2) crucial to orthodoxy, but so is His *tri*-unity. God is not only *one* but He is *three in one*. As we will see, all three members of the Godhead are crucial to the cause of sound doctrine. Indeed, without the tri-unity of God there is no orthodox theology, for the Father, Son, and Holy Spirit each play a crucial role in all the essential doctrines of the Faith.

The Biblical Basis of God's Tri-unity

The Meaning of the Word Trinity

While the *concept* of the Trinity is found in the New Testament (see, for example, Matthew 3:16-17; 28:18-20; 2 Corinthians 13:14), the *term* was not coined until later by Tertullian (b. A.D. 160). The doctrine was defined in the early creeds as a God who is *one in essence* and *three in persons*. As the Athanasian Creed put it, there is "one God in Trinity, and Trinity in Unity....But the Godhead of the Father, of the Son, and of the Holy Spirit is all one, the glory equal, the majesty coeternal....And yet there are not three Gods, but one God." Each member of the Trinity is distinct and yet they are inseparably one in essence.

The Trinity is distinguished, on the one hand, from the heresy of Tritheism, which teaches there are three gods. On the other hand, it is distinguished from the heresy of modalism, which denies there are three distinct persons in God, claiming instead there is only one being who manifests Himself in three different modes. Tritheism denies the absolute simplicity of God's essence, while modalism denies the plurality of the persons in the Godhead. The former claims there are three beings in the Godhead, while the latter denies there are three persons in the one Being who is God.

Biblical Tests Supporting the Trinity

The doctrine of the Trinity is based on two basic biblical teachings: 1) There is one and only one God; and 2) there are three distinct persons who are God: the Father, the Son, and the Holy Spirit. The Trinity is the only logical conclusion from these two premises.

There Is Only One God

The biblical evidence for God's absolute oneness has already been provided in chapter 2, and this evidence need not be repeated here. The point we wish to establish here is that in addition to declaring God to be one in nature or essence, the Scriptures affirm that there are three distinct persons who are God. Each of the three are called God, each possess the same essential divine attributes, and each have the characteristics of personhood.

There Are Three Persons Who Are God

Three different persons are called God in Scripture: the Father, the Son, and the Holy Spirit. Personhood is traditionally defined as one who has an intellect, emotions, and a will. All three of these characteristics are attributed to all three members of the Trinity in Scripture.

The Father is God. Numerous verses speak of the Father being God. Jesus said, "Do not work for food that spoils, but for food that endures to eternal life, which the Son of Man will give you. On him *God the Father* has placed his seal of approval" (John 6:27, emphasis added). Paul added, "To all in Rome who are loved by God and called to be saints: Grace and peace to you from *God our Father* and from the Lord Jesus Christ" (Romans 1:7, emphasis added). And, "Paul, an apostle—sent not from men nor by man, but by Jesus Christ and *God the Father,* who raised him from the dead" (Galatians 1:1, emphasis added).

The Son is God. That Christ is God is affirmed in many passages and in many ways, both directly and indirectly (see chapter 4). In John 1:1 we are told that "the Word [Jesus Christ] was God" (insert added). In John 8:58 Jesus claims to be the great "I AM" of Exodus 3:14. In Hebrews 1:8 we find words spoken by the Father to His Son: "About the Son he says: 'Your throne, O God, will last for ever and ever.'" In Colossians 2:9 the apostle Paul tells us that "in Christ all the fullness of the Deity lives in bodily form." Paul also refers to Jesus as our great God and Savior (Titus 2:13; see also Romans 9:5).

The Holy Spirit Is God. There are many evidences for the deity of the Holy Spirit. First, the Holy Spirit is given names of deity. He is referred to as God or Lord. For example, in Acts 5:3-4, Peter spoke the following words to Ananias in judgment: "Ananias, how is it that Satan has so filled your heart that you have lied to the Holy Spirit....You have not lied to men but to God." In 1 Corinthians 3:16 the apostle Paul exhorts, "Don't you know that you yourselves are God's temple and that God's Spirit lives in you?" Likewise, in 1 Corinthians 6:19 Paul exhorts, "Do you not know that your body is a temple of the Holy Spirit, who is in you, whom you have received from God?" Then in 1 Corinthians 12:4-6 we are told that "there are different kinds of gifts, but *the same Spirit*. There are different kinds of service, but *the same Lord*. There are different kinds of working, but *the same God* works all of them in all men" (emphasis added; see also 2 Corinthians 3:17; Hebrews 9:14).

Second, the Holy Spirit possesses the attributes of deity, such as life (Romans 8:2), truth (John 16:13), love (Romans 15:30), holiness (Ephesians 4:30), eternality (Hebrews 9:14), omnipresence (Psalm 139:7), and omniscience (1 Corinthians 2:11).

Third, the Holy Spirit performs acts of deity, which include the act of creation (Genesis 1:2; Job 33:4; Psalm 104:30), the act of redemption (Isaiah 63:10-11; 1 Corinthians 12:13; Ephesians 4:30), begetting the human nature of Christ (Luke 1:35), performing miracles (Galatians 3:2-5; Hebrews 2:4), inspiring Scripture (2 Timothy 3:16; 2 Peter 1:20-21), and bestowing supernatural gifts (Acts 2:4; 1 Corinthians 12:11).

Finally, the Holy Spirit is associated with God in prayers and benedictions. First Peter 1:2 speaks of "the foreknowledge of *God the Father*, through the sanctifying work of *the Spirit*, for obedience to *Jesus Christ*" (emphasis added). The benediction in 2 Corinthians 13:14 mentions all three members of the Godhead: "May the grace of *the Lord Jesus Christ,* and the love of *God [the Father],* and the fellowship of *the Holy Spirit* be with you all" (insert added, emphasis added). And the baptismal formula of Matthew 28:19 mentions the Holy Spirit along with the Father and the Son, all three subsumed under a singular "name" [=essence]: "Therefore go and make disciples of all nations, baptizing them in the name of *the Father* and of *the Son* and of *the Holy Spirit*" (emphasis added).

All Three Members of the Trinity Are Persons. Each individual member of the Trinity is a person, because each possesses a mind, emotions, and a will.

First, these three elements of personhood are all attributed to the Father. He has intellect (Matthew 6:32), emotions (Genesis 6:6), and a will (Matthew 6:9-10). The Bible also consistently uses the personal pronoun "He" when speaking of God the Father. And personal traits, such as the ability to communicate (John 14:31), are attributed to the Father. Finally, He engages in personal I-thou relationships (John 3:35).

Second, like the Father, the Son has intellect (John 2:25), emotions (John 11:35), and a will (John 6:38). Further, the personal pronoun "He" is used consistently of Him. Finally, He communicates (John 7:17) and engages in I-thou relationships (John 11:41-42).

Third, all the elements of personhood are attributed to the Holy Spirit: mind (John 14:26; 1 Corinthians 2:11), emotions (Ephesians 4:30), and a will (1 Corinthians 12:11). Personal pronouns such as "He" and "His" are used in reference to Him: "But when *he,* the Spirit of truth, comes, *he* will guide you into all truth. *He* will not speak on *his* own; *he* will speak only what *he* hears, and *he* will tell you what is yet to come" (John 14:26, emphasis added). The Holy Spirit even used personal pronouns of Himself: "While they were ministering to the Lord and fasting, the Holy Spirit said, 'Set apart for *me* Barnabas and Saul for the work to which *I* have called them'" (Acts 13:2, emphasis added). Finally, the Holy Spirit engages in actions only a person can do: He searches, knows, speaks, testifies, reveals, convinces, commands, strives, moves, helps, guides, creates, recreates, sanctifies, inspires, intercedes, orders the affairs of the church, and performs miracles (see Genesis 6:3; Luke

12:12; John 3:8; 16:8; Acts 8:29; Romans 8:26; 1 Corinthians 2:11; Ephesians 4:30; 2 Peter 1:20).

All Three Persons Together at Once. In contrast to the heresy of modalism (see below), which claims there is only one person in the Godhead who plays three different roles, several times in Scripture we see all three persons present and operating *at the same time.* For example, in the book of Isaiah we read,

> I will tell of the kindnesses of the LORD, the deeds for which he is to be praised, according to all *the LORD [Father]* has done for us...and so he became their Savior. In all their distress he too was distressed, and *the angel of his presence [Son]** saved them. In his love and mercy he redeemed them....Yet they rebelled and grieved *his Holy Spirit*" (Isaiah 63:7-10, inserts added, emphasis added).

At the baptism of Jesus, all three members of the Trinity were present at once: "As soon as *Jesus* was baptized, he went up out of the water. At that moment heaven was opened, and he saw the *Spirit of God* descending like a dove and lighting on him. And a *voice from heaven [the Father]* said, 'This is my Son, whom I love; with him I am well pleased'" (Matthew 3:16-17, insert added, emphasis added). In the baptismal formula recorded in Matthew 28:19, the three persons of the Trinity are subsumed under a singular name: "Therefore go and make disciples of all nations, baptizing them in the name of the Father and of the Son and of the Holy Spirit." Likewise, in Paul's apostolic benediction, all three persons are present together: "May the grace of the *Lord Jesus Christ,* and the love of *God [the Father],* and the fellowship of *the Holy Spirit* be with you all" (2 Corinthians 13:14, insert added, emphasis added).

Answering Objections to the Trinity

The Trinity Contradicts the Simplicity of God

Since orthodox Christianity affirms that God is absolutely one with

* For proof that appearances of the Angel of the Lord in the Old Testament were preincarnate appearances of Jesus Christ, see Ron Rhodes, *Christ Before the Manger: The Life and Times of the Preincarnate Christ* (Eugene, OR: Wipf and Stock, 2002), chapter 5.

no parts, it is sometimes objected that there cannot be three persons in such a unified Being. To use an analogy mentioned in chapter 2, however, one and the same stick can have two ends. Yet there is only one stick. The two ends are part and parcel of the one stick. Likewise, one and the same triangle has three different corners. The point we are making is that there is no contradiction in affirming both the absolute simplicity of God and His tri-unity. Keep in mind that the doctrine of the Trinity does not divide God into three parts. Rather, each of the three persons in the Trinity is in full possession of the entire divine essence.

The Trinity Is a Logical Contradiction

The most fundamental objection to the teaching of the Trinity is that it violates the law of noncontradiction, which affirms that God cannot be both one and three at the same time. But this argument comes from a misunderstanding of this basic principle of logic.

The law of noncontradiction mandates that for two propositions to be contradictory they must both affirm and deny 1) the same thing, 2) at the same time, and 3) *in the same sense, or in the same relationship.* The doctrine of the Trinity, however, does not affirm that God is both one and three *in the same sense or relationship.* Rather, it affirms that 1) God is one and only one in relation to His *essence,* and 2) God is more than one (that is, three) in relation to His *persons.* Therefore, the Trinity is not contradictory. *Person* and *essence* are different. By person is meant *who* it is, and by essence is meant *what* it is. *Person* is a subjective cognizant center of intentionality and volitionality. *Essence,* by contrast, relates to essential properties and nature. So, by God's tri-unity is meant not that there are *three whos in one who* (which would be a contradiction), but *three whos in one what* (which is not a contradiction). Put another way, there is *one object* and *three subjects.*

Of course, this is not to deny that the Trinity is a mystery that goes *beyond* reason, even though it is not a contradiction that goes *against* reason. That is to say, it is beyond finite ability to *comprehend* how there can be three persons in one nature, but it is not beyond finite ability to *apprehend* the noncontradictory nature of both premises.

It Makes No Sense to Say God Is Both Three and One

Even if the Trinity is not a contradiction, many people have difficulty understanding it because they do not find anything in their experience that corresponds to it exactly. While this may be true, there are some illustrations that are helpful—and some that are not.

Some Bad Illustrations of the Trinity

One oft-used bad illustration is that the Trinity is like water, which has three states—solid, liquid, and gas. The problem with this is that water is not found in all three states at the same time. Yet God is both three and one at the same time. So, despite the good intentions of this analogy, it actually implies the heresy of modalism.

Another bad example of the Trinity is a three-link chain. The problem here is that links are three different things. Despite whatever good intentions may be behind this analogy, it actually points to tritheism (three different gods), not Trinitarianism (three persons in one God). God is one thing (or substance), not three different things joined together in some way.

Yet another bad illustration of the Trinity is that God is like man who has body, soul, and spirit, and yet is one. The problem with this analogy is that the human soul and body separate at death, but the members of the Godhead are inseparable. Further, God has no body. He is pure spirit (John 4:24).

Some Good Illustrations of the Trinity

One helpful analogy is that God is like a triangle which is one figure yet has three different sides (or corners) at the same time. So, there is a simultaneous threeness and oneness. Of course, no analogy is perfect, since in every analogy there is a similarity and a difference. The difference here is that sides or corners are not persons. Nonetheless, a triangle does illustrate how there can be a threeness and oneness at the same time.

Another helpful illustration is that God is like the number 1 to the third power: 1x1x1=1. God is three ones in one. (He is not 1+1+1=3. That would be Tritheism.)

Yet another analogy involves the idea that God is love. Love involves a lover, a beloved, and spirit of love. One advantage of this example is that it involves persons.

Still further, God might be likened to the relation between a person's mind, ideas, and words. They are all one yet distinct. Certainly one's words cannot be separated from his ideas and mind behind them, even though words, ideas, and mind are different.

The Theological Importance of the Trinity

The doctrine of the Trinity is theologically important for a number of reasons. First, as C.S. Lewis once noted, God Himself has told us how to correctly think about Him in His Word, and His Word indicates that He is triune in nature. The primary doctrinal planks of the Trinity—there is one God, the Father is God, Jesus is God, the Holy Spirit is God, and each of the three are distinct persons—virtually permeate divine revelation, especially the New Testament. Second, a proper understanding of the Trinity protects against numerous false beliefs, such as tritheism, modalism, subordinationism (the belief that the Son was inferior in nature to the Father), binitarianism (the belief that there are only two persons in the Godhead), and others. Third, inasmuch as the oneness of God and the absolute deity of Christ are essential doctrines, the Trinity, too, must be considered a correlating essential doctrine. Finally, because the doctrine of the Trinity is necessary to our salvation—with the Father, Son, and Holy Spirit playing distinct roles in the outworking of that salvation—it must be considered an essential doctrine.

The Early Creedal Basis for the Trinity

The Apostles' Creed implies the doctrine of the Trinity, speaking of "one God" which includes "the Father" and "Jesus Christ, the only Son of God...[and] the Holy Spirit." Likewise, the Nicene Creed affirms "one God," which includes "the Father...the only Son of God...[who is] 'of one being with the Father'...[and] the Holy Spirit." The Chalcedonian Creed is even more explicit about the deity of the second person in the Trinity, who is "perfect...in deity" and is "actually God" and "of the same reality as God as far as his deity is concerned," having existed "before time began."

As the Athanasian Creed put it, there is "one God in Trinity, and Trinity in Unity.... But the Godhead of the Father, of the Son, and of the Holy Spirit is all one, the glory equal, the majesty coeternal....And yet there are not three Gods, but one God."

Unorthodox Denials of the Trinity

It almost staggers the mind to contemplate the number of ways the Trinity has either been denied, distorted, or misinterpreted throughout church history. Early in church history, Arius (d. 336), a presbyter of Alexandria who was the founder of Arianism, argued that the Son was created from the nonexistent, and was of a different substance than the Father. There was a time, Arius argued, when the Son was not. Christ, he said, was the highest of all created beings. Athanasius of Alexandria, the champion of orthodoxy, stood against Arius and stressed the oneness of God while maintaining three distinct persons within the Godhead. He correctly (biblically) maintained that the Son was the same substance as the Father, and was hence fully divine. A mediating position was set forth by Eusebius of Caesarea, who argued that the Son was of a similar substance with the Father. After considerable debate, Athanasius won out and Christ was properly recognized by a council as being on a level with the Father as an uncreated Being, thereby supporting the doctrine of the Trinity.

Modalism—the idea that Father, Son, and Holy Spirit are modes of manifestation and not persons—is another heresy that surfaced early in church history. Sabellius, a third-century proponent of this view, taught that the Father was God's mode of manifestation in the work of creation and the giving of the law; the Son was God's mode of manifestation in the incarnation and work as the Redeemer; and the Holy Spirit was God's mode of manifestation in regeneration, sanctification, and the giving of grace. Sabellius was condemned in A.D. 263 for his teachings. Paul of Samosata, another advocate, was condemned in A.D. 269.

These early heresies are worthy of study because they laid the groundwork for the emergence of more modern cultic denials and distortions of the Trinity. For example, the Jehovah's Witnesses followed the lead of Arius in arguing that Jesus was created from the nonexistent (as the archangel Michael), and was of a different (lesser) substance than the Father. They go on to argue that the doctrine of the Trinity is based on the paganism of the ancient Babylonians and Assyrians. The folly of this position becomes evident when it is realized that the Babylonians and Assyrians believed in *triads* of gods who headed up a pantheon of many other gods. These triads constituted *three separate gods* (polytheism), which is utterly different from the doctrine of the Trinity, which maintains there is only one God (monotheism) with three persons within the one Godhead.

The Oneness Pentecostals followed the lead of Sabellius in arguing that Father, Son, and Holy Spirit are modes of manifestation. They argue that the word *Trinity* is not in the Bible, and that Scripture speaks of only one God (Deuteronomy 6:4; 1 Timothy 2:5). They concede that Scripture calls the Father God (Malachi 2:10), the Son God (John 1:1), and the Holy Spirit God (Acts 5:3-4), but their conclusion is that Jesus is the one God who is the Father, the Son, and the Holy Spirit. In Bible passages where three persons are present simultaneously, such as the baptism account of Jesus in Matthew 3:16-17, Oneness Pentecostals bizarrely argue that different modes of Jesus are being manifest at the same time: Jesus was the Son who was being baptized, He was the Father who spoke from heaven, and He was the Holy Spirit who descended on the Son. This is eisegesis at its worst.*

One must note that the lack of the word *Trinity* in the Bible is no more an argument against the doctrine than the absence of the word *Oneness* in the Bible is evidence against Oneness theology. The central issue is, *What does Scripture teach?* We have demonstrated earlier in this chapter that Scripture clearly teaches the Trinity (for example, Matthew 28:19; 2 Corinthians 13:14). One theologian thus wisely asks: "If I believe everything the Bible says about topic X and use a term not found in the Bible to describe the full teaching of Scripture on that point, am I not being more truthful to the Word than someone who limits themselves to only biblical terms, but rejects some aspect of God's revelation?"[1] This is a critically important question—one that Oneness Pentecostals and other cultists would do well to ponder.

---

* *Eisegesis* involves the interpretation of a text by reading into it one's own ideas.

Swedenborgianism, founded by Emanuel Swedenborg (1688–1772), is another belief system that teaches that the Father, Son, and Holy Spirit are mere modes of manifestation of God. "The Christian Trinity of Father, Son, and Holy Spirit are aspects of God just as soul, body, and activities are aspects of each one of us."[2] The Father is God in His essence. The Son is God as manifest among human beings in the flesh. The Holy Spirit is God as a life-giving influence. Swedenborgianism ignores the biblical data presented for the distinct personhood of the Father, Son, and Holy Spirit.

The Christadelphians, founded by Dr. John Thomas (1805–1871), argue against the Trinity by stressing the oneness of God alone: "We reject the doctrine that God is three persons."[3] They argue that the Trinity is nowhere to be found in the Old Testament and is a doctrine that does not make sense. "We reject the idea of a God with multiple independent personalities as not being in harmony with the teachings of Scripture."[4] The big problem with the Christadelphians is their highly selective use of Scripture—they focus only on verses that support God's oneness and ignore those that support His having a triune nature.

One must also challenge the idea that the doctrine of the Trinity is nowhere to be found in the Old Testament. While God's unity and oneness is the clear emphasis in Old Testament revelation, this is not to say there are no hints or foreshadows of the doctrine of the Trinity there, for indeed there are (see, for example, Psalm 110:1; Proverbs 30:4; Isaiah 48:16; 63:7-10). It is noteworthy that the Angel of Yahweh—identified as *being Yahweh* in Exodus 3:1-6—is also seen as *distinct* from Yahweh because He intercedes *to Yahweh* on behalf of the people of God (Zechariah 1:12; 3:1-2). It is by reading the Old Testament under the illumination of the New Testament that we find supporting evidences for the Trinity there.

The metaphysical cults, who use an esoteric method of interpreting Scripture, are among the most bizarre in their interpretation of the Trinity. Christian Science, founded by Mary Baker Eddy (1821–1910), interprets the Trinity as a triply divine principle: Life, Truth, and Love. Religious Science, founded by "Dr." Ernest Holmes, likewise speaks of each person in the Trinity in impersonal terms, the Father being "supreme creative Principle," the Son being the "manifestation of the infinite in any and all planes, levels, states of consciousness," and the Holy Spirit being the "feminine aspect of the Divine Trinity."[5] The Unity School of Christianity, founded by Charles and Myrtle Fillmore in 1891, also describes the Trinity in impersonal terms: "The Father is Principle, the Son is that Principle revealed in creative plan, the Holy Spirit is the executive power of both Father and Son carrying out the creative plan."[6] Such impersonal interpretations of the Father, Son, and Holy Spirit are amply disproved by the evidence provided earlier for the personhood of each.

The Unification Church (also known as the Moonies), founded by Reverend Sun Myung Moon (b. 1920), teaches the existence of multiple trinities. Moon says God's original intention was to form a Trinity with Himself, Adam, and Eve. But Adam and Eve's fall into sin foiled this Trinity. Tragically, a Satanic Trinity was formed that included Satan, Adam, and Eve. Later, however, Jesus was able to perfect Himself spiritually, and a spiritual Trinity was formed with God, Jesus, and the Holy Spirit. A future physical Trinity will involve God, the Lord of the second advent (Moon), and the Lord of the second advent's wife. When this last Trinity is formed, the kingdom of heaven will allegedly be established on earth. All of this, of course, is pure eisegesis.

These various groups with unorthodox views of the Trinity have one fundamental trait in common: They *all* fail to consistently utilize a historical-grammatical approach to interpreting Scripture (see chapter 17). And, tragically, because the Father, Son, and Holy Spirit play such a crucial role in all the essential doctrines of the Faith, it stands to reason that a fallacious view of the Trinity (based on faulty hermeneutics) will lead one far astray in one's broader theology. This is certainly borne out in a study of the cults.

THEOLOGICAL QUICK-REVIEW

Chapter 3 Main Idea: There is only one God, but in the unity of the Godhead are three co-equal and co-eternal persons—the Father, the Son, and the Holy Spirit—equal in divine substance (nature), but distinct in personhood.

Importance: A correct understanding of God is foundational to all other theology. The doctrine of the Trinity is especially important to our salvation, because the Father, Son, and Holy Spirit play distinctive roles in the outworking of that salvation.

Unorthodox Viewpoints: Unorthodox viewpoints include explicit denials, tritheism, modalism, subordinationism, binitarianism, and various cultic distortions.

Course of Action: On the doctrine of the Trinity, there must be conviction without compromise.

4

Christ's Deity

THE DEITY OF CHRIST is part and parcel of the doctrine of the Trinity (see chapter 3). It is a kingpin of Christian orthodoxy. The Bible abounds with evidences of this doctrine, and the early creeds are occupied with defining and defending it.

The Biblical Basis for Christ's Deity

Not only did the Old Testament predict that the coming Messiah would be deity, but Jesus claimed to *be* that Messiah. He declared and defended His deity in numerous ways.

Jesus Claimed to Be Messiah-God

The Old Testament teaches that the coming Messiah would be God Himself. Among the titles of the divine Messiah was "Mighty God" (or *Elohim*, Isaiah 9:6). The Father affirmed of the Messiah, "Your throne, O God, will last for ever and ever" (Hebrews 1:8; compare with Psalm 45:6). In Psalm 110:1 David called Him "my Lord" (compare with Matthew 22:43-44). He is also called the "Ancient of Days" (Daniel 7:22), a phrase used twice in the same passage of God the Father (verses 9,13). Jesus acknowledged He was the Messiah under oath before the high priest. When asked, "Are you the Christ [Messiah], the Son of the Blessed One?" Jesus responded, "I am," at which the high priest tore his robe and said to the others present, "You have heard the blasphemy" (Mark 14:61-64).

Jesus Claimed to Be Jehovah (Yahweh)

Jehovah, or *Yahweh* (YHWH), is the special name given by God for Himself in the Old Testament. It is never used of anyone but God Himself. It is the name revealed to Moses in Exodus 3:14, when God said, "I AM WHO I AM." While other titles also used for God may be used of men (*Adonai* [Lord] in Genesis 18:12) or false gods (*Elohim* [gods] in Deuteronomy 6:14), *Yahweh* is used *only* in reference to the one true God. No other person or thing was to be worshiped or served (Exodus 20:5), and His name and glory were not to be given to another. Isaiah wrote,* "'Thus saith Jehovah...I am the first, and I am the last; and besides me there is no God" (Isaiah 44:6), and, "I am Jehovah, that is my name; and my glory I will not give to another, neither my praise unto graven images" (42:8).

Yet on many occasions, Jesus claimed to be Jehovah. He prayed, "And now, O Father, glorify thou me with thine own self with the glory which I had with thee before the world was" (John 17:5). But Jehovah of the Old Testament said, "My glory will I not give to another" (Isaiah 42:8). Jesus also declared, "I am the first and the last" (Revelation 1:17)—precisely the words used by Jehovah of Himself in Isaiah 42:8. Jesus said, "I am the good shepherd" (John 10:11), but the Old Testament said, "Jehovah is my shepherd" (Psalm 23:1). Further, Jesus claimed to be the judge of all men (Matthew 25:31-46; John 5:27-42), but Joel quotes Jehovah as saying, "I will sit to judge all the nations round about" (Joel 3:12). Likewise, Jesus spoke of Himself as the "bridegroom" (Matthew 25:1), while the Old Testament identifies Jehovah in this way (Isaiah 62:5; Hosea 2:16). While the psalmist declares, "Jehovah is my light" (Psalm 27:1), Jesus said, "I am the light of the world" (John 8:12).

Perhaps the strongest claim Jesus made in reference to being Jehovah is in John 8:58, where He asserted, "Before Abraham was, I am." This statement claims not only existence *before* Abraham, but *equality with* the "I AM" of Exodus 3:14. The Jews who heard Jesus clearly understood His meaning and picked up stones to kill Him for blasphemy (see John 8:58; 10:31-33). Jesus identifies Himself this same way in Mark 14:62 and John 18:5-6.

---

* Quotations in this section are from the American Standard Version (ASV) since it translates LORD (YHWH) as "Jehovah."

Jesus Claimed to Be Equal with God

Jesus claimed to be equal with God in other ways. One was by claiming for Himself the prerogatives of God. He said to a paralytic, "Son, your sins are forgiven" (Mark 2:5). The scribes correctly responded, "Who can forgive sins but God alone?" (Mark 2:7; see also Isaiah 43:25). So, to prove that His claim was not an empty boast, Jesus healed the man, offering direct proof that what He had said about forgiving sins was true also.

Another prerogative Jesus claimed was the power to raise and judge the dead: "I tell you the truth, a time is coming and has now come when the dead will hear the voice of the Son of God and those who hear will live...and come out—those who have done good will rise to live, and those who have done evil will rise to be condemned" (John 5:25,29). Jesus removed all doubt about His meaning when He stated, "For just as the Father raises the dead and gives them life, even so the Son gives life to whom he is pleased to give it" (John 5:21). But the Old Testament clearly teaches that only God is the giver of life (Deuteronomy 32:39; 1 Samuel 2:6). Only God can raise the dead (Psalm 2:7) and judge them (Deuteronomy 32:35; Joel 3:12). Jesus boldly assumed for Himself powers that only God has.

Jesus also claimed that He should be honored as God. He said that all men should "honor the Son just as they honor the Father. He who does not honor the Son does not honor the Father, who sent him" (John 5:23). The Jews who heard this knew that no one should claim to be equal with God in this way, which was why they reached for stones (John 5:18).

Further, Jesus told the disciples, "Do not let your hearts be troubled. Trust in God; trust also in me" (John 14:1). If Jesus was not equal to Jehovah, then placing Himself on an equal par with Jehovah as an object of men's faith would have been blasphemy.

Jesus Claimed to Be God by Accepting Worship

The Old Testament forbids worshiping anyone other than God (Exodus 20:1-4; Deuteronomy 5:6-9). The New Testament agrees, demonstrating that while holy men refused worship (Acts 14:15), as did angels (Revelation 22:8-9), Jesus accepted worship on numerous occasions, in perfect keeping with His claim to be God. A healed leper worshiped Him (Matthew 8:2), as did a ruler (Matthew 9:18). After Jesus stilled a storm, "those who were in the boat worshiped him, saying, 'Truly you are the Son of God'" (Matthew 14:33). A group of Canaanite women (Matthew 15:25), the mother of James and John (Matthew 20:20), and a Gerasene demoniac (Mark 5:6) all worshiped Jesus without a single word of rebuke from Him. Thomas, upon witnessing the risen Christ, cried out in worship, "My Lord and my God!" (John 20:28). It is highly revealing of His identity that Jesus always considered such worship as appropriate.

Jesus Claimed to Be God by Accepting the Titles of Deity

Divine names and titles are often ascribed to Jesus in Scripture. Thomas saw the postresurrected Jesus' wounds and cried out, "My Lord and my God!" (John 20:28). Paul made reference to "Christ, who is God over all" (Romans 9:5). He referred to Jesus as the one in whom "all the fullness of Deity lives in bodily form" (Colossians 2:9). In Titus, Jesus is recognized as "our great God and Savior" (2:13). The heavenly Father says to the Son, in the book of Hebrews, "Your throne, O God, will last for ever and ever" (1:8). Paul says that before Christ existed in the form of man (which clearly refers to Him being really human), He existed in the form of God (Philippians 2:6 NKJV). The parallel phrases suggest that if Jesus was *fully human*, then He was also *fully God*. Moreover, the affirmation in Philippians 2:6 that Jesus existed in the "form of God" is written with a present participle in the original Greek text, which conveys the idea that Jesus *continually and perpetually* existed in the form of God, with the implication that *He still is!*

Colossians 1:15 tells us Jesus is the "image of the invisible God." This description is strengthened in Hebrews, where we read, "The Son is the radiance of God's glory and *the exact representation of his being,* sustaining all things by his powerful word" (Hebrews 1:3, emphasis added). The word "radiance" here literally means "effulgence" or "shining forth," and carries the idea that the very character, attributes, and essence of God shine forth in Jesus Christ.

The prologue to John's Gospel also minces no words, stating, "In the beginning was the Word, and the Word was with God, and *the Word*

[Jesus] was God" (John 1:1, insert added, emphasis added). Note that the verb "was" in this verse is an imperfect tense in the original Greek text, thereby indicating *continued existence* as God.

Jesus Claimed to Have Equal Authority with God

Jesus often put His words on a par with God's. The phrase, "You have heard that it was said to the people long ago...But I tell you..." (Matthew 5:21-22), is repeated several times in Scripture. Moreover, Jesus never said, "Thus saith the Lord...." as did the prophets; He always said, "Verily, verily, I say unto you...." He would later affirm, "*All authority* in heaven and on earth has been given to me. Therefore go and make disciples of all nations" (Matthew 28:18-19, emphasis added).

God had given the Ten Commandments to Moses, but Jesus said, "A new command I give you: Love one another" (John 13:34). Jesus said, "Until heaven and earth disappear, not the smallest letter, not the least stroke of a pen, will by any means disappear from the Law" (Matthew 5:18). Then later, Jesus said of His own words, "Heaven and earth will pass away, but my words will never pass away" (Matthew 24:35). Clearly, Jesus considered His words to have equal authority with God's declarations in the Old Testament. Jesus never retracted anything He said, never guessed or spoke with uncertainty, never made revisions, never contradicted Himself, and never apologized for what He said.

Understandably, Jesus' teachings had a profound effect on people. Many of His listeners surmised that His were not the words of an ordinary man. When Jesus taught in Capernaum on the Sabbath, the people "were amazed at his teaching, because his message had authority" (Luke 4:32). After Jesus taught the Sermon on the Mount, "the crowds were amazed at his teaching, because he taught as one who had authority, and not as their teachers of the law" (Matthew 7:28-29). When some Jewish leaders asked the temple guards why they hadn't arrested Jesus when He spoke, they responded, "No one ever spoke the way this man does" (John 7:46).

One cannot read the Gospels long before recognizing that Jesus regarded Himself and His message as inseparable. The reason Jesus' teachings had ultimate authority is because He is God.

Jesus Claimed to Be God by Requesting Prayer in His Name

Jesus not only asked people to believe in Him and obey His commands, but also asked them to pray in His name: "I will do whatever you ask in my name....You may ask me for anything in my name, and I will do it" (John 14:13-14). "If you remain in me and my words remain in you, ask whatever you wish, and it will be given you" (John 15:7). Jesus even insisted, "No one comes to the Father except through me" (John 14:6). In response to this, Jesus' followers not only prayed in Jesus' name (1 Corinthians 5:4), but prayed directly to Christ (Acts 7:59). Jesus certainly intended that His name be invoked both before God and *as* God in prayer.

In view of these many clear ways in which Jesus claimed to be God, any unbiased observer aware of the Gospels should recognize—whether he accepts the claims or not—that Jesus of Nazareth did indeed claim to be God in human flesh. That is, He claimed to be identical to the Jehovah of the Old Testament.

Jesus' Disciples Acknowledged His Claim to Be God

Not only did Jesus claim to be deity, His disciples also recognized His deity. For example, the apostles referred to Him using divine ascriptions such as "the first and the last" (Revelation 1:17; 2:8; 22:13), "the true light" (John 1:9), the "rock" or "stone" (1 Corinthians 10:4; 1 Peter 2:6-8; compare with Psalm 18:2; 95:1), the "bridegroom" (Ephesians 5:28-33; Revelation 21:2), "the Chief Shepherd" (1 Peter 5:4), and "the great Shepherd" (Hebrews 13:20). The Old Testament role of God as Redeemer (Psalm 130:7; Hosea 13:14) is ascribed to Jesus in the New Testament (Titus 2:13; Revelation 5:9). He is seen as the forgiver of sins (Acts 5:31; Colossians 3:13; compare with Psalm 130:4; Jeremiah 31:34) and "Savior of the world" (John 4:42; compare with Isaiah 43:3,11). Jesus is spoken of as the One "who will judge the living and the dead" (2 Timothy 4:1). He also accepted the title of "Messiah" (John 4:25-26), which the Old Testament said would be God (Psalm 45:6; 110:1; Isaiah 7:14; 9:6; Zechariah 12:10).

Answering Objections to Christ's Deity

Several passages are used by critics to allege that Jesus' disciples did not believe He was God. These texts, however, are consistently taken out of context, as will become clear below:

Mark 10:17. The objection is raised that if Jesus was God, why did He rebuke the rich young ruler for calling Him *good,* saying, "Why do you call me good?...No one is good—except God alone" (verse 18). In response, note that Jesus never denied what the young ruler said. He merely asked a question. As was typical of Jesus, His question was engineered to probe beneath the surface of the glib statement of the young ruler. He was saying, in effect, "Do you realize what you are saying? Are you calling me God?"

John 1:1. John 1:1 is used by Arians to allege that Jesus was only *a* god, not *the* God, because there is no definite article ("the") in the original Greek text of this verse in reference to Jesus. Contrary to such a view, Greek scholars tell us that when the definite article is used, it often stresses the *individual,* and, when it is not present, it refers to the *nature* of the one denoted. In view of this, John 1:1 can be rendered "And the Word was *of the nature of* God." Hence, the best translation is: "The Word was God." Contextually, the full deity of Christ is supported by other references in John's Gospel (see John 8:58; 10:30; 20:28). In John 1:3, for example, we are told that Jesus created the world, which is elsewhere said to be something only God can do (Isaiah 44:24). The rest of the New Testament, too, affirms the full deity of Christ (for example, Colossians 1:15-16; 2:9; Titus 2:13). It is also noteworthy that some New Testament texts actually do use the definite article to speak of Christ as "the God" (for example, Matthew 1:21; John 20:28; Hebrews 1:8). So, it does not matter whether John did or did not use the definite article in John 1:1—the Bible clearly teaches that Jesus is God, not just *a* god.

John 14:28. The objection here is that Jesus said, "The Father is greater than I." How, then, could Jesus be God? Of course, this misses the point of Jesus' total identity in the incarnate state. He is not only God, He is also man. He is the God-man.

As a man, Jesus is clearly less than God. As God, however, He is equal to God. Jesus, in the incarnation, has two natures—one divine, one human. Further, even within the Godhead there is a functional hierarchy. As Son, Jesus had a lesser *position* than the Father, even though He was equal in nature. Just as one's earthly father is greater in *function* or office than is his son (even though both are equally human), even so the heavenly Father is superior to the Son *in office* while being equal in nature.

Colossians 1:15. In this verse Paul refers to Christ as the "firstborn over all creation." Some claim this implies that Jesus was only a creature—that is, the first one born (created) in the universe. Contextually, however, the verse does not mean Jesus is firstborn *in* creation, as if He were created, but rather the firstborn *over* creation (verse 15), since He *created* the creation (verse 16) and "He is before all things" (verse 17). "Firstborn" in this context does not mean the *first one to be born,* but rather the *Heir of all, One who is supreme over all.* As creator of "all things," He could not have been a created thing.

Revelation 3:14. Here John refers to Christ as the "beginning of the creation of God" (NKJV). This may sound to a casual observer like Christ is the first created being. However, "Beginning of the creation of God" refers contextually to Christ being the *Beginner of* God's creation, not the *beginning in* God's creation. While the Greek word in question, *arche,* can mean "beginning," it also carries the important active meaning of "one who begins," "origin," "source," "creator," or "first cause." The English word *architect* is derived from the Greek term *arche.* We might say, then, that Jesus is the architect of all creation (John 1:3; Colossians 1:16; Hebrews 1:2). It is significant that this same Greek word is used of God the Father in Revelation 21:6-7.

The Theological Importance of the Deity of Christ

As noted in chapter 1 of this book, a doctrine is considered essential or fundamental to the Christian Faith if it is necessary to our salvation. This being the case, the deity of Christ is most clearly an essential of the Christian Faith. There are no sinless human beings, but Jesus was sinless. Indeed, He had to be sinless to be a sacrifice for our sins. A sinful savior cannot save sinners. Further, as mediator between God and man (1 Timothy 2:5), Jesus had to be both God *and* man. As God He could reach to God, and as man he could reach to man. So, to bring man to God, God had to be first brought to man. As John put it, "In the beginning was the Word...and the Word was God....The Word became flesh and made his dwelling among us" (John 1:1,14). Had the Son of God not become man, man could not be saved and become a son of God.

The Basis for Christ's Deity in the Early Creeds

The earliest creedal statements are established upon the New Testament. The apostle Paul declared Christ's deity, saying, "God was manifested in the flesh" (1 Timothy 3:16 NKJV).

Later, the Apostles' Creed speaks of Christ as "His [God's] only Son, our Lord" who now "sits at the right hand of God the Father." The Nicene Creed is even more explicit, speaking of "one Lord, Jesus Christ, the only Son of God, eternally begotten of the Father, God from God, light from light, true God from true God, begotten, not made, of one Being with the Father; through whom all things were made" and "who with the Father... is worshiped and glorified." The Creed of Chalcedon confesses "the one and only Son, our Lord Jesus Christ. This selfsame one is perfect both in deity and in humanness; this selfsame one is also actually God." So, from the Old Testament into the New Testament, and into the earliest creeds of the Christian Church, there was no doubt about the full deity of Jesus Christ.

Unorthodox Denials of the Deity of Christ

A near-universal theological characteristic of religious cults is a denial of the absolute deity of Christ. Examples are so plentiful that we can provide only a brief sampling here. One representative cult is the Jehovah's Witnesses, who claim Jesus was created as the archangel Michael billions of years ago, who was then used by Jehovah to create all other things in the universe. "The evidence indicates that the Son of God was known as Michael before he came to earth."[1] "'Michael the great prince' is none other than Jesus Christ Himself."[2] Jesus is viewed as a "mighty god," but He is not God Almighty like Jehovah is.[3]

To support this claim, Witnesses point to passages that seem to indicate Jesus is inferior to the Father. For example, Jesus said, "The Father is greater than I" (John 14:28), and He is the "firstborn over all creation" (Colossians 1:15).[4] (See discussion of these verses on pages 53-54.) Witnesses thus reason that worship is to be "directed only toward God" and not toward Jesus Christ,[5] despite clear New Testament verses in which Jesus *is* worshiped.

The Mormons are another group who deny the absolute deity of Jesus. They argue that Jesus was "begotten" as the first spirit-child of the Father (*Elohim*) and one of His unnamed wives. "Christ, the Firstborn, was the mightiest of all the spirit children of the Father."[6] He then progressed in the spirit world until He became a god—allegedly the Jehovah of the Old Testament (separate from the Father, *Elohim*). Christ, "by obedience and devotion to the truth…attained that pinnacle of intelligence which ranked Him as a God."[7] When it came time for His birth on earth, Jesus was "begotten" through sexual relations between a flesh-and-bone heavenly Father and Mary.

Mormons seem utterly unaware of verses in the Old Testament where Jehovah and *Elohim* are seen to be one and the same God. In Genesis 27:20, for example, Isaac tells his son, "The LORD [Jehovah] your God [*Elohim*] gave me success" (inserts added). Similarly, Jeremiah 32:18 makes reference to the "great and powerful God [*Elohim*], whose name is the LORD [Jehovah] Almighty" (inserts added). Significantly, both Jehovah and *Elohim* are used prophetically of Jesus Christ. In Isaiah 40:3, for example, we read: "In the desert prepare the way for the LORD [Jehovah]; make straight in the wilderness a highway for our God [*Elohim*]" (inserts added). This entire verse was written in reference to John the Baptist preparing the way for the ministry of Christ (John 1:23). Further, contrary to the Mormon view, Mary's conception of Christ's humanity was via a miracle of the Holy Spirit (Matthew 1:20).

The Christadelphians are yet another group who deny the deity of Jesus. They claim Jesus did not exist until He was born in Bethlehem: "We reject the doctrine that the Son of God was co-eternal with the Father."[8] "There is no hint in the Old Testament that the Son of God was already existent or in any way active at that time."[9] Jesus "did not actually come into being until He was begotten of the Holy Spirit and born in Bethlehem."[10] If Jesus were God, they reason, He could not have died on the cross, for God cannot die. Moreover, if Jesus were God, He would be all-knowing, but He did not know the day of His return (Mark 13:32). Further, if Jesus were God, He would be invisible, for God is invisible (1 Timothy 6:16).

Obviously, many Christadelphian arguments against the deity of Christ are based on a misunderstanding of the incarnation. Jesus, in the incarnate state, was 100 percent God and 100 percent man (see chapter 5). Only His human body died on the cross, not His divine nature. Moreover, as God, Jesus was omniscient (John 16:30), but as a man He was limited in His knowledge. It was thus from the perspective of His humanity that He said He did not know the hour of His return. Finally, Jesus in His divine nature is Spirit (John 4:24) and is hence invisible; it is His human body that is visible (John 1:14).

The Unification Church (Moonies) are yet another group who argue that Jesus is not eternal deity. In fact, they argue that the early church was responsible for fabricating teachings about Christ's eternal deity. "After his crucifixion, Christianity made Jesus into God."[11] Jesus did, however, attain a lesser degree of deity in view of His spiritual perfection. Moonies say this deity is not equal to that of the Father. That Jesus was not absolute deity is evident in the facts that He was tempted by the devil and He prayed to the Father.

Like the Christadelphians, Unification arguments against the deity of Christ are based on a misunderstanding of the incarnation. Indeed, it was in His humanity that Jesus was subject to temptation, distress, weakness, pain, sorrow, and limitation. Even though He was tempted, however, Jesus the God-man was completely without sin (Hebrews 4:15). As for prayer, because Christ came as a man—and because one of the proper duties of man is to worship, pray to, and adore God—it was perfectly proper for Jesus to address the Father in prayer. Positionally speaking as a man, as a Jew, *and as our High Priest* ("made like his brothers in every way," Hebrews 2:17), Jesus could pray to the Father. But this in no way takes away from His intrinsic deity.

The Way International is yet another cult that denies the deity of Jesus. Victor Paul Wierwille, cult founder, wrote a book entitled *Jesus Christ Is Not God,* in which he argued that "Jesus Christ is not God, but the Son of God....Jesus Christ was not literally with God in the beginning; neither does he have all the assets of God."[12] We are told that "God is eternal whereas Jesus was born."[13] "Jesus Christ's existence began when he was conceived by God's creating the soul-life of Jesus in Mary."[14] He was a sinless man by virtue of being conceived by the Holy Spirit, but He is not to be worshiped.

Wierwille seems distinctly unaware that the phrase "Son of God" indicates not that Jesus came into being at a point in time but rather that Jesus is *eternal God*. Among the ancients, "Son of" often carried the important meaning "of the same nature as."[15] Hence, when Jesus claimed to be the Son of God, His Jewish contemporaries fully understood He was making a claim to be God in an unqualified sense. This is why, when Jesus claimed to be the Son of God, the Jews insisted, "We have a law, and according to that law he [Christ] must die, because he claimed to be the Son of God" (John 19:7, insert added). Recognizing that Jesus was identifying Himself as God, the Jews wanted to put Him to death for committing blasphemy.

Scripture indicates that Christ's Sonship is an *eternal* Sonship. Hebrews 1:2, for example, says God created the universe *through* His "Son"—implying that Christ was the Son of God prior to the creation. Moreover, Christ *as* the Son is explicitly said to have existed "before all things" (Colossians 1:17; see verses 15-16). As well, Jesus, speaking *as* the Son of God (John 8:54-56) asserts His eternal preexistence before Abraham (verse 58).

We must also point to New Agers as an example of those who deny the absolute deity of Jesus. New Agers typically argue that Jesus was a mere human vessel who embodied the Christ—a cosmic, divine entity who allegedly manifests Himself in all religions. "The vehicle of the Master Jesus, the fairest and most perfect this earth could produce, now became the abode of the Lord Christ for the three years of His earthly ministry."[16] Jesus is viewed as a prototype for humanity, since all other humans can allegedly embody the Christ.

Biblically, however, Jesus is the *singular* Christ/Messiah (John 1:41) whose *sole* coming is prophesied throughout the Old Testament (for example, Isaiah 7:14; 53:3-5; Micah 5:2; Zechariah 12:10). Significantly, when Jesus was acknowledged as *the* Christ in the New Testament, He never said, "You too have the Christ within." Instead, He warned that others would come *falsely claiming* to be the Christ (Matthew 24:5).

There are certainly many other denials of the deity of Christ in the kingdom of the cults. Unitarian Universalists argue that Jesus was a good moral teacher. The Jesus of the spiritists is an advanced medium. The Jesus of psychic Edgar Cayce is a being who in his first incarnation was Adam and in his thirtieth reincarnation became "the Christ" (the sinner and the Savior are found in the same person). The Jesus of UFO cults is said to be half human and half alien—thereby accounting for his seemingly supernatural powers. Eckankar says Jesus was a "great thinker" in the same league as Plato, Muhammad, Buddha, and Lao-Tse, all of whom came to facilitate spiritual evolution.

While these views may try to claim compatibility with Christianity, measuring them against our earlier biblical discussion of Christ's deity shows them to be utterly unorthodox and full of deception. Inasmuch as a counterfeit Christ can only bring a counterfeit salvation, the doctrinal error of the cults on this matter has obvious grave consequences.

THEOLOGICAL QUICK-REVIEW

Chapter 4 Main Idea: Jesus is absolute deity, being fully God in every sense.

Importance: Jesus' deity is an essential doctrine for our salvation. Indeed, Jesus the Savior had to be both God *and* man. As God He could reach to God, and as man He could reach to man. Moreover, His sacrificial death as the God-man was of infinite worth.

Unorthodox Viewpoints: There are a plethora of unorthodox viewpoints on Jesus. Some argue He was a man who *attained* deity. Others argue He was a man who *embodied* deity. Others argue He was a *lesser* deity. Others argue the early church *fabricated* His deity. Still others altogether *deny* His deity.

Course of Action: On the doctrine of Christ's deity, there must be conviction without compromise.

5

Christ's Humanity

CHRIST'S HUMANITY, LIKE HIS DEITY, is an essential to our salvation. As the perfect mediator between God and man, Christ, in the incarnation, was both fully divine and fully human. To deny either is a heresy. Indeed, the Bible labels those "antichrist" who deny His humanity (1 John 4:3; 2 John 7).

The Biblical Basis for Christ's Humanity

The Bible says Christ was human in all points except sin (Hebrews 4:15). This includes all the following characteristics:

Human Parents

Jesus had a human, biological mother named Mary and a legal, but not biological, human father named Joseph:

> This is how the birth of Jesus Christ came about: His mother Mary was pledged to be married to Joseph, but before they came together, she was found to be with child through the Holy Spirit. Because Joseph her husband was a righteous man and did not want to expose her to public disgrace, he had in mind to divorce her quietly (Matthew 1:18-19).

Human Birth

The apostle Paul said Jesus was "born of a woman" (Galatians 4:4). Indeed, His mother conceived Him while a virgin (Matthew 1:23). She had a normal nine-month pregnancy (Luke 1:24,26,31) and a natural child birth (Luke 2:6-7,22-23).

Human Growth

Jesus grew like any other human being. He grew in His mother's womb from an embryo to a fetus, and later from a baby (Luke 2:16) to a young child (Matthew 2:11). He then grew into a young person (Luke 2:42-50). "The child grew and became strong" (Luke 2:40) and He "grew…in stature" (Luke 2:52).

Human Ethnicity

Jesus was Jewish. He was born of the Jewish tribe of Judah (Genesis 49:10; Hebrews 7:14). He was born and reared under the Jewish law (Galatians 4:4). He spoke in the Aramaic language of His time, as did other Jews (see Matthew 27:46). He looked and talked Jewish to the Samaritan woman at the well, who recognized Him as such (John 4:9). There was no question about His human ethnicity.

Human Relatives

Jesus had human relatives. The Bible refers to His "brothers" (John 7:5), specifically affirming that He was "the brother of James, Joses, Judas, and Simon" and that He had "sisters" (Mark 6:3). He was also related to John the Baptist (Luke 1:36).

Human Emotions

As a human person, Jesus had the three dimensions of personality: intellect, emotions, and a will. His emotions were evident in His human desire not to go to the cross, but in His prayer to His Father He said, "Yet, not as I will, but as you will" (Matthew 26:39). He also expressed deep human emotions, for "Jesus wept" at the death of His friend Lazarus (John 11:35). The book of Hebrews informs us that "in the days of His flesh…He had offered up prayers and supplications, with vehement cries and tears" (Hebrews 5:7 NKJV).

Human Hunger

Like any other human being, Jesus got hungry. In Luke 4:2 we read that Jesus fasted for forty days "and afterward, when they had ended, He was hungry" (NKJV). Jesus regularly ate food, including the Passover lamb He ate with His disciples (John 13:1-2). He also drank water from the well in Samaria, being thirsty after His journey (John 4:1-7). On the cross He cried out, "I am thirsty" (John 19:28).

Human Fatigue

John records that "Jesus, being wearied from His journey, sat thus by the well" (John 4:6 NKJV). Jesus sometimes became so fatigued from His contact with crowds that He had to get away from them. Mark tells us that Jesus said to His disciples, "'Come aside by yourselves to a deserted place and rest a while.' For there were many coming and going, and they did not even have time to eat" (Mark 6:31 NKJV).

Human Pain

Death by crucifixion was excruciatingly painful. Jesus was on the cross for over six hours (Mark 15:25-34). He felt the pain of the nails, the pain of thirst (John 19:28), the pain of suffering, and the pain of separation from the Father as He cried out in agony, "My God, My God, why have You forsaken Me?" (Matthew 27:46).

Human Death

What could be more human than to experience death? Jesus died not just any death but a *cruel* death. He experienced the "agony of death" (Acts 2:24). He also experienced being separated from His loved ones (John 19:26-27) as well as being forsaken by the Father (Matthew 27:46). Even in His resurrection body He bore the marks of His death by crucifixion (Luke 24:40; John 20:27).

The only human experience Jesus did not participate in was that of sin. He was "tempted in every way, just as we are—yet was without sin" (Hebrews 4:15). But sin is not of the essence of human nature, because there was no sin before man's Fall into sin, and there will be none in heaven.

Human Spirit

Scripture is also clear that Christ possessed a fully human spirit and soul (John 12:27; John 13:21). When He died on the cross, He *gave up His spirit* to the Father (John 19:30). Hence, as theologian John Walvoord notes,

> It is evident that Christ possessed a true humanity not only in its material aspects as indicated in His human body, but in the immaterial aspect specified in Scripture as being His soul and spirit. It is therefore not sufficient to recognize that Jesus Christ as the Son of God possessed a human body, but is necessary to view Him as having a complete human nature including body, soul, and spirit.[1]

The Theological Importance of Christ's Humanity

Because Christ is the mediator between God and man (1 Timothy 2:5), He must be both God *and* man. As God, He could reach to God. As man, He could reach to man. Further, because He was human and tempted in all points as we are, He can be a sympathetic High Priest, ever living to make intercession for us (Hebrews 4:15).

Christ was also a full revelation of the Father. Jesus said, "Anyone who has seen me has seen the Father" (John 14:9). In Christ, the invisible God became visible. Indeed, the Bible affirms that "the Word became flesh and made his dwelling among us" (John 1:14) for the very purpose of revealing the Father (verse 18). Paul added, "God was manifested in the flesh" (1 Timothy 3:16 NKJV).

So important is the humanity of Christ that Scripture says it is heretical to deny it. As John put it, "Every spirit that does not confess that Jesus Christ has come in the flesh is not of God. And this is the spirit of the Antichrist" (1 John 4:2 NKJV). He repeated the warning in 2 John 7: "Many deceivers have gone out into the world who do not confess Jesus Christ as coming in the flesh. This is a deceiver and an antichrist" (NKJV). It is for this reason that the humanity of Christ must be listed among the great essentials of the Christian Faith.

The Basis for Christ's Humanity in the Early Creeds

Even in tiny creedal statements established upon the New Testament there is evidence that the humanity of Christ is an essential truth. Paul, for example, affirmed that "God was manifested in the flesh" (1 Timothy 3:16). The Apostles' Creed speaks of Jesus' conception, birth, death, and burial, saying, He "was conceived of the Holy Spirit, born of the virgin Mary, suffered under Pontius Pilate, crucified, died, and was buried." The Nicene Creed adds that Jesus "for our sake and for our salvation...came down from heaven, was *incarnate* of the Holy Spirit and the Virgin Mary and became *truly human*. For our sake he was crucified under Pontius Pilate; he *suffered death* and was buried" (emphasis added). As the heretical denials of Christ's humanness increased, the creedal affirmations became more explicit. Indeed, about half of the Chalcedonian Creed is occupied with stressing Christ's human nature. It reads: "This selfsame one is *perfect...in humanness;* this selfsame one is also actually God and *actually man,* with a rational soul and body. He is...*the same reality as we ourselves as far as his humanness* is concerned; *thus like us in all respects,* sin only excepted....This selfsame one was born of Mary the virgin, who is God-bearer in respect of his *humanness*" (emphasis added).

Unorthodox Denials of Christ's Humanity

In most chapters of this book, the "Unorthodox Denials" section deals with *modern* unorthodox denials. In the present case, however, it is instructive to examine a few ancient heresies to illustrate some of the ways Christ's humanity has been denied in the past.

The Docetists in the first century, for example, believed in a form of dualism, the view that matter is evil and spirit is good. Because of this, they believed Jesus couldn't have had a real material human body because that would have involved a union of spirit and matter (good and evil). Jesus therefore must have had a phantomlike body—that is, He only had the *appearance* of flesh, without substance or reality. (*Docetism* comes from a Greek word, *dokeo,* meaning "to seem" or "to appear.") Docetists say Jesus' suffering and death on the cross was not real, for it is inconceivable that a Supreme God (spirit) would give Himself up to the evil and destructive power of matter (evil). Bible passages that specifically refute Docetism include Colossians 1:15-18; 2:9; Hebrews 2:14; 1 John 2:22-23; 4:2-6; 5:1-6; and 2 John 7.

A fourth-century group that compromised the humanity of Christ was the Apollinarians. This group, following the lead of Apollinarius, believed in a trichotomous view of man—that is, they viewed man as having a body, soul, and spirit. In their view, Jesus possessed a human body and soul, but *not* a human spirit, which Apollinarius considered to be the seat of sin in the human being. In place of a human spirit in Jesus was the divine Logos, or divine reason. Jesus was considered human because He possessed a human body and soul; He was considered divine because He possessed divine reason in place of the human spirit. This Logos or divine reason was believed to have dominated the passive human body and soul in Jesus. The obvious problem with this view is that it denies the genuine, full humanity of Christ. Christ, in the incarnation, was 100 percent God and 100 percent man (see Colossians 2:9; 1 Timothy 3:16).

The Eutychians, a fifth-century group, taught that the human and divine in Christ merged to form a single composite nature. "The divine nature was so modified and accommodated to the human nature that Christ was not really divine....At the same time the human nature was so modified and changed by assimilation to the divine nature that He was no longer genuinely human."[2] The Eutychians, then, saw Christ as neither human nor divine.

– ANCIENT HERESIES REGARDING CHRIST'S HUMANITY –

Group	Time	Human Nature	Divine Nature
Docetists	First Century	Denied. Christ only *appeared* to be human. Had a phantomlike body.	Affirmed
Apollinarians	Fourth Century	Compromised. Argued that Jesus had a human body and soul, but said the divine Logos replaced the human spirit.	Affirmed

Eutychians	Fifth Century	Diminished. The human and divine in Christ merged to form a third, compound nature.	Diminished. The human and divine in Christ merged to form a third, compound nature.[3]

While errors relating to the humanity of Christ are not as common today as other theological errors, one still comes upon such errors on occasion, sometimes (sadly) within Christian churches. For example, one of the authors visited a popular independent Bible church in the Dallas area in which a deacon was teaching second graders that in the incarnation, the Holy Spirit came upon Mary, and the Holy Spirit provided the "God part" of Jesus, and Mary provided the "human part" of Jesus. So, Jesus was a hybrid being, part God and part man, but not 100 percent God and not 100 percent human. (The deacon was graciously informed of the biblical view and the class was so instructed.)

A more widely propagated example of a denial of Christ's humanity comes from Eliseo Fernando Soriano (born 1947), an evangelist who presides over the Members Church of God International in the Philippines. In the 1990s Soriano wrote a book titled *Leaving Behind the Fundamental Doctrines of Christ*. In his teachings, which are broadcast over television and radio, he denies the full humanity of Christ based on a misinterpretation of Philippians 2:5-8. He argues that the phrases "form of a bondservant," "likeness of men," and "appearance as a man" (NKJV) prove that Jesus was not truly a man. He only took on the "form" of a man, was made in the "likeness" of a man, and had the "appearance" of a man. If Jesus were truly a man, Soriano reasons, words such as "form," "likeness," and "appearance" would not have been used of Him in the Bible. The doctrinal statement of Soriano's church therefore proclaims, "We believe that Christ descended on earth from the bosom of the Father, suffered for the redemption of sin, died on the cross, resurrected after three days, ascended in heaven and sits on the right side of God."[4]

We noted previously that the apostle John condemns as "the spirit of the antichrist" the teaching that Christ is not a man (1 John 4:2-3).

Soriano is therefore in grave error. Hebrews 2:17 informs us that Christ's humanity is pertinent to our salvation, for "in all things He had to be *made like His brethren,* that He might be a merciful and faithful High Priest in things pertaining to God, to make propitiation for the sins of the people" (NKJV, emphasis added). Without Christ becoming a man, our salvation would not have been possible.

A proper understanding of Philippians 2:5-8 supports the idea that Christ, in the incarnation, was 100 percent God and 100 percent human. The whole point of this passage is that whereas Christ had been God for all eternity, He now had an additional nature—a *human* nature. The incarnation involved a *gaining of human attributes* as opposed to a giving up of divine attributes. That this is meant by Paul is clear in his affirmation that in the incarnation, Christ was "taking the form of a bondservant," "coming in the likeness of men," and "being found in appearance as a man" (Philippians 2:7-8 NKJV). Just as the phrase "form of God" (Philippians 2:6) points to the full deity of Christ, so the phrase "form of a bondservant" points to the full humanity of Christ (Philippians 2:7). There is an intended parallel here. Jesus, as eternal God, took on an additional *complete* nature—a complete human nature. Jesus was 100 percent God and 100 percent human. Hence, as J. I. Packer put it, "He was no less God then [in the incarnation] than before; but He had begun to be man. He was not now God minus some elements of His deity, but God plus all that He had made His own by taking manhood to Himself."[5]

Theologian Robert Lightner suggests there is a reason the phrase "likeness of men" is used of Jesus in this passage. He suggests the word "likeness" indicates *similarity but difference:* "Though His humanity was genuine, He was different from all other humans in that He was sinless."[6] Indeed, this is what Hebrews 4:15 affirms. Hence, contrary to the teachings of Soriano, Philippians 2:5-8 cannot be taken to mean Christ was not fully human.

As we continue our brief survey of the modern-day cults, we find occasional denials of the full humanity of Christ in the New Age movement. One notable example relates to the substantial UFO subculture within New Age circles. Some New Age UFO enthusiasts believe aliens aboard a spacecraft ("Space Brothers") injected Mary with the sperm of a space creature from another world. Others claim the angel Gabriel (of the Gospels) was actually an alien scientist who artificially inseminated the Virgin Mary to create Jesus.[7] In such a scenario, of course, Mary can still obviously be called a virgin, since she had not had sexual relations with anyone. Jesus was, in this view, a mixed breed—part human and part alien.[8] Some suggest this accounts for His seemingly supernatural powers in performing miracles. Such outlandish eisegesis is not even worthy of comment, except to say that this viewpoint—like many others chronicled in this book—fits neatly into the category of "doctrines of demons" (1 Timothy 4:1 NKJV) inspired by the father of lies, Satan (John 8:44).

There are other cults that *claim* to acknowledge Christ came as a human, but one wonders how this can be so, given certain other teachings of the cult. The Mormons are a good example. Mormons teach that Jesus was born as a man from the physical, sexual union of God the Father (an "exalted man" with a flesh-and-bone body) and the Virgin Mary. How, though, can a man be born from a physical union of a physical God and a human? Is not the biblical pattern that like begets like (Genesis 1:24)? The popular Mormon book *Gospel Principles* makes it sound as if Jesus were a hybrid being:

> Jesus is the only person on earth to be born of a mortal mother and an immortal Father. That is why he is called the Only begotten Son. From his mother he inherited mortality and was subject to hunger, thirst, fatigue, pain, and death. He inherited divine powers from his Father.[9]

Biblically, of course, Jesus' human nature was created via the overshadowing ministry of the Holy Spirit (Luke 1:35). This work of the Holy Spirit was necessary because of Christ's eternal deity and preexistence (see Isaiah 7:14; 9:6; Galatians 4:4). The Holy Spirit's supernatural work in Mary's body enabled Christ—as eternal God—to take on a human nature.

Mind Science cults such as Christian Science are also worthy of a hard look. While proponents of Christian Science claim a "human Jesus" embodied the "divine Christ," the Christian Science worldview ultimately causes problems for this idea. After all, Christian Science teaches that *all things* in the universe are ultimately God. Since God is *all* that truly exists, it is reasoned, this means that physical matter ultimately does not exist. If matter does not exist, then neither can a physical human body truly exist—it is ultimately an illusion. It therefore seems fair to suggest that the Christian Science worldview constitutes an implicit denial of the full humanity of Christ—a humanity that includes both a material and immaterial aspect.

In any event, whether unorthodox denials relate to the material or immaterial aspect of Christ's humanity, both denials are in grave error. Because Christ had to be both God *and* man to attain our salvation, the doctrine of Christ's full humanity is truly central to the Christian Faith.

THEOLOGICAL QUICK-REVIEW

Chapter 5 Main Idea: The incarnate Jesus was *fully human.*

Importance: As the perfect mediator between God and man, Christ had to be both fully divine and fully human. As God, He could reach to God. As man, He could reach to man.

Unorthodox Viewpoints: A variety of unorthodox viewpoints are represented in both ancient heresies and modern cults. Such errant viewpoints generally deny either a material or immaterial aspect of Christ's humanity.

Course of Action: On the doctrine of Christ's humanity, there must be conviction without compromise.

6

Human Depravity

THE DOCTRINE OF HUMAN DEPRAVITY is an essential of the Christian Faith. God created all things perfect, but humankind fell into sin. In the wake of Adam's demise, all human beings have subsequently been born into the world as sinners. That this is an essential doctrine of Christianity is evident in the fact that Christ's redemptive mission would not only be diminished apart from the reality of human sinfulness, but it would have been totally unnecessary. Moreover, it is a fact that people generally do not perceive their need for a Savior until they first perceive their sinfulness. Understandably, then, Scripture goes to great lengths to spell out humankind's dire condition.

The Biblical Basis for Human Depravity

From the very beginning of Genesis to the end of Revelation, the doctrine of human depravity permeates all of Scripture. It is one of the great fundamentals of the Christian Faith. Without it the whole plan of redemption is senseless, as are the doctrines of heaven and hell. To illustrate the pervasiveness of divine revelation on this issue, we will start with the book of Genesis and then provide select scriptural highlights throughout the rest of the Bible.

Genesis 2–3: God's perfect creation on earth was interrupted by human sin. We read that "the Lord God commanded man, saying, 'Of every tree of the garden you may freely eat; but of the tree of knowledge of good and evil you shall not eat, for in the day that you eat of it you shall surely die'" (Genesis 2:16-17 NKJV). Eve was soon tempted by Satan, and when she "saw that the tree was good for food, that it was pleasant to the eyes, and a tree desirable to make one wise, she took of its fruit and ate. She also gave to her husband with her, and he ate" (Genesis 3:6 NKJV). The apostle Paul comments on the ramifications of this disobedience for the rest of humanity: "Through one man sin entered the world, and death through sin, and thus death spread to all men, because all sinned" (Romans 5:13 NKJV).

Genesis 4–6: Following the sinful lead of Adam were his children, who were made in his image (Genesis 5:3). His first son, Cain, killed Abel, his brother, and was followed by his wicked descendants (Genesis 4). It was not long before violence filled the earth and "the LORD saw that the wickedness of man was great in the earth, and that every intent of the thoughts of his heart was only evil continually" (Genesis 6:5).

Psalm 51:5: David conceded that he was born into the world with a sin nature: "Behold, I was brought forth in iniquity, and in sin my mother conceived me" (NKJV).

Jeremiah 17:9: The prophet Jeremiah later summed up human depravity well when he wrote: "The heart is deceitful above all things, and desperately wicked; who can know it?" (NKJV). Human beings are *so* sinful that they're not even remotely aware of how badly tainted they are.

Matthew 5:28: Jesus made it clear that sin is not merely a matter of action but also of intention: "I say unto you that whoever looks at a woman to lust for her has already committed adultery with her in his heart" (NKJV). Who can stand under the scrutiny of such standards?

Romans 3:10-12: Not one to mince words, the apostle Paul wrote, "There is none righteous, no, not one; there is none who understands; there is none who seek after God. They have all turned aside...there is none who does good, no, not one" (NKJV). He flatly stated that "all have sinned and fall short of the glory of God" (verse 23).

Ephesians 2:1-3: Paul, addressing redeemed sinners (Christians), paints a realistic picture of fallen human beings apart from God and His grace:

> You He made alive, who were dead in trespasses and sins, in which you once walked according to the course of this world,

> according to the prince of the power of the air, the spirit who now works in the sons of disobedience, among whom also we all once conducted ourselves in the lusts of our flesh, fulfilling the desires of the flesh and of the mind, and were by nature children of wrath, just as the others (NKJV).

Fallen human beings are *by nature* sinful to the core.

1 John 2:15-16: The apostle John exhorted his readers, "Do not love the world or the things in the world...For all that is in the world—the lust of the flesh, the lust of the eyes, and the pride of life—is not of the Father but is of the world" (NKJV). John's exhortation is much needed because man's sinful nature is inclined toward such things.

1 John 3:4: There are sins of commission and sins of omission. John speaks here of the first kind of sin: "Whoever commits sin also commits lawlessness, and sin is lawlessness" (NKJV). That is, sin is breaking the law; it is doing what we know we should not do.

James 4:17: James writes about sins of omission—that is, sins that involve *not* doing what we know we ought to do. He wrote: "Therefore, to him who knows to do good and does not do it, to him it is sin" (NKJV).

James 2:10: All human beings commit sins of both kinds. Some people commit more sins of omission than sins of commission. But *all* are sin. In fact, little sins and big sins are *all* sins and render us guilty before God. James therefore commented, "Whoever shall keep the whole law, and yet stumble in one point, he is guilty of all" (NKJV).

The Theological Importance of Human Depravity

The theological significance of the doctrine of human depravity cannot be overemphasized. Apart from God's grace, human beings are utterly and completely "dead in trespasses and sins" (Ephesians 2:1,3 NKJV). They are "by nature children of wrath" and are "without hope and without God" (Ephesians 2:12). As David put it, "In sin my mother conceived me" (Psalm 51:5 NKJV). And as St. Augustine later put it, human beings have a *propensity to sin* and a subsequent *necessity to die*.

Human depravity means we cannot initiate our salvation (Romans 3:11; 9:16). As John put it, those who have received Christ (John 1:12) are "children born not of natural descent...but born of God" (John 1:13; see also 1 Peter 1:23). Nor can we attain salvation by good works (Romans 4:5; Ephesians 2:8-9; Titus 3:5-6). Salvation is by grace and *grace alone* (Romans 11:6; Titus 2:11-13). Our personal righteousness avails nothing, for Isaiah affirmed, "All our righteous acts are like filthy rags. We all shrivel up like a leaf, and like the wind our sins sweep us away" (Isaiah 64:6).

Recognizing our depravity and inability to attain salvation on our own is an absolute prerequisite to being saved. Realizing the need for a Savior from sin is the first step to salvation. Only drowning people need to be rescued. As Jesus put it, "I have not come to call the righteous, but sinners to repentance" (Luke 5:32).

The Creedal Basis for Human Depravity

The creeds speak of human depravity in two ways—*implicitly* and *explicitly.* The former is contained in statements about Christ's mission to "suffer" and "die" and "rise from the dead." The latter is seen in statements about being saved from God's wrath when "he comes to judge the living and the dead" (Apostles' Creed). Or, in Christ's need to "come for us on behalf of our salvation" (the Chalcedonian Creed) and to provide the "forgiveness of sins" (the Nicene Creed). Christ's coming "is necessary to everlasting salvation" (the Athanasian Creed). Such salvation would be unnecessary if there were no human depravity.

Salvation is the work - Good!! Not atonement

Unorthodox Denials of Human Depravity

There are many denials of human depravity in the kingdom of the cults. For example, many New Agers, who subscribe to what they call "esoteric Christianity" (in which the Bible is interpreted esoterically*), deny that human beings have a sin problem. In fact, the New Age worldview does not even allow for sin. As New Ager David Spangler points out, since humans are viewed as divine, they are essentially a law unto themselves and cannot be held guilty of sin.[1] Further, since New Age monism† blurs the distinction between good and evil, man has no real

* This method of interpretation seeks hidden, secondary, or spiritual meanings of Bible verses.

† The view that all reality is one.

sin problem to deal with. As Shirley MacLaine put it, "There is no such thing as evil or good."[2] "Until mankind realizes that there is, in truth, no good and there is, in truth, no evil, there will be no peace."[3] Indeed, "there is no evil, only the lack of knowledge."[4] Since there is no sin, any talk of salvation becomes meaningless. New Agers tell us we should "surrender all the fallacious ideas of forgiveness...divine mercy, and the rest of the opiates which superstition offers to the sinner."[5] All human beings need, we are told, is an enlightenment regarding their innate divinity.

It has long been recognized that many New Age ideas emerged out of the Mind Science cults, and this is certainly true when it comes to the issue of human depravity. For example, in the New Thought movement, which emerged out of the writings of metaphysician Phineas P. Quimby, there is no sin in the sense of "moral offense against God." Rather, sin is viewed as a succumbing to the illusory world of matter, which is the source of all sickness and death. Right thinking is the cure for the New Thought version of sin.

Mary Baker Eddy, the founder of Christian Science, followed Quimby's lead and taught that sin was just an illusion that could be conquered by correct thinking.[6] Eddy taught that "Christian Science destroys sickness, sin, and death."[7] By the practice of Christian Science, she said, "sin and disease lose their reality in human consciousness and disappear as naturally and as necessarily as darkness gives place to light and sin to reformation."[8] She claimed that "when Mind at last asserts its mastery over sin, disease, and death, then is man found to be harmonious and immortal."[9] Indeed, "when the mechanism of the human mind gives place to the divine Mind, selfishness and sin, disease and death, will lose their foothold."[10] After all, "if sickness and sin are illusions, the awakening from this mortal dream, or illusion, will bring us into health, holiness, and immortality."[11]

Ernest Holmes, the founder of the Religious Science (Mind Science) cult, likewise taught that human beings are part of the divine essence and that humankind's problem is not sin but ignorance of union with the divine: "I have always taught that there is no sin but ignorance."[12] He argues that "there is something Divine about us which we have overlooked. There is more to us than we realize....Man, the real man, is birthless, deathless, changeless; and God, as man, in man, IS man."[13] "But if we are Divine beings," Holmes asks, "why is it that we appear to be so limited, so forlorn, so poor; so miserable, sick, and unhappy? The answer is that we are ignorant of our own nature."[14] We simply need to be enlightened about our divinity!

In this same vein, modern psychics are quite sure that human beings are not sinfully depraved. In fact, psychics claim sin does not even exist. Man is not morally fallen. There is no offense to God that needs fixing, and human beings do not need to be saved. A spirit entity named Seth, communicating through psychic medium Jane Roberts, said, "The soul is not something you must save or redeem."[15] A spirit named Ramtha, communicating through psychic medium J. Z. Knight, said, "The world doesn't need saving—leave it alone....Relinquish guilt....Do not live by rules, live by feelings."[16] A spirit called "Jesus," communicating through psychic medium Helen Schucman, said, "It is so essential that all such thinking be dispelled that we must be sure that nothing of this kind remains in your mind."[17] Rather, psychics say, human beings are perfect in their nature and are "one" with God. Psychic James Van Praagh says, "I believe we are all God...We are all made in the likeness of God....We are all made of the God spark...Each one of us is perfect if we would only seek our divinity."[18] We simply need enlightenment!

Jesus, by stark contrast to such ideas, firmly taught the reality of human sin. In fact, He described sin as a blindness (Matthew 23:16-26), sickness (Matthew 9:12), being enslaved (John 8:34), and living in darkness (John 8:12; 12:35-36). Moreover, He taught that sin is a universal condition and that all people are guilty (Luke 7:37-48). He also taught that both inner thoughts and external acts render a person guilty (Matthew 5:28). And He affirmed that God is fully aware of every person's sins; nothing escapes His notice (Matthew 22:18; Luke 6:8). People thus need not mere enlightenment, but rather to trust in Him (John 3:16-17), the divine Savior (Titus 2:13), who is the "light of the world" (John 8:12)—the "true light that gives light to every man...coming into the world" (John 1:9).

Another group that denies human depravity is the Freemasons. Indeed, Masons deny the Christian doctrine of original sin and reject any suggestion that human beings are depraved. Mason H. L. Haywood comments that man "is not a perfect being...nor is he a debased, rotted creature, wallowing in mire until touched by the arbitrary grace of some supernatural power."[19] Masonry does not teach that "human nature is a depraved thing, like the ruin of a once proud building."[20] L. James Rongstad agrees, noting that "Masonry teaches that humanity is not originally sinful, just imperfect. If a person works faithfully at keeping the principles and teachings of the Lodge, then he will be ushered into the 'Grand Lodge Above,' where the 'Supreme Architect of the Universe' resides."[21] Indeed, Rongstad says, "Masonry teaches its adherence that the candidate coming into the lodge has a 'rough and imperfect nature.' That is why Masonry uses the Ashlar, Gavel, Square, and Compass—to remind the members that they ever must work out their imperfections in order to be found acceptable to the 'Supreme Grand Master' and to achieve a life in paradise, the 'Grand Lodge Above.'"[22] Freemasonry perfectly illustrates the theological dictum that a weak view of sin will always produce a weak view of salvation. Since man is just imperfect, he doesn't need a Savior. He just needs to work off his rough edges!

Yet another group that denies human depravity is Unitarian Universalism. "We do not believe that a person is born and enslaved in the manner that the doctrine of Original Sin teaches."[23] "We do not believe people are born into a state of sin from which they must be saved in order to avoid spending an eternity suffering in hell."[24] "Since we believe in neither original sin nor hell, we do not feel a need to be saved from either."[25]

One can attend a Unitarian Universalist church for years and never hear the word *sin* mentioned a single time. When the word does occasionally surface, it is not taken to be a moral offense against a holy God, but is rather something akin to a simple mistake. Human beings are believed to be essentially good with great potential. This is one reason Unitarian Universalism is so popular among humanists.

Of course, one only needs to watch the evening news for an abundance of empirical proof for human depravity. As G. K. Chesterton once put it, the facts are there for all to see. Original sin is the only Christian doctrine with universal empirical verification. One has only to open his eyes to behold incontestable evidence. Consider that "since 3600 B.C. the world has known only 292 years of peace. In that period, stretching more than 55 centuries, there have been an incredible 14,531 wars in which over 3.6 billion people have been killed."[26] The evidence would suggest that, since the Fall, human beings have manifested "great potential" for ever greater expressions of depravity.

THEOLOGICAL QUICK-REVIEW

Chapter 6 Main Idea: Since the Fall, every human being (except Christ) has been born into the world in a state of total depravity and is thus alienated from God.

Importance: Because human beings are depraved, they cannot initiate their own salvation, nor can they merit salvation or contribute to it by works. Their only hope is a salvation by grace.

Unorthodox Viewpoints: Some argue that sin does not exist. Others argue that sin is an illusion. Still others minimize sin as a mere mistake. It is noteworthy that groups that have a weak view of sin typically have a correspondingly weak view of salvation.

Course of Action: On the doctrine of human depravity, there must be conviction without compromise.

7

Christ's Virgin Birth

SOME HAVE CHALLENGED WHETHER the virgin birth of Jesus is an essential doctrine of the Christian Faith. While the connection is not as explicit as are other doctrines, such as Jesus' death and resurrection, it is nevertheless strong. To put it bluntly, if Jesus had two biological parents like the rest of us, then He would be a sinner like the rest of us. His virgin conception enabled Him to avoid inheriting a sin nature. Hence, the virgin birth is connected with His sinlessness, which is a fundamental doctrine of the Faith.

The Biblical Basis for the Virgin Birth

The virgin birth of Christ is implied in the very first messianic prophecy in the Bible. It is made explicit in later predictions and in the gospel narration of Christ's birth. Let's consider some scriptural highlights:

Genesis 3:15: Speaking to the Tempter (Satan), God said, "I will put enmity between you and the woman, and between your offspring and hers; he will crush your head, and you will strike his heel." That the coming Redeemer was to be the "offspring" or "seed" of the woman is significant in a patriarchal culture. Normally, descendants were traced through their father (see Genesis 5; 11). Even the official genealogy of the Messiah as given in Matthew 1 is traced through Jesus' legal father, Joseph. The implication of being born offspring or seed *of the woman* is that the Messiah would not have a natural father—that is, He would be virgin born.

Jeremiah 22:30: Another intimation of the virgin birth in the Old

Testament is found in the curse placed on Jeconiah: "Record this man as if childless, a man who will not prosper in his lifetime, for none of his offspring will prosper, none will sit on the throne of David or rule anymore in Judah" (Jeremiah 22:30). The problem with this prediction is that Jesus was the descendant of David through Jeconiah (Matthew 1:12). However, because Joseph was only Jesus' *legal* father (by virtue of being engaged to Mary when she became pregnant), Jesus did not inherit the curse on Jeconiah's *actual* descendants. And because Jesus was the actual son of David through Mary according to Luke's matriarchal genealogy (see Luke 3:31), He fulfilled the conditions of coming from the loins of David (2 Samuel 7:12-16) without losing the legal rights to the throne of David by falling under the curse placed on Jeconiah. Thus, the virgin birth is implied in Jeremiah 22:30.

Isaiah 7:14: The virgin birth of Christ is not only implied in the Old Testament, it is actually predicted there, in Isaiah 7:14: "The Lord Himself will give you a sign: The virgin will be with child and will give birth to a son, and will call him Immanuel." Some critics, however, appeal to Isaiah 7:16 in an attempt to place the birth of the child before the invasion of the Assyrian armies and the fall of Samaria in 722 B.C. They also argue that Isaiah 8:3 seems to be a fulfillment of this prophecy in the natural birth of Maher-Shalal-Hash-Baz. If so, Isaiah 7:14 cannot be cited as a prediction of the virgin birth of Jesus. The following evidence is offered in support of the view that Isaiah 7:14 *does* predict the virgin birth:

First, the Hebrew word *almah* in this text should definitely be translated "virgin," because there are no examples in the Old Testament where it means anything but a young unmarried girl. Because she was to conceive and bear the child *as a virgin*, it does not make good sense to say the prediction was fulfilled in someone who conceived in a natural way, such as the mother of Maher-Shalal-Hash-Baz.

Second, the Hebrew word *bethulah* was *not* used in Isaiah 7:14 because it does not always mean a young *unmarried* girl. It can refer to a married person (see Joel 1:8), and hence it is significant that this common word was *not* used.

Third, the Greek Old Testament or Septuagint (LXX), which predates the time of Christ, translated the Hebrew word *almah* by the unambiguous Greek word *parthenos*, which always means "virgin." Hence, the translators of the Greek Old Testament evidently believed Isaiah 7:14 was a prediction of the virgin birth of the Messiah.

Fourth, the inspired New Testament text sanctioned the LXX translation of *almah* as "virgin" when it quoted the LXX of Isaiah 7:14 to show that this prophecy was fulfilled in the virgin birth of Christ (see Matthew 1:23).

Fifth, because *almah* always means a young girl who is not yet married, it follows that to deny that it refers to a virgin demands that she get married before the child is born. But if she is married, then it is no longer a virgin who is conceiving, but a married woman. This, however, is contrary to Isaiah 7:14, which says clearly, "the virgin shall conceive and bear a Son" (NKJV). That is, both the *conception* and *birth* were by a virgin. This would not be true of a natural birth.

Sixth, there are dimensions of this prophecy that can refer only to Christ. For example, the one born of a virgin will be called (not merely named) *Immanuel*, or "God with us," which is quoted in Matthew 1:23 as a reference to the deity of Christ.

Seventh, the prediction obviously goes beyond the time of King Ahaz, since it is given to the whole "house of David" (Isaiah 7:13). Hence, it cannot be limited to a natural birth by a prophetess in Isaiah's day (Isaiah 8:1).

Eighth, because the emphasis is on some wonderful, unheard-of "sign" (see Isaiah 7:11-14), it is best explained by the supernatural birth of Christ, not by the natural birth of Maher-Shalal-Hash-Baz. Why should an ordinary birth be understood as an extraordinary sign of one who was called "God with us"?

Ninth, the entire context of Isaiah 7–11 forms an unbreakable chain of messianic prophecy (for example, Isaiah 7:14; 8:8; 9:6; 11:1-5).

Tenth, the New Testament interprets Isaiah 7:14 as prophetic of the divine Messiah. This is indicated by—

- the phrase "that it might be fulfilled" (Matthew 1:22 NKJV);
- the intensifying phrase used with it, namely, "*all this was*

done that it might be fulfilled" (NKJV, emphasis added); and

- the manner in which the passage is used to show the supernaturalness of the birth and deity of Christ (Matthew 1:23).

Eleventh, one and the same verse cannot refer to both the birth of Maher-Shalal-Hash-Baz in Isaiah's day *and* the birth of the divine Messiah. For the same verse cannot mean two opposing things. In other words, the verse cannot refer to Maher-Shalal-Hash-Baz being born of a *married girl* while at the same time also predicting Jesus will be born of a *virgin*. If both the LXX and the inspired New Testament affirm that the verse refers to someone who was a virgin, then it cannot apply to Maher-Shalal-Hash-Baz. It follows, then, that it *must* refer to Christ.

Matthew 1:18-23: Despite the ongoing debate about Isaiah 7:14, the New Testament clearly affirms that Christ was born of a virgin. Matthew, under the inspiration of the Holy Spirit, wrote:

> This is how the birth of Jesus Christ came about: His mother Mary was pledged to be married to Joseph, but *before they came together*, she was found to be with child through the Holy Spirit. Because Joseph her husband was a righteous man and did not want to expose her to public disgrace, *he had in mind to divorce her quietly*. But after he had considered this, an angel of the Lord appeared to him in a dream and said, "Joseph son of David, do not be afraid to take Mary home as your wife, because *what is conceived in her is from the Holy Spirit*. She will give birth to a son, and you are to give him the name Jesus, because he will save his people from their sins." *All this took place to fulfill what the Lord had said through the prophet: "The virgin will be with child and will give birth to a son, and they will call him Immanuel"*—which means, "God with us" (Matthew 1:18-23, emphasis added).

The emphasized sections of this passage point to four factors that demonstrate Christ was virgin-born:

1. Mary conceived "before they came together," thus revealing hers was not a natural conception.
2. Joseph's initial reaction reveals he had not had sexual relations with Mary, because when he found out she was pregnant, "he had in mind to divorce her quietly."
3. The phrase "what is conceived in her is from the Holy Spirit" reveals the supernatural nature of the event.
4. The citation of the prophet about a "virgin" giving "birth" to a child indicates that Mary had not had sexual relations with anyone. For she was not simply a virgin before the baby was conceived, but also *during* and *after* it was conceived, even when it was *born*.

Luke 1:26-35: Dr. Luke, as one might expect of a physician, gives great attention to Jesus' ancestry, birth, and childhood. He begins with the announcement of Christ's birth:

> In the sixth month, God sent the angel Gabriel to Nazareth, a town in Galilee, to a *virgin* [who was] *pledged to be married* to a man named Joseph, a descendant of David. The *virgin's* name was Mary. The angel went to her and said, "Greetings, you who are *highly favored!* The Lord is with you." Mary was *greatly troubled* at his words and wondered what kind of greeting this might be. But the angel said to her, "Do not be *afraid*, Mary, you have found favor with God. You will be with child and give birth to a son, and you are to give him the name Jesus.... *The Holy Spirit will come upon you, and the power of the Most High will overshadow you.* So the holy one to be born will be called the Son of God" (Luke 1:26-31,35, emphasis added, insert added).

The emphasized text in this passage demonstrates that the conception of Christ was supernatural:

1. Mary was a "virgin" (Greek: *parthenos*) at the time (this

Greek word always connotes someone who has not had sexual relations with a man);

2. Mary's reaction of being "greatly troubled" and being "afraid" reveals that she knew she was a virgin; and
3. The fact that the angel said the conception would be from "the power of the Most High" indicates this was to be a supernatural virgin conception.

John 8:41: In John's Gospel, even the insult of Jesus' enemies provided a backhanded compliment, or indication, that He was born of a virgin. Jesus said to them, "You are doing the things your own father does." They responded, "We are not illegitimate children [as you are]" (insert added). Their response implies they were aware of the claim that Jesus was virgin-born and did not accept it, implying instead that He was born of fornication. Of course, even Joseph thought that until he was supernaturally convinced otherwise by an angel (Matthew 1:20). What's more, how could a person born in sin live a sinless and miraculous life? Jesus boldly asked His enemies, "Can any of you prove me guilty of sin?" (John 8:46).

Galatians 4:4: The epistles are filled with references to Jesus' sinlessness, which, again, implies His virgin birth (2 Corinthians 5:21; Hebrews 4:15; 1 Peter 3:18; 1 John 2:1; 3:3). But Paul's reference to Jesus being "born of a woman" is even more explicit. He wrote, "When the time had fully come, God sent his Son, born of a woman, born under law" (Galatians 4:4). This is a throwback to Genesis 3:15 (see on page 79). In a Jewish patriarchal culture, one is normally said to be begotten of a male (the father). To bring attention to being "born of a woman" is to show that something unusual occurred—in Jesus' case, a virgin birth.

The Theological Importance of the Virgin Birth

Granted that Jesus was virgin-born, the question we must now address is whether this doctrine is essential for our salvation. Certainly the underlying doctrine to which the virgin birth points—*the sinlessness of Christ*—is essential to salvation. For a sinner cannot be the Savior of sinners. He would need a Savior himself. A drowning person cannot save another person who is drowning. Certainly anyone born the natural way would have been—short of divine intervention—a sinner like the rest of us (Romans 3:23; 5:12). The virgin birth was apparently God's way to completely circumvent this problem.

In addition, it was important, if not crucial, to our salvation that God supernaturally signify which of all the persons born of women (Genesis 3:15; Galatians 4:4) was His Son, the Savior of the world.[1] A mere "immaculate conception" of Christ would not have been an outward "sign" that drew attention to the Savior's supernatural and sinless nature from the very beginning. Hence, both by the underlying doctrine of Christ's sinlessness and by its nature as a supernatural sign, the virgin birth was a divinely appointed necessity for our salvation.

The Creedal Basis for the Virgin Birth

Beginning with the very earliest post-New Testament creeds, there are repeated and continual references to the virgin birth. The Apostles' Creed speaks of "Jesus Christ...our Lord: who was conceived of the Holy Spirit, born of the Virgin Mary." Likewise, the Nicene Creed declares Jesus was "incarnate of the Holy Spirit and the Virgin Mary." The Chalcedonian Creed adds, "This selfsame one was born of Mary the virgin, who is God-bearer in respect of his humanness." The Athanasian Creed also affirms the virgin birth, stating that Christ was "God of the substance of the Father...and man of the substance of His mother." Clearly, His humanity came from His mother.

Unorthodox Denials of Christ's Virgin Birth

There have been numerous denials of the virgin birth throughout church history, and there are plenty of such denials in today's kingdom of the cults. For example, in the second century the Ebionites claimed Jesus was a mere man, a prophet who was the natural son of Joseph and Mary. Jesus allegedly distinguished Himself by strict observance of the Jewish law, and was accordingly chosen to be the Messiah because of His legal piety. The consciousness that God chose Him to be the Messiah came at His baptism, when He received the Holy Spirit. Jesus' mission as the Messiah was not to save humankind, but to call all humanity to obey the law. Quite obviously, according to this view, there was no virgin birth. Interestingly, history reveals that this teaching had an influence on how Muhammad, the founder of Islam, viewed Jesus.

Another heresy that surfaced in the second century was Gnosticism, which espoused a dualism between matter and spirit. Among other things, Gnosticism espoused the idea that a special emissary from the kingdom of light was sent into the material world of darkness. This emissary is most often identified with Christ. One influential Gnostic by the name of Cerinthus set forth the idea that a cosmic, spiritual "Christ" came upon a human Jesus at His baptism but departed before His crucifixion. During the interim, the Christ (through the body of Jesus) communicated His secret *gnosis* (knowledge) to His followers. In this viewpoint, there certainly was no virgin birth, for Jesus was a mere (natural) human being. Today this error is repeated in Mind Science cults such as Religious Science and the Unity School of Christianity, as well as in the New Age movement.

Of course, Scripture indicates not that a cosmic Christ came upon an adult human Jesus but that Jesus was the one and only Christ from the very beginning (Luke 2:11; 1 John 2:22). The Old Testament presents numerous prophecies regarding the coming of a single Messiah (for example, Isaiah 7:14; 53:3-5; Micah 5:2; Zechariah 12:10). The New Testament counterpart of the Old Testament word for "Messiah" is "Christ" (John 1:41). Jesus alone fulfilled these prophecies, and hence He alone is the Christ (Luke 9:20), virgin-born (Luke 1:26-35).

Certainly the early Jews denied Christ was virgin-born. We see this in references to Jesus in the Talmud, a collection of ancient rabbinic writings on Jewish law and tradition that constitute the basis of religious authority in orthodox Judaism. Because the Jewish religious leaders were against Jesus, what found its way into the Talmud was understandably unflattering. Keeping this hostility in mind, the Talmudic text indicates that Jesus was born of an adulteress (an attempt at explaining away the virgin birth), and that He practiced sorcery (an attempt to explain away His miracles).[2]

Today it is fashionable for critics to deny the virgin birth by claiming that the concept itself was derived from ancient Greek mythology and paganism. Such critics are distorting the facts. Greek mythology and paganism held that the Greek male gods came down to have sex with human women, who then gave birth to hybrid beings. Christian scholars Ed Komoszewski, James Sawyer, and Daniel Wallace tell us:

> Mythology offers accounts of male deities taking physical form (sometimes human) and impregnating a woman through physical contact. In these stories, the women involved have some sort of sexual relations, so they are not virgins in the strict meaning of the term. By contrast, Gospel accounts of the virgin birth are decidedly non-sexual. Jesus is conceived by the creative power of the Holy Spirit in Mary's womb. He is born of a woman without the seed of man—or god.[3]

Moreover, the chronology for such claims is all wrong. The late Ronald Nash, widely considered an expert on ancient mythology and paganism, noted that "almost all of our sources of information about the pagan religions alleged to have influenced early Christianity are dated very late. We frequently find writers quoting from documents written 300 years [later]." Nash said, "We must reject the assumption that just because a cult had a certain belief or practice in the third or fourth century after Christ, it therefore had the same belief or practice in the first century."[4] Moreover, as the late Bruce Metzger noted, "It must not be uncritically assumed that the Mysteries always influenced Christianity, for it is not only possible but probable that in certain cases, the influence moved in the opposite direction."[5] It should not be surprising that leaders of cults that were being successfully challenged by Christianity should do something to counter the challenge. What better way to do this than by offering a pagan substitute?

Further, the New Testament documents that speak of the virgin birth—all based on eyewitness accounts—do not bear the literary marks of the myth genre. In fact, one Gospel that speaks of the virgin birth, Luke, has been universally lauded by scholars for its historical accuracy.

One modern group known for its denial of the virgin birth is the

Unitarian Universalists, who respect Jesus as a moral teacher and influence, but do not view Him as God. He is viewed as "one of a number of great moral and ethical teachers who have lived on earth."[6] In the Unitarian Universalist book *A Chosen Faith*, we read, "Most of us would agree that the important thing about Jesus is not his supposed miraculous birth or the claim that he was resurrected from death, but rather how he lived. The power of his love, the penetrating simplicity of his teachings, and the force of his example of service on behalf of the disenfranchised and downtrodden are what is crucial."[7] Appealing to human reason, Unitarian Universalists reject Christ's miracles, His virgin birth, and His resurrection from the dead as mythological.[8] The miracle stories recorded in the four Gospels contain embellishments on the part of biased Gospel writers.[9]

The fallacy of the bias charge is to imagine that to give an account of something one believes in passionately necessarily forces one to distort history. This is simply not true. In modern times, some of the most reliable reports of the Nazi Holocaust were written by Jews who were passionately committed to seeing such genocide never repeated. The New Testament is not made up of fairy tales, but is rather based on eyewitness testimony. In 2 Peter 1:16 we read, "We did not follow cleverly invented stories when we told you about the power and coming of our Lord Jesus Christ, but we were eyewitnesses of his majesty." First John 1:1 affirms, "That which was from the beginning, which we have heard, which we have seen with our eyes, which we have looked at and our hands have touched—this we proclaim concerning the Word of life." The New Testament witnesses gave up their lives in defense of what they knew to be the truth.

Yet another modern cult with a warped view of the virgin birth is the Jehovah's Witnesses. According to the Watchtower Society, Jesus was originally created as the archangel Michael—the first being Jehovah-God created in the universe. He allegedly existed in this state for billions of years. At the appointed time, he was born on earth as a human being—ceasing his existence as an angel. In order to "ransom" humankind from sin, Michael willingly gave up his existence as a spirit creature (angel) when his "life force" was transferred into Mary's womb by Jehovah. This was not an incarnation (God in the flesh). Rather, when Jehovah transferred Michael's life force into Mary's womb, Jesus became a perfect human being—nothing more and nothing less. He lived his life as a perfect human, fulfilled the ministry appointed to him by Jehovah, and died faithfully *as a man* for the ransom of humankind.

This view falls short theologically in many ways. First, why send Jesus at all? Since according to Jehovah's Witnesses all that was required for sacrifice was "a perfect human," God could easily have created one from scratch if He wanted. There was certainly no compelling need for God to send His "first and greatest creature," Jesus. Second, Scripture provides plenty of evidence that in the incarnation Jesus was truly God in human flesh. Colossians 2:9 tells us, "In Christ all the fullness of the Deity lives in bodily form." Jesus thus fulfilled the prophecy of Isaiah 7:14: "'The virgin will be with child and will give birth to a son, and they will call him Immanuel'—which means, 'God with us'" (Matthew 1:23). Third, only the death of the *God*-man, not a *mere* man, is sufficient to bear the sins of humankind (Acts 20:28; 1 Peter 1:18-19; Revelation 1:5).

In view of the above, it seems clear that there is a close connection between cultic denials of the virgin birth and the denial of Christ's deity.

THEOLOGICAL QUICK-REVIEW

Chapter 7 Main Idea: Jesus, in the incarnation, was virgin-born.

Importance: Through the virgin birth (or, more accurately, virgin conception), God circumvented Jesus receiving a sin nature, and clearly delineated Jesus as *the* Savior born among humans.

Unorthodox Viewpoints: Throughout church history some have outright denied the virgin birth; others have claimed it is rooted in pagan mythology; and still others have redefined it in a variety of unbiblical ways.

Course of Action: On the doctrine of the virgin birth, there must be conviction without compromise.

8

Christ's Sinlessness

THE SINLESSNESS OF CHRIST is essential to our salvation. To put it boldly, if Jesus had two parents like the rest of us, then He would have been a sinner like the rest of us. Unless He was without sin, then sinners are without salvation. Hence, His sinlessness is a fundamental doctrine of the Christian Faith.

The Biblical Basis for Christ's Sinlessness

The sinless life of Christ was observed by friend and foe (emphasis is added in all the following quotes). Pilate said, "I am innocent of the blood of this *just Person*" (Matthew 27:24 NKJV). The hardened Roman soldier cried out, "Truly, this was a righteous Man!" (Luke 23:47 NKJV). Even Jesus' betrayer recanted, saying, "I have sinned by betraying *innocent blood*" (Matthew 27:4 NKJV). One of Jesus' foremost former enemies declared, "[God] made *him who had no sin* to be sin for us, so that in him we might become the righteousness of God" (2 Corinthians 5:21).

The writer of Hebrews affirmed, "We have one who has been tempted in every way, just as we are—*yet was without sin*" (Hebrews 4:15). Jesus is one who "*loved righteousness* and *hated wickedness*" (Hebrews 1:9). He was "*holy, blameless,* [and] *pure*" (Hebrews 7:26).

One of Jesus' chief disciples, Peter, said, "You know that it was not with perishable things such as silver or gold that you were redeemed...but with the precious blood of Christ, *a lamb without blemish or defect*" (1 Peter 1:18-19). He added, "He committed *no sin,* and *no deceit* was found in his mouth" (1 Peter 2:22, from Isaiah 53:9).

Jesus' beloved disciple John declared He was "Jesus Christ *the Righteous One*" (1 John 2:1). "Everyone who has this hope in him purifies himself, just as *he is pure*" (1 John 3:3). "You know that he appeared so that he might take away our sins. And *in him is no sin*" (1 John 3:5). There is "nothing false" about Jesus (John 7:18), and He always did what pleased the Father (John 8:29).

Certainly there were some in Bible times who tried to argue that Jesus sinned or was unrighteous. For example, the Jewish high priest charged Jesus with blasphemy when Jesus told the truth about His divine identity (Mark 14:61-64). A false witness at Jesus' trial misconstrued what Jesus said about the temple being destroyed and rebuilt in three days (Matthew 26:61). Jesus had actually been speaking about His death and resurrection (John 2:19-22).

There were other such allegations. But the fact is that no one ever successfully laid any sin at the feet of Jesus. He challenged His enemies, "Can any of you prove me guilty of sin?" (John 8:46). The challenge still stands 2000 years later. All who have tried have failed. Bertrand Russell said Jesus was unkind because He warned people of hell. But if there is a hell—and Jesus, the Son of God, was in a better position to know than Russell—then it would be *un*kind *not* to warn people about it. In fact, the most loving thing Jesus could do was to warn people about hell, and let them know the way to escape it.

The Theological Importance of Christ's Sinlessness

Christ's sinlessness is essential to our salvation. The very gospel by which we are saved (Romans 1:16) affirms that He died for our sins (1 Corinthians 15:1-4). How could He have done that if He had sins of His own? Unless He was without sin, then sinners are without salvation. For, as Paul noted, He who died for our sin had to be sinless Himself (2 Corinthians 5:21). Even the Old Testament Passover lamb, which typologically* pointed forward to Christ as the ultimate Passover Lamb of God (1 Corinthians 5:7), had to be "without spot or blemish" (Exodus

---

* A *type* is an Old Testament institution, event, person, object, or ceremony that has reality and purpose in biblical history, but which also—by divine design—foreshadows something yet to be revealed. The Passover lamb was a "type" of Christ.

12:5). Peter confirmed this, noting that we are redeemed by "the precious blood of Christ, a lamb without blemish or defect" (1 Peter 1:19).

The Creedal Basis for Christ's Sinlessness

Christ's sinlessness is everywhere implied in the early creeds. First, His virgin birth—mentioned in almost all the creeds—is a sign of His sinlessness. Second, the fact that He "was crucified," "suffered," and "died" for "our sins"—mentioned in most of the creeds—implies He was sinless Himself. Third, that He will "judge the living and the dead" (mentioned in almost all the creeds) for their sins shows that He must be sinless Himself. Finally, the Chalcedonian Creed says explicitly that Jesus was "perfect both in deity and in humanness" and that He was "like us in all respects, sin only excepted."

Unorthodox Denials of Christ's Sinlessness

The Barna Research Group conducted a nationwide survey of American adults in 1999 and found that 42 percent of adults believe Jesus committed sin during His time on earth. Amazingly, only 67 percent of "Bible readers" believe Jesus was sinless, only 65 percent of "born-again Christians" believe He was sinless, and only 58 percent of "churchgoers" believe He was sinless.[1] One must wonder how Jesus got such a less-than-stellar track record in the minds of some people, especially since everything we read of Him in the Bible shows Him to be altogether sinless.

While it is surprising that some who claim to be Christians deny Jesus was sinless, it is not surprising there are cults and false religions who deny Jesus was sinless. For example, some Hindus and New Agers, who consider Jesus a mere sage, assert that He was not perfect or sinless in view of some of His actions recorded in the New Testament. For example, it is said He demonstrated anger when He drove money changers out of the temple (Mark 11:15-19). As well, He caused a fig tree to wither when He saw there were no figs on it to eat (Matthew 21:19).

Christians answer that Jesus remained sinless in *all* His actions. The Bible indicates that even God demonstrates righteous anger (Exodus 4:14; Numbers 12:9; Psalm 2:5), and it was with a righteous anger that Jesus drove money changers out of the temple. The backdrop is that when people came to Jerusalem from various cities to offer sacrifices, they had to buy animals from vendors in order to sacrifice them. Sometimes families would bring their own animals, only to be told their animals had impurities on them and were hence unacceptable for sacrifice. They were thus forced to purchase suitable animals in Jerusalem, often at exorbitant prices. Further, because people came to Jerusalem from various cities, their money had to be converted into local currency. People were charged extra money for this conversion. The temple, which was a sacred, holy place of God, had been encroached upon by vendors eager to make a lot of money. Thus Jesus demonstrated righteous anger when He drove the money changers out (Matthew 21:12). Clearly, then, Jesus did not engage in sinful behavior here.

Regarding the fig tree episode, it might seem at first glance that Jesus was just responding in anger to the tree, but this is not the case. One must keep in mind the broader backdrop of Jesus' teaching methodology, which often involved parables and word pictures. Scholars agree that Jesus, in the present case, was performing a living parable—an acted-out parable to teach His disciples an important truth. His cursing of the fig tree was a dramatic visual aid. Contextually, it would seem that because the fig tree had leaves on it (Matthew 21:19), it gave the appearance of being fruitful. Upon closer examination, however, it became clear there was no fruit on the tree. It would seem, then, that Jesus' cursing of the fig tree was an acted-out parable that taught the disciples that God will judge those who give an outer appearance of fruitfulness but in fact are not fruitful at all (much like the religious leaders of that day, the Pharisees). Seen in this light, there was no sinful behavior on the part of Jesus.

A representative modern cult that denies the sinlessness of Jesus is the Christadelphians. According to this cult, Jesus was not God in human flesh. He did not exist until He was born in Bethlehem. He "did not actually come into being until He was begotten of the Holy Spirit and born in Bethlehem."[2]

Christadelphians believe Jesus had a sin nature, and was thus in need of redemption himself.[3] "It is not only that Jesus was called a sinner at his trial by his enemies or that he was 'numbered with the transgressors' when he was crucified between two thieves, but more particularly that he shared the very nature which had made a sinner out of every other man who had borne it."[4] Jesus is said to have inherited this sinful nature from Mary: "It was for that very reason—being a member of a sinful race—that the Lord Jesus himself needed salvation."[5] Christadelphians argue that Jesus would have had to possess a sin nature in order to be genuinely tempted.

Christadelphians suggest that Jesus had to engage in self-redemption before seeking to redeem the rest of humanity. They claim "it is equally true that, being 'made sin for us' (2 Cor. 5:21), he himself required a sin offering."[6] We are told that "He [Jesus] saved himself in order to save us."[7] Even then, Jesus did not finally and completely attain human salvation at the cross. "We reject as unbiblical the idea that Christ could die as a replacement for us, thus covering all our sins forever with that one act. Certainly it is through his sacrifice that we may be forgiven, but only if we walk the path of self-denial that he marked out for us."[8]

A number of points can be offered in answering the Christadelphian view of Jesus. First, Jesus was not a mere man who first came into existence in Bethlehem, but is rather eternal God (John 1:1; 8:58), who, in the incarnation, took on a human nature (Philippians 2:5-11).

Second, the biblical record is clear that Jesus was sinless. As noted previously, Scripture refers to Jesus as "him who had no sin" (2 Corinthians 5:21), as one who "loved righteousness and hated wickedness" (Hebrews 1:9), and as being "holy, blameless, [and] pure" (Hebrews 7:26).

Third, not only did Jesus not sin, He did not have a sin nature. As noted in chapter 7, Jesus' virgin conception—via the miraculous work of the Holy Spirit (Matthew 1:18-23; Luke 1:26-35)—enabled Him to avoid inheriting a sin nature.

Fourth, because Jesus was sinless, and had no sin nature, He was not in need of personal redemption. Indeed, it is by virtue of Jesus being sinless that He qualifies as the Lamb of God who takes away the sins of the world. Just as the Passover lamb in Old Testament times had to be without spot or blemish (Exodus 12:5), so Jesus as the Lamb of God was "without blemish or defect" (1 Peter 1:19), and was therefore a perfect sacrifice for the sins of humankind. Contrary to what the Christadelphians say, a fallen, unholy, and sinful Jesus cannot possibly be a pure and perfect sacrifice without defect.

Fifth, the argument that Jesus would have had to possess a sin nature in order to be genuinely tempted is fallacious. After all, Adam was not created with a sin nature, and yet he was tempted and gave in to that temptation. Conversely, Jesus likewise had no sin nature but, unlike Adam, He did not fall into sin: He "has been tempted in every way, just as we are—yet was without sin" (Hebrews 4:15). One must keep in mind that there is a difference between *being* tempted and *yielding to* temptation. Simply being tempted is not sinful. However, allowing oneself to be enticed by temptation and then being "dragged away" by evil desires is sin (James 1:14). One theologian notes, "After struggling, Jesus always resisted temptation because he freely determined to think and do in accord with his sinless human nature and his sinless divine nature."[9]

Sixth and finally, the claim that Jesus saved Himself before saving the rest of humanity is ridiculous. A sinner cannot be the Savior of other sinners. Only a sinless Savior can save sinners. As the apostle Paul put it, "God made him *who had no sin* to be sin for us, so that we might become the righteousness of God" (2 Corinthians 5:21, emphasis added).

Speaking of 2 Corinthians 5:21, one other group we might mention regarding Christ's sinlessness is the Word-Faith movement. Word-Faith leaders interpret 2 Corinthians 5:21 to mean that at the cross, Jesus *actually became sin* and took on the nature of Satan. Kenneth Copeland tells us that Jesus "put Himself into the hands of Satan when He went to that cross, and took that same nature that Adam did [when he sinned]."[10] He adds, "The day that Jesus was crucified, God's life, that eternal energy that was His from birth, moved out of Him and He accepted the very nature of death itself."[11] We are told that Jesus "had to give up His righteousness"[12] and "accepted the sin nature of Satan."[13]

Biblically, of course, Christ did not take on the nature of Satan, for Christ *as God* is immutable and cannot change in His divine nature (Hebrews 13:8; see also Malachi 3:6). In Hebrews 1:12 the Father said of Jesus, "*You remain the same,* and your years will never end" (emphasis added).

Regarding Jesus being "made to be sin" (2 Corinthians 5:21), the correct biblical view is that Jesus was always without sin *actually,* but He was made to be sin for us *judicially.* That is, by His death on the cross, He paid the penalty for our sins and thereby canceled the debt of sin against us. So, while Jesus never committed a sin *personally*, He was made to be sin for us *substitutionally*.

One must keep in mind the Old Testament backdrop of the concept of substitution. The sacrificial victim had to be "without defect" (see Leviticus 4:3,23,32). A hand would be laid on the unblemished sacrificial animal as a way of symbolizing a transfer of guilt (Leviticus 4:4,24,33). Note that the sacrificial animal did not thereby actually *become* sinful by nature; rather, sin was *imputed* to the animal and the animal acted as a sacrificial substitute. In like manner, Christ, the Lamb of God, was utterly unblemished (1 Peter 1:19), but our sin was imputed to Him and He was our sacrificial substitute on the cross of Calvary. The fact our sin was imputed to Jesus does not mean He changed in nature.

Finally, one must note the impossibility of Jesus taking on the "nature of death" to Himself. After all, Scripture asserts that Jesus has "life in himself" (John 5:26), and is the "resurrection and the life" (John 11:25), and is "the way and the truth and the life" (John 14:6). And because Jesus, as God, is immutable (Hebrews 13:8), He cannot change in this regard.

THEOLOGICAL QUICK-REVIEW

Chapter 8 Main Idea: Jesus is absolutely sinless.

Importance: Unless Jesus was completely without sin, sinners are without salvation. As Paul noted, He who died for our sin had to be sinless Himself (2 Corinthians 5:21).

Unorthodox Viewpoints: Some claim that a few actions of Jesus in the New Testament indicate the presence of sin in Him. Others claim Jesus sinned because He had a sin nature, and that He could not really be tempted unless He had a sin nature. Still others claim that Jesus became sin at the cross of Calvary.

Course of Action: On the doctrine of Christ's total sinlessness, there must be conviction without compromise.

9

Christ's Atoning Death

AS THE APOSTLE PAUL NOTED, the atoning death and resurrection of Christ are the heart of the gospel (1 Corinthians 15:1-6), which alone is the power of God unto salvation (Romans 1:16). This places the atonement of Christ at the very heart of the essential doctrines of the Christian Faith.

The Biblical Basis for the Atonement

The biblical words for *atonement* are rich in meaning. The Old Testament Hebrew word is *kaphar* and carries the meaning "to cover, expiate, wipe away, placate, or cancel." The key thought is "to cover over in God's eyes," or "to wipe away." The term is used in verbal form some 100 times in the Old Testament. The New Testament Greek term is *hiloskomai* and carries the meaning "to propitiate, expiate, or conciliate." It is used only twice in the New Testament. In the first instance, a penitent sinner asks God to "be merciful" to him, hearkening back to the Old Testament image where God met the sinner at the Mercy Seat when blood atonement was made for sins (Luke 18:13 NKJV). In the second, we read of Jesus, "For this reason he had to be made like his brothers in every way, in order that he might become a merciful and faithful high priest in service to God, and that he might *make atonement* for the sins of the people" (Hebrews 2:17, emphasis added).

The foreshadowing of Christ's atonement at the cross is evident in the Old Testament sacrificial system, in which blood atonement of innocent animals was regularly required for sins (see Leviticus 4:14-21). This sacrificial system pointed forward to Christ's once-for-all blood sacrifice for our sins (1 Corinthians 5:7). Scripture informs us that blood is necessary for making atonement. In Leviticus 17:11 God said, "The life of a creature is in the blood, and I have given it to you to make atonement for yourselves on the altar; it is the blood that makes atonement for one's life." This points forward to the necessity of Christ's blood sacrifice in the New Testament. As Hebrews 9:22 puts it, "the law requires that nearly everything be cleansed with blood, and without the shedding of blood there is no forgiveness."

Nothing but the blood sacrifice of Jesus, the Lamb of God, could bring atonement for the sins of all humankind (John 1:29). In Hebrews 10 we find an inspired commentary on the Old Testament concept of atonement, especially regarding the ultimate need for Jesus' sacrifice: "It is impossible for the blood of bulls and goats to take away sins....Day after day every priest stands and performs his religious duties; again and again he offers the same sacrifices, which can never take away sins. But when this priest [Jesus] had offered for all time one sacrifice for sins, he sat down at the right hand of God....Since that time he waits for his enemies to be made his footstool, because by one sacrifice he has made perfect for ever those who are being made holy" (verses 4,11-13).

Sacrificial Atonement

Scripture indicates that Christ's atonement is substitutionary in nature. Christ died *in our place*. He was punished for our sins that we might be set free. While all the church fathers believed Christ sacrificed His life for us, not all saw the importance of understanding His work on the cross as a substitutionary atonement. Nonetheless, there are many solid biblical reasons for understanding His atonement this way.[1]

First, God's absolute justice demands a perfect substitute for our sin. He cannot simply overlook sin (Habakkuk 1:13). God is essentially just and cannot be otherwise, since He is, by nature, unchanging (Malachi 3:6; Titus 1:2; Hebrews 6:18; James 1:17).

Second, human depravity (see chapter 6) demands a perfect substitute for human sin. Nothing that human beings can do measures up to God's perfect standard. Only a substitutionary sacrifice can rectify humankind's dilemma.

Third, the Old Testament sacrifices implied a substitutionary atonement. The one who offered the sacrifices laid his hands on the animals, symbolizing a transfer of guilt (Leviticus 1:3-4).

Fourth, Isaiah 53:5-6 speaks explicitly about substitutionary suffering in several phrases: " [1] He was pierced *for* our transgressions, [2] he was crushed *for* our iniquities; [3] the punishment that brought us peace *was upon him,* [4] by *his* wounds *we* are healed…and [5] the LORD has *laid on him* the iniquity of us all" (emphasis added, bracketed numbers added).

Fifth, just as the Old Testament Passover lamb was sacrificed for the sins of Old Testament believers, even so "Christ, our Passover lamb, has been sacrificed" for us (1 Corinthians 5:7). John the Baptist declared, "Look, the Lamb of God, who takes away the sin of the world!" (John 1:29).

Sixth, in keeping with this, Jesus claimed to be the fulfillment of Isaiah 53, which portrayed a substitutionary sacrifice (see Luke 22:37).

Seventh, Jesus presented His death as a ransom (Greek: *lutron*), a term which, in the Greek Old Testament (LXX), usually meant a deliverance from bondage *in exchange for* a payment of compensation or the *offering of a substitute.* Jesus came "to give his life as a *ransom* for many" (Mark 10:45, emphasis added).

Eighth, the book of Hebrews declares,

> Only the high priest entered the inner room, and that only once a year, and never without blood, which he offered *for* himself and for the sins the people had committed in ignorance….For this reason Christ is the mediator of a new covenant, that those who are called may receive the promised eternal inheritance—now that he has *died as a ransom* to set them free from the sins committed under the first covenant (Hebrews 9:7,15, emphasis added).

Similarly, when Christ came into the world, He said to the Father, "Sacrifice and offering you did not desire, but a body you prepared for me; with burnt offerings and sin offerings you were not pleased" (Hebrews 10:5). Jesus Himself died on our behalf, and "we have been made holy through the sacrifice of the body of Jesus Christ once for all" (verse 10).

Ninth, Christ's death was "for" us—that is, *it was on our behalf.* The Greek word for "for" (Greek: *huper*) often implies substitution. In Luke 22:19, for example, we read, "He took bread, gave thanks and broke it, and gave it to them, saying, 'This is my body given *for* you; do this in remembrance of me.'" In the same way, after the supper He took the cup, saying, "This cup is the new covenant in my blood, which is poured out *for* you" (verse 20). Likewise, in John 10:15 the word "for" implies substitution: "I lay down my life *for* the sheep." Many other passages use "for" in a substitutionary sense as well (see Romans 5:8; Galatians 3:13; 1 Timothy 2:6; Titus 2:14; Hebrews 2:9; 1 Peter 2:21; 3:18; 4:1).

Tenth, Christ's death was "for" (Greek: *anti*) us in the sense that He died *instead* of us. In Matthew 20:28, for example, Jesus affirmed that He came "to give his life as a ransom for [*anti*] many" (see also Romans 12:17; Hebrews 12:2; 1 Peter 3:9).

Next, the word "expiation" or "atoning sacrifice," used of Christ's death, implies a substitutionary sacrifice. For instance, in 1 John 2:2 we read, "He is the atoning sacrifice *for* our sins, and not only *for* ours but also *for* the sins of the whole world" (emphasis added).

Finally, appeasing God's wrath by Christ's death implies a substitutionary death. Numerous New Testament passages speak of God's wrath against sin (Romans 1:18; 2:5,8; 5:9; 9:22; 12:19; 13:4-5; Ephesians 2:3; 5:6; Colossians 3:6; 1 Thessalonians 1:10; 2:16; 5:9), thus necessitating Christ's substitutionary sacrifice: "God presented him as a sacrifice of atonement, through faith in his blood" (Romans 3:25).

Combining these arguments, there is a powerful case for the orthodox concept of a substitutionary atonement. "Christ died *for* our sins" (1 Corinthians 15:3). "God made him who had no sin to be sin *for us,* so that in him we might become the righteousness of God" (2 Corinthians 5:21). Indeed, "Christ died *for* sins once for all, the righteous *for* the unrighteous, to bring you to God" (1 Peter 3:18).

The Theological Importance of the Atonement

The sacrificial atonement of Christ lies at the heart of our salvation. As we have seen from Scripture, there is no salvation without it. On this all evangelical theologians agree. Exactly *why* this is the case is a matter of discussion, but there are strong reasons to believe the Reformers made the best sense regarding why a substitutionary atonement was necessary.

Next to Martin Luther, John Calvin is usually regarded as the most important figure in the Reformation. Luther (1483–1546) believed God justified us before Him by giving us the alien righteousness of Christ who died for us. Calvin (1509–1564) held to forensic justification, which stated that "man is not made righteous in justification, but is accepted as righteous, not on account of his own righteousness, but on account of the righteousness of Christ located outside of man."[2]

The reason human beings need justification is that they are completely depraved and totally incapable of attaining their own right standing before God. First, corruption is present at the center of man's being. Second, depravity has extended to every aspect of humanity: physical, social, and spiritual. Third, depravity prevents man from pleasing God unless enabled by grace. Fourth, depravity extends to every corner and culture of the human race.[3]

Borrowing from the apostle Paul's great exposition of this in Romans 3:21-26, it is clear that God is just and cannot overlook sin, and yet He is gracious and wants to forgive it. So, He accepted the payment for our sin when the *Just* (Christ) died for the *unjust* (human beings). The *justice* of God was thereby satisfied, enabling God to be both "just and the justifier" of the unjust who place their faith in Jesus. *This* is why the atonement is so important.

The Creedal Basis for the Atonement

Without spelling out just how the substitutionary atonement worked, the early creeds spoke of Christ's atoning death in many ways. The Apostles' Creed affirms that Christ "suffered under Pontius Pilate, was crucified, died and was buried" for our sins and "He rose again from the dead." By this He brought "forgiveness of sins...and life everlasting." The Nicene Creed repeats almost the same words, adding "for us and for our salvation he came down from heaven," and "for our sake he was crucified" whereby He provided "forgiveness of sins" and "the life of the world to come." Agreeing with the creeds before them in the phrase "following, then, the holy fathers, we unite in teaching all men," the Chalcedon Creed adds that Christ came "in these 'last days,' for us and for our salvation."

However, it was only after long debate that the substitutionary nature of Christ's death was articulated, first through St. Anselm (circa 1033–1109), and then the Reformers. Anselm argued that God cannot forgive sins without the debt being paid: "It is not right to cancel sin without compensation or punishment."[4] But he added that Jesus the God-man "paid for sinners what he owed not for himself."[5]

Unorthodox Denials of the Atonement

There are a variety of denials and distortions of the sacrificial atonement of Christ in the kingdom of the cults. Some cults concede that Christ's atonement *contributes to* salvation, but does not *accomplish* salvation. The Mormons, for example, claim that Jesus "atoned for Adam's sin, leaving us responsible only for our own sins."[6] Salvation, then, *begins* with Jesus' atonement, but each person must complete the process by doing good works. The official *Gospel Principles* manual tells us that Jesus "became our savior and he did his part to help us return to our heavenly home. It is now up to each of us to do our part and to become worthy of exaltation."[7]

The Christadelphians likewise claim Jesus did not attain a complete salvation at the cross. "We reject as unbiblical the idea that Christ could die as a replacement for us, thus covering all our sins forever with that one act. Certainly it is through his sacrifice that we may be forgiven, but only if we walk the path of self-denial that he marked out for us."[8] So, Jesus' atonement is part of the process, but human good works must complete that process.

Contrary to such views, Scripture is clear that Jesus completed the work of atonement at the cross. Upon the cross He uttered, "It is finished" (John 19:30). This proclamation is fraught with meaning. The Lord was doing more than announcing the termination of His physical life. That fact was self-evident. What He was announcing was that God, through Christ, had completed the final sacrifice for sin. The work long contemplated, long promised, long expected by prophets and saints was now accomplished (Isaiah 53:3-5; Zechariah 12:10). Jesus paid in full the price of our redemption (2 Corinthians 5:21). By His death "we have been made holy through the sacrifice of the body of Jesus Christ *once for all*" (Hebrews 10:10, emphasis added). And "after he had provided purification for sins, he sat down at the right hand of the Majesty in heaven" (Hebrews 1:3), where He remains to this day. Human works contribute nothing to our salvation (Romans 3:20; Galatians 2:16; Ephesians 2:8-9; Titus 3:5).

There are other cults today who completely deny or radically reinterpret Christ's atonement. Christian Science, for example, teaches that sin, sickness, and death are illusions. Because sin and death are illusions, Jesus could not have died on the cross for human sin. Mary Baker Eddy, the founder of Christian Science, argued that the blood of Jesus did not and could not cleanse anyone from sin: "The material blood of Jesus was no more efficacious to cleanse from sin when it was shed upon 'the accursed tree,' than when it was flowing in his veins as he went daily about his Father's business."[9] She esoterically explains away the atonement this way:

> One sacrifice, however great, is insufficient to pay the debt of sin....That God's wrath should be vented upon His beloved Son, is divinely unnatural. Such a theory is man-made. The atonement is a hard problem in theology, but its scientific explanation is, that suffering is an error of sinful sense which Truth destroys, and that eventually both sin and suffering will fall at the feet of everlasting Love.[10]

In Eddy's thought, it is not Jesus Himself who saves anyone, but rather we save ourselves through the metaphysical principles He taught. These principles are summarized in Eddy's book *Science and Health with Key to the Scriptures.*

Of course, if Jesus were just a man, as Eddy argues throughout her book, it would be correct to say that the "one sacrifice" of this man would be insufficient to pay the debt of sin. But Jesus, in the incarnation, was the God-man (Philippians 2:5-11; Colossians 2:9), and His sacrifice was therefore of infinite worth (Hebrews 10:4-14; see also John 1:29). Moreover, Jesus didn't teach metaphysical principles. Rather, He taught that human beings are utterly sinful and lost (John 8:34) and that He came to provide salvation through His sacrificial death on the cross (Matthew 20:28; John 3:17).

Another Mind Science cult that denies the atonement of Christ is the United Church of Religious Science, founded by Ernest Holmes. According to Holmes, Jesus did not have to die for any so-called sins. "Jesus made no claim that he had paid Man's debt to God, nor must God's wrath be stayed nor be appeased by a sacrifice of blood."[11]

Contrary to Holmes, Jesus described His mission this way: "The Son of Man did not come to be served, but to serve, and to *give his life a ransom for many*" (Matthew 20:28, emphasis added). "The Son of Man came to seek and to save what was lost" (Luke 19:10). "God did not send his Son into the world to condemn the world, but to save the world through him" (John 3:17). There are multiple such claims by Christ recorded in the New Testament.

Following the lead of the metaphysical cults, New Agers—advocates of "esoteric Christianity"—also completely deny or reinterpret the atoning sacrifice of Christ. New Ager Benjamin Creme, for example, says that "the Christian churches have released into the world a view of the Christ which is impossible for modern people to accept: as the one and only Son of God, sacrificed by a loving Father to save us from the results of our sins—a blood sacrifice, straight out of the old Jewish dispensation."[12] New Agers Mark and Elizabeth Prophet likewise write, "The erroneous doctrine concerning the blood sacrifice of Jesus—which he himself never taught—has been perpetuated to the present hour. God the Father did not require the sacrifice of His son Christ Jesus…as an atonement for the sins of the world; nor is it possible according to cosmic law for any man's sacrifice to balance either the original sin or the subsequent sins of the one or the many."[13] (These fallacious claims are more than adequately answered in our earlier discussion about the biblical basis for the atonement.)

New Agers often interpret the atonement in terms of reincarnation and karma. They argue that because there was so much bad karma on the earth at the time Jesus lived, the planet was in danger of self-destruction. Jesus therefore needed to be crucified to help balance the planetary karma: "Avatars—souls of great Light and spiritual attainment, such as Jesus the Christ and Gautama Buddha—were sent to take upon themselves a certain portion of mankind's planetary karma. This they were able to do because they themselves were 'without blemish and without spot,' having expiated what karma they had, if any, in previous lives."[14]

The folly of reincarnation and karma is evident in the fact that Scripture says we live once, die once, and then face the judgment (Hebrews 9:27). There is no second chance via reincarnation (see 2 Corinthians 6:2). Scripture affirms over and over again that Jesus died not for karma but for human sin (Mark 10:45; John 1:29; 1 Corinthians 5:7; Hebrews 10:4-14; 1 John 2:2). And *only* those who trust in Him during this one life will live with Him forever in heaven (John 3:16-17; Acts 16:31).

Rudolf Steiner, of the Anthroposophy cult, plummets into the bizarre when he argues that humankind fell not into sin but rather into a consciousness that overly focused on the material realm to the exclusion of the spiritual realm. He thus interprets Jesus' shed blood as the cosmic Christ's means of bringing the "Christ presence" into the spiritual earth so that people could now focus on the spiritual:

> The blood flowed from the wounds of Jesus Christ. This blood must not be regarded simply as chemical substance, it must be recognized as something altogether unique. When it flowed from His wounds and into the earth, a substance was imparted to our earth which, in uniting with it, constituted an event of the greatest possible significance; this blood passed through a process of "etherization."...Since the Mystery of Golgotha, the etherized blood of Christ Jesus has lived in the ether of the earth. The etheric body of the earth is permeated by what the blood that flowed on Golgotha became.[15]

Because of this, Steiner says, "ever since the Mystery of Golgotha man lives in a spiritual environment, an environment that has been Christianized because it has absorbed the Christ impulse."[16] Planet Earth now mystically embodies the Christ.

Such a preposterous interpretation of Scripture is hardly worthy of comment. Steiner does illustrate, however, something we said earlier in the book: *A weak view of sin will always produce a weak view of salvation.*

Steiner redefined man's fall in a minimalist way (a fall into a consciousness focused on matter), and he subsequently produced a minimalist view of salvation (restoring a spiritual environment on earth). Human sin is *nowhere* atoned for in Steiner's theology.

Since the cults do not have the *Just* (Christ) dying for the *unjust* (human beings), the unjust *remain* unjust and are therefore—tragically—justifiably condemned.

THEOLOGICAL QUICK-REVIEW

Chapter 9 Main Idea: Jesus sacrificially atoned for human sin at the cross.

Importance: The sacrificial atonement of Christ lies at the heart of our salvation. There is no salvation without it. For, indeed, through the atonement, the *Just* (Christ) died for the *unjust* (human beings), thereby enabling God to be both "just and the justifier" of the unjust who place their faith in Jesus.

Unorthodox Viewpoints: Many believe Christ's atonement *contributes to* but does not actually *accomplish* salvation. Others outright deny Christ's atonement.

Course of Action: On the doctrine of Christ's sacrificial atonement, there must be conviction without compromise.

10

The Bodily Resurrection of Christ

THE RESURRECTION OF CHRIST is at the heart of the Gospel (1 Corinthians 15:1-6). It is necessary to confess for salvation (Romans 10:9-10). Without it, we would yet be in our sins (1 Corinthians 15:12-19). Hence, on any short list of fundamentals of the Christian Faith, the resurrection has a firm position.

The Biblical Basis for the Resurrection

The biblical basis for the resurrection is overwhelming. In what follows, we provide a brief survey of key verses from both the Old and New Testaments:

Psalm 2:7-8: "You are My Son. Today I have begotten You [from the dead]" (NKJV, insert added). This prophetic verse, in which the Father speaks to the Son, is cited in the New Testament in reference to the resurrection of Christ (Acts 13:33; see also Hebrews 1:5).

Psalm 16:10-11: David declared: "You will not abandon me to the grave, nor will you let your Holy One see decay. You have made known to me the path of life; you will fill me with joy in your presence, with eternal pleasures at your right hand." In the New Testament, Peter said of David's prophecy, "Seeing what was ahead, he spoke of the resurrection of Christ, that he was not abandoned to the grave, nor did his body see decay" (Acts 2:31).

Isaiah 53:8-10: We read of the Savior, "He was cut off from the land of the living; for the transgression of my people he was stricken. He was assigned a grave with the wicked, and with the rich in his death...and though the LORD makes his life a guilt offering, he will see his offspring and prolong his days, and the will of the LORD will prosper in his hand." The prolonging of days after the Savior's death refers to His resurrection from the dead.

Daniel 12:2: Old Testament believers were no strangers to a belief in a physical resurrection. Job held it out as his hope (Job 19:25-26). Daniel affirmed that "multitudes who sleep in the dust of the earth will awake: some to everlasting life, others to shame and everlasting contempt." Because it is the body that returns to the dust and will "awake" to "everlasting life" or "everlasting contempt," this is a clear reference to the physical resurrection of both the saved and the lost. Ultimately, this means that predictions by prophets and pronouncements by Christ about His physical resurrection would be no surprise to Jewish believers (Matthew 22:23; see also John 11:23-24; Acts 23:8).

John 2:19-22: "Jesus answered and said to them, 'Destroy *this temple,* and in three days I will raise *it* up.'...But He was speaking of the temple of *His body.* Therefore, when He had risen from the dead, His disciples remembered that He had said this to them" (NKJV, emphasis added).

John 5:28-29: Jesus said, "All those who are in *the graves* will hear his voice and come out—those who have done good will *rise to live,* and those who have done evil will *rise to be condemned*" (emphasis added).

Matthew 12:40: Jesus said, "*As Jonah* was three days and three nights in the belly of a huge fish, *so will the son of Man* be three days and three nights in the heart of the earth."

Matthew 17:9: Jesus predicted His resurrection repeatedly. After His transfiguration He said to His disciples, "Don't tell anyone what you have seen, until the Son of Man has been raised from the dead" (see also verse 23).

Matthew 28 (see also Mark 16; Luke 24; John 20–21): All four Gospels record the bodily resurrection of Christ, as does 1 Corinthians 15. Putting these accounts together, it is clear that Jesus appeared on 12 different occasions over a 40-day period to a total of over 500 people! They saw the empty tomb, the empty grave clothes, and the crucifixion scars on

Christ's body. They touched Him, ate with Him, listened to Him teach, and watched Him do miracles. There is literally no other way Jesus could have convinced them that He had risen physically from the dead.

1 Corinthians 15:1-8: The apostle Paul stated, "I declare to you the gospel...by which also you are saved...that Christ died for our sins according to the Scriptures, and that He was buried, and that He rose again the third day according to the Scriptures, and that He was seen by Cephas, then by the twelve. After that He was seen by over five hundred brethren at once, of whom the greater part remain to the present, but some have fallen asleep. After that He was seen by James, then by all the apostles. Then last of all He was seen by me also" (NKJV).

The Physical Nature of the Resurrection

The Key Evidence

There are numerous lines of evidence to support the conclusion that Jesus was raised in the same physical body in which He was crucified.

1. *The tomb was empty.* All four Gospels (Matthew 28; Mark 16; Luke 24; John 20) report that the tomb in which Jesus was buried and which the Romans guarded was empty three days later.

2. *The grave clothes were left behind.* Not only was the tomb empty, but Jesus' grave clothes were left there as well. In addition, the head cloth was folded and laid in a place by itself (John 20:7). If thieves had raided the tomb, they would not have bothered to do this.

3. *Jesus' resurrection body retained the crucifixion scars.* After Jesus rose from the dead, during the next 40 days He appeared to over 500 people on 12 different occasions, showing on two of these occasions the scars from His crucifixion (Luke 24:39; John 20:27). In one appearance Jesus connected His own self-identity with this body, saying, "Behold My hands and My feet, that it is I Myself. Handle Me and see, for a spirit does not have flesh and bones as you see I have" (Luke 24:39 NKJV). So, either Jesus was in the same body in which He was crucified, or else He was being dishonest!

4. *Jesus' resurrection body had flesh and bones.* As noted above, Jesus' body was not a "spirit" but rather had "flesh and bones" (Luke 24:39).

This reveals that He arose with the *same* body of flesh in which He was incarnated (John 1:14) and in which He continually *lives today* (1 John 4:2; 2 John 7). Indeed, in these latter two texts, John indicates that denials of this are rooted in the spirit of the Antichrist.

5. *Jesus ate food in His resurrection body.* In fact, Jesus ate physical food multiple times after the resurrection (Luke 24:30; 24:42-43; John 21:12-13). This is further proof He had a real physical body.

6. *Jesus' resurrection body was touched by others.* Scripture indicates that on two postresurrection occasions Jesus' body was touched (Matthew 28:9; John 20:27-28) and on another occasion He *offered* His body to be touched (Luke 24:39-40). When doubting Thomas was challenged by Jesus to touch Him, he worshipfully cried out, "My Lord and my God!" (John 20:28).

7. *Jesus' resurrection body was humanly visible and heard.* It was both seen with the human eye (Matthew 28:17) and heard with human ears (John 20:15-16). The same words are used earlier in the New Testament to describe people seeing and hearing Jesus in His preresurrection body. These were not spiritual visions, but *literal observations* with the *natural senses.**

There are good reasons the disciples did not recognize Jesus on occasion. Once, "their eyes were restrained" from recognizing Him (Luke 24.16). Another time, they were perplexed (Luke 24:17-21). Some were in sorrow (John 20:11-15). Once it was still dark (John 20:14-15). On another occasion the distance was great (John 21:4). Those behind a closed door were startled when He suddenly appeared (Luke 24:36-37). Some were disbelieving (John 20:24-25). Others were spiritually dull (Luke 24:25-26). But the fact is that these were only initial and temporary responses. Before the appearance was over in each case, they were so totally convinced of His identity that they were willing to die for Him, and within weeks were turning the world upside down.

---

* The references to the word "vision" in Luke 24:23 and Acts 26:19 do not contradict this conclusion. No resurrection appearance is ever called a "vision" in the Gospels or epistles. Luke 24:23 refers to a vision of *angels* who affirmed Christ was alive, not to a vision of Christ Himself. Visions, such as the one Paul had of paradise in 2 Corinthians 12, are different from *appearances,* such as the appearance of Jesus to Paul in Acts 9 (see verse 17). No physical manifestations are ever associated with a vision. Further, Paul claimed Christ appeared to him just as He had the other apostles (1 Corinthians 15:7-8). Hence, the "vision from heaven" referenced in Acts 26:19 is probably best understood to be Ananias's vision to tell Paul what to do (Acts 9:10), not to Jesus' literal appearance to Paul.

Other Supportive Evidence

There are many other lines of supporting evidence that Jesus was raised in the same physical body of flesh and bones in which He died. For one, in the New Testament, the word "body" (Greek: *soma*), used to describe the resurrection body in 1 Corinthians 15:44, always means a *physical* body when used of individual human beings.[1] Also, only bodies die, not souls. So, it is only bodies that are raised. In addition, using an analogy from planting a seed, the body that is "sown" in death is the same body that is raised (1 Corinthians 15:35-44). What is more, the resurrection is *from among* (Greek: *ek*) the dead. This means Jesus' body was raised from the graveyard (Luke 24:46) where physical corpses are buried (see also Acts 13:29-30). On top of this, Paul alludes to the fact we will recognize our loved ones in heaven (1 Thessalonians 4:13-18).

Of course, the resurrection body has other characteristics, such as immortality and imperishability (1 Corinthians 15:42-54). It is a physical body dominated or energized by the Spirit (1 Corinthians 15:44). That is, it has a spiritual source of power. It is literally a Spirit-dominated physical body. Just as the rock that followed Israel was a literal rock out of which came literal water (1 Corinthians 10:4) but had a supernatural (Greek: *pneumatikos*, "spiritual") source, even so the resurrection body of believers will be a physical body with a spiritual source of energy. Hence, Paul calls it an incorruptible and immortal physical body (1 Corinthians 15:53). The change (1 Corinthians 15:51) that occurs will not be a change of bodies from a *material* to an *immaterial* one at the resurrection, but a change in the material body from a *perishable* physical body to an *imperishable* physical body.

The Theological Importance of the Resurrection

The importance of the resurrection to our salvation cannot be overemphasized. As stated earlier, the resurrection of Christ is at the heart of the gospel (1 Corinthians 15:1-6), and it is necessary to confess for salvation (Romans 10:9-10). The apostle Paul declared that "if Christ is not risen, then our preaching is empty and your faith is also empty.... And if Christ is not risen, your faith is futile; you are still in your sins!" (1 Corinthians 15:14,17 NKJV). Paul affirmed that Jesus "was delivered over to death for our sins and was raised to life for our justification" (Romans 4:25). In short, without a resurrection to confirm His credentials, Jesus' death would have been that of just another false Messiah. Hence, on any short list of truth-essentials to salvation, the resurrection has a permanent place.

The Creedal Basis for the Resurrection

The earliest creeds speak of the resurrection of Christ in the "flesh" (Greek: *sarx*). This is the strongest possible word for a physical resurrection of the same body that died. The Apostles' Creed declared that the one who "suffered under Pontius Pilate, was crucified, and buried"—that same one "the third day rose from the dead." Clearly, this is a reference to the resurrection of the same body that died and was buried. Later, the Creed refers to belief in "the resurrection of the flesh" (*sarx*). The Nicene Creed affirms the same, saying, "He suffered death and was buried. On the third day he rose again." It too speaks of "the resurrection of the dead" for "life in the world to come." The Chalcedonian Creed speaks of "following the holy Fathers" with "one consent" in affirming belief in the resurrection of Christ, and then goes on to stress Christ's deity—the main subject of the creed.

There is a virtually unbroken testimony of the church fathers down to and through the Reformation into the modern world that Christ rose from the dead and that the resurrection was "in the flesh." A few examples will suffice (emphases are added). Irenaeus (A.D. 130–200) declared that "the Church [believes] in...the resurrection from the dead and ascension into heaven *in the flesh* of the beloved Christ Jesus, our lord." Tertullian (A.D. 160–230) concurred, saying, "He rose again the third day," and likewise both the saved and the unsaved will experience "the restoration of their flesh." Justin Martyr added, "Why did he rise in the flesh in which He suffered, unless to show the resurrection of the flesh?" Athenagoras (second century) spoke of God's power to raise from the dead "the same bodies...and their original elements." Cyril of Jerusalem (A.D. 315–386) confessed "the resurrection of the flesh; and eternal life."

In *A Commentary on the Apostles' Creed*, Rufinus (A.D. 345–410) affirmed: "We believe that it is the very flesh in which we are now living which will rise again." At the beginning of the Middle Ages, St. Augustine declared, "The world has come to the belief that the earthly body of Christ was received up into heaven...[They] have believed in the resurrection of the flesh and its ascension to the heavenly places." Near the other end of the Middle Ages, Thomas Aquinas affirmed the same doctrine, specifying that "by conjunction to a soul numerically the same, the man will be restored to matter numerically the same."

This same belief in a physical resurrection of the same body that died was affirmed by the Reformers. The Lutheran Formula of Concord (A.D. 1576) affirms "the same ['human nature'] of Christ doth he raised from the dead." *The Thirty-Nine Articles of Religion* (A.D. 1562) of the Church of England states that "Christ did truly rise again from the dead, and took again his body with flesh and bones." And the *Westminster Confession of Faith* (A.D. 1647) declares that "on the third day he arose from the dead, with the same body in which he suffered; with which he ascended into heaven." Few essentials of the Faith have come down through the centuries with such clarity and unanimity as does the physical resurrection of Christ.

It was not until modern times that the creeds began to translate the word "flesh" as "body"—a term which, in English, is *weaker* than "flesh," and which in recent times has fallen prey to a Gnostic-like spiritualizing of the resurrection body both by influential Christian leaders and cultic groups.

Unorthodox Denials of the Physical Resurrection

George Ladd of Fuller Seminary

In his book *I Believe in the Resurrection of Jesus*, theologian George Ladd wrote, "It was not a revivification of a dead corpse, returning to physical life....Obviously, Jesus had not revived. Obviously, the body had not been stolen. It had simply disappeared."[2] "At his resurrection he entered into the invisible world of God. His appearances to his disciples did not mean the passing of one body through other solid substances; it means that Jesus, who was with them but invisible, made himself visible to their physical senses."[3] "The appearances, then, were condescension of the risen, exalted Lord by which he convinced his disciples that he was no longer dead."[4] Clearly, such statements do not represent the historic orthodox view of the physical resurrection of Christ.

Murray Harris of Trinity Seminary

Professor Murray Harris wrote, "In his resurrected body...his essential state was one of invisibility and therefore immateriality."[5] "Another characteristic of Jesus' resurrection body was the ability to materialize and therefore to be localized at will."[6] "The Ascension vividly dramatized Christ's earlier exaltation to God's right hand—a parable acted out for the benefit of the disciples as a visual and historical confirmation of a spiritual reality."[7] "It is not historical in the sense of being an incident that was observed by witnesses or even an incident that could have been observed by mortal gaze."[8] Here, again, this is a denial of the orthodox view of the resurrection of Christ.

Millard Erickson

Another noted evangelical scholar, Millard Erickson, holds an unorthodox view of the permanent resurrection body, delaying Christ's final transformation for 40 days until the ascension. Erickson writes, "At that time Jesus underwent the remainder of the metamorphosis begun with the resurrection of his body. The significance of the ascension is that Jesus left behind the conditions associated with life on this earth."[9] In short, Jesus was not initially raised immortal; He was raised mortal. He did not receive a glorified body at the time He was first raised; He did not receive that until the ascension.

From a biblical and orthodox creedal perspective, there are serious objections to this view. First, Paul flatly stated, "So also is the resurrection of the dead....[The body] is sown in dishonor, it is *raised in glory*" (1 Corinthians 15:42-43 NKJV, emphasis added). Erickson's view is also opposed to Philippians 3:21, which declares that our resurrection body will be like His glorious body. In addition, it is contrary to Paul's declaration that we will be raised to an immortal and incorruptible body just like Christ our "first fruit" was (1 Corinthians 15:20,53). And it is contrary to 1 Peter 1:11, which speaks of "the sufferings [death] of Christ and the glories that would follow [His resurrection]" (NKJV, inserts added, see also

Acts 26:23). What's more, Paul spoke of the victory over Christ's death on the cross as one of glory, making reference to crucifying "the Lord of glory" (1 Corinthians 2:8). And if the body was not raised immortal, then His resurrection was not a victory over death as the Bible proclaims it to be (1 Corinthians 15:55).

Finally, Christ's resurrection body possessed the characteristics of a glorified body—namely, the ability to appear and disappear (Luke 24:31) and even enter rooms with closed doors (John 20:19). It is important to note that the blinding radiance of His ascended body (Acts 9) was not unique to His postascension state. Jesus was able to do this *before* His ascension on the Mount of Transfiguration (Matthew 17:2).

The Mythology Theory

Some modern scholars claim the concept of the resurrection was derived from Greek mythology and paganism. Such claims, however, are absurd. The late Ronald Nash, considered an expert on alleged myth connections with the New Testament, asked, "Which mystery gods actually experienced a resurrection from the dead? Certainly no early texts refer to any resurrection of Attis. Nor is the case for a resurrection of Osiris any stronger."[10] William Lane Craig agrees, noting that so-called "resurrections" in the stories of Osiris, Attis, and Adonis are not truly resurrections at all: "For example, after Isis gathered together the pieces of Osiris's dismembered body, Osiris became 'Lord of the Underworld.' This is a poor substitute for a resurrection like that of Jesus Christ. And, no claim can be made that Mithras was a dying and rising god."[11]

In view of the evidence, the tide of scholarly opinion has turned dramatically against attempts to make the Christian doctrine of resurrection dependent on the so-called dying and rising gods of Hellenistic paganism. Such mythological resurrections always involved nonhistorical, fictional, mythological characters that came to life "once upon a time," which is in dire contrast to the flesh-and-blood historical Jesus who died and physically resurrected from the dead.

Unlike mythical accounts, the New Testament record is based on eyewitness testimony. In 2 Peter 1:16 we read, "We did not follow cleverly invented stories when we told you about the power and coming of our

Lord Jesus Christ, but we were eyewitnesses of his majesty." First John 1:1 affirms, "That which was from the beginning, which we have heard, which we have seen with our eyes, which we have looked at and our hands have touched—this we proclaim concerning the Word of life." These eyewitnesses gave up their lives defending what they knew to be the truth about Jesus Christ. No one would have made the ultimate sacrifice for what they knew to be a pagan myth.

The Kingdom of the Cults

There are quite a number of cults who have denied or compromised the doctrine of Christ's physical resurrection from the dead. One of the best known of these is the Jehovah's Witnesses. The Watchtower book *Let Your Name Be Sanctified* tells us that "Jesus was raised to life as an invisible spirit. He did not take up again that body in which he had been killed as a human sacrifice to God."[12] In *Studies in the Scriptures* we find the statement, "We deny that He was raised in the flesh, and challenge any statement to that effect as being unscriptural."[13]

In the book *Reasoning from the Scriptures,* the Watchtower Society says it is clear Jesus was raised with a spirit body because in the Greek text of 1 Peter 3:18 the words "flesh" and "spirit" are put in contrast to each other—"He...having been put to death in the flesh, but made alive in the spirit" (NASB).[14] Just as Jesus died *in the flesh,* so He was resurrected *in the spirit.*

In response, 1 Peter 3:18 is better translated, "He was put to death in the body but made alive *by* the [Holy] Spirit" (emphasis added, insert added). The verse indicates that God did not raise Jesus *as* a spirit but raised Him *by* His Spirit. This is in keeping with Romans 1:4, which tells us that it was "through the Spirit of holiness" that Jesus was "declared with power to be the Son of God by His resurrection from the dead." One must also keep in mind that the parallel between *death* and being *made alive* normally refers to the resurrection of the body in the New Testament. For example, Paul declared that "Christ died and returned to life" (Romans 14:9), and "he was crucified in weakness, yet he lives by God's power" (2 Corinthians 13:4).

The Christian Science cult takes a more novel approach in denying

Christ's physical resurrection. This group teaches that because death is an illusion, Jesus did not really die at all on the cross. The disciples "believed Jesus to be dead while he was hiding in the sepulcher, whereas he was alive."[15] When Jesus later spoke of His resurrection body as "flesh and bones" in Luke 24:39, He was simply accommodating Himself to the immature ideas of His disciples.[16]

Of course, the big problem with this view is that if Jesus spoke about a "flesh and bones" resurrection body merely to accommodate Himself to the immature ideas of His disciples, then Jesus was blatantly deceiving His disciples, making them think He had a body when He really did not. Such a view makes a liar out of the Savior—thereby calling into question everything else He said in the New Testament.

There are certainly many other denials of the resurrection that could be examined. But because they are essentially variations on the same theme, the above is more than sufficient to illustrate the concerted effort made by many to deny this central doctrine of the Christian Faith.

THEOLOGICAL QUICK-REVIEW

Chapter 10 Main Idea: Jesus physically rose from the dead in the same body that was laid in the tomb.

Importance: The resurrection of Christ is at the heart of the Gospel (1 Corinthians 15:1-6), and is necessary to confess for salvation (Romans 10:9-10). Without it, we would yet be in our sins (1 Corinthians 15:12-19). It is among the most important essentials of the Christian Faith.

Unorthodox Viewpoints: Some people flat out deny the resurrection. Others claim Jesus left His physical body behind in the grave and was raised as an invisible spirit. Still others claim Jesus was initially raised as a mortal and later received a glorified, immortal body at His ascension.

Course of Action: On the doctrine of Christ's physical resurrection, there must be conviction without compromise.

11

The Necessity of Grace

GOD'S UNMERITED FAVOR, OR grace, is at the heart of the Christian plan of salvation. Without it no one has ever been or ever can be saved. This is affirmed in numerous verses, as we will soon see. All major sections of orthodox Christianity agree with this point. The major disagreements have to do with beliefs about the relation of grace to works, the extent of grace, and the means of obtaining grace—all of which will be addressed later in this chapter.

The Biblical Basis for the Necessity of God's Grace

Scripture is emphatic that fallen, sinful human beings cannot attain their own salvation. In view of this, salvation is possible solely by the grace and aid of God, as the following verses affirm:

- *Acts 15:11:* "We believe it is through the grace of our Lord Jesus that we are saved."
- *Acts 18:27:* "He [Paul] was a great help to those who by grace had believed." (This verse reveals that even our faith is prompted by God's grace.)
- *Romans 4:4-5:* "Now to him who works, the wages are not counted as grace but as debt. But to him who does not work but believes on Him who justifies the ungodly, his faith is accounted for righteousness" (NKJV).
- *Romans 5:8:* "God demonstrates His own love toward

us, in that while we were still sinners, Christ died for us" (NKJV).

- *Romans 5:15:* "For if by one man's offense many died, much more the grace of God and the gift by the grace of the one Man, Jesus Christ, abounded to many" (NKJV).
- *2 Corinthians 8:9:* "You know the grace of our Lord Jesus Christ, that though he was rich, yet for your sakes he became poor, that you through his poverty might become rich."
- *Ephesians 1:7:* "In him we have redemption through his blood, the forgiveness of sins, in accordance with the riches of God's grace."
- *Ephesians 2:8-9:* "By grace you have been saved through faith—and this not from yourselves; *it is* the gift of God—not by works, so that no one can boast."
- *Romans 3:24:* "[We are] justified freely by his grace through the redemption that came by Christ Jesus."
- *Romans 11:6:* "If by grace, then *it is* no longer by works; if it were, grace would no longer be grace."
- *2 Timothy 1:9:* Christ "saved us...not according to our works, but according to His own purpose and grace which was given to us in Christ Jesus before time began" (NKJV).
- *Titus 2:11:* "The grace of God that brings salvation has appeared to all men."
- *Titus 3:5:* "He saved us, not because of righteous things we had done, but because of his mercy."

The clear scriptural testimony is that not only are we totally incapable of saving ourselves, but there is nothing in us that merits God's grace. Grace is God's *unmerited* favor. And our salvation is based *entirely* on God's grace.

An Important Distinction Regarding Grace and Salvation in Roman Catholicism

There is no real debate among orthodox Christians as to the necessity of grace. Everyone who believes in the other essentials of the Faith also believes in the absolute necessity of God's grace. Even Roman Catholics expressed agreement with this at the Council of Trent, stating, "If anyone shall say that man can be justified before God by his own works which are done…without divine grace through Christ Jesus; let him be anathema." Further, "Nothing that precedes justification, whether faith or works, merits the grace of justification. For if it is by grace, it is no more by works; otherwise, as the apostle says [in Romans 11:6], grace is no longer grace."[1]

The debate, then, is not over the *necessity* of grace; both Catholics and Protestants agree on this. The debate is over the *exclusivity* of grace, which Protestants affirm and Catholics deny, insisting that works are also necessary for salvation. But even here Roman Catholics insist that only works inspired by God's grace are sufficient for salvation.

To be more specific, the Roman Catholic view of justification starts out with what they call "first actual grace." This grace is "first" in the sense that it is God who initially reaches out to a person and gives him the grace that will enable him to seek God, to have faith, and prepare his soul for baptism and justification. It is "actual" in the sense that good acts are the goal. This grace does not have an automatic influence; rather, the person must respond to it for it to become effectual. If one cooperates with this grace, one will end up performing "salutary acts." This performing of good works is believed to prepare an adult's soul for baptism and justification. As the Council of Trent put it, when one is "proposing to receive baptism, they are moved to begin a new life and to keep God's commandments."[2]

According to Roman Catholics, when a person is baptized, original sin is removed from one's soul and, in its place, sanctifying grace is infused. It is at this point that one experiences "initial justification." No one can merit or earn this grace, and hence this initial aspect of justification is said to be by grace.

The backdrop, according to Roman Catholics, is that when Adam and Eve fell into sin, they lost the divine life God had bestowed upon them through sanctifying grace. Since then, every human being born into the world has been born without this divine life or sanctifying grace.

This means that for a person to be saved, there must be a *restoration* of sanctifying grace. At the moment of baptism, this is exactly what happens, according to Roman Catholics. Sanctifying grace is infused into the person and he becomes spiritually alive. The actual amount of sanctifying grace that is infused into the soul hinges on one's prebaptismal preparations. One who *fully* cooperates with "first actual grace" prior to baptism is blessed with more sanctifying grace than a lesser-committed person.

The spiritual transformation that takes place at baptism is often referred to as initial "justification" by Roman Catholics. The reasoning goes like this: At baptism the guilt that comes from original sin is removed and the person is infused with sanctifying grace. Hence, because of what this grace accomplishes, it is often called justifying grace. This initial justification involves both the removal of sin and a transition from that state devoid of sanctifying grace to a state of grace.

Hence, baptism is not an optional matter for the Roman Catholic. The Council of Trent stated that "if anyone shall say that baptism is optional, that is, not necessary for salvation: let him be anathema."[3]

Following this initial justification, which occurs at baptism, there is a second aspect of salvation called progressive justification that occurs throughout life as the person continues to cooperate with God's grace and progresses in good works, thereby meriting *further* grace that is necessary for him or her to enter eternal life. The *Catechism of the Catholic Church* tells us, "Since the initiative belongs to God in the order of grace, no one can merit the initial grace of forgiveness and justification, at the beginning of conversion. However, moved by the Holy Spirit and by charity, we can then *merit for ourselves* and for others the graces needed for our sanctification, for the increase of grace and charity, and for the attainment of eternal life."[4] Meritorious works, then, play a major role in the Roman Catholic view of salvation. This brings us back to our original point: While Catholics acknowledge the *necessity* of grace for salvation, they do not acknowledge the *exclusivity* of grace. While Pope John Paul II acknowledged the necessity of grace, he affirmed at the same time that "a good life is the condition of salvation."[5] Protestants, by contrast, believe that salvation is by *grace alone*.

To sum up, then, the Catholic failure of commitment to the *exclusivity* of grace is one of the doctrinal factors that separated the Reformers from the Roman Catholic Church several hundred years ago, and this difference continues to be a cause of some division among Catholics and Protestants today.

This is closely related to another point of division relating to justification. While Catholics view justification as a *process that continues throughout life*, Protestants view it as a *singular and instantaneous event* in which God declares the believing sinner to be righteous (Romans 3:25,28,30; 8:33-34; Galatians 4:21–5:12; 1 John 1:7–2:2), and this justification is based *exclusively* on the grace of God (Romans 3:24). Of course, Protestants believe that the moment one is justified the process of sanctification begins and continues till death. Like justification, Protestants affirm (and Catholics deny) that sanctification is achieved also by faith alone, not by works (Galatians 3:2).

The Theological Importance of the Necessity of Grace

Few doctrines, if any, are more crucial to our salvation than that of the necessity of grace. The Bible verses cited earlier in this chapter make it absolutely clear that this is one of the greatest fundamentals of the Faith. Connected as it is with the complete depravity of man and the inability of our good works to aid in salvation, there is a powerful case for giving this teaching a preeminent place among the salvation essentials of the Christian Faith.

Unorthodox Denials of the Necessity of Grace

Cultic groups almost without exception deny salvation by grace, thus distorting the purity of the gospel. Some groups explicitly claim to believe in the necessity of grace yet implicitly deny it by redefining it to mean something else. Others explicitly deny the necessity of grace or the exclusivity of grace, or so severely compromise on the issue of God's grace that it no longer bears resemblance to the biblical doctrine. Let us consider a few examples.

Grace is certainly a key component in the Mormon view of salvation, but the Mormon concept of grace is substantially different from the biblical concept. Some Mormon literature defines God's grace as God's enabling power that allows people to "lay hold on eternal life and exaltation *after* they have expended their own best efforts."[6] The primary emphasis in Mormonism relates to the individual performing good works as he or she seeks to become increasingly perfect each day. As Mormons succeed in performing good works in varying degrees, they become recipients of varying measures of God's grace. Mormon theologian Bruce McConkie, in his book *Mormon Doctrine,* claims that "grace is granted to men proportionately as they conform to the standards of personal righteousness that are part of the gospel plan."[7]

Mormons are adamant that God's grace is insufficient in itself to bring salvation. Spencer W. Kimball made the point that "one of the most fallacious doctrines originated by Satan and propounded by man is that man is saved alone by the grace of God; that belief in Jesus Christ alone is all that is needed for salvation."[8]

In keeping with this, Mormonism teaches that salvation *begins* with Jesus' atonement, but each person must *complete the process* by doing good works throughout life. The official *Gospel Principles* manual tells us that Jesus "became our savior and he did his part to help us return to our heavenly home. It is now up to each of us to do our part and to become worthy of exaltation [to godhood]."[9]

Eventually, if and when such exaltation to godhood occurs, one then attains the attribute of grace for oneself. McConkie wrote:

> Grace is an attribute of perfection possessed by Deity...and Christ himself "received grace for grace" until finally he gained the fullness of the Father. The same path to perfection is offered to man. "If you keep my commandments," the Lord says, "you shall receive of his fullness, and be glorified in me as I am in the Father; therefore, I say unto you, you shall receive grace for grace" (D. & C. 93:6-20.).[10]

The Jehovah's Witnesses also claim to teach the necessity of grace to be saved. However, while they speak of salvation as a "free gift," they redefine it in such a way that salvation is impossible apart from a lifetime of good works. Practically speaking, true grace never comes into the picture. A former Jehovah's Witness put it this way:

> What the Watchtower means by "free gift" is that Christ's death *only* wiped away the sin inherited from Adam. They teach that without this work of atonement, men could not work their way toward salvation. But the "gift" of Christ's ransom sacrifice is freely made available to all who desire it. In other words, without Christ's sacrifice, the individual wouldn't have a chance to get saved. But in view of His work, the free gift which removed the sin inherited from Adam, the individual now has a chance.[11]

So, the Watchtower view is that by the grace of God that is displayed in Christ taking away the sin inherited by Adam, human beings now have the wonderful and free opportunity to go out and *earn* salvation by *performing a lifetime of good works*. Part of the process of "working out" salvation involves distributing Watchtower literature door to door. Full-time "pioneer ministers" (dedicated Jehovah's Witnesses) can be required to spend 100 hours each month preaching from house to house and conducting home Bible studies. The Watchtower Society teaches that Jehovah's Witnesses must dedicate their lives to Jehovah and *remain* faithful to Him *to the very end* for fear of losing their salvation. The Watchtower warns that "to get one's name written in that Book of Life will depend upon one's works."[12] Witnesses are to continually be "working hard for the reward of eternal life."[13]

With such a view of grace and salvation, Jehovah's Witnesses cannot know for sure whether they have salvation during this life. Only an unbending stance against sin and *total* obedience to the Watchtower gives the Witness any hope of salvation. Even then, the Witness is told that if he should fail during the future millennium, he will be annihilated. However, if he faithfully serves God throughout this 1000-year period, eternal life *might* finally be granted.

The biblical concept of grace as unmerited favor is certainly absent in Unification Church theology. The Unification Church's doctrine of indemnity involves people atoning for their own sins through specific acts of penance. While God is said to accomplish the majority of the work of salvation, people must do their part. "The providence of restoration cannot be fulfilled by God's power alone, but it is to be fulfilled by man's joint action with God."[14] The Unification view is that "as one atones for his own sins through constant effort, he can build up enough indemnity merit to be freed from guilt."[15]

Taking an entirely different slant, the Mind Science cults deny the necessity of grace. As an example, let us consider the United Church of Religious Science, founded by "Dr." Ernest S. Holmes (1887–1960). The Religious Science teaching that God is in all things means God is in man, and hence man is divine. Man is a personification of the infinite. "There is that within us which partakes of the nature of the Divine Being, and since we partake of the nature of the Divine Being, we are divine."[16] "Every man is an incarnation of God."[17]

But if we are divine beings, Holmes asks, why do we appear to be so limited, so forlorn, so miserable and sick? The answer, Holmes says, is that "we are ignorant of our own nature."[18] The *only* "sin" is ignorance of one's divinity. Through Religious Science, this ignorance can be rectified, and man—as a divine being—can become the master of his own destiny. When any individual, through Religious Science, recognizes his union with the infinite, he automatically becomes the Christ.

Salvation in Religious Science, then, is simply a matter of the mind—*no grace required*. Everyone is already saved—if they will only realize it. "There is no need to seek unity with God and the Universe. We already have it. It is something we must become aware of."[19] "There must come a new impulse to the mind, a new way of looking at things. This is what Jesus called the new birth."[20] Understanding alone constitutes true salvation. Hence, any talk of the necessity of grace is a waste of time.

The cultic views described above are a mere sampling of those found among groups that either completely deny the necessity of grace or so distort the doctrine of grace that it is no longer recognizable from a biblical point of view. We have noted that *grace* literally means "unmerited favor." The very meaning of the word goes against these cultic views, for it refers to the undeserved, unearned favor of God. Romans 5:1-11 tells us that God gives His incredible grace to those who actually deserve the opposite—that is, condemnation. The word *unmerited* means this favor cannot be worked for. Indeed, if grace is not free, it is not truly grace. "If by grace, then it is no longer of works; if it were, grace would no longer be grace" (Romans 11:6).

Scripture is thus emphatic that eternal life cannot be earned. Verse after verse in the Bible indicates that eternal life is a free gift that comes as a result of believing in the Savior, Jesus Christ. We read, for example, that "the *gift of God* is eternal life in Christ Jesus our Lord" (Romans 6:23, emphasis added). Ephesians 2:8-9 likewise states, "By grace you have been saved, through faith—and this not from yourselves; it is the gift of God—not by works, so that no one can boast." Titus 3:5, in like manner, affirms that God saved us "not by works of righteousness which we have done, but according to His mercy" (NKJV).

Romans 3:20 asserts that "by the deeds of the law no flesh will be justified [or declared righteous] in His sight" (NKJV, insert added). In Galatians 2:16 the apostle Paul tells us that "a man is not justified by observing the law, but by faith in Jesus Christ...by observing the law no one will be justified."

All this points to the absolute necessity of grace in salvation. Of course, orthodox Christians believe that a life of good works and holiness is important. However, holiness *follows* the salvation that is by grace alone, not *causes* it. Works are not the *condition* of our salvation, but a *consequence* of it. While we are saved *by* grace through faith, we are saved *for* good works.

THEOLOGICAL QUICK-REVIEW

Chapter 11 Main Idea: God's unmerited favor, or grace, is at the heart of the Christian plan of salvation. Without it no one has ever been or ever can be saved.

Importance: God's grace, connected as it is with the complete depravity of man and the inability of our good works to aid in salvation, is one of the most important essentials of the Faith.

Unorthodox Viewpoints: There are a plethora of unorthodox viewpoints on the necessity of grace. Some religious groups outright deny any need for grace. Quite a number of groups claim the need for grace, but so redefine it that it bears no real resemblance to the biblical doctrine.

Course of Action: On the doctrine of the necessity of grace, there must be conviction without compromise.

12

The Necessity of Faith

THE ESSENTIALS WE HAVE EXAMINED in chapters 2 through 11 constitute the grounds on which a Christian's salvation is made possible. According to Scripture, however, no one can realize this salvation in his or her own life apart from faith. For "without faith it is impossible to please God" (Hebrews 11:6). Paul said, "By grace you have been saved through faith" (Ephesians 2:8), and "the righteous will live by faith" (Romans 1:17). When the jailer asked, "What must I do to be saved?" Paul and Silas answered, "Believe in the Lord Jesus, and you will be saved" (Acts 16:30-31). John repeatedly calls on people to believe in order to receive God's gift of salvation (John 3:16,18,36; 5:24). So without faith, no one is saved.

The Biblical Basis for the Necessity of Faith

The debate about the relation of faith and works notwithstanding, all sides agree that faith is absolutely necessary for salvation. This is borne out by numerous texts of Scripture:

- *Genesis 15:6*: "Abram believed the LORD, and credited it to him as righteousness." This text is repeated in the New Testament to establish the same point (Romans 4:3; James 2:23).
- *Habakkuk 2:4*: "The righteous will live by his faith." This verse is cited three times in the New Testament to show the necessity of faith in salvation (Romans 1:17; Galatians 3:6; Hebrews 10:38).

- *Romans 1:16-17:* "I am not ashamed of the gospel of Christ....For in it the righteousness of God is revealed from faith to faith; as it is written, 'The just shall live by faith'" (NKJV).
- *Galatians 3:11:* "That no one is justified by the law in the sight of God is evident, for 'the just shall live by faith'" (NKJV).
- *Hebrews 10:38:* "Now the just shall live by faith" (NKJV).
- *Hebrews 11:6:* "Without faith it is impossible to please Him [God], for he who comes to God must believe that He is, and that He is a rewarder of those who diligently seek Him" (NKJV).
- *John 3:16:* "God so loved the world that he gave his one and only Son, that whoever believes in him shall not perish but have eternal life."
- *John 3:18:* "Whoever believes in him is not condemned, but whoever does not believe stands condemned already because he has not believed in the name of God's one and only Son."
- *John 3:36:* "Whoever believes in the Son has eternal life, but whoever rejects the Son will not see life, for God's wrath remains on him."
- *John 5:24:* "Most assuredly, I say to you, he who hears My word and believes in Him who sent Me has everlasting life, and shall not come into judgment, but has passed from death into life" (NKJV).
- *Acts 16:30-31:* "The jailer asked, 'Sirs, what must I do to be saved?' So [Paul and Silas] said, 'Believe on the Lord Jesus Christ, and you will be saved, you and your household'" (NKJV, insert added).
- *Romans 3:21:* "Now a righteousness from God, apart

from law, has been made known....This righteousness from God comes through faith in Christ Jesus to all who believe."

- *Romans 4:5:* "To him who does not work but believes on Him who justifies the ungodly, his faith is accounted for righteousness" (NKJV).
- *James 2:23:* "The scripture was fulfilled that says, 'Abraham believed God, and it was credited to him as righteousness.'"*

The Theological Importance of Faith

Biblically, no one can be saved apart from faith. To reiterate a few highlights from the above cited verses, "without faith it is impossible to please God" (Hebrews 11:6), and "by grace you have been saved through faith" (Ephesians 2:8; see also Romans 3:21). In every age (see Galatians 3:8) the one and only fundamental requirement for receiving God's gift of salvation has been and still is faith. Hence, the necessity of faith is a fundamental of the Faith.

The Basis for the Necessity of Faith in the Early Creeds

Even in the tiny creeds imbedded in the New Testament, faith for salvation is an essential component. In 1 Timothy 3:16 Paul declares that Christ was "believed on in the world." Likewise, in 1 Corinthians 15:1, Paul speaks of basic Christian truths as being "received" by faith. The Apostles' Creed begins with "I believe." The Nicene Creed begins with the confession, "We believe." Later, in the Chalcedonian Creed, the necessity of faith is implied in the phrase, "We unite in teaching all men to confess [their faith]." The Athanasian Creed ends by declaring, "This is the catholic [universal] faith, which except a man believe faithfully he cannot be saved." In short, the creeds are clear that one simply cannot be saved apart from faith.

---

* James goes on to say that "faith without deeds is dead" (2:26) because he believed we are saved by faith alone, but the faith that saves us is not alone; it is accompanied by good works. We do not work *for* grace, but we work *from* grace. We are not saved *by* good works, but *to* good works (see Ephesians 2:10).

Some Important Distinctions

Some important distinctions are necessary before we proceed further. First, we need to recognize a crucial distinction between what is necessary to make salvation *possible* and what is necessary to *believe* in order to receive the gift of salvation.

Necessary to Be True *versus Necessary to* Believe

Salvation in the broad sense—embracing justification, sanctification, and glorification—is not possible unless all the doctrines addressed in Part One of this book (chapters 2 through 17) are true. All these teachings are the foundations of one of the three stages of salvation. But what is necessary to be *true* for salvation to be possible and what is necessary to *believe* to be saved are two separate things.

To be frank, there is some disagreement even among orthodox Christians on this point. Many Christian scholars take a somewhat simplistic approach and point to the bare essentials in Hebrews 11:6—namely, that everyone in every age must believe that God *is*, and that He rewards with salvation those who diligently seek Him. Even here there are many doctrines involved, some being implied: (1) one must recognize his or her need of salvation (acknowledging human sinfulness); (2) he or she must believe in one God; (3) he or she must recognize that salvation is dependent on God's grace; and (4) he or she must have faith in God.

Others make a distinction between what is *minimally* necessary to believe in all ages (such as the four "bare essential" doctrines listed above*) and what is *normatively* necessary to believe *today* (that is, since the time of the fuller revelation given in the New Testament) in order to be saved. The latter appears to explicitly include far more than the "bare essentials," including the deity of Christ as well as His death and resurrection. This seems to be apparent from the following verses:

Acts 4:12: "Nor is there salvation in any other, for there is no other name under heaven given among men by which we must be saved" (NKJV). This text affirms that it is necessary to believe in the name of Jesus in order to be saved.

---

* There is no convincing evidence that it was normatively necessary for everyone in Old Testament times to believe in (for example) God's triunity, the virgin birth, or Christ's sinlessness, bodily resurrection, bodily ascension, and second coming in order to be saved.

John 8:24: "If you do not believe that I am He, you will die in your sins" (NKJV). The original Greek text for this verse does not have the word "He." The verse literally reads, "If you do not believe that I AM, you shall die in your sins." The verse points to faith in Christ as God (see John 8:58; Exodus 3:14).

Romans 10:9: "If you confess with your mouth the Lord Jesus and believe in your heart that God has raised Him from the dead, you will be saved" (NKJV). It appears here that confessing Jesus as "Lord" (= God) as well as believing in His resurrection are both necessary for salvation.

1 Corinthians 15:1-6: Here Paul defines the "gospel" (which is the power of God to save—Romans 1:16) as including the death and resurrection of Christ. He says, "By this gospel you are saved" (verse 2).

John 3:18: Here John declares not only that belief in Christ is necessary for salvation, but that disbelief brings condemnation. For "whoever does not believe stands condemned already because he has not believed in the name of God's one and only Son."

We favor the view that one's faith should embrace the theological content in the above verses. The backdrop is that God's revelation is progressive in nature. It is therefore not surprising that the fuller revelation of the New Testament brought with it an apparent increase in "mandatory saving-faith content." This increase, we believe, includes information about Christ's deity, death, and resurrection (see John 8:24; Acts 4:12; Romans 10:9; 1 Corinthians 15:1-6). Based on the New Testament evidence, it would seem that belief in these doctrines is normatively necessary for New Testament salvation.

There are other doctrines, by contrast, that are necessary to be *true* but not necessary to *believe* (at least not explicitly) in order to attain salvation. An example might be the humanity of Christ. While Christ's humanity is absolutely necessary to make salvation *possible* (He became a man to die on the cross), it does not appear to be an explicitly necessary faith condition for *receiving* the gift of eternal life.

Implicit Faith versus Explicit Faith

Through the ages, the vast majority of Christendom (Roman Catholicism, Eastern Orthodoxy, Anglicanism, and Lutheranism) has believed in baptismal regeneration for infants. An infant, however, is not old enough to express explicit faith in Christ, let alone the other doctrines essential to being saved. Many proponents of baptismal regeneration believe this regeneration is only temporary or needs confirmation later when the child is old enough to make a faith decision for himself. Most Christians who oppose infant baptism (us included) favor belief in God's salvation of infants who die and who are not yet able to believe.* So, even here there is no explicit faith expressed by the infant—at least none *while* the individual is an infant. Thus, if not an implicit faith in the infant, at least there must be an explicit faith expressed later. If this were not the case, we would be forced to conclude that explicit faith is not an absolute essential to salvation. Rather than sacrificing this important truth, some evangelicals believe there will be an opportunity for infants to express faith after they get to heaven. Some believe the same applies to heathen peoples who have never heard the gospel.[1] All of this is heavily debated among Christians. Because there is no normative view among evangelicals on this point, it should therefore fall into the category of a nonessential issue. Of course, the necessity of faith is an essential doctrine.

Denial in Principle versus Denial in Practice

Many in the Anabaptist, Baptist, or independent traditions believe that infant baptismal regeneration is a denial of a fundamental doctrine—the necessity of faith for salvation. While the authors disagree with the doctrine of infant baptismal regeneration, we also recognize that if this view denies the necessity of faith for salvation, it does so primarily *in practice*, not necessarily *in principle*. What we mean is that proponents of this position hold to a kind of implicit faith by the infant or at least a "wait and see" attitude with regard to his or her eventual explicit faith and subsequent salvation. Because almost all these groups believe that regeneration can be lost, it is no irreconcilable problem *within their system* to account for a baptized infant *not* having explicit faith as an adult and,

* Some believe that only *elect* infants go to heaven. Others hold that only those infants God *foreknew* would believe go to heaven. Those who believe that *all* infants who die go to heaven must either believe that explicit faith is not an absolute condition for salvation or else that they will be given an opportunity to believe after they die. Verses often cited in support of the salvation of all infants include Isaiah 7:15; Matthew 19:14; Mark 10:14; John 3:16; Romans 5:18-19; 2 Corinthians 5:19; 1 Timothy 2:4; and 2 Peter 3:9.

therefore, not eventually making it to heaven. As such, there is no denial of the necessity of faith *in principle* among those who believe in infant baptismal regeneration.

Unorthodox Denials of the Necessity of Faith

When it comes to the issue of the necessity of faith in the kingdom of the cults, things become a bit complicated because, on the one hand, there are cultic groups that outright deny the necessity of faith when it comes to the issue of salvation. On the other hand, there are cultic groups who hold to the necessity of faith, but because they completely redefine the *object* of faith—believing in a different God or a different Jesus—their views are just as unbiblical. Some cultic groups deny both the necessity of faith for salvation as well as set forth an unbiblical God or Jesus. To clarify all this, let's take a look at some representative examples.[2]

The Unitarian Universalist Association, a cult whose membership claims to include professing Christians (albeit liberal), denies the necessity of faith for salvation. In fact, the group's members do not have to believe anything at all in order to be a part of this eclectic cult. "We have no specific doctrines to which members are expected to subscribe....We do not believe that any religious precept or doctrine must be accepted as true simply because some religious organization, tradition, or authority says it is."[3] "Ours is a non-creedal, non-doctrinal religion which affirms the individual's freedom of belief."[4] "Ours is a *creedless* faith....We do not require our members to subscribe to a particular theology or set of affirmations in order to join our congregations."[5] Indeed, "Unitarian Universalists can believe anything they like."[6] Church members openly admit that "since individual freedom of belief is one of our basic principles, it follows that there will be differing beliefs among us."[7] They claim their religion "excludes all exclusiveness" and that truth changes over time.[8] They thus claim, "We do not have a defined doctrine of God. Members are free to develop individual concepts of God that are meaningful to them."[9] Clearly, faith is not a necessity in this religious group—not faith in God, not faith in Christ, not faith in *anything!*

We cannot resist noting, in passing, that Unitarian Universalists seem blind to the philosophical problems inherent in their theology.

For example, the Unitarian Universalist claim that truth "changes over time" is meaningless, for what if the position that truth changes over time is itself one of the "truths" that changes over time? Moreover, it is impossible for Unitarian Universalists to "exclude all exclusivistic positions" because the very act of excluding these positions is itself an act of exclusivism.

The Masonic Lodge is another example of a group that essentially denies the necessity of faith for salvation. We say "essentially" because Masonic leaders *do* require that initiates believe in God in order to become a Mason, but this "God" can be any god one prefers—Yahweh, Allah, Shiva or any Hindu god, or any other god of any other religion. Moreover, while faith in a god is a requirement for initially joining the lodge, faith itself is not viewed as necessary for salvation.

Masons do not believe human beings are fallen in sin, but are rather just imperfect beings who are fully capable of working their own way to heaven (no faith is necessary). James Rongstad notes that "Masonry teaches that humanity is not originally sinful, just imperfect. If a person works faithfully at keeping the principles and teachings of the Lodge, then he will be ushered into the 'Grand Lodge Above,' where the 'Supreme Architect of the Universe' resides."[10] Rongstad says:

> Masonry teaches its adherents that the candidate coming into the lodge has a "rough and imperfect nature." That is why Masonry uses the Ashlar, Gavel, Square, and Compass—to remind the members that they ever must work out their imperfections in order to be found acceptable to the "Supreme Grand Master" and to achieve a life in paradise, the "Grand Lodge Above."[11]

Masons believe that human beings can, in and of themselves, improve their somewhat flawed or unpolished character and behavior and attain the moral perfection necessary to go to heaven.[12] W. L. Wilmhurst writes, "Human nature is perfectible by an intensive process of purification and initiation."[13] Masonry's purpose is "to make good men better."[14] Albert G. Mackey, in the *Revised Encyclopedia of Freemasonry,* writes, "All [Masons] unite in declaring it to be a system of morality, by the practice of which its members may advance their spiritual interest, and mount by the theological ladder from the Lodge on earth to the Lodge in heaven."[15]

In the Masonic view, one earns salvation by ethical living based on whatever holy book one subscribes to—the Christian Bible, the Hindu Vedas, or the Muslim Koran, for example. *Faith plays no role.* Just follow the ethical principles in whatever holy book, and everything will be fine for the Mason. William Hammond writes, "Through the fellowship of a moral discipline Masons are taught to qualify for the fellowship of eternal life."[16] John Robinson states, "The Masonic leaning is to encourage the individual to advance toward the hope of resurrection and immortality through personal merit and acts of charity."[17] Jack Harris, a former Worshipful Master Mason, affirms that "in all the rituals that I taught for eleven years, Masonry did teach how to get to heaven. They taught it with the apron that I wore, by my purity [of] life and conduct....Never at any Masonic ritual did they point out that Jesus is the way of salvation."[18]

One of the closing prayers used in the lodge includes the words, "May we so practice thy precepts, that we may finally obtain thy promises, and find an entrance through the gates into the temple and city of our God."[19] Likewise, the following words are often spoken at a Masonic burial service:

> May the present instance of mortality remind us of our own approaching fate, and, by drawing our attention toward Thee, may we be induced so to regulate our conduct here that when the moment of dissolution shall arrive at which we must quit this brief scene, we may be received into Thine everlasting kingdom, there to enjoy that uninterrupted and unceasing felicity which is allotted to the souls of just men made perfect.[20]

Again, then, there is no necessity of faith in Masonic theology.

The Mormons are an example of a cult that *claims* to hold to the necessity of faith, but there are significant problems with their views regarding this issue. First, the *object* of Mormon faith is completely unbiblical. More specifically, while Mormons claim it is necessary to have faith in "Jesus Christ" for salvation,[21] the Jesus they believe in is not the Jesus of the Bible.

Their Jesus is not eternal God, but rather, came into being at a point in time when he was born as the first and greatest spirit child of the heavenly Father and one of His unnamed wives. In his pre-existent state as a spirit, he allegedly worked his way toward—and then *attained*—deity. This same Jesus was later *physically* born on earth as a result of physical sexual relations between the Father (who is said to have a physical body) and Mary, His daughter. This is not the same object of faith that is portrayed in the Christian Bible.

A second problem with Mormon teaching on the necessity of faith is that even though they concede faith is necessary for attaining salvation, *faith alone* certainly does not save, and faith is often so overshadowed by a continual emphasis on works that one is forced to wonder how much a role faith really does play. Mormon leader Legrand Richards, in his book *A Marvelous Work and a Wonder,* said,

> One erroneous teaching of many Christian churches is: *By faith alone we are saved.* This false doctrine would relieve man from the responsibility of his acts other than to confess a belief in God, and would teach man that no matter how great the sin, a confession would bring him complete forgiveness and salvation. What the world needs is more preaching of the necessity of abstaining from sin and living useful and righteous lives, and less preaching of forgiveness of sin...The truth is that men must repent of their sins and forsake them before they can expect forgiveness.[22]

Likewise, Mormon theologian Bruce McConkie wrote,

> Many go so far...as to pretend and, at least, to believe that if we confess Christ with our lips and avow that we accept Him as our personal Savior, we are thereby saved. His blood, without other act than mere belief, they say, makes us clean...Finally in our day, he has said plainly: "My blood shall not cleanse them *if they hear me not.*" Salvation in the kingdom of God is available because of the atoning blood of Christ. But it is received only on condition of faith, repentance, baptism, *and enduring to the end in keeping the commandments of God.*[23]

Mormon James Talmage, in his *Study of the Articles of Faith,* refers to "justification by belief alone" as "a most pernicious doctrine." He laments that "dogmas of men have been promulgated to the effect that by faith alone may salvation be attained."[24] One must of necessity engage in perpetual works. Talmage asserts, "There is no difference in meaning between *true faith* and *works of faith*. In the Bible the two terms mean the same thing."[25]

We see this same mentality of unceasing works overshadowing faith among the Jehovah's Witnesses. In the Watchtower book *You Can Live Forever in Paradise on Earth,* we read that "you must have faith in Jehovah and in his promises....However, more than faith is needed. There must also be works to demonstrate what your true feelings are about Jehovah."[26] We then read:

> Suppose you wanted to become a citizen of another country. In order to do so, you would have to meet the requirements set by the rules of that country's government. But before you could do this, you would have to learn what these requirements are. In a similar way, you need to learn what God requires of those who want to become subjects of his government. And then you need to meet these requirements....It is obvious that human governments do not want criminals as new citizens. And Jehovah has even higher standards....If persons do not keep God's laws, they will not be permitted to live under his kingdom.[27]

While Jehovah's Witnesses might talk about the necessity of faith, in actuality, it is works and unceasing obedience to the Watchtower Society that brings salvation. "To get one's name written in that book of life will depend upon one's works."[28] "It is for the reward of eternal life that every last person on earth should now be working. Are you?"[29] This hardly sounds like the good news of salvation by grace through faith as found in the Bible.

Finally, there are Mind Science cults that affirm the necessity of faith, but they do not mean by this what the Bible means. For example, Mary Baker Eddy, founder of the Christian Science cult and author of *Science and Health with Key to the Scriptures,* relates "faith" or "belief" to overcoming the errors of mortal mind (such as belief in the reality of sin, disease, and death—which are really just illusions). She notes that "the Hebrew verb *to believe* means also *to be firm.*"[30] She claims that "firmness in error will never save from sin, disease, and death."[31] "Faith," she says, "is a chrysalis state of human thought, in which spiritual evidence, contradicting the testimony of material sense, begins to appear, and Truth, the ever-present, is becoming understood."[32] What she means by this is that faith is that state of mind which recognizes that sin, disease, and death are errors of mortal mind and can be overcome by right thinking (the kind of thinking taught in Christian Science). It is in this sense that "faith" is necessary.

Another example is Religious Science, a Mind Science cult founded by Ernest Holmes. In his thinking, faith is necessary not in order to be saved, but in order to bring about changes in the material realm by the power of the mind. Holmes wrote,

> "Faith is the substance of things hoped for, the evidence of things not seen." The thought of faith molds the undifferentiated substance, and brings into manifestation the thing which was fashioned in the mind. This is how faith brings our desires to pass....When we use our creative imagination in strong faith, it will create for us, out of the One Substance, whatever we have formed in thought. In this way man becomes a Co-Creator with God.[33]

In Religious Science, the necessity of faith relates more to having the "faith of God" rather than "faith in God." In view of Religious Science's pantheism (all is God), man himself *is* God, and therefore exercises the *faith of* God in calling things into being. It is only in this sense that "faith" is a necessity.

Closing Observation

Over 100 times in the New Testament, salvation is said to be by faith alone—with no works in sight. Here are three examples just from the Gospel of John:

- "God so loved the world that he gave his one and only Son, that whoever believes in him shall not perish but have eternal life" (John 3:16).
- "Whoever hears my word and believes him who sent me has eternal life and will not be condemned; he has crossed over from death to life" (John 5:24).
- "I am the resurrection and the life. He who believes in Me, though he may die, he shall live" (John 11:25 NKJV).

If salvation were not by faith alone, then Jesus' message in the Gospel of John—manifest in the above quotations—would be deceptive. That is, if salvation is obtained by both faith *and* good works, then it would have been wrong of Jesus to say so many times that there is only one condition for salvation—faith.

At the same time, Scripture is clear that while we are saved *by* faith, we are saved *for* good works. That is, works are not the *condition* of our salvation, but are a *consequence* of it (see Ephesians 2:10; Titus 3:8). We are saved not *by* works, but by the kind of faith that *ends up producing* works (James 2:18-20). A life of holiness is important, but it *follows* salvation, not *causes* it. In short, we are saved by faith alone, but the faith that saves us is not alone—it is accompanied by good works.

It is at this point that Protestants and Roman Catholics diverge. Roman Catholics believe works are a condition of one's ultimate salvation. Just as in the question of grace (see chapter 11), Roman Catholicism affirms the *necessity* of faith but not the *exclusivity* of faith in obtaining salvation. And it is at this point that we believe their teaching is in serious error. However, what saves the Catholic view from utter heresy is its acknowledgment that these works necessary for salvation are prompted by God's grace, which is obtained by the necessity of faith.

THEOLOGICAL QUICK-REVIEW

Chapter 12 Main Idea: No one can realize salvation in his own life apart from faith in God.

Importance: In every age the one and only fundamental requirement for receiving God's gift of salvation has been and still is faith. Good works merit nothing in terms of salvation, but rather follow salvation. Hence, the necessity of faith is a fundamental of the Faith.

Unorthodox Viewpoints: Some cultic groups outright deny the necessity of faith in regard to salvation. Other cultic groups claim the necessity of faith, but the object of their faith (a counterfeit God or a counterfeit Jesus) renders their view unbiblical. In almost all cultic groups, works grossly overshadow any talk of the necessity of faith.

Course of Action: On the doctrine of the necessity of faith, there must be conviction without compromise.

13

The Bodily Ascension of Christ

CHRIST'S BODILY ASCENSION TO the right hand of the Father signals the beginning of the basis of the second state of our salvation, called *sanctification.* For by the ascension, Christ received His position in heaven at the right hand of the Father, from which He intercedes on our behalf and from which He sent the Holy Spirit to enable us to live a Christlike life. Thus, the bodily ascension of Christ is an essential doctrine for our salvation from the power of sin in our life in the present.

The Biblical Basis for the Ascension and Its Significance

1 John 2:1: "If anyone sins, we have an Advocate with the Father, Jesus Christ the righteous" (NKJV). The backdrop here is that Satan accuses believers before God's throne because of our sins (Revelation 12:10). In heaven, the resurrected and ascended Christ is our advocate or attorney pleading our case before the Father. His defense hinges entirely on His once-for-all atonement in which He paid for all our sins—past, present, and future (Hebrews 10:12-14). Because of Christ's work on our behalf, the Father's verdict is, "Case dismissed."

John 14:2-3: "In My Father's house are many mansions; if it were not so, I would have told you. I go to prepare a place for you. And if I go and prepare a place for you, I will come again and receive you to Myself; that where I am, there you may be also" (NKJV). If Christ had not ascended bodily, He would not be preparing our eternal abode in heaven.

John 20:17: "Jesus said to her [Mary], 'Do not cling to Me, for I have not yet ascended to My Father'" (NKJV, insert added). Following the crucifixion, Jesus' spirit was with the Father in heaven (Luke 23:46) while His body was yet in the tomb on earth. At the resurrection, His spirit was reunited with His physically resurrected body. In John 20:17, Jesus affirmed to Mary that He would soon ascend into heaven, where He would again be with the Father not just in His spirit, but in His physically resurrected body as well.

John 16:7: Jesus said, "I tell you the truth. It is to your advantage that I go away; for if I do not go away, the Helper [the Holy Spirit] will not come to you; but if I depart, I will send Him to you" (NKJV, insert added). This statement is emphatic about the need for Christ's ascension, for without it, we would not have the Holy Spirit in our lives.

Luke 24:50-51: "He led them [some disciples] out as far as Bethany, and He lifted up His hands and blessed them. Now it came to pass, while He blessed them, that *He was parted from them and carried up into heaven*" (NKJV, insert added, emphasis added).

Acts 1:9-11: "When He had spoken these things, while they [some disciples] watched, *He was taken up*, and a cloud received Him out of their sight...they looked steadfastly toward heaven as *He went up*" (NKJV, insert added, emphasis added).

Acts 2:33: Peter, in the sermon he gave on the day of Pentecost, said this about Jesus: "Therefore *being exalted to the right hand of God*, and having received from the Father the promise of the Holy Spirit, He poured out this which you now see and hear. For David did not ascend into the heavens [as Christ has], but he said himself: 'The LORD said to my Lord, Sit at My right hand, till I make Your enemies Your footstool'" (NKJV, insert added, emphasis added).

Ephesians 4:8-12: "Therefore He says: '*When He ascended on high*, He led captivity captive, and gave gifts to men.'...(He who descended is also *the One who ascended* far above all the heavens, that He might fill all things). And He Himself gave some to be apostles, some prophets, some evangelists, and some pastors and teachers, for the equipping of the saints for the work of ministry, for the edifying of the body of Christ" (NKJV, emphasis added). Spiritual gifts, which come to us as a result of Christ's ascension, are used of God to bless believers and to help them overcome the power of evil in their lives, which is part of the ongoing process of sanctification.

Hebrews 1:3: This verse makes reference to the Son of God, who, "when He had by Himself purged our sins, *sat down at the right hand of the Majesty on high*" (NKJV, emphasis added). This position of honor and preeminence was a direct consequence of Christ's bodily ascension into heaven.

Hebrews 10:12: "This Man [Jesus], after He had offered one sacrifice for sins forever, sat down at the right hand of God" (NKJV) after His physical resurrection and bodily ascension into heaven. Again, His position of authority in heaven comes as a result of His ascension.

Note that Christ's ascension into heaven was bodily. For Christ rose immortal in the same physical body in which He was crucified (Luke 24:39; John 20:27). He ascended into heaven in this same physical body (Acts 1:10-11), remains in the "flesh" in heaven even now (1 John 4:2; 2 John 7; Revelation 5:6), and will one day return in this physical body (Zechariah 14:4; Revelation 1:7).

The Theological Importance of the Ascension

It is clear from all these texts that the bodily ascension of the resurrected Christ is an important doctrine in connection with our salvation. That Christ is seated at the position of honor and preeminence at the right hand of the Father shows the divine acceptance of His death for our sins. Further, the ascension put Christ in the position to fulfill His promise to send the Holy Spirit, who accomplishes our sanctification. Without the bodily ascension of Christ, this important aspect of our salvation would not be possible.

The Creedal Basis for the Bodily Ascension

The creedal basis of the bodily ascension is strong from the very beginning. Even in the incipient creed imbedded in 1 Timothy 3:16 we find mention of Christ being "received up in glory": "God was manifested in the flesh, justified in the Spirit, seen by angels, preached among the Gentiles, believed on in the world, *received up in glory*" (NKJV, emphasis added). The

Apostles' Creed expressed it clearly in these words: "He ascended into heaven and sits at the right hand of God the Father." The Nicene Creed repeats the same phrase. The Chalcedonian Creed, in turn, reaffirms the Nicene Creed.

Many early church fathers placed strong emphasis on the bodily nature of the ascension, as do later confessions. Irenaeus (A.D. 130–200) declared, "The Church [believes] in...the resurrection from the dead and ascension into heaven in the flesh of the beloved Christ Jesus, our Lord." St. Augustine said, "The world has come to the belief that the earthly body of Christ was received up into heaven....[They] have believed in the resurrection of the flesh and its ascension to the heavenly places." The Thirty-Nine Articles of Religion (A.D. 1562) of the Church of England proclaimed, "Christ did truly rise again from the dead, and took again his body with flesh and bones...wherewith he ascended into heaven." Likewise, the *Westminster Confession of Faith* (A.D. 1647) stated, "On the third day he arose from the dead, with the same body in which he suffered; with which he ascended into heaven."

Unorthodox Denials of the Bodily Ascension

In view of the importance of this doctrine, it is sad to observe that many groups throughout church history have denied both Christ's bodily resurrection and His bodily ascension into heaven. Within the confines of this chapter, we can do little more than provide a representative sampling.

One heresy that emerged early in church history is Gnosticism. For our purposes, the Gnostic Cerinthus serves as a good example. Cerinthus drew a distinction between the human Jesus and the Christ, a cosmic spirit. We learn of the unique views of Cerinthus from the writings of a premier heresiologist, Irenaeus (A.D. 130–200), who tells us:

> [Cerinthus] represented Jesus as having not been born of a virgin, but as being the son of Joseph and Mary according to the ordinary course of human generation, while he nevertheless was more righteous, prudent, and wise than other men. Moreover, after his baptism, Christ descended upon him in

> the form of a dove from the Supreme Ruler, and that then he proclaimed the unknown Father, and performed miracles. But at last Christ departed from Jesus, and that then Jesus suffered and rose again, while Christ remained impassible [inaccessible to harm or pain], inasmuch as he was a spiritual being.[1]

According to Cerinthus, when Jesus was taken captive in order to be crucified, "Christ ascended up on high," so that Jesus alone was subject to the pain of crucifixion. This "ascension" of "the Christ" is hardly that described in the Bible. Irenaeus goes on to tell us that the apostle John specifically directed his Gospel against Cerinthus.[2] In fact, not only John's Gospel but also his epistles effectively refute the Gnostic view of Christ, providing convincing proof of the full humanity of the Christ.

For example, "The Word became flesh and dwelt among us" (John 1:14 NKJV). "By this you know the Spirit of God: Every spirit that confesses that Jesus Christ has come in the flesh is of God, and every spirit that does not confess that Jesus Christ has come in the flesh is not of God. And this is the spirit of the Antichrist, which you have heard was coming, and is now already in the world" (1 John 4:2). "Many deceivers have gone out into the world who do not confess Jesus Christ as coming in the flesh. This is a deceiver and an antichrist" (2 John 7).

John's Gospel provides evidence for the bodily, physical resurrection of Christ. The tomb where Jesus was buried was empty (John 20:5-6). Jesus appeared to the disciples and "showed them his hands and side" (John 20:20). He invited doubting Thomas to "put your finger here; see my hands. Reach out your hand and put it into my side. Stop doubting and believe" (John 20:27). He also spoke of His bodily ascension to Mary (John 20:17).

Some elements of Cerinthus's Gnostic view are repeated in the modern New Age movement, with many in this movement espousing what is called "esoteric Christianity." This form of Christianity claims to offer the true meaning of the Bible yet offers an entirely different understanding of the resurrection and ascension of Christ. According to this view, there is a distinction between the cosmic Christ and the human Jesus, who was a mere vehicle for the Christ for three years. While this view is similar to that of Cerinthus, who distinguished between the cosmic Christ and the human Jesus, it is different in that the New Age view does not portray the Christ as departing from the human Jesus before the crucifixion but rather as participating in it. More specifically, some New Agers teach that at the crucifixion, the etheric (or spiritual) blood of Christ/Jesus flowed into the spiritual earth. This served to increase "the divine immanent within the world."[3]

Later the Christ experienced an occult "resurrection" and "ascension." This basically refers to the outflowing of Christ energies (divine energies) from the etheric (spiritual or astral) realm to the physical realm. This, in turn, allegedly enabled the Christ to make an impact on the spiritual evolutionary development of humankind. In other words, as a result of the "resurrection" of the Christ (the outflowing of the Christ energies from the etheric realm), an "ascension of consciousness would take place in the life-streams of the planet, especially those of the human kingdom."[4] This consciousness centers on the inner divinity of all things. So, basically, the ascension refers to the rise of Christ consciousness among human beings on planet Earth. This, allegedly, is true Christianity.

There are other New Age enthusiasts who speak more generally of Ascended Masters—also known as Cosmic Masters—who allegedly seek to help lesser-attuned human beings usher in a New Age of peace and enlightenment in the world. The Ascended Masters are said to be a group of formerly historical persons who have finished their earthly evolutions and have moved on (ascended) to higher planes of existence. They now voluntarily seek to help lesser-evolved human beings reach their exalted level. Jesus is said to be one of these Ascended Masters. Many believe that Jesus and other Ascended Masters live in Tibet; others claim they live on Venus. Attuned New Age leaders can allegedly initiate psychic contact with the Ascended Masters and serve as their mouthpieces on earth via channeling (a New Age form of spiritism).

Obviously, this version of the "ascension" bears no resemblance to that portrayed in the Bible. This New Age view is based on a faulty, subjective, mystical form of Bible interpretation—"esoteric hermeneutics"—which seeks hidden or secondary meanings of Scripture verses. (In chapter 17 we will address proper biblical hermeneutics.)

Yet another mystical cultic group that denies the bodily ascension of Christ into heaven is Christian Science, founded by Mary Baker Eddy. In Christian Science theology there is no death, which means any discussion of a physical resurrection and ascension is a moot point. Eddy, utilizing esoteric methodology, interpreted the resurrection and ascension of Christ in terms of a consciousness focused on the material realm transforming into a consciousness focused on spirit. In Eddy's book *Science and Health with Key to the Scriptures,* we read this:

> Jesus' unchanged physical condition after what seemed to be death was followed by his exaltation above all material conditions; and this exaltation explained his ascension, and revealed unmistakably a probationary and progressive state beyond the grave. Jesus was "the way"; that is, he marked the way for all men. In his final demonstration, called the ascension, which closed the earthly record of Jesus, he rose above the physical knowledge of his disciples, and the material senses saw him no more.
>
> His students then received the Holy Ghost. By this is meant, that by all they had witnessed and suffered, they were roused to an enlarged understanding of divine Science, even to the spiritual interpretation and discernment of Jesus' teachings.... They no longer measured man by material sense. After gaining the true idea of their glorified Master, they became better healers, leaning no longer on matter, but on the divine Principle of their work.[5]

Clearly, then, there is no physical bodily ascension of Jesus Christ in Christian Science theology. All is interpreted in terms of mental enlightenment and deliverance from illusion.

A more mainstream example of a cultic denial of Christ's bodily ascension is that of the Jehovah's Witnesses. According to Watchtower theology, Jesus was resurrected spiritually from the dead. "We deny that he was raised in the flesh, and challenge any statement to that effect as being unscriptural."[6] "Jesus Christ was not made a human creature at his resurrection but was made a spirit."[7] He allegedly proved the reality of this resurrection to His followers by materializing bodies, much like the angels did in biblical times. "Jesus must be a spirit being. He simply materialized bodies."[8] "Usually [the people to whom Jesus appeared] could not at first tell it was Jesus, for he appeared in different bodies. He appeared and disappeared just as angels had done, because he was resurrected as a spirit creature."[9] "In order to convince Thomas of who He was, He used a body with wound holes."[10]

When it came time for Jesus to ascend into heaven, He allegedly dissolved whatever material body He was in at the moment and assumed spiritual form. In the Watchtower book *Aid to Bible Understanding,* we read,

> While Jesus began his ascent in a physical form, thus making possible his being seeable by his watching disciples, there is no basis for assuming that he continued to retain a material form after the cloud interposed itself. The apostle Peter states that Jesus died in the flesh but was resurrected "in the spirit" (1 Pet. 3:18). Paul declares the rule that "flesh and blood cannot inherit God's kingdom" (1 Cor. 15:50).[11]

Likewise, the Watchtower book *The Greatest Man Who Ever Lived* declared of the ascension: "While they are still looking on, Jesus begins rising heavenward, and then a cloud obscures him from their sight. After dematerializing his fleshly body, he ascends to heaven as a spirit person."[12]

Clearly, the Watchtower view on the ascension is based on a faulty exegesis of key Bible verses relating to the resurrection. Consider 1 Peter 3:18 as an example (Jesus was resurrected "in the spirit"). This verse is actually better translated, "He was put to death in the body but made alive *by* the [Holy] Spirit" (insert added, emphasis added). The passage is translated with this same understanding in the New King James Version and other reliable translations. God did not raise Jesus *as* a spirit, but raised Him *by* His Spirit.

The entire New Testament emphasizes that Jesus was resurrected bodily (Acts 4:33; Romans 1:4; 1 Corinthians 15:21; 1 Peter 1:3). In Luke 24:39 the resurrected Christ said, "Look at my hands and my feet.

It is I myself! Touch me and see, a ghost does not have flesh and bones, as you see I have" (Luke 24:39). The resurrected Christ also ate physical food on four different occasions to prove He had a real physical body (Luke 24:30,42-43; John 21:12-13; Acts 1:4). Hence, 1 Peter 3:18 cannot be interpreted in such a way that it contradicts this massive New Testament evidence. And because Jesus rose bodily—that is, *physically*—His ascension was bodily as well.

As for 1 Corinthians 15:50—"flesh and blood cannot inherit the kingdom of God"—the Watchtower misinterprets this verse as well. The phrase "flesh and blood" is simply an idiom used in Scripture to refer to mortal humanity. This verse is saying that mortal humanity cannot inherit the kingdom of God. Mortal humanity must be made immortal humanity in order to survive in heaven. The physical resurrection body will be endowed with special qualities that will make it perfectly adapted to life in God's presence.

In support of this position, the latter part of verse 50 makes reference to *perishable* human flesh. This sets the proper context for interpreting the entire verse. Clearly, Paul is not speaking of flesh as such, but of *perishable* flesh not inheriting God's kingdom. Hence, Paul is not affirming that the resurrection body will not have flesh, but that it will not have perishable flesh. In view of such facts, the Watchtower has virtually no basis for arguing that the ascension of Christ was spiritual and not bodily (physical).

Not only do many cults deny the physical bodily ascension of Christ, but an astonishing number of contemporary evangelicals do as well. These include such notables as George Ladd, Murray Harris, and Millard Erickson. Harris referred to the ascension of Christ as a "parable," saying: "The Ascension *vividly dramatized* Christ's earlier exaltation to God's right hand [at the resurrection]. It was a *parable* acted out for the benefit of the disciples as a visual and historical confirmation of a *spiritual reality*."[13] Harris affirmed that "in his normal or customary bodily state after the Resurrection, Jesus was neither visible to the human eye nor composed of 'flesh and bones.'"[14] Then, "when his appearances on earth were ended, Jesus assumed the sole mode of being visible to the inhabitants of heaven but having a nonfleshly body."[15] However, both the Bible (Acts 1:1-11; 1 John 4:2) and the creeds consistently affirm that Jesus went to heaven in the same body of "flesh" (Greek: *sarx*) in which He was raised.

Millard Erickson, former professor at Wheaton College and Bethel Seminary, wrote, "At that time [of the ascension] Jesus underwent the remainder of the metamorphosis begun with the resurrection of his body. The significance of the ascension is that Jesus left behind the conditions associated with life on this earth."[16] This is clearly contrary to the great creeds and confessions of the Christian Faith, as well as to the teaching of the New Testament.

New denials of Christ's bodily ascension continue to surface. Novelist Dan Brown's book *The Da Vinci Code* argues that the doctrines of Christ's resurrection and ascension were borrowed from pagan mythology. The book *The Jesus Family Tomb,* written by Simcha Jacobovici and Charles Pellegrino and promoted by film director James Cameron (of the blockbuster movie *Titanic*), states that a set of ossuary-urns—engraved with the names Jesus, Mary, a second Mary, Matthew, Joshua, and Judah—"proves" that the divine Savior did not rise from the dead then ascend to heaven. Rather, He married Mary Magdalene and had a son named Judah. Such ideas have been thoroughly and irrefutably debunked by numerous reliable scholars.[17] The evidence remains decisively on the side of the bodily ascension of Jesus Christ.

THEOLOGICAL QUICK-REVIEW

Chapter 13 Main Idea: Christ's bodily ascension to the right hand of the Father signals the beginning of the basis of the second state of our salvation, called sanctification.

Importance: By the ascension, Christ received His position in heaven at the right hand of the Father, from which He intercedes on our behalf and from which He sent the Holy Spirit to enable us to live a Christlike life. Hence, the bodily ascension of Christ is an essential doctrine for our salvation from the power of sin in our life in the present.

Unorthodox Viewpoints: Some cultic groups outright deny the bodily ascension of Christ. Others offer mystical reinterpretations. Still others hold to only a spiritual ascension of Christ. Even some evangelicals have said Christ had a nonphysical, spiritual ascension.

Course of Action: On the doctrine of the bodily ascension of Jesus Christ, there must be conviction without compromise.

14

Christ's Priestly Intercession

AS NOTED IN CHAPTER 1, all the "essential" doctrines are necessary for salvation. And salvation comes in three stages: *justification* (salvation from the penalty of sin), *sanctification* (salvation from the present power of sin), and *glorification* (salvation from the future presence of sin). All the doctrines discussed in chapters 2 through 12 constitute the basis for the three stages of salvation. The chapter on Christ's ascension (chapter 13) and this chapter examine the basis for our sanctification.

When Christ ascended bodily on high and was seated at the right hand of the Father, He was then able to send the Holy Spirit (John 16:7) to empower us to live a holy life (Acts 1:8). He was also enabled, by His position before the Father, to make intercession for our sins. More specifically, as our advocate before the Father and on the basis of His finished work on the cross (John 19; Hebrews 10:12-14), Christ is able to plead the efficacy of His once-for-all sacrifice for our sins in the present (Hebrews 7:25; 1 John 2:1). Without this we would not be able to enter heaven, for God is absolutely holy (Leviticus 11:45; Isaiah 6:1-7; Habakkuk 1:13) and no sin will be tolerated in His holy presence (Revelation 2:27; 22:14-15).

The Biblical Basis for the Priestly Intercession of Christ

Although the Bible does not say as much about it as other aspects of salvation, Christ's high priestly intercession for us is a very important doctrine for our salvation from the power of sin in the present. It is closely related to the lifelong process of sanctification, which involves progressively being made more and more like Christ. Without Christ's intercession on our behalf, this would not be possible.

1 John 2:1: "My dear children, I write this to you, so that you will not sin. But if anybody does sin, we have one who speaks to the Father in our defense—Jesus Christ, the Righteous One." As the accuser of believers (Satan) attacks us before God's throne because of our sins (Revelation 12:10). Christ is our attorney in heaven pleading our case before the Father based on His once-for-all payment for all our sins—past, present, and future (Hebrews 10:12-14).

Hebrews 1:3: Christ is the Son of God who, "after he had provided purification for sins, he sat down at the right hand of the Majesty in heaven." No priest in the Old Testament sat down while on duty, for two reasons: First, there were no chairs in the tabernacle or temple. Second, their work was never done. By contrast, the first thing Christ did when He entered the heavenly tabernacle was to sit down, for He had fully and completely accomplished the work of redemption.

Hebrews 4:15-16: "We do not have a High Priest who cannot sympathize with our weaknesses, but was in all points tempted as we are, yet without sin. Let us therefore come boldly to the throne of grace, that we may obtain mercy and find grace to help in time of need" (NKJV). As a human being who was tempted in every way that we are, Christ can fully sympathize with our infirmities. Thus, His high priestly duties are invariably effective for us.

Hebrews 7:25: "He is also able to save to the uttermost those who come to God through Him, since He always lives to make intercession for them" (NKJV, see also John 17:6-26). Complete salvation is more than justification. That is just the beginning. It also necessarily includes sanctification, which Christ aids us in achieving.

The Theological Importance of the Priestly Intercession of Christ

As noted earlier, when Christ ascended into heaven and was seated at the right hand of the Father, He was then able to send the Holy Spirit (John 16:7) to empower us to live a holy life. He was also enabled, by His position before the Father, to make intercession for our sins. More specifically, as our advocate before the Father and on the basis of His finished work on the cross (John 19:30; Hebrews 10:12-14), He is able to plead the efficacy of His once-for-all sacrifice for our sins in the present. That Christ is our advocate carries the idea that He is our defense attorney. A defense attorney becomes necessary when someone has been charged with a crime or a wrongdoing.

Who is our accuser? Revelation 12:10 says it is Satan, "the accuser of our brethren" (NKJV). This is illustrated in the book of Job, where we find Satan going before God's throne to bring accusations against Job (1:5-12). Satan does the same thing with us. Without Christ's faithful advocacy, we would not be able to enter heaven because God is absolutely holy (Habakkuk 1:13) and no sin can be tolerated in His holy presence. As our advocate, Jesus makes sure that no sin bars us from heaven.

The Creedal Basis for the Priestly Intercession of Christ

The creedal basis of the intercession of Christ follows on the ascension, which introduced Christ to His high priestly position at the right hand of the Father. Even the tiny creed stated in 1 Timothy 3:16 mentions it in the phrase "received up in glory." It reads: "God was manifested in the flesh, justified in the Spirit, seen by angels, preached among the Gentiles, believed on in the world, *received up in glory*" (NKJV, emphasis added). This implies an act of approval by the Father to Christ's new role in heaven. The Apostles' Creed implies Christ's intercession when it speaks of His return to the Father in these words: "He ascended into heaven and sits at the right hand of God the Father" and when it refers to the "forgiveness of sins." The Nicene Creed repeats the same phrase, and the Chalcedonian Creed reaffirms the Nicene Creed.

Christ's intercession in heaven is *bodily*, for He rose immortal in the same physical body in which He was crucified (Luke 24:39; John 20:27). He ascended into heaven in this same physical body (Acts 1:10-11) and will return to Earth in this body (Zechariah 14:4; Revelation 1:7). He remains in the "flesh" in heaven now (1 John 4:2; 2 John 7; Revelation 5:6), ever living to make intercession for us (Hebrews 7:25; 1 John 2:1). Summing up the view of the creeds and church fathers before him, St. Augustine declared, "The world has come to believe that *the earthly body of Christ was received up into heaven*."[1] The Anglican creed, the Thirty-Nine

Articles of Religion (A.D. 1562), stated, "Christ did truly rise again from death, and took again *his body with flesh and bones…wherewith he ascended into Heaven,* and there sitteth, until he return the judge of all Men" (emphasis added). Likewise, the *Westminster Confession of Faith* (A.D. 1647) says, "On the third day he arose from the dead, *with the same body in which he suffered; with which he ascended into heaven*" (emphasis added).

Unorthodox Denials of the Priestly Intercession of Christ

For the most part, the cults do not speak much about the priestly intercession of Jesus Christ. This is largely because they have a diminished view of Jesus, both in His identity and His work of redemption on the cross. However, the little they do reveal clearly crosses outside the line of historic, orthodox Christianity.

To begin, as noted in the previous chapter, there have been groups throughout church history that have denied Christ's physical ascension into heaven, and therefore any discussion of His postascension ministries—such as His priestly intercession in heaven—becomes a moot point. Consider, for example, the ancient Gnostics, who claimed that a cosmic Christ descended upon a human Jesus, communicated secret knowledge to people for a period of three years, and then departed from the body of Jesus prior to the crucifixion.[2] In such a scenario, there is no physically ascended Christ in heaven who acts as our advocate with the Father (see 1 John 2:1).

Some New Agers, such as David Spangler, hold to a view similar to that of the Gnostics.[3] Spangler says, the Christ remained with the human Jesus at the crucifixion. That is, the Christ's etheric or spiritual blood flowed into the etheric Earth at the crucifixion, after which the Christ experienced an occult "resurrection" and "ascension." This basically refers to the outflowing of Christ energies (divine energies) from the etheric (spiritual or astral) realm to the physical realm, which allegedly results in human beings coming to recognize their inner divinity. This means there is no physically ascended Christ in heaven who acts as our advocate with the Father and who sends the Holy Spirit to minister among us (see John 16:7).

We also noted in the previous chapter that many New Agers speak more generally of Ascended Masters or formerly historical persons who have finished their earthly evolutions (they died) and have moved on (ascended) to higher planes of existence. They now voluntarily seek to help lesser-evolved human beings reach their exalted level, and Jesus is allegedly one of these Ascended Masters. Thus Jesus *did not* uniquely ascend to a position of authority at the right hand of the Father, where He could then make intercession for us and send the Holy Spirit to us. Rather He, like many other supposedly enlightened individuals throughout human history, simply ascended to a higher plane of existence (in the astral realm), where He now seeks to influence and aid those still on the earthly plane.

We can also point to Mind Science groups, such as Christian Science (founded by Mary Baker Eddy), which flatly deny the reality of death. In this death-denying theology, there is no place for any discussion of a physical resurrection and ascension. Eddy, utilizing esoteric methodology, interprets the resurrection and ascension of Christ in terms of the disciples having a consciousness focused on the material realm transforming into a consciousness newly focused on spirit.[4] It is something that took place *in the minds of the disciples*. Consequently, there can be no physically ascended Christ who acts as our advocate with the Father and sends the Holy Spirit to us.

Hypothetically speaking, even if these groups were to admit that Jesus Christ ascended into heaven, what good would it do for us to have, acting as our advocate before the Father, a cultic and impotent "Jesus Christ" who is not deity? As noted earlier, New Agers and Mind Science groups say that Jesus was not unique, but was a mere human who embodied the Christ like all other humans can. Jesus was allegedly just a prototype for the rest of us. Can such a Jesus really help us at all? It's hard to see how. Biblically, the reason Jesus is a perfect advocate and mediator is that He is 100 percent God and 100 percent man (since the incarnation). He can therefore perfectly represent man to God as our advocate (1 Timothy 2:5; 1 John 2:1), especially because He Himself paid the full price for our sins at the cross.

The Mormons are a good case study in this regard. In Bruce McConkie's *Mormon Doctrine* we read, "To Christ, the Father has given 'power to make *intercession* for the children of men' (Mosiah 15:8), that is, he has the role of interceding, of mediating, of praying, petitioning and entreating the Father to grant mercy and blessings to men (Rom. 8:34; Heb. 7:25)."[5] But who is this Jesus who is interceding for us? He was first born as a spirit child of the heavenly Father and one of his unnamed wives. He is thus not eternal God but came into being at a point in time. Later, when Jesus was to be physically born on earth, the heavenly Father (in his physical body) came down and had sexual relations with his daughter Mary, and Jesus was physically born nine months later.[6]

Many Mormons believe this Jesus grew up to be a polygamist, and that the wedding at Cana—where He turned water into wine—was his own wedding. This same Jesus did die to atone for sin, but this atonement served only to secure man's resurrection from the dead (something Mormons call "general salvation").[7] Human beings must engage in good works to accomplish "individual salvation."

The point we thus want to emphasize is this: The Jesus of the Bible is eternal God, and in heaven He pleads the efficacy of the *full and finished* redemption He purchased with His blood on the cross. By contrast, the plea of the Mormon Jesus seems to ring hollow because he was not eternal God, and he did not accomplish a full and completely finished redemption for man regarding all human sin. (Bottom line: The Mormon Jesus was a *lesser person* who accomplished a *lesser work*, and hence his plea carries a *lesser weight*.)

There is another point that bears mentioning: Many cultic groups deny the reality of sin altogether, and therefore there is no need for either a purchased redemption on Earth or the advocacy of Jesus Christ in heaven. For example, Mind Science groups such as Christian Science, Religious Science, and the Unity School of Christianity all say that sin is just an illusion; it doesn't really exist. As well, New Agers typically hold to a monistic worldview and therefore blur the distinction between good and evil, resulting in an ultimate denial of the reality of sin. Sin is denied by many other cultic groups, including the Unitarian Universalists. Obviously, if there is no sin—*if there is no offended God*—then there is no need for us to have an advocate pleading our case before God. Nor is there any need for the Holy Spirit to help us to overcome sin.

This brings up yet another point. Even if (in cultic theology) human beings *did* have a bad sin problem, and the impotent Jesus of the kingdom of the cults *did* somehow manage to send the Holy Spirit, what kind of "Holy Spirit" would be here to help us? The reality is that the cults have so distorted the doctrine of the Holy Spirit that their "Holy Spirit" bears little or no resemblance to the Holy Spirit in the Bible. Let's consider a few examples:

The Unity School of Christianity has a completely warped interpretation of all three persons of the Trinity: "The Father is Principle, the Son is that Principle revealed in creative plan, the Holy Spirit is the executive power of both Father and Son carrying out the creative plan."[8] It is hard to see how such an impersonal Holy Spirit could be of any real benefit to the people of God.

Ernest Holmes, who founded the Religious Science cult, writes that "the Spirit of Truth is in all people—not unto Jesus alone—but unto all alike." Holmes' all-is-divine theology teaches that "as the Holy Comforter comes, He makes all things known to us. Intuition is the speech of this Comforter. 'I am in my Father, and ye in me, and I in you.' The eternal Father begets the eternal Son. This Son is generic, all are members of this Universal Sonship, all are members of the one Tree of Life, from which every individual shoot springs."[9] If we are the Son like Jesus is, and we are divine like Jesus is, why do we even need help from this "Holy Comforter"?

Eckankar teaches that the Holy Spirit is an impersonal life force that sustains all life. More specifically, Eckankar teaches that one can obtain enlightenment, over the course of many lifetimes (via reincarnation), by practicing the spiritual exercises set forth by the ECK Master. *ECK* refers to the "Life Force" or "Divine Spirit" or "the Holy Spirit" that sustains all life.[10] Eckankar claims to provide spiritual exercises that open one's heart to the Divine Spirit, bring purification, and enable one to experience the Light and Sound of God (also known as the Holy Spirit). We are told that "the inner Sound is the Voice of God calling us home. The inner Light is a beacon to light our way. All the Spiritual Exercises of ECK are built on these two divine aspects of the Holy Spirit."[11] As one obeys the teachings of the ECK Masters, the ECK (the Holy Spirit or "Life Force") can purify one of bad karma and speed one's spiritual progression. Such teaching bears no resemblance at all to the work of the Holy Spirit as described in the Bible.

The Children of God cult, led by Moses David Berg, believed the Holy Spirit was the feminine aspect of God, and often referred to "her" as the "Holy Queen of Love" and God's "Elixir of Love." The Holy Spirit was often portrayed in the *Mo Letters* (the educational newsletters of the cult) as an enticing and sensual young woman (often nude).

The Unification Church, founded by Reverend Moon, describes the ascension of Christ and the subsequent sending and role of the Holy Spirit in terms far removed from the teachings of the Bible: "Jesus ascended...to the position of the spiritual Messiah and sent the Holy Spirit. Thereupon, Jesus and the Holy Spirit became the spiritual True Parents....Ever since the descent of the Holy Spirit at the Pentecost, the resurrected Jesus as the spiritual True Father and the Holy Spirit as the spiritual True Mother have worked in oneness to grant spiritual rebirth by spiritually engrafting believers with themselves."[12] We are told, "Since the Holy Spirit is the feminine aspect of divinity, without first receiving her we cannot go before Jesus as his brides. Being feminine, the Holy Spirit consoles and moves the hearts of people. She cleanses people's sin, thereby atoning for the sin which Eve committed. Jesus, the masculine Lord, works in heaven (yang), while the Holy Spirit, his feminine counterpart, works on earth (yin)."[13] This is a hybrid theology that mixes Christianity with Eastern religious elements. We might add that the Jesus of the Unification Church can hardly carry on an effective advocacy on our behalf in heaven, for, according to Moon, Jesus only accomplished *spiritual* salvation but failed to accomplish *physical* salvation. Reverend Moon must now succeed where Jesus failed—that is, he himself must now accomplish physical salvation.

Paul Wierwille, founder of The Way International cult, drew a distinction between the Holy Spirit (with capital letters) and the holy spirit (with lowercase letters). The Holy Spirit is another name for the Father, and is hence God. The holy spirit is the gift—an inanimate, impersonal force—that the Holy Spirit (the Father) gives to individual Christians to empower them. It is important to understand this distinction, we are told, for "many confuse the Giver, Holy Spirit, with the gift, holy spirit."[14]

This convoluted theology is supposed to yield the "abundant life" to followers of the cult.

There are other examples we could share. The above is sufficient, however, to illustrate how the cults distort or deny Christ's bodily ascension, His work of advocacy at the right hand of the Father, the role of the Holy Spirit among us, and whether or not there's even a need for Christ's advocacy and the Holy Spirit's ministry because there is allegedly no sin to begin with. There can be no true salvation in such theology.

THEOLOGICAL QUICK-REVIEW

Chapter 14 Main Idea: When Christ ascended to heaven and was seated at the right hand of the Father, He sent the Holy Spirit (John 16:7) to empower us to live a holy life (Acts 1:8). He was also enabled, by His position before the Father, to make intercession for our sins (Hebrews 7:25; 1 John 2:1).

Importance: Jesus—as our advocate before the Father and on the basis of His finished work on the cross (John 19; Hebrews 10:12-14)—is able to plead the efficacy of His once-for-all sacrifice for our sins in the present (Hebrews 7:25; 1 John 2:1). Without this we simply would not be able to enter heaven, because God is absolutely holy (Leviticus 11:45; Isaiah 6:1-7; Habakkuk 1:13), and no sin can be tolerated in His holy presence (Revelation 2:27; 22:15).

Unorthodox Viewpoints: Many cults distort or deny Christ's ascension, His work of advocacy at the right hand of the Father, and the role of the Holy Spirit among us. Some deny there's even a need for Christ's advocacy and the Holy Spirit's ministry because there is allegedly no sin to begin with in human beings.

Course of Action: On the doctrine of Christ's priestly intercession, there must be conviction without compromise.

15

Christ's Bodily Second Coming

THE SECOND COMING OF CHRIST brings us to the third and final stage of salvation—deliverance from the very presence of sin. *Justification* (chapters 2–12) deals with salvation from the past penalty of sin; *sanctification* (chapters 13 and 14) deals with salvation from the present power of sin; and *glorification* will deliver us from the very presence of sin in the future. So, at Christ's return, the final stage of our salvation becomes complete.

Of course, not all people will be saved. Nonetheless, end-time events associated with the second coming (such as the judgment) will signal the defeat of sin, which involves heaven for the saved and hell for the lost. Thus the flip side of the final salvation doctrine is that it ushers in the final condemnation as well. This, too, has been part of orthodox Christian teaching from the earliest times.

The Biblical Basis for the Second Coming of Christ

While significant differences exist among Christians regarding the end times, the key characteristics of historic Christianity's essential beliefs about the end times include the following: 1) a literal return of Christ to earth to end the dominion of sin and bring in righteousness and peace; 2) the separation of humankind into two groups forever, wherein a) the saved will enjoy conscious eternal life, and b) the lost will be condemned to suffer conscious everlasting doom; and 3) in conjunction with point 2, there will be a bodily resurrection of all the saved and the unsaved. The saved will undergo a personal transformation into a state of perfect and permanent righteousness.

Beyond these basics, there has been a broad range of disagreements over the timing, nature, and details of the events surrounding the second coming. So the main focus in this chapter will be on the essential areas of agreement among orthodox Christians from the earliest centuries. Some key passages will make the point. First, let us consider some biblical texts about the personal effect of the second coming on believers (emphasis is added in some verses):

Romans 8:18-23: "I consider that the sufferings of this present time are not worthy to be compared with *the glory which shall be revealed in us.* For the earnest expectation of the creation eagerly waits for the revealing of the sons of God. For the creation was subjected to futility, not willingly, but because of Him who subjected it in hope; because the creation itself also will be delivered from the bondage of corruption into the *glorious liberty* of the children of God. For we know that the whole creation groans and labors with birth pangs together until now. Not only that, but we also who have the firstfruits of the Spirit, even we ourselves groan within ourselves, eagerly waiting for the adoption, the redemption of our body" (NKJV).

1 John 3:2-3: The apostle John stated, "Beloved, now we are children of God; and it has not yet been revealed what we shall be, but we know that *when He is revealed, we shall be like Him,* for we shall see Him as He is. And everyone who has this hope in Him purifies himself, just as He is pure" (NKJV).

*1 Corinthians 13:10,12: "When perfection comes, the imperfect disappears...*Now we see but a poor reflection as in a mirror; then we shall see face to face. Now I know in part; *then I shall know fully,* even as I am fully known" (emphasis added). In view of this approaching day, hymn writer Charles H. Gabriel exulted, "O that will be glory for me, glory for me, glory for me. When by His grace I will look on His face. That will be glory, be glory for me!"

There are several things we as Christians look forward to in this third and final stage of salvation. First, our sin nature will be abolished. Currently, "if we claim to be without sin, we deceive ourselves and the truth is not in us" (1 John 1:8). But then we will be perfect (1 Corinthians 13:10), for "we know that when he appears, we shall be like him, for we shall see him as he is" (1 John 3:2). On that day, Christ "will transform our lowly bodies so that they will be like his glorious body" (Philippians 3:21).

Second, the beatific (blessed) vision will be accomplished. We will see God face-to-face. This is something that no mortal man can do in this life. For "no one has ever seen God, but God the One and Only, who is at the Father's side, has made him known" (John 1:18). Even Moses—the great mediator who spoke directly with God—was forbidden to see His face. When he asked to do so, God said, "You cannot see My face, for no one may see me and live" (Exodus 33:20).

While mortal man cannot behold God and live, by contrast, immortal man will see God and live forever. John wrote, "*They will see his face,* and his name will be on their foreheads" (Revelation 22:4, emphasis added). Paul wrote, "When perfection comes, the imperfect disappears...Now we see but a poor reflection as in a mirror; then we shall see *face to face*" (1 Corinthians 13:10-12, emphasis added). Jesus said, "Blessed are the pure in heart, for they will *see God*" (Matthew 5:8, emphasis added).

The Eternal State for the Saved Is Heaven

Revelation 21: John's vision of our future salvation included this glorious description:

> Now I saw a new heaven and a new earth, for the first heaven and the first earth had passed away. Also there was no more sea. Then I, John, saw the holy city, New Jerusalem, coming down out of heaven from God, prepared as a bride adorned for her husband. And I heard a loud voice from heaven saying, "Behold, the tabernacle of God is with men, and He will dwell with them, and they shall be His people. God Himself will be with them and be their God. And God will wipe away every tear from their eyes; there shall be no more death, nor sorrow, nor crying. There shall be no more pain, for the former things have passed away."...And he carried me away in the Spirit to a great and high mountain, and showed me the great city, the holy Jerusalem, descending out of heaven from God, having

> the glory of God. Her light was like a most precious stone, like a jasper stone, clear as crystal....The construction of its wall was of jasper; and the city was pure gold, like clear glass. The foundations of the wall of the city were adorned with all kinds of precious stones....The twelve gates were twelve pearls: each individual gate was of one pearl. And the street of the city was pure gold, like transparent glass. But I saw no temple in it, for the Lord God Almighty and the Lamb are its temple. The city had no need of the sun or of the moon to shine in it, for the glory of God illuminated it. The Lamb is its light (verses 1-4,10-11,18-19,21-23 NKJV).

The Eternal State for the Lost Is the Lake of Fire

Revelation 20:11-15: In this passage, John declared:

> Then I saw a great white throne and Him who sat on it, from whose face the earth and the heaven fled away. And there was found no place for them. And I saw the dead, small and great, standing before God, and books were opened. And another book was opened, which is the Book of Life. And the dead were judged according to their works, by the things which were written in the books. The sea gave up the dead who were in it, and Death and Hades delivered up the dead who were in them. And they were judged, each one according to his works. Then Death and Hades were cast into the lake of fire. This is the second death. And anyone not found written in the Book of Life was cast into the lake of fire (NKJV).

The Saved: Free from Sin Forever

Among the most glorious doctrinal teachings of Scripture is that the saved, in heaven, will be *free from sin forever.* For there, our freedom will be perfect and made more like God's. Being absolutely perfect, God does not have the freedom to do evil. It is impossible for Him to sin or even be tempted by sin (Hebrews 6:18; James 1:13). Likewise, at the beatific vision, when we see Absolute Good face-to-face, we too will no longer be able to sin.

Currently by God's grace, we are *able* not to sin (1 Corinthians 10:13), but in the future, we will *no longer* be able to sin. This is not a loss of true freedom; it is the gaining of perfect freedom. Perfect freedom is not the freedom to be in bondage to sin; rather, it is the freedom of being delivered from sin. Just as one who is truly in love makes the free choice to "forsake all others" and cling only to his or her beloved, even so heaven, like marriage, involves not a loss of freedom but a fulfillment of it.[1]

We will be liberated from all bondage, including the bondage to Satan. By His first coming, Jesus defeated Satan *officially* (Colossians 2:14; Hebrews 2:14). But at His second coming, Christ will defeat Satan *actually* and *finally* (Matthew 25:41; Revelation 20:10).

The Theological Importance of the Second Coming of Christ

Without this final stage of salvation, there is no victory over sin. In short, without the second coming and the judgments that follow, Satan would have won and God would have lost the final battle between good and evil. But with the final victory over the very presence of sin in the world, the *paradise lost* will become the *paradise regained*. Satan and all his hosts will be expelled from the Garden of God. Good and evil will be separated eternally. Evil will be quarantined in hell; good will reign in heaven and on earth forevermore. The prayer our Lord gave us will be finally fulfilled: "Your kingdom come. Your will be done on earth as it is in heaven" (Matthew 6:10)! Our personal salvation will be complete, for we will be forever delivered from the very presence of sin (1 Corinthians 13:10; Philippians 3:21; 1 John 3:2).

The Creedal Basis for the Second Coming of Christ and Judgment

Later forms of the Apostles' Creed spoke explicitly of hell. The earliest forms spoke of heaven and of Christ coming to "judge the living and the dead" and of "life everlasting." The Nicene Creed spoke of Christ who "came down from heaven" and "ascended into heaven" and is coming again "to judge the living and the dead." It adds that His "kingdom will have no end," and speaks of "the resurrection of the dead" and "the life of the world to come." The Chalcedonian Creed affirms the Nicene Creed. The Athanasian Creed speaks of "everlasting salvation" and of "hell" and "heaven," spelling out more precisely that this means an everlasting conscious existence of both the saved (in heaven) and the lost (in hell): "They that have done good shall go into life everlasting and they that have done evil into everlasting fire."

Other than Origen, who denied eternal conscious punishment and whose view was condemned by later church councils, the standard orthodox teaching of the church fathers affirmed both the eternal conscious bliss of the saved and the eternal conscious woe of the unsaved. This was true of the early, medieval, and Reformation church. Most denials of conscious suffering in hell came later and were generally connected with denials of other orthodox essentials of the Christian Faith.

Unorthodox Denials of the Second Coming of Christ

As a preface, there are some groups that altogether deny the reality of sin—cults such as Christian Science, Religious Science, the Unity School of Christianity, and the Unitarian Universalists. Groups such as these also deny that there is any need for salvation, including a final and complete deliverance from the presence of sin at the second coming. Most of these groups redefine the second coming and deny the existence of a real heaven and a real hell.

Beyond this, there are a number of groups that claim that references to the second coming in the Bible refer not to Jesus but to someone (or something) else.[2] For illustration purposes, let us consider the Baha'i Faith. The "prophet" Baha'u'llah was claimed by Baha'is to be the second coming of Christ, the promised Spirit of truth of John 14:16, and a new revelation from God, following in the footsteps of such spiritual luminaries as Moses, Buddha, Jesus, and Muhammad. Not only is Baha'u'llah viewed as the second coming of Christ, he is viewed as the coming of Maitreya the Buddha (prophesied in Buddhist scripture), the new incarnation of Krishna for the Hindus, and a fulfillment of the "Day of God" spoken of in the Muslim Koran.[3] All the world's major religions have allegedly been pointing to the coming of Baha'u'llah. He alone is "the Promised One of all these Prophets—the Divine Manifestation in Whose era the reign of peace will actually be established."[4]

Baha'is realize that Christians talk about the second coming in terms of the personal return of Jesus Christ. But Christians are viewed as being mistaken. The Bible has purportedly been misunderstood for several millennia by Christian clergy, and the proper understanding comes through Baha'i, which is viewed as the true form of Christianity.

It is often argued that just as the ancient Jews misunderstood the Old Testament Scriptures and therefore opposed Jesus, so Christians today have misunderstood Scripture and are thus in opposition to Baha'u'llah. "Today, Christians make the same mistake the Jews made 2000 years ago. They are so concerned with their own ideas of what Christ is that they cannot see the spirit of Christ in Baha'u'llah."[5] Of course, if the Baha'is are correct, then the second coming occurred a long time ago, and it had virtually nothing to do with final deliverance from the presence of sin. Rather, it had only to do with new revelation from Baha'u'llah.

Christians, according to Baha'is, have also been pitifully misled about the afterlife. Heaven and hell are not literal places; rather, they are states of being. "Heaven is knowing about God and doing what he wants. Hell is not knowing about God or not doing what he wants. A person who is happy and is obeying God is in heaven. A person is in hell when he dislikes others or himself, or is always unhappy."[6] Hence, we can experience our own heaven or hell while yet on earth.

A cursory scan through the pages of the Bible shows just how far off-base these Baha'i teachings are. In terms of the second coming, for example, Scripture indicates with absolute clarity that the very same Jesus who ascended into heaven will one day personally return (Acts 1:9-11). Scripture also prophesies a number of dramatic and highly visible signs that will accompany the second coming—the sun will be darkened, stars will fall from the sky, and heavenly bodies will shake (Matthew 24:29)—none of which were present when Baha'u'llah arrived on the scene in utter obscurity. Further, Scripture indicates that every eye will see Jesus when He comes (Revelation 1:7). There will be no possibility of mistaken identity on that day.

Further, Jesus was most certainly not referring to Baha'u'llah in John 16:12-13 when He made reference to the "Spirit of truth" when speaking to the disciples. Jesus clearly identifies the Spirit of truth as being the Holy Spirit (John 14:16-17,26). And Jesus said, almost 2000 years ago, that His promise of the Holy Spirit would be fulfilled "in a few days" (Acts 1:5), not in the 1800s, when Baha'u'llah was born. Indeed, the fulfillment came in Acts 2 on the Day of Pentecost. Moreover, Jesus said a primary function of the Holy Spirit would be to *make known* Jesus' teachings, not *replace* them with those of another prophet (John 16:14). And, finally, Jesus said the Holy Spirit will "be with you forever" (John 14:16). Baha'u'llah lived a mere 75 years and died in 1892. This hardly constitutes "forever." Clearly, the Baha'i interpretation of Christian Scripture—especially as pertaining to the second coming—is completely unreliable.

There are other groups who deny that the New Testament references to the second coming refer to Jesus Christ. Some New Agers, such as Benjamin Creme, believe that verses about the second coming refer not to Jesus but rather to Maitreya, who will allegedly take the primary leadership role in the coming New Age. Maitreya is said to be the leader of the "Planetary Hierarchy"—a group of alleged exalted Ascended Masters who guide humankind's spiritual evolution.[7] Maitreya does not teach that man has a sin problem from which he needs to be delivered. Maitreya does not teach the need for a Savior who died for any so-called sins. Rather, Maitreya teaches that human beings possess an innate divinity, and they simply need to be enlightened by him and other Ascended Masters.

Other New Agers interpret the second coming as a mass "incarnation" of the cosmic Christ in all of humanity. This is the view of David Spangler and George Trevelyan. Spangler says that "the second coming is occurring now in the hearts and minds of millions of individuals of all faiths as they come to realize this spiritual presence within themselves and each other."[8] Spangler refers to this second coming as a "mass" coming. He writes, "The second coming of the Christ in our age will be fundamentally, most importantly, a mass coming. It will be the manifestation of a consciousness within the multitudes."[9] Jesus "was the prototype or the expression of the reality of the Christ consciousness which is inherent in us all."[10] As such, human beings can become "the Word made flesh"—that is, *all* flesh. In this scenario, there is no such thing as a final stage of salvation (glorification) that takes place at the second coming because there is nothing to be saved from in the first place. Human beings are not sinners,

Spangler says; they are actually Christ or God, and simply need to raise their consciousness in this regard.

We must repeat that from a scriptural perspective, the very same Jesus who ascended into heaven will come again at the second coming. Moreover, the second coming will not involve an invisible cosmic Christ coming upon all of humanity, but will rather be a visible, physical coming of the glorified Jesus (see Daniel 7:13; Zechariah 12:10; Matthew 16:27-28; 24:30; John 1:51). Revelation 1:7 speaks prophetically: "Behold, He is coming with clouds, and every eye will see Him, even they who pierced Him. And all the tribes of the earth will mourn because of Him" (NKJV). The second coming will be a glorious event accompanied by magnificent signs in the heavens (Matthew 24:29-30). It is at this time that believers will finally and ultimately experience full deliverance from the presence of sin (Romans 8:18-23; 1 John 3:2-3).

The Jehovah's Witnesses also have an unbiblical view of the second coming. Early in its history, the Watchtower Society declared—based on convoluted prophetic calculations—that the spiritual (nonphysical) second coming of Christ occurred in October 1874.[11] Jehovah's Witnesses do not like to admit this, because the Society now teaches that Christ "returned" invisibly and spiritually in 1914.[12] Watchtower literature asserted that the year 1914 would mark the overthrow of human governments and the full establishment of the kingdom of God on earth,[13] which clearly did not happen.

There are other things that did not happen at this cultic, spiritual kind of second coming of Christ. For example:

- The third aspect of salvation, in which believers are finally and completely delivered from the presence of sin, did not happen. Ever since this obscure and utterly unnoticed *spiritual* second coming of Christ took place in 1914, Jehovah's Witnesses have remained on earth busily seeking to work out their salvation with fear and trembling.
- There was no resurrection of either believers or unbelievers from the dead. In fact, Jehovah's Witnesses teach that unbelievers will not be permanently resurrected

> from the dead because, according to them, hell is not a place of conscious eternal suffering, but rather, is the common grave of humankind. The wicked are simply annihilated. Not even all the righteous will be physically resurrected from the dead. In fact, there are two classes of Jehovah's Witnesses, and only the "other sheep" class will be physically resurrected so they can live forever on a physical paradise Earth. The other elite class of Jehovah's Witnesses—the "anointed class"—will be spiritually resurrected in the same way as Jesus was so they can rule with Him in heaven. Watchtower teachings about the second coming, then, bear no resemblance to those found in the Bible.

Compare these cultic distortions of the second coming to what is described in Revelation 19:11-16:

> Now I saw heaven opened, and behold, a white horse. And He who sat on him was called Faithful and True, and in righteousness He judges and makes war. His eyes were like a flame of fire, and on His head were many crowns. He had a name written that no one knew except Himself. He was clothed with a robe dipped in blood, and His name is called The Word of God. And the armies in heaven, clothed in fine linen, white and clean, followed Him on white horses. Now out of His mouth goes a sharp sword, that with it He should strike the nations. And He Himself will rule them with a rod of iron. He Himself treads the winepress of the fierceness and wrath of Almighty God. And He has on His robe and on His thigh a name written: KING OF KINGS AND LORD OF LORDS (NKJV).

We are assured, "Behold, He is coming with clouds, and every eye will see Him" (Revelation 1:7 NKJV). What an awesome moment that will be!

THEOLOGICAL QUICK-REVIEW

Chapter 15 Main Idea: The literal physical second coming of Christ brings us to the third and final stage of salvation—complete and final deliverance from the presence of sin.

Importance: Without this final stage of salvation, there is no victory over sin. Without the second coming and the judgments that follow, Satan would have won and God lost the final battle between good and evil. But with the final victory over the presence of sin in the world, the *paradise lost* will become the *paradise regained*. Satan and all his hosts will be expelled from the garden of God. Good and evil will be separated eternally. Evil will be quarantined in hell; good will reign in heaven and on Earth forevermore. Our personal salvation will be complete because we will be forever delivered from sin (1 Corinthians 13:10; 1 John 3:2).

Unorthodox Viewpoints: Some cults altogether deny the reality of sin, and hence they perceive no need for a final deliverance from the presence of sin at the second coming. Other groups hold that Bible verses relating to the second coming refer not to Jesus but to someone (or something) else, and, again, is completely unrelated to final deliverance from the presence of sin. One major cult argues for a spiritual second coming that occurred a long time ago, and it too is unrelated to final deliverance from the presence of sin. There are a variety of other cults that have generally convoluted views of the second coming that deny various aspects of the biblical viewpoint.

Course of Action: On the doctrine of Christ's literal physical second coming, and its relationship to the third and final stage of salvation (permanent deliverance from the presence of sin), there must be conviction without compromise.

16

The Inspiration of Scripture

WE NOTED IN CHAPTER 1 that there are different kinds of essentials. There are *salvation* essentials, a *revelation* essential, and an *interpretation* essential. There are also ethical and metaphysical essentials.* But the focus in this book is on essentials that deal specifically with salvation.

We also noted earlier that not all essentials are directly related to salvation. The doctrine of Scripture is in this category. For example, one does not have to believe in the inspiration of the Bible in order to be saved. But if there were not an inspired Bible, we would have no sure foundation for the essentials that *are* necessary to believe in order to be saved. So, the doctrine of Scripture is fundamental to the other fundamental doctrines. In this sense, it can be called the *fundamental of the fundamentals*. Hence, it is of fundamental importance to know what is meant by the divine inspiration of the Bible.

The Biblical Basis for the Inspiration of Scripture

Space limitations permit only an outline of the topic before us.[1] Both the Old and New Testaments clearly and repeatedly claim to be of divine origin. Some scriptural texts refer only to specific biblical books being inspired, while others refer to the whole canon of Scripture up to the time the passage was written.

Zechariah 7:12: The prophet makes reference to "the law [of Moses] or to the words that the LORD Almighty had sent by his Spirit through the earlier prophets." This is a claim that the writings ("words") of Moses and

* Metaphysical (worldview) essentials include theism and creation. Moral or ethical essentials focus on moral absolutes based on the moral nature and will of God.

all the prophets up to the end of the Old Testament were of divine origin. That is, they came by way of the inspiration of "his [God's] Spirit."

2 Samuel 23:2: David wrote: "The Spirit of the LORD spoke through me; *his word was on my tongue*" (emphasis added). Both the divine origin and the human instrument of Scripture are mentioned here. The writings came from God, but were mediated through a prophet of God.

2 Timothy 3:16-17: Looking back on the whole Old Testament, the apostle Paul wrote, "*All Scripture is God-breathed* and is useful for teaching, rebuking, correcting, and training in righteousness, so that the man of God may be thoroughly equipped for every good work" (emphasis added).

Several things are important to note in that passage: First, Paul is speaking of the whole Old Testament—he refers to "all Scripture," which Timothy learned from his Jewish parentage (verse 15). Second, it is the *written text* that has divine authority—the "Scripture" (Greek: *grapha*). Third, these writings were literally "God-breathed." That is, they were breathed out by God. Finally, they had divine authority for faith and practice. Because the Scriptures were the Word of God, they were authoritative for the people of God.

2 Peter 1:20-21: Peter asserted that "no prophecy of Scripture came about by the prophet's own interpretation. For prophecy never had its origin in the will of man, but men spoke from God as they were carried along by the Holy Spirit." Inspired Scripture did not originate with human beings, but with God. It came from God, to and through prophets of God, to the people of God. In short, Spirit-moved men uttered God-breathed writings.

Jesus' View of the Divine Authority of Scripture

Perhaps the best way to summarize what is meant by the inspiration of the Word of God is to consider the very words of the Son of God. Christ's view of Scripture can be stated briefly as follows:

Scripture Is Divinely Authoritative

Jesus declared to Satan: "It is written, 'Man does not live on bread alone, but on *every word that comes from the mouth of God*'...It is also written: 'Do not put the LORD your God to the test.... Away from me, Satan! For it is written: 'Worship the LORD your God, and serve him only'" (Matthew 4:4,7,10, emphasis added).

Scripture Is Imperishable

Jesus declared: "Do not think that I have come to abolish the Law or the Prophets; I have not come to abolish them but to fulfill them. I tell you the truth, until heaven and earth disappear, not the smallest letter, not the least stroke of a pen, will by any means disappear from the Law until everything is accomplished" (Matthew 5:17-18). In short, the Bible is imperishable.

Scripture Is Infallible

Jesus clearly affirmed that the Bible is infallible when He asserted that "Scripture cannot be broken" (John 10:35).

Scripture Is Inerrant (Without Error)

Jesus said to some Jewish leaders: "You are in error because you do not know the Scriptures or the power of God" (Matthew 22:29). Jesus also affirmed to the Father: "Your Word is truth" (John 17:17).

The reasons the Bible cannot err are clear: 1) The Bible is the Word of God; 2) God cannot err; 3) therefore, the Bible cannot err. The Bible is clear about both premises, and the conclusion logically follows from them:

First, the Bible is the Word of God.

- *Matthew 4:4:* "It is written...live...on every word that comes from the mouth of God."
- *2 Peter 1:20-21:* "No prophecy of Scripture came about by the prophet's own interpretation. For prophecy never had its origin in the will of man, but men spoke from God as they were carried along by the Holy Spirit."

Second, God cannot err.

- *Hebrews 6:18:* "It is impossible for God to lie."

- *Romans 3:4:* "Let God be true, and every man a liar."
- *John 17:17:* Jesus asserted: "Your word is truth."

From this it follows that the Bible cannot err.

It is broken logic to claim that because the Bible is also the words of human beings (who err), the Bible must have errors in it. First, humans do not *always* err. Second, they *never* erred when guided by the Holy Spirit, who *cannot* err (John 16:13).

Scripture Is Historically Reliable

Jesus confirmed the historicity of specific Old Testament events. For example: "As Jonah was three days and three nights in the belly of a huge fish, so the Son of Man will be three days and three nights in the heart of the earth" (Matthew 12:40). "As it was in the days of Noah, so it will be at the coming of the Son of Man. For in the days before the flood, people were eating and drinking, marrying and giving in marriage, up to the day Noah entered the ark; and they knew nothing about what would happen until the flood came and took them all away. That is how it will be at the coming of the Son of Man" (Matthew 24:37-39).

Scripture Is Scientifically Accurate

In Matthew 19:4-5 Jesus said: "Haven't you read…that at the beginning the Creator 'made them male and female,' and said, 'For this reason a man will leave his father and mother and be united to his wife, and the two will become one flesh'?" Jesus thus confirmed the scientific accuracy of the creation account of Adam and Eve, over against the theory of evolution. He did the same for the story of Noah and the Flood (Matthew 24:37-39) and numerous other Old Testament events associated with individuals such as Jonah (Matthew 12:40), Moses (John 3:14), and David (Matthew 22:43-44).

Scripture Has Ultimate Supremacy

In Matthew 15:3,6, Jesus said to some Jewish leaders: "Why do you break the command of God for the sake of your tradition?…Thus you nullify the word of God for the sake of your tradition." Such verses affirm that Scripture is supreme over human tradition. Having said that, we wish to emphasize that creeds and confessions of the fathers (that is, traditions) are fine as long as they are based on Scripture. As the great Catholic theologian Thomas Aquinas put it, "We believe the prophets and apostles because the Lord has been their witness by performing miracles....And we believe the successors of the apostles and prophets *only in so far as* they tell us those things which the apostles and prophets have left in their writings."[2]

We also wish to emphasize that the characteristics addressed above—which, in context, are written in regard to Jesus' view of the Old Testament Scriptures—apply to the prophetic nature of the New Testament as well. For example, Peter calls Paul's writings "Scriptures" along with the inspired writings of the Old Testament (2 Peter 3:15-16). And Paul refers to the Gospels as "Scripture" alongside the Old Testament (1 Timothy 5:18). This makes sense, because the New Testament writers were prophets as well (Ephesians 3:5).

The Theological Importance of the Inspiration of Scripture

While one does not have to believe in the inspiration of the Bible in order to be saved, nonetheless, the Bible is the foundation for all the doctrines that *are* necessary for salvation. In this sense, the divine inspiration of the Bible is a revelational essential of the Faith. For if there were no inspired Bible, then we would have no sure foundation for the essentials that are necessary to believe in order to be saved. So, to repeat what we stated earlier, the doctrine of Scripture is fundamental to the other fundamental doctrines. Thus, it is not only appropriate but necessary to list the inspiration and inerrancy of Scripture as one of the essential doctrines of the Christian Faith.

The Creedal and Patristic Basis for the Inspiration of Scripture

The Apostles' Creed makes no explicit reference to Holy Scripture, but it is everywhere implied and assumed. Some of its key phrases are directly dependent on the Bible, including "Creator of heaven and earth," "born of the Virgin Mary," "Pontius Pilate," "the third day He arose," "ascended into heaven," "judge the living and the dead," "forgiveness of sins," "the right hand of God," and "life everlasting." Indeed, all its truths are directly dependent on Scripture as a divine revelation. The Nicene Creed, like the Apostles' Creed, is also directly dependent on Scripture for all its teaching and much of its phraseology. In addition, it makes explicit reference to Scripture by the phrases "in accordance with the Scriptures" and what was "spoken through the prophets." Likewise, the Chalcedonian Creed bases its teachings on the Bible, reaffirms the Nicene Creed, which refers explicitly to Scripture, and then adds, "Thus have the prophets of old testified; thus the Lord Jesus Christ himself taught"—a phrase that refers to the authority of both the Old and New Testaments.

The reason the doctrine of Scripture never became an explicit object of confession in the early creeds is because it was universally accepted that it did not need to be stated. That it was the obvious authoritative basis of the church fathers' teachings is evident from their writings which cite it over 36,000 times in only the first few centuries![3] St. Augustine summarized the early fathers' view of Scripture by calling it "the words of God," "infallible Scripture," "divine revelation," and "the oracles of God."[4] From the above it is evident that the early fathers of the church believed the Scriptures were the divinely authoritative and written Word of God.

Unorthodox Denials of the Inspiration of Scripture

There are many denials of the inspiration and inerrancy of the Bible among the cults. Here we will provide a representative sampling of cultic distortions. We begin by recognizing that one favorite tactic among many cults is to claim that the Bible is not uniquely inspired, but is rather just one of many holy books.

The Unitarian Universalists, for example, have little respect for the Bible. While some Unitarian Universalists would say there are some inspiring truths in it, most say it is a fallible human book. It is viewed as one among many other religious books—right alongside the Hindu Vedas and the Muslim Koran.[5] "We regard the Bible as one of many important religious texts but do not consider it unique or exclusive in any way."[6]

Drawing on liberal higher criticism, Unitarian Universalists believe there are textual errors in the "very imperfect" Bible such that we cannot trust that it accurately records the actual words of Jesus. Indeed, the Jesus of the four Gospels is said to be more a reflection of the theological biases of the Gospel writers—who were fallible and ignorant men—than of historical reality.[7]

This prevalent view is worthy of response. The fallacy here is to imagine that to give an account of something one believes in passionately necessarily forces one to distort history. This is simply not true. As stated earlier, in modern times some of the most reliable reports of the Nazi Holocaust were written by Jews who were passionately committed to making sure such genocide never happens again.

The New Testament is not made up of fairy tales, but is rather based on eyewitness testimonies. In 2 Peter 1:16 we read, "We did not follow cleverly invented stories when we told you about the power and coming of our Lord Jesus Christ, but we were eyewitnesses of his majesty." First John 1:1 affirms, "That which was from the beginning, which we have heard, which we have seen with our eyes, which we have looked at and our hands have touched—this we proclaim concerning the Word of life."

Further, it is highly relevant that many of the New Testament writers gave up their lives in defense of the truths they witnessed. "Theological biases" hardly explain why these individuals were so committed to their beliefs that they were willing to make the ultimate sacrifice by defending them.

Further, the claim that the biblical writers were biased and influenced by theological motives seems incompatible with the embarrassing details they provide about themselves in the Bible. For example, the Old Testament was written by Jews, yet it includes reports of their total unfaithfulness during the wilderness sojourn as well as their participation in idolatry. And the New Testament was written by Christians, yet it includes reports of Peter denying Christ three times, Peter being addressed as "Satan" by Jesus, the disciples scattering like a bunch of faithless cowards when Christ was arrested, and Thomas's doubt about the resurrection of Jesus. Surely if the biblical documents were influenced by biases, these biases would have caused the biblical writers to remove such unflattering information from the Old and New Testaments.

Finally, one cannot help but be impressed that the Bible's historical accuracy and reliability have been verified over and over again by archaeological finds produced by both believing *and* nonbelieving scholars and scientists. This includes verification for numerous customs, places, names, and events mentioned in the Bible. Scholar Donald J. Wiseman notes, "The geography of Bible lands and visible remains of antiquity were gradually recorded until today more than 25,000 sites within this region and dating to Old Testament times, in their broadest sense, have been located."[8] Nelson Glueck, a specialist in ancient literature, did an exhaustive study and concluded, "It can be stated categorically that no archaeological discovery has ever controverted a biblical reference."[9] Scholar William Albright, following a comprehensive study, wrote, "Discovery after discovery has established the accuracy of innumerable details, and has brought increased recognition of the value of the Bible as a source of history."[10] This hardly sounds like the Bible is an error-packed book, as taught by the Unitarian Universalists.

The Masons are another cultic group with a low view of the Bible. Masons say they believe the Bible is a significant book, but they do not believe it is the exclusive Word of God. It is not viewed as God's only revelation to humankind, but as one of many holy books that contain religious and moral truth. Masons say the Bible is not uniquely inspired and inerrant, and they often refer to it as a *symbol* of God's will.[11] "The prevailing Masonic opinion is that the Bible is only a symbol of divine will, law, or revelation. So far, no responsible authority has held that a Freemason must believe the Bible or any part of it."[12] Other "symbols" of God's will include the Muslim Koran, the Hindu Vedas, and the Jewish Pentateuch.

All such holy books are acceptable within the confines of any Masonic Lodge. These books provide not just religious truth but moral truth and hence constitute ethical guides by which to govern one's life. The Masonic view of the Bible is in keeping with Masonic openness to all religions.

Still another group with a low view of the Bible is Religious Science, a Mind Science cult founded by Ernest Holmes. Proponents of this group say the Bible is not God's only revelation. Holmes believed that many other holy books are just as legitimate as the Christian Bible, including the

Koran, the Talmud, the Bhagavad-Gita, the Vedas, and the Upanishads. "It is unreasonable to suppose that any one person, or race, encompasses all truth, and alone can reveal the way of life to others. Taking the best from all sources, Religious Science has access to the highest enlightenment of the ages. Religious Science reads every man's Bible and gleans the truths therein contained."[13]

It is claimed that even though the holy books of various religions may seem to contain different ideas, in reality, they are all speaking of the same ultimate truth. Holmes exclaimed, "It has been well said that 'religions are many'; but Religion is one....There is One Reality at the heart of all religions, whether their name be Hindu, Mohammedan, Christian or Jewish."[14]

Of course, such claims reveal a nearly unfathomable level of ignorance. It is fair to say that if one of these books is correct (the Bible, the Muslim Koran, or the Hindu Vedas), then the others must necessarily be wrong because they set forth diametrically opposing ideas on basic religious concepts—the doctrine of God being a good example. The Christian Bible teaches a triune concept of God; the Muslim Koran denies the Trinity, says God cannot have a Son, and says Allah is the one true God; the Hindu Vedas recognize the existence of many gods. Also, the Koran and Vedas speak of a works-oriented salvation, whereas the Bible says salvation is a free gift for those who trust in Christ (Ephesians 2:8-9). The many radical and irreconcilable points of difference between these books forces us to conclude that if one of them is right, the others must be wrong.

Other cults have taken a different approach in regard to the Bible. Their argument is that the Bible in its *original* form was God's Word, and in *that* form it agreed with the cult's doctrines. Since then, however, the Bible has been corrupted in the process of transmission such that the Bible, as it now exists, has many disagreements with the cult's doctrines. Thus, the Bible can no longer be trusted.

That is the case with the Mormons. Their eighth "Article of Faith" affirms, "We believe the Bible to be the Word of God, as far as it is translated correctly."[15] Mormons teach that because of poor manuscript transmission, large portions of the Bible have been lost through the centuries, and the portions that have survived have become corrupted because of faulty transmission.

Mormon apostle Orson Pratt once went so far as to ask, "Who, in his right mind, could, for one moment, suppose the Bible in its present form to be a perfect guide? *Who knows that even one verse of the Bible has escaped pollution?*"[16] This seems an odd statement to make given the fact that the Book of Mormon plagiarizes extensively (over 27,000 words, sometimes whole paragraphs) from the King James Version of the Bible—so much so that one cannot disparage the Bible *en toto,* as Pratt essentially did, without substantially implicating the Book of Mormon in the process. Pratt apparently was oblivious to the hole he dug for himself.

One wonders how knowledgeable Mormons could claim today's Bible is the product of poor transmission in view of the substantial manuscript support that proves the reliability of Bible transmission through the ages. Unlike the Book of Mormon, which has absolutely no manuscript support proving its reliability, the Bible has overwhelming manuscript evidence that affirms its reliability. There are nearly 5700 known partial and complete manuscript copies of the New Testament. These manuscript copies are very ancient and they are available for inspection today. Following are some highlights:

- The Chester Beatty papyrus (P45) dates to the third century A.D. and contains the four Gospels and the book of Acts (chapters 4–17) (P = papyrus).
- The Chester Beatty papyrus (P46) dates to about A.D. 200 and contains ten Pauline epistles (all but the pastorals) and the book of Hebrews.
- The Chester Beatty papyrus (P47) dates to the third century A.D. and contains Revelation 9:10–17:2.
- The Bodmer Papyrus (P66) dates to about A.D. 200 and contains the Gospel of John.
- The Bodmer Papyrus (P75) dates to the early third century and contains Luke and John.

- The Sinaiticus uncial manuscript dates to the fourth century and contains the entire New Testament.
- The Vaticanus uncial manuscript dates to the fourth century and contains most of the New Testament except Hebrews 9:14ff., the pastoral epistles, Philemon, and Revelation.
- The Washingtonianus uncial manuscript dates to the early fifth century and contains the Gospels.
- The Alexandrinus uncial manuscript dates to the fifth century and contains most of the New Testament.
- The Ephraemi Rescriptus uncial manuscript dates to the fifth century and contains portions of every book except 2 Thessalonians and 2 John.
- The Bezae/Cantabrigiensis uncial manuscript dates to the fifth century and contains the Gospels and Acts.
- The Claromontanus uncial manuscript dates to the sixth century and contains the Pauline epistles and Hebrews.

If one adds into the mix over 10,000 Latin Vulgate manuscripts and at least 9300 other early versions—including Ethiopic, Slavic, Armenian, and other versions—the total approximates 25,000 manuscripts that cite portions of the New Testament. This far exceeds the number of manuscripts available of other ancient documents, which, in most cases, numbers less than ten copies. And in the case of the Book of Mormon, *zero* copies.

By the way, Joseph Smith, the founder of Mormonism, is credited with the "translation" of the Inspired Version of the Bible. Actually, Smith did not come up with a new translation. Rather, he took the King James Version (KJV) and added to and subtracted from it—not by examining Bible manuscripts, but allegedly by "divine inspiration." Smith "corrected, revised, altered, added to, and deleted from" the KJV.[17] Virtually thousands of changes were introduced. While it took a large group of the world's greatest Bible scholars (who knew Hebrew and Greek) years to finish their work on the KJV, it took Smith a mere three years to complete his work—despite the fact that he had virtually no knowledge of the biblical languages. Smith even added a passage in Genesis 50 that predicted his own coming: "That seer will I bless...and his name shall be called Joseph."[18]

The Jehovah's Witnesses also claim the original Bible was accurate and today's copies are not. For example, Watchtower publications assert that God's true name is Jehovah, and that superstitious Jewish scribes long ago removed this sacred name from the Bible. But there is no need to worry, the Watchtower Society says, for their New World Translation has "faithfully" restored the divine name in the Old Testament where the Hebrew consonants "YHWH" appear.[19]

Moreover, the name *Jehovah* has been inserted in the New Testament by the Watchtower translation committee in verses where the text is believed to refer to the Father.[20] They have taken the liberty to do this despite the fact doing so goes blatantly against what actually appears in the thousands of Greek manuscripts of the New Testament that we possess. (The New Testament always uses the words "Lord" [Greek: *kurios*] and "God" [Greek: *theos*], never "Jehovah"—even in quotations from the Old Testament.[21])

The New World Translation also alters many verses that, in other versions, clearly point to the deity of Jesus Christ. In fact, the New World Translation was created specifically to support the Watchtower Society's unorthodox doctrines. It is fair to say that this translation is radically biased in favor of the theology of the cult.

Understandably, the New World Translation has received a universal "thumbs down" from reputable Bible scholars. Dr. Julius Mantey, author of *A Manual Grammar of the Greek New Testament,* called the New World Translation "a shocking mistranslation."[22] Dr. Bruce M. Metzger, former professor of New Testament at Princeton University, called it "a frightful mistranslation," "erroneous," "pernicious," and "reprehensible."[23] Dr. William Barclay concluded that "the deliberate distortion of truth by this sect is seen in their New Testament translation....It is abundantly clear that a sect which can translate the New Testament like that is intellectually dishonest."[24]

Yet another recent example of a low view of the Bible is found in the recent blockbuster book *The Da Vinci Code* by Dan Brown. In the book it is claimed that "the Bible is a product of man...not of God."[25] We are told that "the New Testament is false testimony" and that "the New Testament is based on fabrications."[26] It is further asserted that "the Bible...has evolved through countless translations, additions, and revisions. History has never had a definitive version of the book."[27]

It is claimed in *The Da Vinci Code* that "history is always written by the winners. When two cultures clash, the loser is obliterated, and the winner writes the history books—books which glorify their own cause and disparage the conquered foe."[28] In this line of thought, the true version of Christianity was Gnostic Christianity, but orthodox Christianity became more powerful and won out over the Gnostics. Because the orthodox Christians won over the Gnostics, *they* wrote history—and the Bible—in a way favorable to their version of Christianity.

Most of Brown's claims have already been adequately answered by the material in this chapter. We wish to close, however, by briefly addressing Brown's claim regarding orthodox Christians "winning" over the Gnostic Christians.

Such a claim is truly preposterous and shows how out of touch Brown is with the hard facts of history. To begin, anyone who knows anything about Christian history knows that the early Christians were anything but "winners." The early Christians were fiercely persecuted by both Roman and Jewish authorities. Christianity itself was outlawed by the Romans in the second century, and in the third and early fourth centuries, there was widespread persecution and murder of Christians. Some Christians were thrown into an arena to be eaten by lions, to the entertainment of Roman citizens who were watching. Other Christians were tied to poles, drenched with fuel, and lit as street lamps at night.

According to tradition, at the end of his life, Peter was crucified upside-down in Rome during Emperor Nero's persecution in A.D. 64. Previous to this, Peter had written two epistles to help other Christians who were facing persecution. Peter probably wrote from Rome at the outbreak of Nero's persecution. Having already endured a beating at Herod's hands, Peter wrote his brethren in Asia—probably to encourage and strengthen those who faced the Neronian persecution. It may well be that in doing so, Peter recalled his Lord's injunctions, "Strengthen your brothers" (Luke 22:32), and "Feed my sheep" (John 21:16-17). Paul, too, suffered persecution and was put to death during the Neronian persecution in A.D. 64. The fact that New Testament writers gave their lives in defense of their biblical writings says something. No one chooses to die for something that was made up out of thin air!

One of the purposes of the book of Revelation was to comfort Christians who were suffering persecution. The author is the apostle John, who himself had been imprisoned on the isle of Patmos (in the Aegean Sea) for the crime of sharing Jesus Christ with everyone he came into contact with (Revelation 1:9). The recipients of the book of Revelation were undergoing such severe persecution that some of them were being killed (see Revelation 2:13). Things were about to get even worse, and John wrote this book to give his readers a strong hope that would help them patiently endure in the midst of suffering.

Despite all this heavy persecution, the church survived and spread around the world. Christianity grew not because the Christians were "winners" and wrote a "winner's history," but rather, Christianity grew *despite* the fact Christians were big losers under Roman persecution. The Gnostic Gospels are dated centuries later than the historically verified New Testament Gospels, were obvious forgeries, contain false doctrine and historical errors, and give every evidence of being man-made. They are completely unlike the New Testament Gospels, which were inspired by God, written close in time to the events on which they report, and have been substantiated by historical and archaeological evidence as well as many thousands of manuscript copies. Such false gospels have an uphill battle against the incumbent!

A final modern-day challenge worthy of mention relates to the low view many have of the Bible in the emerging church movement. Many in this movement deny that there is any such thing as absolute truth and deny that the Bible is infallible. They choose not to use an objective approach to interpreting Scripture, but rather, believe there is a multiplicity of valid perspectives as opposed to a single valid meaning of the text. Many in the movement say we can no longer look to the Bible alone as a guide for spiritual living. It is claimed we cannot reach the new generation using the old ways.

We are told that postmoderns want a God they can feel, taste, touch, hear, and smell—in short, they want a full sensory immersion into the divine. Many are thus open to various forms of mysticism, including deep breathing, yoga, chanting (like Benedictine monks), the use of mantras (involving the repetition of holy words in order to induce a deep meditative state), and contemplative prayer (which typically involves an altered state of consciousness and a sense of oneness with all things).

Evangelical Christians respond that the so-called *emerging* church is more accurately called the *diverging* church because it diverts from orthodoxy on its view of the Bible and its openness to Eastern mysticism. It seems clear that what this movement has "emerged" into is not Christian in any traditional, historic, or orthodox sense of the word. Indeed, it has emerged from orthodoxy to unorthodox, from objectivism to subjectivism and mysticism, and from absolutism to relativism.

There are, of course, notable dangers in engaging in mystical practices. First, mysticism is insufficient as a ground upon which to build our knowledge of God. The Bible stresses the importance of objective, historical revelation (see, for example, John 1:18 and 14:7). Second, those who place faith in mysticism seem blind to the possibility of spiritual deception. What if that which mystics assume to be genuine "God-consciousness" is in fact less than God, or at worst Satan, the great impersonator of God and the father of lies (John 8:44; 2 Corinthians 11:14)? Third, altered states of consciousness can be dangerous and can lead to harmful consequences. Studies have shown that such altered states can hinder logical thought processes and cause people to fear losing grip on reality, not to mention causing them to develop increased anxiety, confusion, and depression. And fourth, contemplative prayer's emphasis on attaining a sense of oneness with all things (including a sense of oneness with God) lies in direct contradiction to the biblical view of the eternal distinction between God the Creator and His creatures (Isaiah 44:6-8; Hebrews

2:6-8). This mystical component in the emerging church movement, along with its low view of the Bible, should be a concern to all Bible-believing Christians.

THEOLOGICAL QUICK-REVIEW

Chapter 16 Main Idea: The Bible is inspired and inerrant.

Importance: One does not have to believe in the inspiration of the Bible in order to be saved. But if the Bible were not inspired, we would have no sure foundation for the essentials that *are* necessary to believe in order to be saved. So, the doctrine of Scripture is fundamental to the other fundamental doctrines. In this sense, it can be called the fundamental of the fundamentals. Hence, it is of fundamental importance to know what is meant by the divine inspiration of the Bible. Historically, orthodox Christianity has pronounced the Bible the infallible and inerrant Word of God.

Unorthodox Viewpoints: The cults hold to many strange views about the Bible. Some flat-out deny that the Bible is inspired by God, arguing instead that it is a man-made book. Others argue that the Bible is not uniquely inspired, but is simply one of many holy books. Still others argue that we can't trust the Bible of today because, even though it was originally inspired by God, human beings through the centuries have introduced so many changes into the text that it can no longer be trusted. Some neo-pagans today argue that history has always been written "by the victor." In this line of thought, orthodox Christianity allegedly won out over the Gnostic form of Christianity, and hence we have an orthodox Bible. Had the Gnostics won, we would have an entirely different Bible.

Course of Action: On the doctrine of the divine inspiration and inerrancy of Scripture, there must be conviction without compromise.

17

The Literal Interpretation of Scripture

ALL THE ESSENTIAL DOCTRINES expressed in the Bible and in the early creeds are dependent on another doctrine—the historical-grammatical method of interpretation. Without it there would be no such list of essential doctrines. For it is only by understanding the Scriptures through this historic method of interpretation that there *are* any essential doctrines. If the opposing allegorical method of interpretation were used on Scripture, it would yield results so different that there would be no such fundamentals of the Faith. Hence, the literal or historical-grammatical interpretation of the Bible must be listed as one of the great essentials of the Christian Faith.

Of course, one need not believe in the literal method of interpretation of the Bible to be saved. But without this method there would be no means of understanding the essential teachings about salvation that must be believed to be saved. So, while the historical-grammatical method of interpretation is not a *salvation* essential (see chapters 2–15) or even a *revelation* essential (see chapter 16), nonetheless, it is an *interpretation* essential.

The Basis for Literal Interpretation

What the Literal Method Is

By the "literal" method is meant the historical-grammatical method of interpreting Scripture. This method can be understood by what it is and by what it is not. We will first discuss what the method is.[1]

Literal. The word *literal* as used in hermeneutics (the science of interpretation), comes from the Latin *sensus literalis,* meaning the literal sense of the text, as opposed to a nonliteral or allegorical sense of it. It refers to the understanding of a text that any person of normal intelligence would understand without the help of any special keys or codes.

Normal. Another way to describe the literal meaning of Scripture is that it embraces the normal, everyday, common understanding of the terms in the Bible. Words are given the meaning they normally have in common communication. This speaks of the basic, normal, or plain way of interpreting a Bible passage.

Historical. The word *historical* means that the sentences of Scripture should be understood in their historical setting. They should not be taken out of the space-time, cultural context in which they were uttered. It is the means by which the interpreter mentally transfers himself into the context in which the author uttered the words. This guards against the interpretive error of making the *reader's* historical or cultural context the norm for understanding the text.

Grammatical. This term indicates that the proper meaning of a sentence is rooted in its grammar. The sense of the passage emerges from the grammatical structure wherein all parts of speech—including nouns, verbs, adjectives, adverbs, articles, prepositions, and the like—are placed in a proper form from which only a certain meaning can be derived. This method involves giving each word the same exact basic meaning it would have in the normal, ordinary, customary usage of its day.

Contextual. Every sentence in Scripture should be understood in the context of its paragraph, and every paragraph in the context of its whole book. And each book of the Bible should be understood in the context of the whole Bible. So, meaning is discovered by context—from the *immediate* to the *broader* context.

Authorial. Finally, the historical-grammatical meaning is the author's expressed meaning. It is the author who gives the meaning to the text, not the reader. It is the reader's obligation to *discover* the meaning that the author *determined.* To put it another way, only a *meaner* can give *meaning* to a text. Hence, what is *meant* in the text is what the *meaner meant* by it, not what the reader desires for it to mean.

What the Literal Method Is Not

The literal method of interpretation does not mean that everything in the Bible is *true literally;* rather, it means that everything is *literally true* (we'll clarify this distinction below). Also, it does not mean that there are no figures of speech, such as metaphors and anthropomorphisms. Figures of speech can be used to communicate a literal truth, as the following discussion will demonstrate.

The Literal Method Does Not Eliminate Figures of Speech. When the Bible speaks of the eye, arms, or wings of God (Psalm 34:15; 91:4; Isaiah 51:9), such expressions should not be taken as true literally. God does not have these physical features because "God is Spirit" (John 4:24). Likewise, He cannot literally be a rock (Psalm 42:9), which is material. But we would not know what is *not* literally true of God unless we first know what *is* literally true. For example, if it were not literally true that God is Spirit and infinite, then we would not be able to say that certain things attributed to God elsewhere in the Bible are not literally true, such as materiality and finitude. For example, when Jesus said, "I am the true vine" (John 15:1), the literal method of interpretation does not take this to mean He is a physical vine. What He said is literally true (namely, that believers derive their spiritual life from Him, the vine), but it is not true literally that Jesus is a physical vine.

Of course, sometimes it is difficult to determine when a passage should not be taken literally. Certain guidelines are helpful in making this determination. Briefly put, a text should be taken figuratively 1) when it is *obviously* figurative, as when Jesus said He was a gate (John 10:9); 2) when the text itself authorizes the figurative sense, as when Paul said he was using an "allegory" (Galatians 4:24 NKJV); or 3) when a literal interpretation would contradict other truths inside or outside the Bible, as when the Bible speaks of the "four corners of the earth" (Revelation 7:1). In short, as the dictum puts it, "When the literal sense makes good sense, seek no other sense, lest it result in nonsense." Likewise, "When the literal sense does not make good sense [such as the claim that God is Spirit and yet has eyes, ears, and arms], then we should seek some other sense lest it result in nonsense."

The Literal Method Does Not Eliminate the Use of Types. A type may be defined as "an Old Testament institution, event, person, object, or ceremony which has reality and purpose in biblical history, but which also by divine design foreshadows something yet to be revealed."[2] The New Testament clearly affirms that Christ is the fulfillment of many Old Testament types that prefigured Him. These types passed away when they were fulfilled by Christ—such as the Passover lamb (1 Corinthians 5:7) and the Levitical sacrificial system (Hebrews 10:12-14). These Old Testament types found their literal fulfillment in Christ the antitype, being only the shadow of the substance that was ultimately found in Him (Colossians 2:17). This fulfillment is in no way a spiritualization or allegorization of any literal thing or event.

The Literal Method Does Not Eliminate the Use of Symbols. The Bible is filled with symbols. But each symbol is emblematic of something literal. For example, the book of Revelation contains many symbols that represent literal things. For instance, John said the "seven stars" in Christ's right hand were "the angels [messengers] of the seven churches" (Revelation 1:20), "the seven golden lampstands" were "the seven churches" (1:20), "the bowls full of incense" were "the prayers of the saints" (5:8), and "the waters" were "peoples, multitudes, nations and languages" (17:15). Clearly, then, each symbol represents something literal. There are often textual clues that point us to the literal truth found in a symbol—either in the immediate context, or in the broader context of the whole of Scripture.

The Literal Method Does Not Eliminate the Use of Parables and Allegories. Jesus often used parables that were not to be taken literally. Yet each parable always conveys a literal point. That Jesus wanted His parables to be clear to those who were receptive to them is evident by the fact He carefully interpreted two of them for the disciples—the parables of the sower (Matthew 13:3-9) and the tares (13:24-30). He did this not only so there would be no uncertainty as to their meaning, but to guide believers as to the proper method to use when interpreting the other parables. The fact that Christ did not interpret His subsequent parables indicates that He fully expected believers to understand the literal truths intended by His parables by following the methodology He illustrated for them.

Allegorical language also sometimes appears in Scripture. Paul, for example, used an allegory and labeled it as such (Galatians 4:24). Comparing different Bible translations on this verse shows Paul's meaning: "This may be interpreted allegorically" (ESV); or: "These things may be taken figuratively" (NIV); or: These "things are symbolic" (NKJV). But even allegorical statements such as this communicate a literal truth that can be understood.

Let us also keep in mind that the historical-grammatical method of Bible interpretation recognizes that there are different genres of literature in the Bible, each of which have certain peculiar characteristics that must be recognized in order to interpret the text properly. Biblical genres include the historical (for example, Acts), the dramatic epic (Job), poetry (Psalms), wise sayings (Proverbs), and apocalyptic writings (Revelation). An incorrect genre judgment will lead one far astray in interpreting Scripture. A parable should not be treated as history, nor should poetry or apocalyptic literature (both of which contain many symbols) be treated as straightforward narrative.

Having made this point about literary genres, we offer a warning to the wise. When studying the text of Scripture, genre decisions should *follow* an examination of the total context via the historical-grammatical method of interpretation. In other words, genre decisions should not be made prior to examining the total context via the historical-grammatical method of interpretation. The need for this warning is evident in that one might decide up front that the book of Genesis is an allegorical genre, and therefore we need not take the creation account seriously but are free to believe in the theory of evolution. An examination of the total context of the Genesis creation account via the historical-grammatical method of interpretation would prevent such a hermeneutical error. Those who seek to import ideas alien to Scripture via their up-front (and fallacious) genre decisions end up violating the intended meaning of the biblical authors. Such a practice is no more than a covert way to read one's theological biases into Scripture under the guise of adding a "literary" element to the historical-grammatical hermeneutic. Indeed, this is a subtle means of reading antisupernatural or other biases *into* Scripture rather than deriving the correct meaning *out of* Scripture.

The Literal Method Does Not Eliminate Spiritual Applications. Denying allegorism as a basic hermeneutical method does not mean there are no legitimate spiritual applications of biblical texts. Once the literal meaning is determined, it can then be applied spiritually in a number of legitimate ways. The New Testament provides examples of this in its use of the Old Testament. For instance, Hosea spoke of God literally bringing Israel, the messianic nation (whom God called "my son"), out of Egypt (Hosea 11:1). Matthew spiritually applied this passage to Jesus, the son of the messianic nation (Matthew 2:15). The generic meaning of God's "son" is the same, but in the New Testament it is applied to the product predicted for the messianic nation—namely, to the Messiah Himself. This is clearly a legitimate spiritual application of an Old Testament text.

There are, of course, limits to legitimate spiritual applications. For one, such an application cannot be allowed to destroy the basic meaning of the text. While there may be *many applications* of a text, there is only *one proper interpretation* of the text. For another, the application must not contradict any other revealed truth. Finally, while there is only *one interpretation* of a text—the literal one intended by the author—nonetheless, there are *many implications* in a text. The New Testament authors often draw such implications from Old Testament texts (again, compare Hosea 11:1 with Matthew 2:15).

The Reasons for a Literal Approach to Interpretation

There are many reasons for adopting a literal interpretation of Scripture: 1) It is the normal approach in all languages; 2) the greater part of the Bible makes sense when taken literally; 3) it will take the secondary meaning when demanded; 4) all secondary meanings actually depend on the literal meaning; 5) it is the only "sane and safe check on the imagination of man"; and 6) it is the only approach in line with the nature of inspiration.[3]

Biblical Confirmation of a Literal Interpretation

There are numerous confirmations of the literal method of interpretation found in the Bible. Following are some representative examples:

1. *Later biblical texts take earlier ones as literal.* For example, the creation events in Genesis 1–2 are taken literally by later books (for example,

Exodus 20:10-11). This is likewise the case regarding the creation of Adam and Eve (Matthew 19:4-6; 1 Timothy 2:13), the fall of Adam and his resulting death (Romans 5:12,14), the Flood (Matthew 24:38), and the accounts of Jonah (Matthew 12:40-41), Moses (1 Corinthians 10:2-4,11), and many other historical figures.

2. *Prophecies about the Messiah were literally fulfilled.* Over 100 Old Testament predictions about the Messiah were fulfilled literally in Jesus' first coming, including the facts He would be 1) the seed of a woman (Genesis 3:15); 2) from the line of Seth (Genesis 4:25; see also Luke 3:38 and compare with Genesis 3:15); 3) a descendant of Shem (Genesis 9:26); 4) the offspring of Abraham (Genesis 12:3); 5) from the tribe of Judah (Genesis 49:10); 6) the son of David (Jeremiah 23:5-6); 7) conceived of a virgin (Isaiah 7:14); 8) be born in Bethlehem (Micah 5:2); 9) be the heralded Messiah (Isaiah 40:3); 10) the coming king (Zechariah 9:9); 11) the One suffering for our sins (Isaiah 53); 12) the One pierced in His side (Zechariah 12:10); 13) the One dying about A.D. 33 (Daniel 9:24-25); and 14) the One rising from the dead (Psalm 2,16).

3. *By specifically indicating within the text the presence of parables* (see Matthew 13:3) or an "allegory" (Galatians 4:24), the Bible thereby indicates that the ordinary meaning is a *literal* one.

4. *By giving the interpretation of a parable,* Jesus revealed that there is a literal meaning behind them (Matthew 13:18-23).

5. *By rebuking those who did not interpret the resurrection literally,* Jesus indicated the literal interpretation of the Old Testament was the correct one (Matthew 22:29-32; see also Psalm 2, 16).

6. *By interpreting prophecy literally* (Luke 4:16-21), Jesus indicated His acceptance of the literal interpretation of the Old Testament.

Unorthodox Denials of the Literal Interpretation of the Bible

The allegorical method of interpretation denies that the basic meaning of a text is literal. It favors a nonliteral, deeper, or mystical meaning that is not rooted in the historical-grammatical use of language. In fact, it spiritualizes away the literal truth of Scripture in favor of an interpretation that denies essential orthodox doctrines of the Christian Faith.

The two methods can be contrasted as follows:

	Literal	**Allegorical**
Locus	In the words	Beneath the words
Nature	Objective	Subjective
Approach	Common	Mystical
Meaning	Ordinary	Special
Clarity	Obvious	Obscure
Sense	One	Many
Key	Context	Special code or key
Result	Truth	Heresy

By creating their own special allegorical or mystical interpretations of Scripture, many heretical and cultic groups make the Bible say anything they want it to say. For example, consider Jesus' words in Matthew 11:29. New Ager Elizabeth Clare Prophet tells us that when Jesus said "Take my yoke upon you and learn from me" (Matthew 11:29), He was teaching His disciples to "take my yoke, *yoga,* upon you and learn of me—take my consciousness of my sacred labor, my Christhood bearing the burden of world karma…and learn of my Guru, the Ancient of Days—for I am meek and lowly in heart, and ye shall find rest unto your souls. For my yoke, *yoga,* is easy and my burden in heaven and on earth is truly Light."[4] Of course, in context, Jesus was referring not to yoga but to His followers finding spiritual rest in their relationship with Him. The word *yoga* is not mentioned nor even remotely implied in the Bible text.

Prophet allegorizes further by asserting that when Jesus said to some of His Jewish critics, "I tell you the truth…before Abraham was born, I am!" (John 8:58), He did so "in the full awareness that the 'I AM' of him had always been the Christ. And he also knew that the permanent part of each one of you was and is that same Christ."[5] She says that "Jesus' I AM Presence looks just like yours. This is the common denominator. This is the coequality of the sons and daughters of God. He created you equal in the sense that he gave you an I AM Presence—he gave you a Divine Self.[6] In her allegorized approach to Scripture, Prophet is clearly reading her own New Age theology *into* the text instead of deriving the correct meaning *out of* the text. Contrary to Prophet's view, by following the historical-grammatical system of Bible interpretation summarized in this chapter, we quickly see that Jesus was making a unique claim to absolute deity (see Exodus 3:14-15).

John 10:34 is another Scripture passage that has been given a twisted meaning. In this verse, Jesus said to some of His Jewish critics, "Is it not written in your Law, 'I have said you are gods'?" New Ager David Spangler exults that "we can be the God that Jesus proclaimed us to be: 'Ye are Gods.'"[7] Spangler explains that such godhood is *the* revelation for the New Age: The divinity of man "ultimately is the revelation, the eternal revelation, the only revelation. Everything else leads to that, contributes to it in some fashion."[8] Like Prophet, Spangler is clearly reading his New Age theology into a Bible text.

Contrary to Spangler's view (which is representative of millions of New Agers), the historical-grammatical system of Bible interpretation points us to a number of reasons John 10:34 cannot be taken to teach the deity of human beings. (We include the following discussion to illustrate the kinds of hermeneutical factors that guide us to the correct interpretation of Scripture, as well as to demonstrate the folly of the Scripture-twisting tactics of the cults.)

1. Such a New Age interpretation is contrary to the overall context. Jesus is not speaking to *pantheists* (who believe that God is everything and everything is God) or *polytheists* (who believe in many gods). Rather, He is addressing strict, Jewish *monotheists* who believe that only the Creator of the universe is God. So, His statement should not be wrenched out of this monotheistic context and given a pantheistic or polytheistic twist.

2. Jesus' statement must be understood as part of His overall reasoning here, which is an *a fortiori* argument. Christ had just pronounced Himself *one* with the Father, saying, "I and My Father are one" (John 10:30). The Jews wanted to stone Him because they thought Christ was blaspheming, making Himself out to be equal with God (verses 31-33). Jesus therefore appealed to Psalm 82:6, which says, "I said, 'You are gods.'" Christ's argument amounts to saying, "If God even called finite human judges 'gods' because of the works they do (pronouncing life and death

decisions over human beings), then how much more can I call Myself the Son of God—especially in view of the works I am doing (mighty divine miracles)?"

3. In the context of Psalm 82, notice that not everyone is called "gods," but only a special class of persons—namely, divinely appointed judges "to whom the word of God came" (verse 35). Jesus was showing that if the Old Testament Scriptures could give some limited divine status to divinely appointed judges, why should His Jewish listeners find it incredible that He should call Himself the Son of God?

4. Even though these judges were called "gods" in the sense that they stood in God's place judging over life-and-death matters, they were never considered to be divine beings. In fact, the text Jesus cites (Psalm 82) goes on to say that they were "mere men" and would "die" as the men they really were (verse 7).

5. Finally, it is possible, as many scholars believe, that when the psalmist Asaph said "You are gods" of the unjust judges, he was speaking in irony. He indicated to these judges, "I have called you 'gods,' but in fact you will die like the men that you really are." If this is so, then when Jesus alluded to this psalm in John 10, He was saying that what the Israelite judges were called *in irony* and *in judgment*, He is *in reality*. So, using the historical-grammatical method, the correct interpretation of John 10:34 is that Jesus was giving a defense for His own deity, not a defense for the deification of man.

There are other cults that misinterpret Scripture by taking anthropomorphisms in a literal fashion. For example, one reason the Mormons believe God the Father has a physical body is that Moses spoke to God "face to face" (Exodus 33:11). They reason that if God has a face, then He must have a physical body. Contrary to this view, the broader context of Scripture indicates that God is a spirit (John 4:24), and a spirit does not have flesh and bones (Luke 24:39). Hence, it is incorrect to think of God as a physical being that has a literal face. In keeping with this, the Bible indicates that God should not be depicted by any likeness whatever (Exodus 20:4).

In the Hebrew mind-set, "face to face" metaphorically meant "directly" or "intimately." Moses did not see any physical part of God, such as a literal face, but rather entered into God's direct presence and spoke with Him in an intimate way. Even a blind person can speak "face to face" with someone else—that is, directly and personally, without ever actually seeing a face.

Perhaps the most common hermeneutical violation in the kingdom of the cults is taking verses out of context. The Oneness Pentecostals, for example, often claim that Isaiah 9:6 proves Jesus is the Father. After all, the verse refers to Jesus as "Mighty God, Everlasting Father." If Oneness Pentecostals would use the historical-grammatical method of interpretation, and approach this verse from the broader context of the whole of Scripture, they would not come to this conclusion.

Foundationally, the Father is considered by Jesus as someone other than Himself over 200 times in the New Testament. And over 50 times in the New Testament, the Father and Son are distinct within the same verse (for example, Romans 15:6; 2 Corinthians 1:3; Galatians 1:1-3; Philippians 2:10-11; 1 John 2:1; 2 John 3). Further, the word "Father," as a title of God, did not emerge into prominence until New Testament times, when Jesus taught that God was the Father. It certainly was not a common title of God in Old Testament times. This would argue against the idea that the use of "Father" in Isaiah 9:6 was intended to be a New Testament-like reference to God. Rather, the term is used in a different sense.

If the Father and the Son are distinct, as Scripture clearly indicates, then in what sense can Jesus be called "Everlasting Father" (Isaiah 9:6)? There are two primary options. First, many scholars believe this phrase is better translated "Father of eternity," carrying the meaning "possessor of eternity." Father of eternity is here used in accordance with a Hebrew and Arabic custom in which he who possesses a thing is called the father of it. Thus, "father of strength" means strong; "father of knowledge," intelligent; "father of glory," glorious. According to this common usage, the meaning of "Father of eternity" in Isaiah 9:6 is eternal. Christ as the "Father of eternity" is an eternal being.

A second plausible view suggests that the first part of verse six refers to the incarnation of Jesus. The next part, which lists the names by which He is called, then expresses Jesus' relationship to His people. He is *to us* a Wonderful Counselor, Mighty God, the Father of eternity, and the Prince of Peace. In this sense of the usage of the word "Father," Jesus may be viewed as a provider of eternal life. By His death, burial, and resurrection, He has brought life and immortality to light (2 Timothy 1:10). Jesus is the Father or *provider* of eternity for His people. Whichever of the two above views are correct, the historical-grammatical system of Bible interpretation renders the Oneness Pentecostal view impossible.

One final group we can point to for illustrative purposes is the Jehovah's Witnesses, who are notorious for taking verses out of context. One example of this is their citation of 1 Corinthians 14:33 as a disproof of the doctrine of the Trinity. First Corinthians 14:33 tells us that God is not a God of confusion. Jehovah's Witnesses reason that because the doctrine of the Trinity is difficult to understand and is confusing, it cannot possibly be correct.

If the Jehovah's Witnesses were to utilize the historical-grammatical method of interpretation, they would never come to this faulty conclusion. Consulting the context of 1 Corinthians reveals that the Corinthian church was plagued by internal divisions and disorder (1 Corinthians 1:11), especially in regard to the exercise of spiritual gifts—such as prophesying and speaking in tongues. Because God is a God of peace and not a God of confusion, Paul says, the church itself must seek to model itself after God by seeking peace and avoiding disharmony and disorder in its services. By so doing, the church honors God. First Corinthians 14:33 doesn't even remotely have anything to do with the Trinity.

There are many other examples we could point to that illustrate how cults consistently fail in the area of hermeneutics. And because of their failures, it is inevitable that they end up denying essential doctrines of the Christian Faith and subscribe to many strange doctrines, as we have illustrated throughout this book.

THEOLOGICAL QUICK-REVIEW

Chapter 17 Main Idea: It is only by understanding the Scriptures through the historical-grammatical method of interpretation of the Bible that we know there are any essential doctrines.

Importance: One need not believe in the literal method of interpretation of the Bible to be saved. But without this method of interpreting Scripture, there would be no means of understanding the essential teachings about salvation that *must* be believed to be saved. So, while the historical-grammatical method of interpretation is not a *salvation* essential or even a *revelation* essential, the doctrine is an *interpretation* essential.

Unorthodox Viewpoints: The primary reason so many cults deny one or more of the essentials of the Christian Faith and end up embracing strange doctrines is that they do not use the historical-grammatical system of interpretation. Among the errors cults resort to are allegorizing the text of Scripture, taking anthropomorphisms literally, ignoring grammatical considerations, ignoring historical considerations, and taking Bible verses out of context.

Course of Action: On the necessity of the historical-grammatical means of interpreting the Bible, there must be conviction without compromise.

Part Two:

In Nonessentials, *Liberty*

THIS SECTION FOCUSES ON the second part of the dictum, *In essentials, unity;* ***in nonessentials, liberty;*** *and in all things, charity*. As we learned in Part One, majors should not be reduced to minors, nor, as demonstrated here, should minors be made into majors. All too often Christian groups, large and small, have made fundamentals out of nonfundamentals, thus unnecessarily dividing the body of Christ.

18

The Procession of the Holy Spirit

ODDLY ENOUGH, THE GREATEST and earliest major division in Christendom was over what appears to be a relatively minor difference in doctrine. Unlike early heresies that denied important doctrines such as the deity of Christ or the essential equality of all members of the Trinity, this dispute was over the order and procession in the Godhead.

The Bible speaks of Christ returning to the Father and the Father sending the Holy Spirit into the world. Jesus said, "I will pray the Father, and He will give you another Helper, that He may abide with you forever" (John 14:16 NKJV). He later added, "The Helper, the Holy Spirit, whom the Father will send in My name, He will teach you all things" (John 14:26). Clearly, then, the Holy Spirit proceeded from the Father. But Jesus also said, "When the Helper comes, whom *I shall send to you* from the Father, the Spirit of truth who proceeds from the Father, He will testify of Me" (John 15:26, emphasis added). Herein lies the dispute. Did the Holy Spirit proceed *only* from the Father, as the Eastern church holds, or also from the Son, as the Western church believes?

The History of the Disagreement

The Eastern and Western branches of Christianity were united until the eleventh century. The Eastern church is called the Church of the Seven Councils because it agreed with Rome on the pronouncements of all these General Councils of the church. (Most Protestants agree only with the first four.)

1. First Council of Nicea (A.D. *325)*

This council, called by professing Christian Emperor Constantine, affirmed the Trinity as well as the full deity of Christ as eternal and of the same nature as the Father. The council formulated the famous Nicean Creed, by which the heresy of Arianism, which denied the deity of Christ, was condemned.

In addition, Nicea set forth numerous canons that claim to be universally binding on the whole church. These include that bishops should be appointed only by other bishops (Canon 4), that excommunication is to be done by a bishop (Canon 5), and that the bishops have jurisdiction over their own geographical areas (Canon 6).*

2. First Council of Constantinople (A.D. *381)*

This council, convened by Emperor Theodosius I (A.D. 379–395), reaffirmed the Nicean Creed, proclaimed the deity of the Holy Spirit, and united the Eastern church (divided by the Arianism controversy). The emperor is said to have "founded the orthodox Christian state. Arianism and other heresies became legal offenses, sacrifice [to pagan gods] was forbidden, and paganism almost outlawed."[1]

3. Council of Ephesus (A.D. *431)*

This council condemned Nestorianism, which taught there were two natures and two persons in Christ. Because Christ is only one person with two natures, the council concluded that Mary was truly the mother of God—that is, the "God-bearer," or the one who gave birth to the person (Jesus), who is God as well as man. Extracts from Cyril to Nestorius in Session I read, "This was the sentiment of the holy Fathers; therefore they ventured to call the holy Virgin, the Mother of God, not as if the nature of the Word or his divinity had its beginning from the holy Virgin, but

* The claim that this canon gives primacy of the Bishop of Rome over the whole church is without justification. The context makes it clear that it speaks only about different bishops having jurisdiction in their respective geographical areas, naming three centers: Alexandria, Antioch, and Rome. The text is clear: "Let the ancient customs in Egypt, Libya and Pentapolis prevail, that the Bishop of Alexandria have jurisdiction in all these, since it is customary for the Bishop of Rome also. Likewise in Antioch and the other provinces, let the Churches retain their privileges" (Philip Schaff, *A Select Library of Nicene and Post-Nicene Fathers of the Christian Church* [Grand Rapids: Eerdmans, 1964], p. 15). As Hefele put it, "It is evident that the Council has not in view here the primacy of the bishop of Rome over the whole Church, but simply his power as a patriarch" (cited by Schaff, p. 16).

because of her was born that holy body with a rational soul, to which the Word being personally united is said to be born according to the flesh."[2]

4. Council of Chalcedon (A.D. 451)

This council, called by Emperor Marcian, dealt with the Eutychianis (Monophysite) heresy, which merged the two natures of Christ, making a logically incoherent combination of an infinite-finite nature. The council agreed with Archbishop [Pope] Leo I to "anathematize" this as "absurd," "extremely foolish," "extremely blasphemous," and "impious."[3] The council reaffirmed the decisions of all three general councils that preceded it (Session 4) as well as "the writings of that blessed man, Leo, Archbishop of all the churches who condemned the heresy of Nestorius and Eutyches, [to] shew what the true faith is."[4]

The most controversial canon of this council (number 28) affirms that "Constantinople, which is New Rome...enjoys equal privileges with the old imperial Rome" and hence "should in ecclesiastical matters also be magnified as she is, and rank next after her."[5] (That is, the Eastern church should rank right after the Western church in Rome.) This canon was rejected by Archbishop Leo of the old Rome. But of historic importance is the statement that gives the reason any primacy was given to Rome in the first place: "For the Fathers rightly granted privileges to the throne of the old Rome, because it was the royal city."[6] Louis-Sébastien Le Nain de Tillemont's comment is to the point: "This canon seems to recognize no particular authority in the Church of Rome, save what the Fathers had granted it, as the seat of the empire."[7]

5. Second Council of Constantinople (A.D. 553)

This council was convened by the Emperor Justinian. It contains 14 anathemas, the first 12 directed at Theodore of Mopsuestia. A later insert placed Origen's name in the eleventh anathema, which was accepted by later popes. Among the heresies condemned are Arianism, Nestorianism, Eutychianism, and Monophysitism (Statements I–XI) as well as Adoptionism (XII). The perpetual virginity of Mary was affirmed, being called the "ever-virgin Mary, the Mother of God" (Statements V and XIV). It is this council, and those that followed, that most Protestants deny as being authoritative. Most Protestants accept only the first four general councils.

6. Third Council of Constantinople (A.D. 680)

This council was convened by Emperor Constantine IV (Pogonatus). It affirmed the "five holy ecumenical councils."[8] In addition, it reaffirmed that Christ had two natures united in one person, and that He had two wills—one human and one divine—which had a moral unity resulting from the complete harmony between the two natures of the God-Man (as opposed to the Monothelites). In condemning the Monothelite heresy (that Christ had only one will), the council warned that "no one henceforth should hold a different faith, or venture to teach one will [in Christ] and one energy [operation of the will]."[9] It also referred to Mary as "our Holy Lady, the holy, immaculate, ever-virgin and glorious Mary, truly and properly the Mother of God."[10]

This council is noteworthy for condemning Honorius, "some time Pope of Old Rome,"[11] for teaching heresy, a fact that seriously undermined the later Catholic claim of infallibility when popes speak on doctrinal matters.

This council claimed to be not only "illuminated by the Holy Spirit" but also "inspired by the Holy Spirit." Thus, it claimed to provide "a definition, clean from all error, certain, and infallible."[12] This infallibility would later be claimed by the pope for himself at Vatican I (1870).

7. Second Council of Nicea (A.D. 787)

This council was called by the emperors Constantine and Irene and was attended by legates of Pope Hadrian. It dealt with the iconoclastic controversy (about the use of visual images or icons in worship) and ruled in favor of venerating images, stating, "Receiving their holy and honorable residues with all honor, I salute and venerate these with honor...Likewise also the venerable images of the incarnation of our Lord Jesus Christ... and of all the Saints—the Sacred Martyrs, and of all the Saints—the sacred images of all these, I salute, and venerate."[13] Further, it pronounced "anathemas to those who do not salute the holy and venerable images" and "anathemas to those who call the sacred images idols." With seeming zealous overkill, it added: "To those who have a doubtful mind and do not confess with their whole heart that they venerate the sacred images, Anathemas!"[14]

This council also encouraged prayer to Mary and the saints: "I ask for the intercession of our spotless Lady the Holy Mother of God, and those of the holy and heavenly powers and those of all the Saints."[15] The council attempted to distinguish this practice in theory (if not in practice) from true worship that is due to the Trinity alone. It affirmed, "The worship of *adoration* I reserve alone to the supersubstantial and life-giving Trinity."[16]

The contemporary iconoclasts' objections to the council's decisions were expressed in another council claiming to be the *true* seventh ecumenical council. They declared flatly that "Satan misguided men, so that they worshiped the creature instead of the Creator."[17] They argued that the only admissible figure of the humanity of Christ, however, is bread and wine in the holy Supper. They cited Exodus 20:4: "Thou shalt not make thee any graven image, or any likeness of anything that is in heaven" and affirmed, "Supported by the Holy Scriptures and the Fathers, we declare unanimously, in the name of the Holy Trinity, that there shall be rejected and removed and cursed out of the Christian Church every likeness which is made out of any material and color whatever by the evil art of painters."[18] The council concluded: "If anyone does not accept this our Holy and Ecumenical Seventh Synod, let him be Anathema." The council also condemned Emperor Germanus of Constantinople, calling him "the double-minded worshiper of wood."[19]

8. Fourth Council of Constantinople (A.D. 869)

This council explicitly affirmed the Second Council of Nicea (A.D. 787) and condemned the schism of Photius, Patriarch of Constantinople. He had challenged the *filioque* (Latin: "and the Son") clause of Nicea II in the creed (which affirmed the Holy Spirit also proceeded from the Son, not just the Father).

The Great Schism (A.D. 1054)

This issue of whether the Holy Spirit proceeded from the Son as well as from the Father became a bone of contention between the Western and Eastern churches in A.D. 1054 and was at the root of the great schism between Eastern Orthodoxy and Roman Catholicism.

9-12. The First (A.D. 1123), Second (1139), Third (1179), and Fourth Lateran Councils (1215)

These continued the development of the Roman church. The later councils pronounced the Roman doctrines of transubstantiation, the seven sacraments, the primacy of the Bishop of Rome, and condemned heretics and turned them over to the state for punishment. This further solidified the split between East and West.

13. Second Council of Lyons (A.D. 1274)

This council made a brief attempt to heal the wounds between East and West. It was called by Pope Gregory X to bring about union with the Eastern church, to liberate the Holy Land, and to bring moral reform in the church. It unsuccessfully demanded affirmation of the double procession of the Holy Spirit from the Father and the Son, which the Eastern church rejected. Albert the Great and St. Bonaventure attended, but Thomas Aquinas died on his way to the council in A.D. 1274. This council defined the procession of the Holy Spirit (the *filioque* clause) and imposed it on Eastern Orthodoxy, but the union with the East was short-lived, ending in 1289.

This *filioque* clause ("and the Son") was later added to the Nicene-Constantinople Creed and appears at the Council of Toledo (A.D. 589). In A.D. 796 it was defended by Paulus of Aquileia at the Synod of Friuli, and from around A.D. 800 it was generally chanted at Mass throughout the Frankish Empire. It was introduced by their monks in A.D. 847 at their Jerusalem monastery, where it met with strong opposition by Eastern monks, who followed the chief orthodox teacher John of Damascus in denying it. Nonetheless, Pope Leo III approved the doctrine while attempting to suppress its use liturgically. It continued to be sung, however, and was adapted by Rome soon after A.D. 1000. Because Photius, Patriarch of Constantinople, strongly denounced it, it remained at the center of the dispute between the Eastern and Western churches. Even though it was imposed on the Eastern church at the councils at Lyons

(A.D. 1224) and Florence (A.D. 1439), this imposed union was short-lived and is still a point of division between East and West to this day. Following the Thirty-Nine Articles of the Church of England, most Western theologians have accepted it.[20]

The Two Parties of the Dispute: Roman Catholicism and Eastern Orthodoxy

As noted previously, the Bible affirms that the Father sent the Holy Spirit into the world (John 14:16,26). However, we also read that Jesus would send the Holy Spirit (John 15:26). So, to review, the heart of the issue is whether the Holy Spirit proceeds only from the Father, as the Eastern church holds, or also from the Son, as the Western church believes.

There are, of course, other differences between the Eastern and Western churches. For example, the Eastern church accepts the authority of only the first seven general councils, whereas Rome holds to all 21, right up to and through Vatican II (1962–1965). This, in turn, means that Eastern Orthodoxy rejects the Roman Catholic claim of the infallibility of the Bishop of Rome, pronounced at Vatican I in 1870.

Most Protestants accept the doctrinal teaching of only the first four councils. They also reject other Catholic doctrines such as the perpetual virginity of Mary, the veneration of images, purgatory, and the elevation of tradition alongside Scripture, which denies the Protestant principle of *sola Scriptura* (the Bible alone).

Majoring on a Minor

This major split in Christianity—the first and the biggest—is a classic example of the significant problem that can be caused by majoring on a minor doctrine. Neither view on the procession of the Holy Spirit is unorthodox or heretical. Both sides of the dispute are orthodox in their view of the Trinity. Neither one denies that there are three distinct and eternal persons who are coequal in nature and glory. None of the major heresies condemned in the first four church councils relate to this issue. Why, then, make such a big deal over such a minor doctrinal difference?

Someone has well said that the devil's strategy is to unite what God has divided and to divide what He has united. This division in Christendom is a tragic example of the latter. In short, those involved in this dispute made a dogmatic mountain over a doctrinal molehill.

Areas of Agreement Between the Parties

As noted previously, there are areas of agreement both on the underlying doctrine of the Trinity as well as on the procession of the Holy Spirit. First, both sides agree that the Holy Spirit proceeds from the Father. Second, both agree that Christ is involved in this procession process. He is the One who prays to the Father for the Spirit to proceed. Jesus said, "I will *pray the Father,* and He will give you another Helper, that He may abide with you forever" (John 14:16 NKJV, emphasis added). The Spirit is also sent in Christ's name. He said, "the Helper, the Holy Spirit, whom the Father will send *in My name,* He will teach you all things" (John 14:26 NKJV, emphasis added). Finally, the Bible clearly says that Christ will send the Holy Spirit: "But when the Helper comes, whom *I shall send to you from the Father,* the Spirit of truth who proceeds from the Father, He will testify of Me" (John 15:26 NKJV, emphasis added). As to whether the Holy Spirit is sent through Christ *indirectly* or *directly,* there is no real reason to quibble—at least not to the degree of separating fellowship between two groups who hold in common all 16 of the essentials of the Christian Faith. Over nonessentials such as the doctrine of the procession of the Holy Spirit, we should simply agree to disagree agreeably.

19

Forms of Church Government

EARLY IN THE HISTORY of the Christian church, there emerged a controversy over the proper form of church government. The controversy continues to this day.

Whole denominations have split over this issue. Some churches have canonized one form of church government, making it into a kind of fundamental of the Faith. Other denominations have insisted that one must belong to their particular church or else one is not a true representative of the Christian Faith. The sad fact is that whether the form of church government has been dogmatized on the local level (for example, by the so-called Church of Christ) or on the universal level (such as in the Roman Catholic Church), an important principle has been violated—namely, in nonessentials, *liberty.*

The Danger of Extreme Views on Church Government

The error of making the minor doctrine of church government into a major issue and a test of fellowship with other believers comes in two basic forms: universal and particular. On the universal level, the Roman Catholic canonizing of the episcopal form of government and making the Bishop of Rome infallible in faith and practice is a prime example of attempting to establish one true visible and universal form of church government on earth. On the particular (or local/individual) level, radical authority is assigned to the individual local churches. Let us now consider these in greater detail, first turning our attention to the Roman Catholic extreme.

The Roman Catholic Extreme

There are giant leaps from the local, self-governing, autonomous churches of the New Testament to the Roman Catholic claim to be the one true and infallible repository of Christian truth (Vatican I, 1870). Even granted the validity of the episcopal form of government (which many sectors of Christianity do not accept), it takes a number of unjustified leaps from one bishop over a local church (late second century), to one bishop over a region (early third century), to one bishop over all the earth (late third century), to coercive authority of the pope (early fifth century), to one pope with authority to define doctrine in a creed (thirteenth century), to (finally) one infallible bishop (when speaking *ex cathedra*) over the whole world (nineteenth century)![1]

While Rome has not officially denied any of the 16 essentials of the Faith (see chapters 2–17), it has obscured many of them, and added as well as elevated nonfundamental teachings such as the Roman episcopal form of government, reaching a crescendo with the infallibility of the pope when teaching as the official interpreter of the church on matters of faith and practice. At the Third Council of Constantinople (A.D. 680), its pronouncements were said to have been "illuminated by the Holy Spirit" and provided "a definition, clean from all error, certain, and infallible." At the First Vatican Council (A.D. 1870), the pope assumed this infallibility for himself, asserting that his official statements on faith and practice are "irreformable of themselves, and not from the consent of the Church." The Fourth Lateran Council (A.D. 1215) had already declared "the primacy of the Bishop of Rome" (the pope).

Reading this view of the church back into earlier ecumenical creeds, which affirmed no salvation outside the "Catholic Church" (meaning the *universal* church), Rome has been able to make the unjustified claim that "there is no salvation outside the *Roman Catholic* Church."[2] So, for example, while the Athanasian Creed declared that "whoever will be saved, before all things it is necessary that he hold the catholic faith," Rome takes this to mean the Roman Catholic Church.

Thus, by a gradual development over the centuries of an episcopal form of government not found in the New Testament, an exclusivistic authoritarian structure eventuated that institutionalized salvation in the Roman Catholic sacraments, mediated through the Roman Catholic priesthood, thus obscuring the exclusivity of grace and faith and replacing it with a system of salvation accentuated by good works. In the practical sense of the term, the word "cultic"[3] is not inappropriate to use for describing the Roman Catholic authoritarian structure. This is a classic example of making a major out of a minor and legislating it for the whole Christian church.

There are numerous reasons for rejecting the Roman Catholic teaching regarding infallibility. Because many arguments for such infallibility are rooted in the alleged supremacy of Peter (the alleged first bishop of Rome), we begin by addressing his place in the early church:

1. Contrary to Roman Catholic claims, Peter was not the foundation of the church but only part of it with the other apostles (Ephesians 2:20).
2. Except for the one-time use of the "key" to "open the kingdom" to Jews (Acts 2) and Gentiles (Acts 10), Peter did not have any greater power than the other apostles who were given the same power as he (Matthew 18:18).
3. Jesus promised the "key" *only to Peter,* not to his successors (Matthew 16:19).
4. Peter did not have authority to commission others, but was himself commissioned by the other apostles (Acts 8:14).
5. Peter had no authority over the church, but was held accountable by it (Acts 11:1-18).
6. Peter was rebuked by another apostle for his error (Galatians 2:11-14).
7. After the church was born, when apostles died, they were not replaced by other apostles (Acts 12:3). Rather,

they appointed elders in each church, not apostles over all the churches (Acts 14:23).

8. Moreover, popes were far from infallible in what they taught:

    - Pope Honorius I (A.D. 625–638) taught heresy.
    - Others made grave errors (for example, in condemning Galileo for positing the now-well-established scientific theory that the sun, not the earth, is the center of the solar system).
    - There were two or more popes at the same time who mutually excommunicated each other.
    - Popes were excommunicated by the ecumenical Council of Constance (A.D. 1413–1418).
    - Pope Sixtus (A.D. 1590) published an inspired version of the Bible with thousands of errors in it that had to be corrected.
    - Because there is no infallible list of infallible statements of popes, there is no infallible way to know what is infallible.
    - Some alleged infallible statements are unbiblical—for example, the veneration of Mary, her sinlessness, her bodily assumption into heaven, the worship of the communion host (bread and wine), and the teaching that works are necessary for salvation.

We are compelled to observe that by making a minor doctrine (church government) into a major teaching, a major teaching (salvation by grace through faith) has thereby officially been made into a minor teaching and, in practice, is often denied. This reveals the significant effect of failing to abide by the dictum "in nonessentials, liberty." Had Rome followed this, there would likely have been no need for a Reformation, for there would have been liberty on the nonessential issue of the form of church government. Allowing diversity within essential unity is not evil (see chapter

30). Governmental and ritualistic diversity is no more evil than ethnic diversity is. It adds color to commitment and variety to basic virtue. Sadly, the exclusivistic and dogmatic claim of Rome has prompted unnecessary division within the true Christian church. While evangelicals share real unity in doctrine and spirit with all born-again believers, including Roman Catholics, this true unity has been vitiated by the cultic claim of exclusivistic and infallible authority by Rome, to say nothing of the numerous Christian leaders (such as William Tyndale and Martin Luther) who were falsely proclaimed to be heretics by Rome, many of whom were even sentenced to death, with thousands of martyrs ultimately sacrificed (such as John Huss and Jerome Savanarola) by the Roman Inquisition.

Other Church Extremes

While the episcopal form of government went to seed in medieval Romanism, the congregational form of government of the Church of Christ degenerated in the opposite extreme. Both groups claim to be the true church, but each has a different form of government. In the case of Roman Catholicism, the final authority rests in a monarchial rule over all the churches. In the case of the Church of Christ, there is a radical authority of the individual local churches. Unfortunately, the Church of Christ is not alone in this extreme. Many Landmarkian Baptist churches, for example, lay claim to their group being the unique descendants of true Christianity, whose properly baptized converts *alone* comprise the bride of Christ. In this view, the local churches and the "kingdom of God" are viewed as essentially synonymous terms.[4]

The so-called Local Church movement of Witness Lee claims there is only one true local church in each city—*theirs*. This movement, noted for its doctrinal deviations on the Trinity favoring the heresy of modalism, has described all the rest of Christianity in the most negative of terms. In their failed appeals to the Texas Supreme Court (2006) to reconsider their lawsuit against two evangelical authors and their publisher, the Local Church included, with the appeal, an appendix containing chapter 3 from a book by Witness Lee titled *The God-Ordained Way to Practice the New Testament Economy*. In this chapter Witness Lee engages in particularly inappropriate and utterly self-incriminating language for a group that resents being called a cult.[5] He denounces all of organized Christianity with strong language, referring to the object of his scorn as "all of Christianity," "all Christians," "today's Christendom" (pages 25-26), "all Christianity," "today's Catholic Church" (26), and "the Catholic Church and all the denominations" (29). His attack is delivered with a devastating vehemence and by sweeping indictments against organized Christianity, which he describes in these terms: It is "altogether negative," "deformed and degraded," and "absolutely far off from God's eternal plan" (25). It has "false teachers" who are "in their apostasy" (26). The Roman Catholic Church is infested with "Satan's evil spirits" and "full of all kinds of evils. Evil persons, evil practices, and evil things are lodging there" (26). It is an "adulterous woman who added leaven (signifying evil, heretical, and pagan things)." It is "the Mother of the Prostitutes" and an "apostate church" (27). Again, it is "full of idolatry," "against God's economy," and "saturated with demonic and satanic things" (28-29). It is ironic that a group that strongly objects to being called a cult would use such vitriolic language to describe all of Christianity.

One final group we might mention in this regard is the Church of Jesus Christ of Latter-day Saints (the Mormons). Because, according to Joseph Smith's First Vision account, all the churches were corrupt in God's sight, Smith was allegedly instructed by the Father and Jesus Christ not to join any of them. Moreover, through Smith, the one true church was to be restored on Earth.

Mormons claim that proper church organization with its respective offices had been lost, along with continual revelation through God's appointed representatives (prophets and apostles). The true gospel had also been lost in its completeness from the Bible due to "designing priests" removing its "plain and precious" truths. Further, the Melchizedek priesthood had allegedly been lost from the Earth after the death of the last apostle.

Joseph Smith allegedly restored proper church organization, the true gospel, the offices of prophets and apostles, and the "eternal" Melchizedek priesthood. Mormons believe the presence or absence of this priesthood establishes the divinity or falsity of a professing church. Because the Mormon church exclusively possesses this "restored" priesthood, *it alone* is claimed to be the one true church. Here again we witness the cultic tendency to pronounce one's own group to be the sole faithful repository of God's truth.

Today the Mormon church—which denies numerous essential doctrines of the Christian Faith, such as the Trinity, the deity of Christ, and salvation by grace alone through faith alone—is led by a First Presidency (a "collective trio" made up of the president of the church and a first and second counselor), the Council of Twelve Apostles (who hold lifetime positions), the First Quorum of the Seventy and the Second Quorum of the Seventy (stemming from Moses's calling of 70 elders to assist him). The 15 men at the top—the First Presidency and the Council of Twelve Apostles—rule with unchallenged authority in the church.

Areas of Agreement on Church Government

Evangelical Christians disagree with Witness Lee's Local Church movement and the Church of Jesus Christ of Latter-day Saints because of their denial of essential doctrines of the Christian Faith (see chapters 2–17). But when it comes to differences and disagreements over the nonessential doctrine of church government among churches that subscribe to the biblical essentials of the Faith, two areas of agreement should emerge. First, we should agree to disagree agreeably on this matter, for no specific form of church government is a fundamental of the Christian Faith. There are only 16 of these (see chapters 2–17), and the form of church government is not among them.

Second, all can agree that there should be *some* form of government in the church. The apostle Paul said, "Let all things be done decently and in order" (1 Corinthians 14:40 NKJV). God is the author of peace, not confusion. Some structure is therefore needed in the local church. And regardless of the specific title, some—often called bishops or elders—should be responsible for the spiritual oversight of the church, and others—often called deacons—should care for the material needs of the congregation (Acts 6). Likewise, there should be congregational involvement in the ministry of the church, for each member is gifted for the good of the whole body, and each should exercise their respective gifts (1 Corinthians 12).[6]

Beyond this, just how the governance of the church is understood and exercised—and what the names of the officers are—is a matter of intramural differences. On these we can agree to disagree, and when we do, it should be in love (1 Corinthians 13:4-7) as well as respect for one another's views (1 Peter 3:15).

20

Grace, Faith, and Works

THE ABSOLUTE NECESSITY OF GOD'S GRACE in relation to salvation is one of the essentials of the Christian Faith (see chapter 11), as is the necessity of faith as opposed to works (see chapter 12). However, there has been much debate about the relation of works to faith and about the exclusivity of grace. Roman Catholics believe in the *necessity* of grace but not in its *exclusivity* in salvation. They believe good works are also a condition of salvation. Protestants deny this. The same is true of the relation between faith and works. Strong Augustinians and Calvinists believe God's grace is *operative* apart from human free will. More moderate Augustinians and Calvinists believe human free will is *cooperative* with God's grace. Both views, however, believe in the necessity of grace and faith as fundamental to salvation. Let's consider the details.

The History and Parties of the Disagreement

Although the debate over grace and works was central to the Reformation, it has always been present to some degree and was first accented in the Augustinian-Pelagian controversy in the late fourth and early fifth centuries. While Pelagianism was dealt with at church councils, no ecumenical council has ever ruled on Semi-Pelagianism, except the Council of Trent (1445–1463), which Catholics accept as authoritative but Protestants do not. Hence, the debate continues unabated.

Pelagianism

The roots of the later Reformation are found in the fifth-century Pelagian controversy. Pelagianism has been defined as "the heresy which holds that man can take the initial and fundamental steps toward salvation by his own efforts, apart from divine grace."[1] Pelagianism was condemned as heretical at two local councils at Carthage and Milevis, both in A.D. 416. Later, at the Council of Carthage in A.D. 418, the Augustinian doctrine of the fall of man and original sin were affirmed in opposition to Pelagianism. Other Pelagians were condemned at the Council of Ephesus in A.D. 431.

St. Augustine

The basis of the condemnation of Pelagius is found in Augustine's anti-Pelagian writings, such as *On the Grace of Christ, On Grace and Free Will, On Predestination of the Saints, On Original Sin, Enchridion*, and *On the Gift of Perseverance.*

In his earlier writings, Augustine designated a greater role to man's free will: "Sin is so much a voluntary evil that it is not sin at all unless it is voluntary."[2] He also said that the will to believe comes from ourselves. Augustine thus asked: "If [salvation is] from God's gift, then again, why is not the gift open to all; since 'He will have all men to be saved, and to come unto the knowledge of the truth'?" He answered, "God no doubt wishes all men to come into the knowledge of the truth; but yet not so as to take away from them free will."[3] "For the soul cannot receive and possess these gifts, which are here referred to, except by yielding its consent...and yet the act of receiving and having belongs, of course, to the receiver and possessor."[4]

Augustine's radical shift on the issue of free will and the need for God's irresistible grace occurred after his controversy with Pelagius and the Donatists, and begins in his work *On the Correction [Coercion] of the Donatist* (A.D. 417), in which he concluded that even heretics could be coerced to believe the Catholic faith against their will.[5] He uses words such as "violence" and "compulsion"[6] to describe this irresistible grace of salvation. Such irresistible grace is needed in view of man's loss of free will:

> It was by the evil use of his free will that man destroyed both it and himself. For, as a man who kills himself must, of course, be alive when he kills himself, but after he has killed

> himself ceases to live, and cannot restore himself to life; so, when man by his own free will sinned, then sin being victorious over him, the freedom of his will was lost.[7]

As to the necessity of grace, Augustine affirmed, "God created man such a free will, but once that kind of freedom was lost by man's fall from freedom, it could be given back only by Him who had the power to give it."[8] Faith is a gift of God given only to some. This was done "lest men should arrogate to themselves the merit of their own faith at least, not understanding that this too is the gift of God."[9] For Augustine, God's predestination is double, for "as the Supreme good, he made good use of evil deeds, for the damnation of those whom he had justly predestined to punishment and for the salvation of those whom he had mercifully predestined to grace."[10] Of course, God by His irresistible grace can change any evil will He wishes, for "who would be so impiously foolish as to say that God cannot turn evil wills of men—as he willeth, when he willeth, and where he willeth—toward the good?"[11]

As to why God does not do this for all, Augustine responded that God would have been perfectly just even if He had done it *for none:* "The whole human race was condemned in its rebellious head by a divine judgment so just, that if not a single member of the race had been redeemed, no one could justly have questioned the justice of God."[12]

As for God's grace before salvation, Augustine commented, "Let compulsion be found outside, the will will arise within."[13] For "great indeed is the help of the grace of God, so that He turns our heart in whatever direction He pleases."[14] Augustine reversed his earlier interpretation of 1 Timothy 2:4, which says that God "wants all men to be saved," and now claimed it means "no man is saved unless God wills his salvation," but "we know well that all men are not saved."[15]

It is only after salvation, Augustine claimed, that there is *cooperative* grace. So, "He [God] operates [in regeneration], therefore, without us, in order that we may will [in sanctification], and so will that we may act, He cooperates with us."[16] That is, God's grace in regeneration is operative and monergistic (God's operation alone), but His grace after we are believers is synergistic (cooperating with our free will).

Semi-Pelagianism

Semi-Pelagianism developed in response to the extreme predestinationism and infallible perseverance in the late Augustine, yet it did not approve of Pelagianism. This view teaches that while Adam's sin had a universal effect on the nature and will of all human beings, it only resulted in a *weakened* state, not one of *total* inability to do good. Man is therefore sick but not dead in his sins. Both Pelagianism and Semi-Pelagianism were condemned together at the Council of Orange in A.D. 529. In 25 dogmatic canons, the council upheld many of Augustine's doctrines on the nature of grace against the Semi-Pelagianism then being advocated by Faustus of Riez, though it also repudiated the doctrine of double-predestination.

The council pronounced that: 1) God gives only some the grace to believe; 2) human free will is so depraved that it cannot even receive the gift of salvation; 3) regeneration is thus necessary *before* one can believe; 4) all those who are elect can persevere to the end; 5) no act of freedom or good work is done apart from the prompting of God's grace; 6) the whole man—body and soul—is dead in sin which he inherited from Adam; 7) not only faith, but the very *desire* for faith, comes from God; 8) no one can come to faith by free will apart from the grace of God working on it first; 9) when we do a good work, it is God doing that work in us; 10) freedom is "destroyed" in fallen human beings (Canon 13) and can be restored only by the grace of baptism; 11) grace is not preceded by any merit on our part; rather, all good works are preceded by God's grace; 12) no man has anything of his own but untruth and sin (Canon 22); 13) even when we comply with God's will by our will, we do so because God prepared and instructed our will (Canon 23); 14) even our love for God is wholly a gift from God (Canon 25); 15) nonetheless, we "do not believe that any are foreordained to evil by the power of God" ("Conclusion").

Most of these statements boil down to the underlying teachings of total depravity and God's grace being *operative* but not *cooperative* with human free will. In other words, God works salvation in fallen human beings *monergistically* (by His energy alone), not *synergistically* (in co-operation with our free will). This teaching was reversed by Rome until the Council of Trent (1545–1563), which sided with the Semi-Pelagians on cooperative grace for salvation.

The Reformation on Grace and Free Will

Martin Luther

This same debate re-emerged at the Reformation. Luther's response to the Catholic view, expressed by Erasmus, is found in his *On the Bondage of the Will*, in which he repeated the position of the late Augustine and the Council of Orange. According to Luther, man's "Free-will is overruled by the Free-will of God alone, just as He pleases: but that God-ward, or in things which pertain unto salvation or damnation, he has no 'Free-will,' but is captive, slave, and servant, either to the will of God, or to the will of Satan."[17] Free will conceived any other way, Luther said, is a kind of good works by which we cannot be saved. Free will "could neither receive nor believe" the gospel, "so far is it from possibility that it should either will it, or believe it."[18] Citing Augustine with approval, Luther proclaimed that "'Free-will,' of its own power, cannot do anything but fall, nor avail unto anything but to sin."[19] So, free will in all, is alike defined to be "that which cannot will good."[20] "Indeed, if it were not so, God could not elect anyone, nor would there be any place left for election."[21] "If, therefore, 'Free-will' be of one and the same nature and impotency in all men, no reason can be given why it should attain unto grace in one, and not in another."[22]

As to why God does not move by grace on *all* human wills to be saved, Luther said, "This belongs to those secrets of Majesty."[23] For "God is that Being for whose will no cause or reason is to be assigned, as a rule or standard by which it acts."[24] Luther further commented, "What God wills, is not therefore right, because He ought or ever was bound so to will; but on the contrary, what takes place is therefore right, because He so wills."[25]

Luther's views were strongly monergistic. However, the Lutheran systematic theologian of the Reformation, Philip Melanchthon, reversed Luther's view, and Lutherans since the Reformation have adopted Melanchthon's more synergistic view.

John Calvin

Another major Reformer, John Calvin, was not as bombastic as Luther, but he was just as strong on the crucial issues pertaining to salvation. Calvin believed that because of human depravity, man's free choice is not capable of understanding or receiving God's saving grace. God gives the ability to respond by regenerating some (the elect), thus enabling them to believe. This saving grace is given *only* to some (the elect), not to all. This giving of grace is necessary, Calvin said, because "the will, so far as regards divine things, chooses only what is evil."[26] Of course, God gave Adam the power of choice, but it was lost for him and his posterity in the fall. Further, while the remnant of God's image is still in fallen man, it was "so corrupted, that anything which remains is fearful deformity; and, therefore, our deliverance begins with that renovation which we obtain from Christ."[27]

Calvin defended the idea that God's grace is operative, not cooperative, in the redeemed. He rejected even those who "insinuate that man, by his own nature, does good in some degree, though ineffectually."[28] He believed that

> our freedom is not to the extent of leaving us equally inclined to good and evil in acts or in thought, but only to the extent of freeing us from compulsion. This liberty is compatible with our being depraved, the servant of sin, able to do nothing but sin. In this way, then, man is said to have free will, not because he has a free choice of good and evil, but because he acts voluntarily, and not by compulsion.[29]

In brief, then, man—by making a bad use of free will—lost both himself *and* his free will. That free will having been made captive, can do nothing in the way of righteousness. No will is free that has not been made so by divine grace.

The Danger of the Extremes

The Pelagian Extreme

As in the case with other doctrinal controversies, there are dangers within the extremes. The Pelagian extreme is clearly heretical because it denies several essential doctrines—including the depravity of man, the necessity of grace, and the need for faith, to say nothing of undermining the necessity of Christ's atonement.

The Late Augustinian Extreme

On the other end of the spectrum, the late Augustine and later

Reformers reacted to Pelagianism. Likewise, Arminianism and Wesleyanism are a reaction to strong Calvinism. And the beat goes on. The pendulum never seems to stop in the middle.

Regardless of where one is on the spectrum of these non-Pelagian views, they are all within the borders of orthodoxy. None of them are heretical. Yet theological literature is filled with the anathemas of one group against another. Brethren, these things ought not to be so. These Augustinian and Semi-Pelagian issues do not deny *any* of the 16 essentials of the Christian Faith addressed in chapters 2–17. Thus, they fall into the category of a nonessential, and, as the famous dictum states, our attitude ought to be "in nonessentials, *liberty*."

This does not mean one cannot hold a view on this issue. The authors do (we are moderate Calvinists). What it means is that we should not use our particular view as a test of fellowship with other believers, nor should we call their view heretical. We should exercise the last third of the dictum—namely, "in all things, *charity*."

The Core of Agreement Among the Various Orthodox Views

All orthodox participants in this intramural debate agree—or *should* agree—on certain common related doctrines:

1. Man is so depraved that he cannot save himself (see chapter 6).
2. God's grace is absolutely necessary to our salvation (chapter 11).
3. Faith is absolutely essential to receive the gift of salvation (chapter 12).
4. Not our works, but only Christ's death can procure our salvation (chapter 9).

In addition to these fundamental doctrines all orthodox Christians hold in common, there are other core truths all parties can or should agree on:

5. Apart from God's grace, no one would even seek to be saved.
6. Our faith is not the source of our salvation; God's grace is.
7. We cannot merit our salvation by doing good works alone; God's grace is necessary.
8. Even the good works we perform after salvation are not performed apart from God's grace.

Of course, there are many more issues on which there are disagreements. But they are not fundamentals of the Faith, and should not be treated as such. Even though we may have strong beliefs about some of these nonessential doctrines, they should not hinder us from fellowshipping and cooperating with those who disagree. Life is too short and eternity is too long to make minors into majors and essentials out of nonessentials so that we cannot fulfill God's commands to edify believers and evangelize unbelievers.

21

The Extent of Salvation

AMONG THE MORE CONTROVERSIAL issues related to the doctrine of the atonement is this question: For whom did Christ die? There are two theological camps regarding this issue. One camp argues that Jesus' death was intended to secure salvation for a limited number of people. This is called the "limited atonement" view because God is said to have limited the effect of Christ's death to a specific number of elect persons. This is also called the "particular redemption" view because advocates of this view believe redemption was provided solely for a particular group of people—that is, the elect. The second camp is called the "unlimited atonement" or "general redemption" view. This camp argues that God did not limit Christ's redemptive death to the elect, but allowed it to be for humankind in general. In this view, Christ's death made the *provision* of salvation for all humanity, but salvation becomes *effective* only for those who exercise faith in Christ. Salvation becomes effective only for God's elect.

The History of the Debate

Limited Atonement

Limited atonement is the view that Christ's atoning death was only for the elect. Reformed theologian Louis Berkhof explains it this way: "The Reformed position is that Christ died for the purpose of actually and certainly saving the elect, and the elect only. This is equivalent to saying that He died for the purpose of saving only those to whom He actually applies the benefits of His redemptive work."[1]

Verses Offered in Support of Limited Atonement

Following are some of the key verses Berkhof and others cite in favor of limited atonement. We've italicized the relevant portions of each verse:

- *Matthew 1:21:* "She will give birth to a son, and you are to give him the name Jesus, because he will save *his people* from their sins."
- *Matthew 20:28:* "The Son of Man did not come to be served, but to serve, and to give His life as a ransom *for many.*"
- *Matthew 26:28:* "This is my blood of the covenant, which is poured out *for many* for the forgiveness of sins."
- *John 10:15:* "I lay down my life *for the sheep.*"
- *Acts 20:28:* "Keep watch over yourselves and all the flock of which the Holy Spirit has made you overseers. Be shepherds of *the church of God, which he bought with his own blood.*"
- *Ephesians 5:25:* "Husbands, love your wives, just as Christ loved *the church* and *gave himself up for her.*"
- *Hebrews 9:28:* "Christ was sacrificed once to take away the sins *of many.*"
- *John 15:13:* "Greater love has no one than this, that he lay down his life *for his friends.*"

Proponents of limited atonement believe the above verses support the idea that Christ died not for all people but for a particular group of people—His "people," the "many," the "church of God," His "sheep," His "friends."

Arguments Offered in Support of Limited Atonement

Proponents of limited atonement, such as late Reformed scholars Louis Berkhof and Charles Hodge, set forth a number of arguments that they believe conclusively prove the truth of the doctrine. Following are eight of the more notable arguments:

1. As Berkhof puts it, "Scripture repeatedly qualifies those for whom Christ laid down His life in such a way as to point to a very definite limitation. Those for whom He suffered and died are variously called His 'sheep,' John 10:11, 15; His 'Church,' Acts 20:28; Eph. 5:25-27; His 'people,' Matt. 1:21; and the 'elect,' Rom. 8:32-35."[2]
2. Because the elect were chosen before the foundation of the world, how could Christ honestly be said to have died for all human beings? Put another way, how could Christ design something that, by virtue of His omniscience, He knew would never come to pass? Hodge clarifies this line of argument by suggesting that "if God from eternity determined to save one portion of the human race and not another, it seems to be a contradiction to say that the plan of salvation had equal reference to both portions."[3]
3. Christ is defeated if He died for all men and not all men are saved.
4. If Christ died for all people, then God would be unfair if He sent people to hell for their own sins. No court of law allows payment to be exacted twice for the same crime, and God would never do that, either. Christ paid for the sins of the elect; the lost pay for their own sins.
5. Because Christ didn't pray for everyone in His high priestly prayer in John 17, but only prayed for His own, Christ must not have died for everyone. Because the intercession is limited in extent, the atonement must be, too.
6. Some proponents of limited atonement charge that unlimited atonement tends toward universalism. Hence, unlimited atonement cannot be the correct view.

7. In the Middle Ages, scholars such as Prosper of Aquitaine, Thomas Bradwardine, and John Staupitz taught limited atonement. Many Calvinists claim that even though John Calvin did not explicitly teach the doctrine,* it is implicit in some of his writings. Calvin's successors, especially Theodore Beza, made limited atonement explicit and included it in Reformed confessions of faith such as the Canons of Dort and the *Westminster Confession of Faith*.
8. Though terms such as "all," "world," and "whosoever" are used in Scripture in reference to those for whom Christ died (for example, John 3:16), these words are to be understood in terms of the elect. "All" refers to "all of the elect" or "all classes of men" (Jew and Gentile).[4] "Whosoever" refers to "whosoever of the elect." "World" refers to the "world of the elect" or to people without distinction (Jews and Gentiles).[5]

Unlimited Atonement

In notable contrast to the doctrine of limited atonement, the doctrine of unlimited atonement says that Christ's redemptive death was for all persons. Christ died not just for the elect, but for the nonelect as well.

Verses Offered in Support of Unlimited Atonement

Following are some of the verses used to support the unlimited atonement view, along with some expositional commentary. Again, we've italicized the relevant words in each verse.

- *Luke 19:10:* "The Son of Man came to seek and to save *what was lost*." It is argued by unlimited atonement proponents that the word "lost" in this verse refers to the collective whole of lost humanity, not just the lost elect. That is the most natural understanding of this verse.

---

* See N.L. Geisler, *Chosen But Free* (Minneapolis, MN: Bethany House, 2001), Appendix 2.

- John 1:29: "The next day John saw Jesus coming toward him and said, 'Look, the Lamb of God who takes away the sin *of the world!*'" Reformer John Calvin says of this verse, "He uses the word *sin* in the singular number for any kind of iniquity; as if he had said that every kind of unrighteousness which alienates men from God is taken away by Christ. And when he says *the sin of the world,* he extends this favor indiscriminately to the whole human race."[6] Though Calvin is often cited in favor of limited atonement, here unlimited atonement is in view.

J. C. Ryle similarly states,

> I hold as strongly as anyone that Christ's death is profitable to none but the elect who believe in His Name. But I dare not limit and pare down such expressions as the one before us....I dare not confine the intention of redemption to the saints alone. Christ is for every man....The atonement was made for all the world, though it is applied and enjoyed by none but believers.[7]

- John 3:16: "God so loved *the world* that he gave his one and only Son, that *whoever* believes in him shall not perish but have eternal life." Advocates of unlimited atonement point out that Greek lexicons are unanimous on the fact that "world" here denotes humankind, not the "world of the elect."

  Further, it is reasoned that John 3:16 cannot be divorced from the context that is set in verses 14 and 15, wherein Christ alludes to Numbers 21. In this passage, Moses is seen setting up the brazen serpent in the camp of Israel so that "everyone" who looked to it experienced physical deliverance. In verse 15 Christ applies the story spiritually when He says that "everyone" who believes on the uplifted Son of Man will experience spiritual deliverance. As John Calvin notes, John "has employed the universal term *whosoever,* both to invite all indiscriminately to partake of life, and to cut off every excuse from unbelievers....He invites all men without exception...to the faith of Christ."[8]

- John 4:42: "They said to the woman, 'Now we believe, not because of what you said, for we ourselves have heard Him and we know that this is indeed the Christ, *the Savior of the world*" (NKJV). It is reasoned that when the Samaritans called Jesus "the Savior of the world," they were not thinking of the world of the elect. To read such a meaning into this text would be sheer eisegesis.

  Likewise, it is argued that when Jesus said, "I am the light of the world" (John 8:12), He was not thinking of Himself as the light of the world of the elect. "The sun in the heavens shines on all men, though some, in their folly, may choose to withdraw into dark caves to evade its illuminating rays."[9]

  First Timothy 2:4-6 declares that God "wants all men to be saved and to come to a knowledge of the truth." It adds immediately that "the man Christ Jesus...gave himself a ransom for *all.*" According to proponents of unlimited atonement, this clearly indicates that Christ provided a ransom for all men and desires for all of them to be saved.

- 1 Timothy 4:10: "We have put our hope in the living God, who is the *Savior of all men, and especially of those who believe.*" It is noted that there is a distinction in this verse between "all men" and "those who believe." Apparently the Savior has done something for all human beings, though it is less in degree than what He has done for those who believe. In other words, it is concluded that Christ has made a provision of salvation for all men, though it becomes effective only for those who exercise faith in Christ.

- Hebrews 2:9: "We see Jesus, who was made a little lower than the angels, now crowned with glory and honor because he suffered death, so that by the grace of God he might taste death *for everyone.*" The Greek word for "everyone" (*pantos*) is better translated "each." The singular brings out more emphatically the applicability of Christ's death to *each individual person.*
- Romans 5:6: "When we were still powerless, Christ died *for the ungodly.*" Advocates of unlimited atonement believe that it doesn't make much sense to read this verse as saying that Christ died for the ungodly among the elect. Rather, the verse plainly indicates that Christ died for the ungodly of all the earth.
- Romans 5:18: "As through one man's offense judgment came to *all men,* resulting in condemnation, even so through one Man's righteous act the free gift came to *all men,* resulting in justification of life" (NKJV). Those who affirm unlimited atonement believe that impartial exegesis demands that the phrase "all men" must have the *same extent* in both clauses. In other words, just as *all men* on the earth were brought to a state of condemnation through one sin (Adam's), so salvation was made available for *all men* by Christ's death on the cross—though the reception of this salvation depends upon exercising faith in Jesus.
- 2 Corinthians 5:14-15: "The love of Christ compels us, because we judge thus: that if One died for *all,* then all died; and He died for *all,* that those who live should no longer live for themselves" (NKJV). So, according to the unlimited atonement view, the "all" refers to all mankind since in the same context the "all [that] died" are all mankind.
- 2 Corinthians 5:19: "God was reconciling *the world* to himself in Christ, counting men's sins against them." If

so, then it is argued that Christ's work on the cross was not just for the elect but for the whole world.

- 1 John 2:2: "He is the atoning sacrifice for our sins, and not only for ours but also for the sins of *the whole world*." Here too, it is reasoned that a natural reading of this verse supports unlimited atonement. It would not make sense to interpret it as saying, "He is the atoning sacrifice for our [the elect] sins, and not only for ours [the elect] but also for the sins of the whole world [of the elect]."
- Isaiah 53:6: "*All we* like sheep have gone astray; we have turned, *every one*, to his own way; and the LORD has laid on Him the iniquity of *us all*" (NKJV). According to proponents of unlimited atonement, this verse does not make sense unless it is read to say that the same "all" that went astray is the "all" for whom the Lord died.
- 2 Peter 2:1: "There were also false prophets among the people, just as there will be false teachers among you. They will secretly introduce destructive heresies, *even denying the sovereign Lord who bought them*—bringing swift destruction on themselves." The argument here is that Christ's salvation is *provided* for all (even false teachers), though not all will accept it.
- John 3:17: "God did not send his Son into the world to condemn *the world*, but to save *the world* through him." Commenting on this verse, Calvin said that "the word *world* is again repeated, that no man may think himself wholly excluded, if he only keeps the road of faith."[10] Unlimited atonement advocates conclude here that God has made the provision of salvation available to all human beings.

The Universal Proclamation of the Gospel

In keeping with the above verses, there are also many verses that are used to indicate that the gospel is to be universally proclaimed to all human beings (Matthew 24:14; 28:19; Acts 1:8; 17:30; Titus 2:11; 2 Peter 3:9). In view of such verses, those who embrace unlimited atonement ask: If Christ died only for the elect, how can an offer of salvation be made to all persons without some sort of insincerity, artificiality, or dishonesty being involved in the process? Is it not improper to offer salvation to everyone if, in fact, Christ did not die to save everyone? As Norman Douty put it, "How can God authorize His servants to offer pardon to the non-elect if Christ did not purchase it for them? This is a problem that does not plague those who hold to General (Unlimited) Redemption, for it is most reasonable to proclaim the Gospel to all if Christ died for all."[11]

Putting the Limited and Unlimited Verses Together

Proponents of unlimited atonement believe that seemingly restrictive references can be logically fit into an unlimited scenario much more easily than universal references can be made to fit into a limited atonement scenario. Lewis Sperry Chafer explained it this way:

> To the unlimited redemptionist the limited redemption passages present no real difficulty. He believes that they merely emphasize one aspect of a larger truth. Christ did die for the elect, but He also died for the sins of the whole world. However, the limited redemptionist is not able to deal with the unlimited redemption passages as easily.[12]

Thus, it is reasoned that the two sets of passages are not irreconcilable from an unlimited atonement perspective. While it is true that the benefits of Christ's death are referred to as belonging to God's "sheep," His "people," and the like, it would have to be shown that Christ died *only* for them in order for limited atonement to be true. Unlimited atonement proponents do not deny that Christ died for God's "sheep" and His "people." It is only denied that Christ died *exclusively* for them. Certainly if Christ died for the whole of humanity, there is no logical problem in saying that He died for a specific part of the whole—such as when the apostle Paul declared that Christ "loved me and gave himself for me" (Galatians 2:20).

Of course, the limited atonement proponents point out that the unlimited texts can be explained in the light of limited atonement. They point out that Christ's death was sufficient for all, but efficient only for the elect. Limited atonement advocates support their view by reference to the "many" versus the "all" passages. In Matthew 26:28 Jesus said, "This is my blood of the covenant, which is poured out *for many* for the forgiveness of sins." However, the reference to "many" in Christ's words do not support limited atonement, but rather, unlimited atonement. Unlimited redemptionists point out that earlier in Matthew's Gospel, Jesus had said that *few* find eternal life (Matthew 7:14) and *few* are chosen (22:14). But Christ did not say His blood was poured out for a *few*, but for *many*. John Calvin thus declares, "By the word *many* He means not a part of the world only, but the whole human race."[13]

Unlimited redemptionists note this same meaning appears in Romans 5:15: "If by the one man's offense *many* died, much more the grace of God and the gift by the grace of the one Man, Jesus Christ, abounded to *many*" (NKJV). The "many" in the second clause of the verse is coextensive with the "many" in the first clause. It is pointed out that the "many" of verse 15 is defined in verse 18 as *all men:* "Just as the result of one trespass was condemnation for *all men*, so also the result of one act of righteousness was justification that brings life for *all men*."

Responding to Four Common Objections to Unlimited Atonement

There are four objections often raised in opposition to the doctrine of unlimited atonement. Proponents of unlimited atonement respond as follows:

Objection #1: If Christ died for those who go to hell, what benefit have they from His death?

Answer: In response it could be asked, What good did the bitten Israelites obtain from the brazen serpent to which they refused to look (Numbers 21:8–9)? None, of course, but nevertheless, God in His omnibenevolence received the glory for being generous in making provision for them.

Objection #2: If satisfaction has been made for all, how can any go to hell?

Answer: Unlimited proponents respond by noting that God has *provided* atonement for all, but He has stipulated that this atonement becomes *effective* only for those who exercise faith in Jesus Christ. Deliverance from doom depends not on the atonement alone, but on the reception of it. It is a fact that human beings can starve in the presence of a free feast if they refuse to partake of it.

Objection #3: Why would God have Christ die for those whom He, in His omniscience, knew would never receive His provision?

Answer: Opponents ask a similar question in regard to numerous other events in Scripture. For example, Why did God send Noah to preach to his contemporaries if He knew they would not listen (2 Peter 2:5)? Why did God send the prophets to preach to the rebellious Israelites, knowing that on many of those occasions they would refuse to listen? The fact is, God made a provision for all people because He is benevolent and seeks their highest good.

Objection #4: Doesn't unlimited atonement lead to universalism?

Answer: Unlimited atonement proponents claim their perspective does not lead to universalism. One can distinguish between the *provisional* benefits of Christ's death and the *appropriation* of those benefits by the elect. Although the provision of atonement is unlimited, the application of it is limited. In his book *The Death Christ Died,* Robert Lightner rightly explains that

> the cross does not apply its own benefits but that God has conditioned His full and free salvation upon personal faith in order to appropriate its accomplishments to the individual. This faith which men must exercise is not a work whereby man contributes his part to his salvation, nor does faith...improve in any way the final and complete sacrifice of Calvary. It is simply the method of applying Calvary's benefits which the sovereign God has deigned to use in His all-wise plan of salvation.[14]

Unlimited atonement proponents hold that God is not unfair in condemning those who reject the offer of salvation. *He is not exacting judgment twice*. Because the nonbeliever refuses to accept the death of Christ as his own, the benefits of Christ's death are not applied to him. He is lost not because Christ did not die for him, but because he refuses God's offer of forgiveness.

A Survey of Church History

Proponents of unlimited atonement appeal to the fact that the vast majority of theologians, Reformers, evangelists, and church fathers from the beginning of the church until the present day have supported their view. Following is a representative sampling:

- Clement of Alexandria (A.D. 150–220) said that "Christ freely brings...salvation to the whole human race."[15]
- Eusebius (A.D. 260–340) said that "it was needful that the Lamb of God should be offered for the other lambs whose nature He assumed, even for the whole human race."[16]
- Athanasius (A.D. 293–373) said that "Christ the Son of God, having assumed a body like ours, because we were all exposed to death, gave Himself up to death for us all as a sacrifice to His Father."[17]
- Cyril of Jerusalem (A.D. 315–386) said, "Do not wonder if the whole world was ransomed, for He was not a mere man, but the only-begotten Son of God."[18]
- Gregory of Nazianzen (A.D. 324–389) said "the sacrifice of Christ is an imperishable expiation of the whole world."[19]
- Basil (A.D. 330–379) said that "the holy and precious blood of our Lord Jesus Christ" was "poured out for us all."[20]
- Ambrose (A.D. 340–407) said that "Christ suffered for all, rose again for all. But if anyone does not believe in Christ, he deprives himself of that general benefit."[21]
- Not unlike John Calvin (discussed earlier), Martin

Luther (A.D. 1483–1546) said that "Christ hath taken away the sins, not of certain men only, but also of thee, yea, of the whole world."[22]

- Philip Melanchthon (A.D. 1497–1560) said, "It is necessary to know that the Gospel is a universal promise, that is, that reconciliation is offered and promised to all mankind. It is necessary to hold that this promise is universal, in opposition to any dangerous imaginations on predestination, lest we should reason this promise pertains to a few others and ourselves. But we declare that the promise of the Gospel is universal."[23]

Limited atonement proponents respond by noting that truth is not determined by majority vote. Further, since the time of late Augustine and especially since the Reformation, the strong Calvinist's position of limited atonement has grown considerably. As noted above, both the Synod of Dort and the *Westminster Confession of Faith* advocate the strong Calvinist view.

It is important to note that there is a common core of belief between both sides of this debate. First, both believe that Christ did die for all who will believe. Second, both sides believe Christ's salvation was sufficient for all mankind. Third, both believe that the benefits of Christ's death will be applied only to the elect. Fourth, both sides of the debate believe it is our obligation to preach the gospel to all men. Finally, both sides hold that not everyone will be saved, but only the elect. And while the authors favor the unlimited view, we recognize that this point is not one of the historic fundamentals of the Faith over which Christians should cease fellowship. Nor should anyone condemn the opposing view as a heresy.

A Related Debate: Divine Sovereignty versus Human Freedom

A kindred issue we need to address briefly pertains to divine sovereignty versus human freedom as related to the salvation of the elect. Foundationally, Scripture portrays God as being absolutely sovereign over all things, including the salvation of the saints and the condemnation of unrepentant sinners. All forms of existence are within the scope of God's absolute dominion. Psalm 50:1 makes reference to God as the Mighty One who "speaks and summons the earth from the rising of the sun to the place where it sets." Psalm 66:7 affirms that "he rules forever by his power." We are assured in Psalm 93:1 that "the LORD reigns" and He "is armed with strength."

God asserts, "My purpose will stand, and I will do all that I please" (Isaiah 46:10). God assures us, "Surely, as I have planned, so it will be, and as I have purposed, so it will stand" (Isaiah 14:24). Proverbs 16:9 tells us, "A man's heart plans his way, but the LORD directs his steps" (NKJV). Proverbs 19:21 says, "There are many plans in a man's heart, nevertheless the LORD's counsel—that will stand" (NKJV). Proverbs 21:1 asserts: "The king's heart is in the hand of the LORD, like the rivers of water; He turns it wherever He wishes" (NKJV). God is the One "who works out everything in conformity with the purpose of his will" (Ephesians 1:11). In short, God's providence controls every particular of the universe.

Scripture is equally clear regarding the fact of human freedom. Human beings are viewed as being responsible for their moral choices as well as their eternal destiny. For example, God commanded Adam and Eve not to eat the forbidden fruit (Genesis 2:16-17), and after they disobeyed, God asked them: "What is this *you have done?*" (Genesis 3:13, emphasis added). Adam acknowledged his personal responsibility in wrongly using his free will by saying, "I ate it [the forbidden fruit]" (verse 12), after which God pronounced judgment: "Because you listened to your wife and ate from the tree...cursed is the ground" (verse 17).

Human responsibility regarding choices is evident throughout the Bible. Joshua exhorted Israel, "Choose for yourselves this day whom you will serve" (Joshua 24:15). Elijah prodded Israel, "How long will you waver between two opinions?" (1 Kings 18:21). Jesus said to some Jews, "O Jerusalem, Jerusalem, you who kill the prophets and stone those sent to you, how often I longed to gather your children together, as a hen gathers her chicks under her wings, but *you were not willing*" (Matthew 23:37, emphasis added). Second Peter 3:5 tells us that some people deliberately and willfully ignore what God says. Romans 6:16 tells us that humans can *choose* to be slaves to sin or to righteousness.

Some verses mention both divine sovereignty *and* human responsibility. For example, in Acts 2:23 (NKJV) we read regarding Jesus' death that He was "delivered by the determined purpose and foreknowledge of God" (divine sovereignty) while at the same time was the One whom the Jews had "taken by lawless hands, have crucified, and put to death" (human responsibility). In John 6:37 we read, "All that the Father *gives Me* will come to Me, and *the one who comes to Me* I will by no means cast out" (NKJV, emphasis added). We see the same in Acts 13:48: "All who were *appointed* for eternal life *believed*" (emphasis added). There are other verses as well (for example, Genesis 45:8 with 50:20; Luke 22:22; Acts 4:27-28; 1 Peter 2:8).

The problem, of course, is this: How do we reconcile divine sovereignty and human freedom? Below we summarize three theological views that have been suggested:[24]

1. Extreme Calvinism: Predetermination Is in Spite of *Foreknowledge*

According to extreme Calvinism, God operates with such unapproachable sovereignty that His choices are made with no consideration of the choices made by human beings. God sovereignly saves whomever He wishes to save. God even sovereignly gives the faith to believe to those whom He is saving. Without this act on God's part, human beings could not and would not believe. Because human beings are so dead in sin, they are unable to believe, and hence they must be regenerated by God before they can believe. The moment of conversion is totally a result of God's operation, without any cooperation on the human side. Regeneration is thus said to be a *monergistic* act (meaning "His work alone"). God's irresistible grace—grace that is irresistible even on the unwilling—plays a key role in this view.

The big problem with extreme Calvinism is that it denies free choice on the part of human beings. Scripture indicates that God is love (1 John 4:16), but love is *persuasive,* not *coercive.* True love does not force itself on others. Further, God is portrayed in Scripture as being *all*-loving (John 3:16). But how can God be all-loving if He demonstrates that love only *to some* (the elect), desiring *only them* to be saved?

2. *Arminianism: God's Predetermination Is* Based on *His Foreknowledge*

According to Arminianism, God, in His omniscience (all-knowingness), knows in advance what choices every human being will make, including whether they will accept or reject salvation. On the basis of this foreknowledge, God elects to salvation those whom He knows in advance will, by their free choice, accept Christ. In this system of thought, then, human beings are completely free to accept or reject God, and are under no coercion from Him. Yet because He is all-knowing, He is also sovereign over the universe. This sovereign control is based not on coercion of events but on God's foreknowledge of what free agents will do under whatever persuasive means He may employ.

In addition to the fact that the Bible never says God's election is *based on* His foreknowledge, the big problem with Arminianism is that the Bible doesn't just indicate that God knows things in advance; it says He actually *determines* what will happen (Proverbs 16:9; 19:21; 21:1; Isaiah 14:24; 46:10; Philippians 1:6; 2:13). That God is sovereign involves more than just having foreknowledge—it means God has *absolute control* of all that happens in the universe. Further, if God's choice to save is based merely on the free-will decisions of those who accept Him, then salvation would not be based on divine grace, but on human decisions—an idea that flies in the face of numerous Scriptures (for example, John 1:13; Romans 9:16; 11:6; Ephesians 2:8-9; Titus 3:5-7).

3. *Moderate Calvinism: God's Predetermination Is* in Accord with *His Foreknowledge*

According to this view (held by the authors), God's election is based neither on His foreknowledge of man's free choices (Arminianism) nor in spite of God's foreknowledge (extreme Calvinism), but rather is "*according to* the foreknowledge of God" (1 Peter 1:2, emphasis added). In this view, there is no chronological or logical priority of election and foreknowledge. All aspects of God's eternal purpose are equally timeless. Both foreknowledge and predetermination are *one* in God's indivisible essence. Both must be simultaneous, eternal, and coordinate acts of God. Whatever He knows, He determines. Whatever He determines, He knows.

We thus might speak of God as *knowingly determining* and *determinately knowing* from all eternity everything that happens, including the free acts of human beings. In this view, then, God is completely sovereign in the sense of actually determining what occurs, and yet human beings are completely free and responsible for what they do.

The debate between these respective schools of thought remains intense. It is crucial to keep in mind, however, that one's view on this matter—while important—is not an essential of the Faith.

The Dangers of Extreme Views

As with other nonessential doctrines, there are dangers rooted in extreme views related to the extent of the atonement. One such problem relates specifically to limited atonement. According to this view, when doing the work of evangelism, a Christian could not say to a potential convert, "Christ loves *you* and died *for your* sins." After all, this prospect may be one of the nonelect. Reformed counselor Jay Adams is forthright in saying, "As a reformed Christian, the writer believes that counselors must not tell any unsaved counselee that Christ died for him, for they cannot say that. No man knows except Christ himself who are his elect for whom he died."[25] Berkhof candidly admits, "It need not be denied that there is a real difficulty at this point."[26]

Another danger related to limited atonement is that this doctrine could very possibly undermine one's trust in the love of God. After all, according to this view, God ultimately loves *only* the elect. Consequently, any diminution of God's love in any one area (such as the doctrine of election) may eventually corrode one's overall confidence in God's love.

There are also a number of dangers rooted in extreme views related to divine sovereignty versus human freedom. An example rooted in extreme Calvinism's view of unconditional election involves a lack of any real role on man's part. Even the faith that the elect must exercise (John 3:16; Acts 16:31; Romans 5:1) is an unconditional gift to the elect. In this view, then, the condition of faith turns out to be no condition at all, because God sovereignly brings it all about. Critics of this view have noted that there are many verses that contradict monergism (for example, Matthew 23:37; Acts 7:51; 2 Peter 3:9).

A related problem is that extreme Calvinism seems to minimize personal responsibility for the actions of human beings. After all, if we do something bad, it is only because we are so dead in sin that we are unable to do good. If we do something good, it is only because God has sovereignly caused that good in our life.

There are problems with the Arminian position as well. Perhaps the greatest problem is that it ultimately sacrifices God's sovereignty on the altar of man's free choice. If trust in God's sovereignty is undermined, then trust in God's control of the universe wanes as well. It is hard to feel secure in a universe in which God is not completely sovereign. It also overlooks the fact that salvation is unconditional (Romans 11:29; 2 Timothy 2:13), not conditional. It is not dependent on our faithfulness but on God's.

Areas of Agreement

The issues addressed in this chapter have led to some of the most heated and even vitriolic debates among Christians. It is good to remind ourselves that there is some general agreement in the midst of our diversity on these issues:

1. Each side of the "extent of the atonement" debate can agree that the opposing view has at least some scriptural support. (The difficulty is in reconciling seemingly limited and unlimited verses.)
2. Human beings are fallen in sin and are in need of salvation.
3. God is sovereign.
4. God has elected a people unto salvation for all eternity.
5. Jesus atoned for our sins at the cross.
6. Faith is a necessary component in salvation.
7. The benefits of Christ's atonement will certainly be applied to the elect.
8. Not everyone will be saved—only the elect.

9. The saved (the elect) will spend eternity in heaven, while the unsaved (the nonelect) will spend eternity in hell.

Granted, the different schools of thought may interpret the above points in different ways, but at least there are some generalized commonalities. Because life is very short and eternity is very long, we ought to make every effort to show liberty to our brothers and sisters on these nonessential issues during our brief time on Earth. Let us agree to disagree in an agreeable way—such behavior is befitting of the elect.

22

The Candidate, Mode, and Efficacy of Baptism

THROUGH THE CENTURIES, the Christian church has been divided over these questions about baptism: Is water baptism for today? Who should be baptized? How should they be baptized? Is baptism necessary for salvation?

Many insist that children should be baptized. Others contend that only those old enough to believe should be baptized. Further, in both camps there is division over how or by what mode one should be baptized—sprinkling, pouring, or immersion. There is also a strong difference of opinion over the efficacy of baptism. Many believe it is necessary for salvation, while many others believe it is not. Large sections of Christendom believe baptism is the instrument of salvation (regeneration). On the other end of the spectrum are those who deny that water baptism should be practiced at all. Still further, while most baptize in the name of the Father, the Son, and the Holy Spirit (Matthew 28:19), others baptize in the name of Jesus only (Acts 2:38). Let's consider the details.

The Areas of Disagreement

As noted, Christians disagree on several areas about baptism: 1) the candidate, 2) the mode, 3) the efficacy, and 4) the necessity. Sad to say, there are groups that have taken these minor points and made major issues out of them—even to the point of using them as a test for faith.

Disagreement over the Need to Baptize—E. W. Bullinger

Some Christians deny the need to baptize altogether. In the broad spectrum of Christendom, this group is almost infinitesimal, but it does illustrate the primary point of Part Two of this book—namely, that we should not make theological mountains over practical molehills. Several groups do not practice water baptism.

E. W. Bullinger (1837–1913), a noted Greek scholar of the late nineteenth century, was the father of the ultradispensational movement, which placed the origin of the Christian church *after* Acts 28, contending that the earliest believers were a Jewish church (in an earlier dispensation) in which baptism and the Lord's Supper were practiced. All references to water baptism or the Lord's Supper during those early years, prior to Acts 28, allegedly do not apply to our present dispensation. The true church—the mystery body of Christ (Ephesians 3:3-5)—allegedly did not appear until Paul's prison epistles (such as Ephesians and Colossians), which Bullinger contends have no reference to water baptism or communion.[1] Bullinger's argumentation is weak. For example, the point that there are no references to water baptism in any epistle written after the time of Acts 28 is an argument from silence. *Omission* does not mean *exclusion*. Just because an ordinance is not mentioned in some books does not mean it was not in effect. Even the resurrection of Christ is not mentioned in some books (for example, James, Philemon, 2 John, 3 John, and Jude), but this does not mean that the author of those books did not believe the event took place.

Moreover, many argue that the apostle Paul refers to water baptism in Colossians 2:12. There, Paul refers to baptism as burial with Christ, which depicts immersion, a mode of water baptism mentioned in the New Testament (compare with Matthew 3:16-17 and Romans 6:1-4). Likewise, in Ephesians 4:5, Paul refers to "one baptism" after he has *already* spoken of "one body and one Spirit" (which would be Spirit baptism) *and* after the confession of "one Lord, one faith" (mention of these items in this order would be the logical sequence for water baptism to be referred to last).

Further, Bullinger's argument collapses if it can be shown that the church as the "body" of Christ occurs earlier than Acts 28, and some indeed believe there is good evidence that it existed earlier. They point out:

1. The church as Christ's body resulted from the baptism of the Holy Spirit (1 Corinthians 12:13). This baptism of the Holy Spirit first occurred only "days" after Jesus' ascension (Acts 1:5), which was the day of Pentecost (Acts 2:1-4).

2. In Acts 9, Jesus told Saul that he was persecuting His body when He said: "Saul, Saul, why do you persecute me?" (verse 4). Paul later conceded, "I am the least of the apostles and do not even deserve to be called an apostle, because *I persecuted the church of God*" (1 Corinthians 15:9, emphasis added).

Finally, ultradispensationalism misses the point of Acts 10, where Peter was called to witness to Gentiles, who were baptized into the body of Christ. Also, in Acts 15, the apostles—who are part of the foundation of the church (Ephesians 2:20)—issued a declaration that Gentiles were fellow heirs of the gospel along with the Jews, and this is precisely what the "mystery" of the body of Christ is (see Ephesians 3:6 and Colossians 1:27). The mystery of the body of Christ, then, clearly existed at least as early as Acts 10, which Peter clearly relates to what happened on the day of Pentecost in Acts 2 (compare with Acts 11:15).

Disagreement over the Need to Baptize—The Berean Church

This view, expressed today by Cornelius Stam, Charles Barker,[2] and the Berean [Grace] movement, claims that the Christian church began sometime between Acts 9 and 13. They say that because there is no reference to water baptism after this time frame, water baptism does not apply to us today.

Critics point out that this view suffers from many of the same problems as found in the Bullingerite view described above.[3] First, this view involves a fallacious argument from silence. Second, it makes *distinctions* (related to the alleged earlier and later church) without real *differences*. For example, the ministry of circumcision (Peter's ministry to Jews) and the ministry of uncircumcision (Paul's ministry to Gentiles) involve different *audiences* but not different *gospels*. Third, even granting that the mystery of the church was not *revealed* to anyone before Paul, it does not mean the church did not *exist* before Paul spoke about it. Fourth, Scripture indicates that the Church existed from the time the Holy Spirit baptized people into the body of Christ (1 Corinthians 12:13), and this first occurred on the Day of Pentecost (Acts 1:5; 2:1-4,42-47). Following this time, the *same* church continued to grow whenever another person was baptized into the body of Christ. Fifth, Christian water baptism took place *after* Acts 9–13, when the Bereans say the New Testament church began. In Acts 19, for example, converts who had already undergone an earlier Jewish baptism were rebaptized in Christ's name. Sixth, Jesus commanded that we "make disciples of all nations, baptizing them" (Matthew 28:19). He would remain with us in this work "to the very end of the age" (verse 20), and not just the first century. Finally, we note that this view is not very significant either numerically or theologically in the broad sweep of Christendom.

Disagreement over the Mode of Baptism

The mode of baptism is a more hotly disputed issue throughout the Christian church. Congregationalists, Baptists, and others springing from the Anabaptist tradition insist on baptism by immersion. Others, such as Roman Catholics, Anglicans, Lutherans, Presbyterians, and Methodists, baptize by sprinkling or pouring. Let's consider the arguments on both sides.

The Arguments for Pouring or Sprinkling

Many arguments have been offered for the pouring or sprinkling of water as an appropriate mode of baptism. The following are noteworthy:

Baptism Is Symbolized by Pouring. Jesus said, "John baptized with water, but...you will be baptized with the Holy Spirit" (Acts 1:5). But when this was fulfilled, we read that the Holy Spirit descended on their heads (Acts 2:3), and Peter said this was a fulfillment of what Joel said: "I will *pour out* of my Spirit on all people" (Acts 2:17, emphasis added). Hence, baptism by pouring best symbolizes this truth.

Salvation Is Symbolized by Sprinkling. Sprinkling was a common figure of speech in reference to salvation both in the Old Covenant (Exodus 29:20; Ezekiel 36:25) and the New (Hebrews 9:13; 11:28; 1 Peter 1:2), which fulfilled the Old. Hebrews makes reference to "Jesus the mediator of the new covenant" and to "the *sprinkled* blood that speaks a better word than the blood of Abel" (Hebrews 12:24, emphasis added). Because baptism is a symbol of salvation, and salvation is described as sprinkling, then sprinkling with water is an appropriate symbol of salvation.

Isaiah Speaks of Sprinkling Many Nations. The prophet Isaiah said of the Messiah, "So will he *sprinkle* many nations, and kings will shut their mouths because of him. For what they were not told, they will see, and what they have not heard, they will understand" (Isaiah 52:15, emphasis added). This is the very passage the Ethiopian was reading when he was saved and said, "Look, here is water. Why shouldn't I be baptized?" (Acts 8:36). It is possible that this would have been prompted by Isaiah's reference that the Messiah will "sprinkle many nations." Hence, his baptism by sprinkling would follow naturally from the context.

The Arguments for Baptism by Immersion

Those who favor immersion as the proper mode of baptism also offer many arguments from Scripture. The following is a summary:

Jesus Was Baptized by Immersion. We read that "as soon as Jesus was baptized [in the Jordan River], he went up out of the water" (Matthew 3:16, insert added). To be *in* the river and *come up out of* the water speaks of having been *immersed* in it. Why a river, if a cup of water would do? Why wade into a river and come up out of the midst of it, if all that happened was that a handful of water was poured on His head?

John Was Baptizing Where There Was Much Water. The Bible says, "John also was baptizing in Aenon near Salim, because there was *much water* there. And they came and were baptized" (John 3:23 NKJV, emphasis added). Why go to a place with a lot of water if only a handful would do? The description here fits better with immersion as the mode of baptism.

The Eunuch's Baptism Was by Immersion. The book of Acts speaks of Philip and the Ethiopian eunuch: "As they traveled along the road, they *came to some water* and the eunuch said, 'Look, *here is water.* Why shouldn't I be baptized?'...both Philip and the eunuch went *down into the water* and Philip baptized him" (Acts 8:36-38, emphasis added). They then "came up out of the water" (verse 39). It is not difficult to see that going *down into* the water and *coming up out* of it involves an act of immersion.

Baptism Is Depicted as Burial. The New Testament describes baptism as "burial" and "resurrection" (Romans 6:4; Colossians 2:12). Burial and resurrection involve going down into a grave and then coming up out of it, which is precisely what immersion depicts. Paul wrote,

> Do you not know that as many of us as were baptized into Christ Jesus were *baptized into His death?* Therefore we were *buried with Him through baptism* into death, that just *as Christ was raised from the dead* by the glory of the Father, even so we also should walk in newness of life. For if we have been *united together in the likeness of His death,* certainly we also shall be *in the likeness of His resurrection"* (Romans 6:3-5 NKJV, emphasis added).

Thus, baptism by immersion is a perfect picture of what Christ did for us, which is the heart of the gospel (1 Corinthians 15:1-8).

Early Church Baptismal Tanks Support Immersion. There is evidence that the very early church practiced immersion; archaeologists have unearthed some baptismal tanks. Some churches with the earliest roots in church history still baptize by immersion, such as the Eastern Orthodox Church. Even as late as the Reformation, Martin Luther prescribed baptism by immersion.

Disagreement over the Candidate for Baptism

There are also differences over the candidate for baptism. Baptist and other baptistic groups insist on believers' baptism only, whereas the Eastern Orthodox, Anglicans, Lutherans, Presbyterians, Methodists, and some others baptize infants. The debate over who can or should be baptized falls into two basic categories. Pedobaptists (literally, child-baptizers) argue that infants should be baptized. Anabaptists (literally, rebaptizers) argue that a person should not be baptized until after he or she becomes a believer. For this reason, their practice is to rebaptize those who were baptized in infancy.

Reasons Offered for Baptizing Infants

There are several arguments offered for baptizing infants. Among them, the following are the most significant:

Baptism Is Like Old Testament Circumcision, Which Was Performed on Infants. Proponents of this view appeal to verses such as Colossians 2:11-12: "In Him you were also circumcised with the circumcision made without hands, by putting off the body of the sins of the flesh, by the circumcision of Christ, buried with Him in baptism, in which you also were raised with Him through faith in the working of God, who raised Him from the dead" (NKJV). It is reasoned that if circumcision (the sign of the Old Covenant) was done on children, then there is no reason to prohibit baptism (the sign of the New Covenant) being performed on children as well.

Many Household Baptisms Are Mentioned in the New Testament. Four times in the New Testament we read of whole households being baptized (Acts 16:15,33; 18:8; 1 Corinthians 1:16). Because whole families usually include infants or small children, it is reasonable to conclude that infant baptisms may have taken place in these instances.

Baptism Is Essential to Salvation, Including the Salvation of Little Children. The mainline families of Christianity, East and West, believe in baptismal regeneration—that is, baptism is the means of regeneration (or salvation) (John 3:5; Acts 2:38; 22:16; Titus 3:5-7). Because Jesus said little children will be in heaven (Matthew 18:3; Mark 10:14), baptism must therefore be for little children as well.

Reasons Given for Not Baptizing Infants

In response, Baptists argue that infant baptism is an unbiblical practice:

Household Baptisms Did Not Necessarily Include Children. Nowhere does the text of Scripture say that any infants were baptized when household baptisms took place. This is a supposition. Second, it is argued that there is evidence in every case that there were no infants. In the Philippian jailer's case, for example, everyone who was baptized had previously believed: "He rejoiced, *having believed* in God *with all his household*" (Acts 16:34 NKJV, emphasis added). Further, members of the household of Crispus were apparently all older because Crispus "and his entire household *believed in the Lord*" (Acts 18:8, emphasis added). Finally, when Paul said he baptized the "household of Stephanas" (1 Corinthians 1:16), it is clear that there were no infants present, for we later read "that the household of Stephanas were the *first converts in Achaia,* and they have *devoted themselves to the service of the saints*" (1 Corinthians 16:15, emphasis added). Infants are obviously not old enough to serve. Finally, in Lydia's case, she was clearly a woman of means and had her own household. Because no husband is mentioned and because she was a virtuous woman, she would have had no children. Being a woman of commerce (Acts 16:14), she undoubtedly had servants, which would constitute her "household" members who were also baptized.

Opponents of infant baptism also point out that every instance of baptism in the New Testament involved an adult. This is especially important, given that there are many baptisms mentioned in the New Testament (for example, Matthew 3; John 3; Acts 2; 8; 10; 19). Moreover, there are no cases of Jesus or His disciples ever baptizing an infant. Baptists argue that given Jesus' love and compassion for little children (Matthew 18:1-6), surely there would be a command to engage in infant baptism if it were intended to be a normative practice. But there is no such command. Nor is there an example of such a baptism taking place.

Belief Is a Condition for Being Baptized, and Infants Cannot Believe. Perhaps the most fundamental reason given by anti-pedobaptists for not baptizing infants is that infants are not old enough to believe, and belief in Christ is a condition for being saved.[4] Repeatedly the New Testament affirms the essence of what Paul declared: "*Believe* in the Lord Jesus, and you will be saved—you and your household" (Acts 16:31). Jesus said, "Whoever *believes* in him is not condemned, but whoever does not *believe* stands condemned already because he has not *believed* in the name of God's one and only Son" (John 3:18, emphasis added; see also 3:36; 20:31; Romans 10:9). Infants are not old enough to make a conscious decision to believe. Therefore, baptism should be reserved for those who are old enough to believe.

Baptism Is an Outward Symbol of an Inner Reality. Baptists also argue that baptism is a symbolic representation of salvation. It is an outward sign of what happens inwardly when a person becomes saved. As Paul put it,

> Do you not know that as many of us as were baptized into Christ Jesus were baptized into His death? *Therefore we were buried with Him through baptism into death, that just as Christ was raised from the dead by the glory of the Father, even so we also should walk in newness of life.* For if we have been united together in the likeness of His death, certainly we also shall be in the likeness of His resurrection, knowing this, that our old man was crucified with Him, that the body of sin might be done away with, that we should no longer be slaves of sin (Romans 6:3-6 NKJV, emphasis added).

It is reasoned that we cannot outwardly symbolize what we have not inwardly experienced. Hence, baptism should *follow* salvation, not *precede* it. To do otherwise is to put the cart before the horse. Baptists argue that just as we do not put on a wedding ring until after we have made a commitment to marriage, even so, we should not baptize a person until that person believes.

Circumcision Is Not Analogous to Baptism. Baptists insist that New Testament baptism is not the equivalent of Old Testament circumcision. They point out that only males were circumcised in the Old Testament, but proponents of infant baptism insist on baptizing girls, too. So, not only do proponents of infant baptism have a weak argument from analogy, but an inconsistent one at that. Further, baptism is never said to be a sign of the New Covenant. Rather, communion is the sign of the New Covenant (1 Corinthians 11:25).

Arguments from the Practice of the Church Are Inadequate. In response to the proponents of infant baptism claiming that large portions of Christendom practice infant baptism, Baptists say that this is not a sound ground for teaching it. They go on to say that Christian practice should be based on the Bible, which is the only infallible written source of Christian teaching. Many false doctrines, even heresies, appeared early in the church, even in New Testament times (1 Timothy 4:1-5; 1 John 4:1-6). Simply because a teaching appeared does not make it true.

As for the argument that infant baptism is necessary for salvation, that leads us to the next area of disagreement.

The Disagreement over the Efficacy of Baptism

This is by far the most important debate within the Christian church on baptism. There are two basic views: 1) Baptism is necessary for salvation; and 2) baptism, though important, is not necessary for salvation.

The view that baptism is necessary for salvation breaks into two categories: a) Some believe that baptism is the instrument by which God actually saves (or regenerates) the individual; and b) some, like those in the Church of Christ, do not believe water is the instrument through which God regenerates, but nevertheless water baptism is a necessary command to obey in order to be saved—along with the commands to repent, believe, and confess Christ. The first view is held by Roman Catholics, the Eastern Orthodox, Anglicans, and Lutherans. It is a sacramental view, insisting that God has ordained water baptism as a means of grace—a means by which one receives the grace of initial salvation (regeneration). The other view, that of the Christian Church and Church of Christ, is nonsacramental, denying any efficacy in baptism itself as a means of God's grace.

Arguments in Favor of Baptism Being Necessary for Salvation. While various families of denominations have differing views on sacramentalism, many of the arguments for the necessity of baptism are the same. These include the following:

1. Baptism is a command (Matthew 28:18-20; Acts 2:38), and it is necessary to obey God's commands to be saved (John 14:15; 1 John 2:4).
2. Peter commanded baptism as a condition of receiving the Holy Spirit (Acts 2:38).
3. Peter later said that "baptism" by water "saves you" (1 Peter 3:21).
4. Paul was told to "get up, be baptized and wash your sins away, calling on his name" (Acts 22:16).
5. Jesus said, "No one can enter the kingdom of God unless he is born of water [interpreted as baptism] and the Spirit" (John 3:5, insert added).

Arguments Against Baptism Being Necessary for Salvation. Those who oppose baptismal regeneration argue that:

1. *Faith alone* is portrayed as the single condition of salvation many times throughout the New Testament (for example, John 3:16,18,36; Acts 16:31).
2. There is a clear example in Scripture of an individual receiving the Holy Spirit *before* he was baptized, indicating he was saved prior to baptism (Acts 10:47).
3. Paul affirmed that the gospel was the means of salvation (Romans 1:16), and that baptism was not part of the gospel (1 Corinthians 1:17).
4. We are saved by Christ's death and resurrection, and baptism is only a sign or symbol of that (Romans 6:1-4).
5. Baptism is a work of "righteousness" (Matthew 3:15), but we are not saved by works of righteousness (Ephesians 2:8-9; Titus 3:5-7).

The Dangers of Extremes on Baptism

Clearly, there are radically different views on baptism. On the one end of the spectrum are the Bullingerites and Bereans, who do not believe in water baptism at all. On the other end of the spectrum are Roman Catholics, who believe baptism is *so* necessary for salvation that, even if one is baptized by an unbeliever or a heretic, he is still regenerated by it. There is also the Church of Christ, which believes that one must not only be baptized but must be baptized *by immersion* to be saved. Then there are the Landmarkian Baptists, who hold that one must be baptized by an *unbroken chain of Baptists* that goes all the way back to John the Baptist or else they are not in "the bride of Christ," but only friends of the bride. Clearly, all these proponents have taken a nonessential doctrine and made it essential to believe what *they* believe about it. This is clearly a case of majoring on the minors.

The Roman Catholic Church, for example, ruled that "if anyone shall say that baptism is optional, that is, not necessary for salvation: let him be anathema."[5] When one remembers that *anathema* means that if one rejects the Roman Catholic view of baptism, one will go to hell, one can easily see that a nonessential teaching has been set up as an essential dogma. Likewise, a Church of Christ minister known to one of the authors said he believed that even if a person repented from his sins, believed Christ died for his sins and rose again, confessed all this before a congregation, and was on his way to be baptized and suddenly dropped dead, he would go to hell! To teach such is to make a theological mountain out of a molehill.

Basic Areas of Agreement on Baptism

Despite the great divergency of opinion on the doctrine of baptism, there is wide agreement on several things. First, there is no doubt that Christians should practice water baptism. Second, baptism is a command of Christ, and it should be obeyed. Third, baptism should be done today in the name of the Father, the Son, and the Holy Spirit. Fourth, it should be done by water. Fifth, even as exclusivistic and emphatic as Catholic dogma may seem, even Catholics admit that one can be saved apart from baptism (by the *intent* to be baptized). This means that baptism is not an *absolute* necessity to be saved, but rather, a *normative* one.

These issues related to baptism are not among the fundamentals of the Faith. Regardless of how strongly one holds a given view, the candidate and mode of baptism is not a doctrine over which Christians should break fellowship and stop cooperating together on spreading the Faith once for all committed to the saints. The efficacy of baptism, particularly by those who consider it necessary for salvation, is a more serious doctrinal matter. But even here, as long as one believes in the necessity of God's grace and our faith, the debate need not involve a heresy on either side.

23

The Nature and Function of Communion

NOT ONLY HAS THERE BEEN a great deal of controversy in the church over the nature and function of baptism, but the same exists with regard to the other universally accepted ordinance—communion. Disagreements exist over the name, number, nature, participants, and efficacy of communion. Some call it the Lord's Table (1 Corinthians 10:21); others refer to it as the Lord's Supper (1 Corinthians 11:20) or communion (1 Corinthians 10:16 NKJV); others call it the breaking of bread (Acts 2:42; 20:7); and the more liturgical churches label it the Eucharist, after the Greek word *eucharisteo,* which means "to give thanks" (Matthew 26:27; 1 Corinthians 11:24). The Roman Catholic use of the term *Mass* is not found in the New Testament but comes from the Latin word *missa,* from *mittere,* meaning "to dismiss"—which is what the priest did to the participants after the ceremony was over. Space limitations permit only discussion about the differences over the nature and function of the communal elements. In this area alone there are five major views.

Disagreements over Communion

There are five different ways to understand what Jesus meant when He said, "This is my body" (Matthew 26:27): 1) physically (Roman Catholic); 2) really (Eastern Orthodox); 3) consubstantially (Lutheran); 4) spiritually (Reformed); and 5) symbolically (Zwinglian and Baptist).

Another crucial difference is that Catholics, Lutherans, and Anglicans hold a sacramental view of the elements, claiming that they are actual means of God's grace for the recipient, whereas both Presbyterians and Zwinglians deny the sacramental view, insisting that the efficacy of the communal elements depends on the recipient's faith.

The Roman Catholic View

The Nature and Function of Communion

Roman Catholics define a sacrament as a cause of grace. Catholic authority Ludwig Ott said that by "its etymology the word 'sacramentum' means a sacred or holy thing."[1] "The Roman Catechism (II, I, 8) defines a sacrament as 'a thing perceptible to the senses, which on the grounds of divine institution possesses the power both of effecting and signifying sanctity and righteousness' (= sanctifying grace)."[2] We are told, "If anyone shall say that the sacraments of the New Law do not contain the grace which they signify, or that they do not confer that grace on those who do not place any obstacle in the way, as though they were only outward signs of grace or justice, received through faith...let him be anathema." And this "grace is...conferred from the work which has been worked and not from 'faith alone.'"[3] Catholics believe that "the sacraments...not only point externally to salvation; they contain and bestow the salvation they signify."[4] Thus, "if anyone shall say that the sacraments of the New Law are not necessary for salvation, but are superfluous, and that, although all are not necessary individually, without them or without the desire of them through faith alone men obtain from God the grace of justification: let him be anathema."[5]

According to Catholic theology, "the Eucharist is that sacrament, in which, under the forms of bread and wine, is truly present, with [Christ's] body and blood, in order to offer Himself in an unbloody manner to the Heavenly Father, and to give Himself to the faithful as nourishment for their souls."[6] Thus, "after the consecration of the bread and the wine our Lord Jesus Christ, true God and man, is truly, really, and substantially...contained under the species of those sensible things."[7*] So, "by the consecration of the bread and wine a conversion takes place of the

---

* The bread and wine are "sensible" in that they are perceivable by the senses.

whole substance of the bread into the substance of the body of Christ our Lord, and of the whole substance of the wine into the substance of His blood. This conversion is appropriately called transubstantiation by the Catholic Church."[8]

Because transubstantiation is said to turn the elements of communion into the actual body and blood of Christ, Catholics believe it is appropriate to worship the consecrated elements as God. The Council of Trent pronounced emphatically that "there is, therefore, no room left for doubt that all the faithful of Christ...offer in veneration...the worship of *latria* which is due to the true God, to this most Holy Sacrament."[9] Catholics reason that because Christ in His human form is God, and, therefore, appropriately worshipped (for example, John 20:28), and because in the Mass the bread and wine are transformed into the actual body and blood of Christ, then there is no reason that this sacrament should not be worshipped as God. Thus, Trent affirmed that "if anyone says that in the holy sacrament of the Eucharist the only-begotten Son of God is not to be adored even outwardly with the worship of *latria* (the act of adoration)...and is not to be set before the people publicly to be adored, and that the adorers are idolaters; let him be anathema."[10]

Catholics argue that the necessity of accepting transubstantiation is found in a literal interpretation of Jesus' statements "this is my body" and "this is my blood" (Matthew 26:26-28). This, they believe, is evident a) from the nature of the words used; b) from the difficulties created by a figurative interpretation; and c) from the reaction of Jesus' listeners and His confirmation of their literal acceptance of His words.

A Protestant Response to the Catholic View

Protestants strongly reject the Roman Catholic view of the nature and function of the sacrament of communion. The following reasons are given:

1. *It is not necessary to understand these phrases in a physical sense.* Jesus' words need not be taken to mean we are ingesting His actual physical body and blood. Jesus often spoke in metaphors and figures of speech. For example, in this same book Jesus said, "I am the true vine" (John 15:1) and "I am the gate" (John 10:9). There is no reason, then, to understand

Jesus in a literal, physical sense when He said "this is my body." Jesus often spoke in graphic parables and figures, as He Himself noted (Matthew 13:10-11).

2. *It is not plausible to understand Jesus' words in a physical sense.* Jesus often used vivid phrases when speaking figuratively, and such phrases are not meant to be taken literally. This follows the Old Testament pattern. The Psalms, for example, are filled with vivid figures of speech. God is depicted as a rock (Psalm 18:2), a bird (Psalm 63:7), a tower (Proverbs 18:10), and in many other ways. Further, the Bible often uses the language of ingesting in a figurative sense. "Taste and see that the LORD is good" is a case in point (Psalm 34:8). The apostle Peter tells young believers, "Like newborn babies, crave pure spiritual milk" (1 Peter 2:2). And the writer of Hebrews speaks of "solid food" for mature Christians (5:14), and of others who "have tasted the heavenly gift" (6:4). Likewise, in Jesus' very words about the ordinance of communion, He used words metaphorically. When speaking about the New Covenant, He said, "This cup is the new covenant" (Luke 22:20). Clearly the *literal* cup was not the New Covenant, but what it *symbolized*.

3. *It is not possible to hold to a literalistic view.* In at least one very important respect, it is not physically or theologically possible for an orthodox Christian to hold to a literalistic interpretation of Jesus' words, "This is my body." For when Jesus said this in regard to the bread in His hand, no apostle present could possibly have understood Him to mean that the bread was *actually* His physical body, since He was still with them in His physical body. Otherwise, we must believe that Christ was holding His own body in His own hands.

4. *It is idolatrous to worship the host.* Many Protestants believe worship of the host is a form of idolatry—it is the worship of something that is a finite creation of God, namely, bread and wine. The worship of God under a physical image is clearly forbidden in the Ten Commandments (Exodus 20:4).

5. *It undermines belief in the resurrection and sense knowledge in general.* To claim that the consecrated host is anything but a finite creation undermines the very epistemological basis by which we know anything in the empirical world and, indirectly, the very historical basis of support

for the truth about the incarnate Christ, His death, and resurrection. For if the senses cannot be trusted when they experience the communion elements, then neither can the apostles' senses be trusted to verify Christ's claims to be resurrected. Jesus said in proof of His resurrection, "*Look* at my hands and my feet. It is I myself! *Touch me* and *see;* a ghost does not have flesh and bones, as you *see* I have" (Luke 24:39, emphasis added; see also John 20:27). The apostle John said of Christ that He was "that which was from the beginning, which we have *heard,* which we have *seen* with our eyes, which we have *looked at and our hands have touched*" (1 John 1:1, emphasis added).

The Catholic view of the communion elements not only undermines the resurrection but the reliability of our senses in general. For if what we see, touch, taste, and smell in the host is not real bread, then how do we know whether anything else we see, touch, taste, and smell is really what it seems to be?

6. *It claims one and the same body is in many places at the same time.* This represents a significant problem for most evangelicals.[11] "In order to be bodily present at thousands of altars, the body of Christ must possess one of the so-called attributes of the majesty of God, namely, omnipresence or ubiquity."[12] Simply put, "to believe that Jesus was in two places at once is something of a denial of the incarnation, which limited his physical human nature to one location."[13] Indeed, it is akin to the monophysite heresy that held that following the incarnation, Christ possessed only one incarnate divine nature—combining and commingling His two natures. If this heresy was condemned, why shouldn't the commingling of the divine and human in the substance of the communion elements be condemned as unorthodox as well?

7. *It diminishes the value and finality of Christ's sacrifice.* Roman Catholics (and Anglicans[14]) view the Eucharistic feast as a "sacrifice," although an "unbloody" one.[15] This term is found as early as Gregory the Great (A.D. 540–604), who was elected pope in A.D. 590.[16] In A.D. 831, a Frankish monk, Paschasius Radbertus, in a work titled *On the Body and Blood of the Lord,* addressed this issue. Radbertus taught that Christ is "corporeally" present during communion. Early in the church, the Eucharist was considered a fellowship meal. Hence, "the new emphasis on the corporeal

presence of Christ permitted the Church to begin to treat Christ as a victim, rather than as the host [of the feast], to think of itself as offering him to the Father, rather than as coming to be nourished at his table."[17]

Protestants strongly object to viewing communion as a sacrifice because it is done repeatedly, while Christ's actual sacrifice was a *once-for-all* event (Hebrews 10:12-14). Jesus said on the cross, "It is finished" (John 19:30). Thus, unfortunately, the Lord's Supper—which the early church viewed as simply a *fellowship* meal—became in Roman Catholicism a *sacrifice*. The *remembrance* of the sacrifice became a new *enactment* of that sacrifice.[18] Contrary to such a view, Jesus very clearly said that when we participate in communion, we are *remembering* His sacrifice on the cross, not *reenacting* it (Luke 22:19).

The Eastern Orthodox View

Eastern Orthodoxy is more mystical and less rational than the Western, and makes no attempt to explain Christ's presence in the communion service. However, Eastern Orthodox believers do believe He is really present. But His presence is mystical, not transubstantial.[19]

While Eastern Orthodox believers genuflect before the consecrated host, this does not mean they agree with the Roman Catholic view. Only Catholics believe the host is actually the body of Christ and can and should be worshipped as God. Eastern Orthodox believers say that Christ is really present *in* the host, but this is very different from saying He *is* the host and should be worshipped as such.

The Lutheran View

In contrast to Catholics, Lutherans reject the concept of the Mass as a sacrifice: "Since Christ died and atoned for sin once and for all, and since the believer is justified by faith on the basis of that one-time sacrifice, there is no need for repeated sacrifices."[20] Sacerdotalism, which is the belief that priests act as mediators between God and humans, is also rejected: "The presence of Christ's body and blood is not a result of the priest's actions. It is instead a consequence of the power of Jesus Christ."[21] In brief, the whole concept of re-enacting and re-presenting Christ's sacrifice on the cross is contrary to the clear teaching of Hebrews that this sacrifice was a once-for-all event (Hebrew 10:12-14).

The Lutheran position on communion is known as consubstantiation, though Luther himself never called it that. Luther believed that the actual body of Christ is *in* and *under* the elements, penetrating these elements in the same way that fire penetrates metal.[22] He rejected Catholic transubstantiation, stating rather that "it is not that the bread and wine have become Christ's body and blood, but that we now have the body and blood *in addition* to the bread and wine."[23] Lutherans believe that Christ is present *permeationally*, not *transformationally*, in that He penetrates and permeates the bread and the wine.

Lutheran scholar Theodore Mueller stated that "what the words of institution declare in particular is that, 'in, with, and under' the bread and the wine Christ presents His true body and blood to be truly and substantially eaten and drunk by us." In other words, "the words of the institution say: 'that which I offer you, which you are to receive and eat, is *not only* bread, but *also* My body. That which I offer you, which you are to receive and drink, is *not only* wine, but *also* My blood.'"[24]

The Lutheran view differs from the Roman Catholic view in at least two respects. First, while Christ's body and blood are believed to be physically present, there is no transubstantiation of the bread into Christ's body or wine into His blood. That is, they coexist and are concurrently present with the elements. Luther used the illustration of an iron bar heated in fire. The iron does not cease to exist, but the fire penetrates it and exists *in*, *with*, and *under* it. Second, Luther rejected Catholic sacerdotalism, insisting that priestly action is in no sense responsible for the physical presence of Christ in the elements, but rather involves the action of God. Nonetheless, Luther did accept the idea of *manducation*—that is, the real eating of Jesus' body. He took Jesus' statement, "Take and eat; this is my body," literally. Finally, the Lutheran view is not clearly contrary to the senses, nor does it involve a form of idolatry in worshipping a part of the creation (the elements). Nonetheless, the Lutheran view is subject to the criticism of being literalistic.

The Reformed (Calvinistic) View

The Reformed Calvinistic view of the Lord's Supper is that the bread and the wine contain the body and blood of Christ *spiritually*. More specifically, Christ is found in the sacrament in a spiritual, dynamic sense, rather than a physical or bodily sense. John Calvin used the sun as an illustration, stating that "the sun remains in the heavens, yet its warmth and light are present on earth. So the radiance of the Spirit conveys to us the communion of Christ's flesh and blood."[25] So, through Christ's spiritual presence, the elements partaken do have efficacy. They are not mere symbols. In short, Christ is spiritually present through the Holy Spirit in such a way that His entire body and blood is enjoyed through the Lord's Supper.

Theologian Charles Hodge explains that "anything is said to be present when it operates duly on our perceiving facilities. A sensible object [that is, an object capable of being perceived by the senses] is present...when it affects the senses. A spiritual object is present when it is intellectually apprehended and when it acts upon the mind." Plainly stated, "it is present to the mind, not to our bodies. It is perceived and received *by faith* and not otherwise. He is not present to *unbelievers*."[26] Thus, "Christ is present when He thus fills the mind, sheds abroad His love in our hearts by the Holy Ghost given unto us."[27]

Further, the elements not only communicate the spiritual presence of Christ, they also seal the believer with assurances of God's promises. That is, there are real, objective spiritual benefits from the elements that do not come from them but from Christ, although they depend in large part on the faith and receptiveness of the participant. In this sense they are not sacraments, which are a means of grace, but are simply elements through which Christ is present dynamically and spiritually to the believer in the communion service.

The Memorial View

According to the Reformation leader Ulrich Zwingli, the memorial view of the Lord's Supper states that the communion service is primarily a commemoration of Christ's death on the cross, in light of Jesus' words, "Do this in remembrance of me" (Luke 22:19). Although Zwingli himself acknowledged that Christ was spiritually present to those of faith, his view is primarily characterized by its emphasis on the memorial aspect and the symbolic significance of the elements. The value of the elements lies in their ability to symbolize and remind us of the benefits of Christ's death. Like a sermon, the event proclaims the death of Christ, except that, unlike a sermon, communion is a *visual* reminder. The backdrop to Zwingli's view is that because Jesus was present with the disciples in bodily form when the Lord's Supper was instituted, it is absurd to claim that the elements He held in his hand—the bread and the wine—were actually the physical body and blood of Christ.

Zwingli taught that "the Lord's Supper is nothing else than the food of the soul, and Christ instituted the ordinance as a memorial of Himself."[28] Moreover, "the natural substantial body of Christ in which He suffered, and in which He is now seated in heaven at the right hand of God, is not in the Lord's Supper eaten corporeally, or as to its essence, but spiritually only."[29] Zwingli added, "We teach that the great design and end of the Lord's Supper, that to which the whole service is directed, is the remembrance of Christ's body devoted, and of his blood shed, for the remission of our sins. This remembrance, however, cannot take place without true faith."[30] In brief, then, according to the memorial view, Christ is not present physically, neither transubstantially (Roman Catholics), nor consubstantially (Lutherans), nor spiritually (Reformed), but only symbolically and commemoratively.

Adherents of the memorial view include the Anabaptists, modern Baptists, Restorationists (such as the Church of Christ and Christian Church), other baptistic churches, and many independent churches. These groups generally prefer to use the term *ordinance* rather than *sacrament* when referring to the Lord's Table or communion.

The Dangers of Extreme Views

One extreme view on communion is that of E. W. Bullinger (1837–1913), who denied the ordinance altogether, claiming it was an observance of an early Jewish church that existed before Acts 9 (see chapter 22). On the other end of the spectrum is the Roman Catholic view that literally worships the consecrated elements. Lesser extremes exist in the Catholic sacramental view that the elements of communion are effective means of grace even if one does not participate in faith, and the symbolic view that sees no spiritual significance in the elements themselves. We also note the problematic claim of the Roman Catholic, Eastern Orthodox, and Lutheran views that Christ is *bodily* present in some sense (biblically, Christ's human body is *not* omnipresent at altars around the world), in contrast to the Reformed view, which asserts that He is spiritually present, and the Zwinglian position, which says that He is only present symbolically.

Another extreme relates to the efficacy of the communion elements. The sacramental view holds that the communion elements are a special means of grace. But nonsacramentalists see significant problems with this view. First, they believe it is contrary to the claim of the passage that the event is basically *memorial* and *proclamational*. Jesus said, "Do this in remembrance of me" (Luke 23:19), and the apostle Paul said that, by our participation, we "proclaim the Lord's death" (1 Corinthians 11:26). Second, nonsacramentalists ask the question, If the ritual itself has some spiritual efficacy, then why is it that some who partook became sick or died, rather than being spiritually edified by it (1 Corinthians 11:30)? There was nothing automatic about the effects of the communion elements. Those who responded to communion in the proper way by faith were edified, while those who did not were not edified. The efficacy of the communion experience did not depend on the elements or rite, but on the faith and reception of the participant.

The Common Elements in Virtually All Christian Views of Communion

With the exception of the Bullingerites (see chapter 22)—a tiny sect of Christendom—virtually all Christians hold in common a number of facts about communion. First, it was ordained by Christ for His followers to practice until He returns to earth (Matthew 26:26-30; 1 Corinthians 11:23-26). Second, unlike baptism, it is a perpetual ordinance to be performed over and over again in memory of Christ's death for us. Third, the basic elements are bread and wine, the former representing His body and the latter His blood. Fourth, only believers should participate in communion, because it focuses on His death for them. Fifth, communion should be celebrated regularly. In the early church, it was observed at least once a week on the first day of the week (Acts 20:7). Sixth, communion is effective only by the grace of God. Mere bread and wine in themselves (as physical elements) have no efficacy apart from God's grace.

It is this latter point that saves the Roman Catholic view from heresy. Orthodoxy demands the necessity of God's grace in *every* saving act, whether it is in justification, sanctification, or glorification (see chapter 11). The fact that God uses physical means to channel His grace is neither logically impossible nor heretical. Whether it is true or not is an intramural debate on which there is liberty within orthodoxy, and in which charity should be exercised by the differing parties.

24

The Nature of Sanctification

ALL CHRISTIANS BELIEVE IN what many call *sanctification*—that is, the process by which believers become more Christlike in this life between the moment of regeneration and death (or Christ's coming, whichever comes first). They also believe that Christ's death on the cross (see chapter 9) and high priestly ministry in heaven (see chapter 14) are crucial to the sanctifying process. Within this broad framework, however, there are some significant differences among Christians.

For example, the Eastern Orthodox call this process "Christification" or "deification," not to be confused with the New Age pantheistic belief that we can actually come to realize that we are God. Nor is sanctification to be confused with the Mormon idea that believers may become gods in the world to come.

The Roman Catholic terminology for sanctification is also different. What many Protestants call *justification*—that is, the initial act of salvation from the penalty of sin when one is regenerated—Roman Catholics refer to as *initial justification*. What many Protestants call sanctification—salvation from the power of sin in our lives—Roman Catholics label *progressive justification*.[1]

To make matters even more confusing, many Wesleyans believe that sanctification need not be a lifelong process, but can be an instantaneous act by which one reaches a state of sinless perfection. In this case there is not only a difference in terminology, there is also a difference in the belief being proclaimed. However, we must remind ourselves again that these differences are not fundamental. That is, they affect no essential doctrine of the Christian Faith (listed in chapters 2–17).

The History of the Disagreement

The different views on sanctification lay relatively dormant for many centuries, then surfaced during the Reformation period. They came to focus when Martin Luther stressed that justification comes to believers by faith alone, resulting in Christ's righteousness being accounted to them, by which they are made fit for heaven. John Calvin likewise taught forensic justification—whereby a person, by faith alone, is accounted righteous before God and thereby made fit for heaven.

This, of course, cut across the grain of Roman Catholic doctrine, which, "infallibly" interpreted at the Council of Trent, held that one is not made fit for heaven until he has both an initial infusion of righteousness (at regeneration) *plus* a life of good works in which no mortal sin is committed (otherwise known as progressive justification). On the basis of *both* of these, one is given ultimate justification and is thereby made ready for heaven. Roman Catholics add, however, that those who, at death, have nonmortal sins (called venial sins) must suffer in purgatory for the temporal consequences of these sins, for which no penance was paid on earth.

It is obvious that there is considerable difference in both terminology *and* truth claimed in these various views. To gain proper appreciation for these differences, let's consider some specifics about these views.

Before the Reformation

Before Luther's time, one can find strains of various views on the doctrine of sanctification, largely interpreted in terms of the role of good works in one's ultimate salvation. One was similar to the Catholic view, speaking of infused righteousness for justification and continued growth in actual righteousness after that. Another, identified by Thomas Oden, was akin to the later Reformation view that spoke of justification by faith.[2] What confuses the matter is that some other views involved belief in 1) baptismal regeneration, 2) sacramentalism, or 3) the view that not all the regenerate were elect (that is, one could lose his salvation). These beliefs tended to make one's ultimate salvation hinge on whether one continued in a life of good works. Thus, in these views, one's ultimate salvation—*getting into heaven*—seems to hinge on sanctification.

Martin Luther's View

Before Luther, the standard Augustinian position stressed *intrinsic* justification. The believer was *made* righteous by God's grace. Extrinsic justification, by which a sinner is *legally declared* righteous, was, at best, a minority view in pre-Reformation Christendom. With Luther the situation changed dramatically. However, as Peter Toon notes, "Luther does not employ forensic terms to explain this imputation or alien righteousness. This development came later from Calvin and his followers."[3]

Luther's mentor, Johann von Staupitz, assigned him to lecture on Paul's letters to the Romans and Galatians from the fall of A.D. 1515 to 1517. Luther discovered that in the Greek used by the apostle Paul, the word *justice* has a double meaning: the first involves a strict enforcement of the law, and the second involves "a process of the sort which sometimes takes place if the judge suspends the sentence...and thereby instills such resolve that the man is reclaimed."[4] This latter meaning of the word *justice* is necessary because "the sinner cannot ever attain any righteousness of his own: he merits or deserves only condemnation." But God has "freely opted to receive us to Himself...to a fellowship that we from our side had broken and could never mend."[5]

When studying the meaning of Romans 1:16-17, Luther came to a life-changing conclusion:

> Night and day I pondered until I saw the connection between the justice of God and the statement that "the just shall live by faith." Then I grasped that the justice of God is that righteousness by which through grace and sheer mercy God justifies us through faith. Thereupon I felt myself to be reborn and to have gone through open doors into paradise. The whole of Scripture took on new meaning, and whereas before the "justice of God" had filled me with hate, now it became to me inexpressibly sweet in great love. This passage became to me the gate to heaven.[6]

It is sometimes forgotten, however, that Luther also believed in a progressive sense of justification (= sanctification). For example, he said, "For we understand that a man who is justified is not already righteous but moving toward righteousness." Further, "Our justification is not yet complete....It is still under construction. It shall, however, be completed in the resurrection of the dead."[7] This sense of progressive justification is what many Protestants today call sanctification, the process by which we are *made* righteous, not an act by which one is *declared* righteous. Toon adds that for Luther, "justification by faith is both an event and a process. What later Protestants were to divide, Luther kept together. He is quite clear that there is a moment when a sinner is actually justified by faith. He then has the righteousness of another, the alien righteousness of Christ, imputed to him."[8]

Catholic Response to Luther

The Council of Trent was the Catholic response to Lutheranism. On January 9, 1547, the council participants agreed on a final formula for justification. First, although several council members recognized an extrinsic element in justification (thereby approaching the Reformers on this point), the consensus view was that "the opinion that a sinner may be justified solely as a matter of reputation or imputation...is rejected."[9] Therefore, "justification is thus defined in terms of a man becoming, and not merely being reputed as, righteous."[10]

Second, in that Trent understood justification in two senses (the second corresponding to the Reformed doctrine of sanctification), this second justification required good works. "It is thus both possible and necessary to keep the law of God."[11]

Third, Trent, taking into account original sin, affirmed that sin has affected the entire human race. Therefore, "man is incapable of redeeming himself. Free will is not destroyed, but is weakened and debilitated by the Fall"[12]—an idea Luther rejected in his book *Bondage of the Will.* Trent asserted, "If anyone shall say that man's free will moved and aroused by God does not cooperate by assenting to God who looses and calls...let him be anathema."[13] So, for Trent, "the sinner indeed cooperates with this grace, at least in the sense of not sinfully rejecting it."[14]

Fourth, the subject of the sacraments was addressed at Session VII (March 3, 1547). In order to understand these pronouncements, one must remember that Trent understood justification in two ways, involving first and second phases. Baptism is said to be operative in the first way, because grace to overcome original sin is said to be "mediated" to us through baptism.[15] Both the Eucharist and penance pertain to the second sense of justification, and such justification (that is, righteousness) is said to be increased by participation in these sacraments.

Fifth, Trent stated that our initial justification must be seen as a gift. Thus it comes as a surprise to many Protestants that Roman Catholics believe that "if anyone shall say that man can be justified before God by his own works which are done...without divine grace through Christ Jesus: let him be anathema."[16] Further, "[N]othing that precedes justification, whether faith or works, merits the grace of justification. For if it is by grace, it is no more by works; otherwise, as the apostle says, grace is no more grace."[17] On the other hand, Trent does assert that works are necessary for salvation in the progressive and eventual senses, for it made it dogma that "by his good works the justified man really acquires a claim to supernatural reward from God."[18] And it is precisely here that Catholics and evangelicals strongly disagree.

Trent held that ultimately, eternal life is given to us on the grounds of our good works.[19] Thus the Council of Trent declared that "those who work well 'unto the end' [Matt. 10:22], and who trust in God, life eternal is to be proposed, both as a grace mercifully promised to the sons of God through Christ Jesus, 'and as a recompense' which is...to be faithfully given to their good works and merit."[20] It adds that "if anyone shall say that the good works of the man justified are in such a way the gift of God that they are not also the good merits of him who is justified, or that the one justified by the good works...does not truly merit increase of grace, eternal life, and the attainment of eternal life (if he should die in grace), and also an increase of glory; let him be anathema."[21]

John Calvin's View

While Martin Luther held that by faith alone one could receive the alien righteousness of Christ, he did not spell this out in terms of forensic justification. This was left to John Calvin.[22] Whereas Roman Catholics believe that initial justification (regeneration) involves an actual infusion of righteousness, Calvin believed that justification is forensic and involves an imputation of righteousness. The Old Testament Hebrew word *hitsdiq,* usually rendered "justify," more often than not is "used in a forensic or legal sense, as meaning, not 'to make just or righteous,' but 'to declare judicially that one is in harmony with the law.' "[23] Also, "he is righteous who is judged to be in the right (Ex. 23:7; Deut. 25:1); i.e., who in judgment through acquittal thus stands in a right relationship with God."[24] Even the Catholic scholar Hans Küng agrees that "according to the original biblical usage of the term, 'justification' must be defined as a *declaring just by court order.*"[25]

In the New Testament, the Greek verb translated "to justify" is *dikaioó.* This word is used by the apostle Paul in a forensic or legal sense; the sinner is *declared* to be righteous (see Romans 3–4). It is the opposite of condemnation. As Anthony Hoekema notes, the opposite of condemnation is "not 'making righteous' but 'declaring righteous.' " Therefore, by *dikaioó* Paul means the "legal imputation of the righteousness of Christ to the believing sinner."[26]

When a person is justified, God pronounces that one *acquitted*—in advance of the final judgment. As the apostle Paul put it, God was "reconciling the world to himself in Christ, not counting men's sins against them" (2 Corinthians 5:19). Therefore, "the resulting righteousness is not ethical perfection; it is 'sinlessness' in the sense that God no longer counts a man's sin against him (II Cor. 5:19)."[27] Thus we find in the New Testament that "justification is the declarative act of God by which, *on the basis of the sufficiency of Christ's atoning death,* he pronounces believers to have fulfilled all of the requirements of the law which pertain to them."[28]

This has significant implications for the role of sanctification. First, because forensic justification totally prepares one for heaven, sanctification—whatever its role—*is not* a condition for entrance into heaven. Thus, even if sanctification were achieved by good works for Protestants—and it is *not*—it would still not have anything to do with one's entrance into heaven.

What, then, is the role of sanctification for a Protestant? Sanctification does not determine whether one gets into heaven (justification alone does that); rather, it determines what one's rewards will be in heaven. In short, sanctification—by *making* one more righteous (rather than simply *declaring* one righteous, as justification does)—makes one more Godlike, and therefore more capable of appreciating and absorbing into one's life all that God desires, as well as subsequently increasing one's level of reward in heaven. As someone put it, in the Protestant view, when we get to heaven all our cups will be running over, but not everyone will have the same-size cup. That will be determined by our sanctification.

John Wesley's View

In addition to the significant differences between Catholics and Protestants on sanctification, there is an important difference of views within Protestantism itself. According to John Wesley, the founder of the Methodist Church, it is possible to attain a state of sinless perfection in this life. He describes it as a "habitual disposition of the soul which, in the sacred writings, is termed holiness; and which directly implies that being cleansed from sin, 'from all filthiness both of flesh and spirit;' and, by consequence, the being endued with those virtues which were in Christ Jesus; the being so 'renewed in the image of our mind,' as to be 'perfect as our Father in heaven is perfect.'" In short, it involves "deliverance from inward as well as from outward sin."[29] Following are some specifics of Wesley's view:

Perfectionism is a state of sinlessness. Wesley asks:

> What is it to be sanctified? To be renewed in the image of God, "in righteousness and true holiness." What is implied in being a perfect Christian? The loving God with all our heart, and mind, and soul (Deut. vi. 5). Does this imply that all inward sin is taken away? Undoubtedly; or how can we be said to be "saved from all our uncleanness"? (Ezek. xxxvi. 29).[30]

Wesley thus implored, "Now, Savior, now the power bestow, and let me cease from sin!"[31]

Perfection is possible in this life. Wesley stated: "'True,' say some, 'but not till death, not in this world.' Nay, St. John says, 'Herein is our love made perfect, that we may have boldness in the day of judgment; because, as He is, *so are we in this world.*'" It is "not only at or after death, but '*in this world,'* they are 'as their Master.' "[32] "When does inward sanctification begin? In the moment a man is justified. (Yet sin remains in him, yea, the seed of all sin, *till he is sanctified throughout.*) From that time, a believer *gradually dies to sin,* and grows in grace."[33] So, while all will be made perfect at death, it can be expected sooner.

Perfection is attained by faith after salvation. Wesley believed that perfection is "receivable by mere faith" and is "hindered only by unbelief." Further, "this faith, and consequently the salvation which it brings, is spoken of as given in an instant." Indeed, "it is supposed that instant may be now."[34]

Perfectionism does not guarantee no mistakes. In what sense are Christians *not* perfect? Wesley affirmed, "They are not perfect in knowledge. They are not free from ignorance, no, nor from mistake. We are no more to expect any living man to be infallible, than to be omniscient. They are not free from infirmities, such as weakness or slowness of understanding, irregular quickness or heaviness of imagination." They are not free from "impropriety of language, ungracefulness of pronunciation; to which one might add a thousand nameless defects, either in conversation or behavior. From such infirmities as these none are perfectly freed till their spirits return to God; neither can we expect till then to be wholly freed from temptation; for 'the servant is not above his master.'"[35]

Reformed Critique of Perfectionism

The classic critique of perfectionism was made by Reformed theologian B. B. Warfield in his book titled *Perfectionism.*[36] He does not directly address John Wesley so much as some of Wesley's more remote disciples in Warfield's day, such as C. G. Trumbull, A. B. Simpson, and Robert Pearsall Smith and his wife. Among other things, Warfield argued that 1) perfectionism amounts to a quick-fix sanctification; 2) it sharply separates justification and sanctification; 3) by its own admission, it is a new doctrine, thus making it dubious; 4) it is a form of spiritual passivism that can lead to a ceasing of moral effort on our part; 5) it is a form of quietism, reducing victory to surrender on our part; 6) it is self-contradictory, claiming that those free from sin can still resist Christ; and 7) it minimizes sin to make perfection possible.

In addition to Warfield's critique, Wesley's own admissions about perfectionism are revealing. He admitted 1) it does not eliminate "a thousand nameless defects."[37] 2) Even chief apostles had not attained perfection.[38] 3) Death to sin is only gradual.[39] Further, he acknowledged 4) it does not mean that we will never sin again; 5) it does not mean we cannot lose our salvation; 6) no more than a small minority of all believers of all time have ever attained it; 7) most who get it do so not much before death; and 8) the apostle Paul rarely, if ever, used the term *sanctified* in this unique Wesleyan sense. Indeed, some Wesleyan scholars have viewed perfectionism not as eradication but as empowerment, thus making it more like some non-Wesleyan views of sanctification.

The Dangers of Extremes on Sanctification

Like other nonessentials, the various views on sanctification are not immune to extremes. The Roman Catholic view is a prime example.

The Roman Catholic Extreme

The Roman Catholic view of sanctification comes the closest to denying a major doctrine of any major orthodox group in Christendom. Indeed, were one to apply what Catholics believe about sanctification to justification, it would be a heresy. What salvages their view from being heretical are two factors: First, they believe in the exclusivity of grace for the initial stage of salvation (initial justification). Second, even in the second stage (sanctification) they believe in the necessity of grace. More specifically, even though they believe works are necessary along with grace to enter heaven, nonetheless, they believe even these works are prompted by and empowered by God's grace. In the interest of accuracy, however, we must note that in practice, the Catholic emphasis on works often seems to overshadow Catholic teachings on grace.

The Protestant Extremes

While some evangelicals come close to lawlessness with their overemphasis on free grace, others tend toward the legalistic end of the spectrum in demanding rules, the keeping of which is believed to merit grace. The truth abides between antinomianism and legalism.

Wesleyanism, at least in its more extreme forms, diminishes, if not destroys, the important emphasis on continued sanctification. It can engender a quick-fix mentality that hinders Christian spiritual growth. On the other hand, it offers a goal that is worthy of pursuit—holiness.

Areas of Agreement on Sanctification

There are some areas in which divergent groups in Christendom agree on sanctification. Four points of agreement are especially important:

1. Even among Protestants, there is the acknowledgment that, while justification opens the door of heaven to us, it is not all that God desires for us; it is only the first stage of salvation—namely, deliverance from the penalty of sin. Most acknowledge that God also desires sanctification (deliverance from the power of sin) for every believer.
2. There is general agreement, whatever name is attached to it, that all believers should seek to become more Christlike.
3. All agree that sanctification cannot be attained without God's grace.
4. All hold that faith is a vital part of the sanctification process. Mere works, apart from faith, cannot achieve an effective sanctifying work in our lives.

These and other points of agreement can serve as our motivation to show liberty on this nonessential doctrine of the Christian Faith. On points of difference, let us agree to disagree in an agreeable fashion. Let us also observe that the very act of showing liberty to others on this and other nonessential doctrines may, in fact, itself be an evidence of the effectiveness of the sanctification process in our lives.

25

The Use of Musical Instruments in Worship

CHRISTIANS THROUGHOUT HISTORY HAVE universally sung hymns and songs as a part of their corporate worship and praise to God. Within this broad framework, however, a division has long existed within the body of Christ: Some Christians believe hymns and songs should be sung in church without instrumental accompaniment (*a cappella* singing); most Christians believe it's permissible for hymns and songs to be sung with instrumental accompaniment.

Representative churches among those who are against instrumental accompaniment are the Primitive Baptists, the Churches of Christ, and the Church of God in Christ, Mennonite. Many traditional Baptist, Methodist, Presbyterian, Roman Catholic, and churches of other mainstream denominations use an organ, piano, or both to accompany singing, and there are an increasing number of churches within each of these denominations that use partial or full bands or orchestras. There is wide diversity on this issue, and the differences regarding the use of musical instruments are not fundamental. That is, they affect no essential doctrine of the Christian Faith (chapters 2–17).

The History of Disagreement

Many churches throughout history have included hymns and songs in their worship services with no musical accompaniment. This was apparent especially so during the patristic period. Hymns featured the human voice alone.

The most famous musical instrument that eventually made its way into church services is the church organ, which most believe was first introduced by Pope Vitalian in Western Europe in the seventh century. During the eighth century the organ became common in the Latin church, though there were quite a number of monks who resisted its use. By the fifteenth century, the use of organs was well established in monastic churches and cathedrals throughout Europe. Even the Gregorian chant, which was sung for the previous nine centuries with no musical accompaniment, eventually incorporated use of the organ. Following the fifteenth century, other kinds of musical instruments began to be used in liturgical compositions.

History reveals that it was through Ludovico Grossi da Viadana (1564–1627) that the use of various instruments became more common in churches. He composed liturgical pieces for voice which incorporated use of the organ, violins, and wind instruments. It was not long after this that other musicians wrote pieces to be performed in churches by instruments alone.

During this same general time frame, the use of both voices and instruments became common in opera, and because of the enormous emerging popularity of opera, the use of instruments in church services became not just acceptable but also desirable. The simplicity of liturgical chants gave way to more elaborate musical art forms that mixed both voices and instruments. Not unexpectedly, the acceptance of musical instruments became so widespread that, eventually, most music written for churches was with orchestral accompaniment. At some cathedrals and large churches, large orchestras became permanently endowed.

Some churches, however, continued to resist the use of the organ and other instruments—especially full orchestras—including a number of Reformed, Presbyterian, and Methodist churches. John Calvin once commented, "Musical instruments in celebrating the praise of God would be no more suitable than the burning of incense, the lighting up of lamps, [and] the restoration of the other shadows of the law. The Papists, therefore, have foolishly borrowed this, as well as many other things, from the Jews."[1] John Wesley made his feelings known in the comment, "I have no objection to instruments of music in our chapels, provided they are neither heard nor seen."[2] One reason some Christian leaders resisted the use of musical instruments in church was that musical instruments were also used for the purposes of social dancing and entertainment.

It is interesting to observe that some authorities issued regulations for the use of musical instruments in churches or in religious communities. For example, Benedict XII in 1728 chastened some Benedictine nuns in Milan for using instruments other than the organ during Mass. He also forbade the Franciscans to use any instrument other than the organ in their churches. Benedict XIV tolerated in church *only* the organ, stringed instruments, and bassoons. He forbade use of kettle drums, horns, trombones, oboes, flutes, pianos, and mandolins.[3] And the beat goes on...(the debate continues).

Churches That Are Against Instrumental Music

The Primitive Baptists

A more recent group to reject use of instrumental music is the Primitive Baptists—primitive not in the sense of being backward, but rather in the sense of originality, the goal being to recapture the original faith and practice of the New Testament apostles. The reason musical instruments are not used in their church services is because they were not said to be used in the New Testament churches. (There are no Sunday school classes in Primitive Baptist churches for this same reason.) It is interesting to observe that though this group prohibits instrumental music, sermons are typically delivered in a dramatic singsong voice. (We say interesting not only because this is an unusual method of sermon delivery, but because such sermon delivery was not a practice of the New Testament apostles.)

The Churches of Christ

Among the key figures of the Restoration movement of the early 1800s were Barton Stone, whose followers were called simply "Christians," and Thomas and Alexander Campbell, whose followers called themselves the Disciples of Christ. Members of both groups did not want to be bound by human creeds. The Bible was clear enough for anyone to understand, they asserted, and there was no need for creeds. They felt the Bible alone should be the rule of faith and practice, and they believed church membership should be based solely on the beliefs and practices of New Testament Christianity.

A historic union took place in 1832 between Barton Stone's 10,000 followers and Thomas and Alexander Campbell's 12,000 followers. The merged group was known as both "Christians" and "disciples." In the latter part of the nineteenth century, however, a conflict between conservatives and progressives emerged within the movement. The conservatives withdrew in protest against the development of missionary societies—a development interpreted as a step toward centralization that would weaken the autonomy of the local church. The conservatives also opposed the use of instrumental music in church services. They felt that because neither missionary societies or musical instruments were found within the pages of the New Testament, they should not be part of the church. In 1906, the conservative dissenters formed a new denomination called the Churches of Christ, while the progressives who allowed instrumental music and missionary societies became known as the Disciples of Christ.

The Church of God in Christ, Mennonite

In the middle of the nineteenth century, some within the Mennonite movement felt their denomination had drifted away from sound doctrine, and that the movement was experiencing a general spiritual decline. Among the concerns: 1) Individuals were being baptized whose personal conversions were in serious doubt; 2) the church had fallen away from a strong stand on church discipline of erring members; 3) church members were not making enough effort to avoid apostates; 4) there was a lack of true spirituality in general. Thus in 1859, concerned members separated from the Mennonite church and founded the Church of God in Christ, Mennonite.

Members of the Church of God in Christ, Mennonite—in seeking to be biblical—believe in simple homes, simple and modest clothing, devotional head coverings for women (symbolizing submission to male leadership), and beards for men. Christians are not to participate in politics or hold government offices. The members practice nonresistance—meaning they should not quarrel with other people or file lawsuits, evil should not be returned for evil, one should not participate in civil law enforcement, and one should not participate in the armed forces. They believe in a clear separation between church and state. Church members are to be a separate people, not conformed to the world. This means that such things as fashion, pleasure and entertainment, professional sports, idolatrous art, television, radio, movies, popular music, dancing, and the like must be avoided. In terms of church services, worship and Sunday school take place on Sunday mornings in plain buildings. Musical instruments are never used. All singing is *a cappela.*

Churches That Are Open to Instrumental Music

Many other churches scattered across numerous Christian denominations are open to the use of instrumental music. They do not see the use of musical instruments as a manifestation of worldliness. Moreover, they are not bothered by a lack of mention of musical instruments at church services in the New Testament. They believe that to prohibit musical instruments simply because they are not mentioned in the context of New Testament church services is an argument from silence, which, of course, is not a valid argument. *Omission* does not mean *exclusion.*

The broader context of the whole of Scripture reveals quite a bit about the use of musical instruments. People in Old Testament times, for example, played music and sang songs for a variety of purposes—including the celebration of military victories, including God's victory over the Egyptians at the exodus (Exodus 15:1-18). Another example relates to the men of Judah and Jerusalem, who celebrated their victory over Ammon and Moab by going into the temple of the Lord "with harps and lutes and trumpets" (2 Chronicles 20:27-28).

Music was played for the homecoming party of the prodigal son (Luke 15:25), and was also used at banquets and feasts (Isaiah 5:12) as well as for laments (Matthew 9:23). Music was performed at the coronation of kings (2 Chronicles 23:11-13) and at temple ceremonies (1 Chronicles 16:4-6; 2 Chronicles 29:25). Music was also often performed during pilgrimages (2 Samuel 6:5).

There were a variety of musical instruments used in ancient Israel, including wind, stringed, and percussion instruments. Examples of wind instruments include the *halil,* which was basically a hollow pipe of cane or wood that utilized a reed to make a musical sound. The *geren* was a form of trumpet, made from the horn of an animal (see Leviticus 25:9; Joshua 6:4). Trumpets made from a ram's horn were called *shofar,* and were used for special occasions during the Jewish year, particularly on New Year's Day and the Day of Atonement. *Flutes* were common as well (1 Samuel 10:5; Isaiah 5:12; Jeremiah 48:36).

Stringed instruments included the *kinnor,* which is essentially a harp or lyre (see 2 Samuel 6:5; 1 Kings 10:12). It was a wooden frame that had strings within it, and may have been plucked like the modern harps of today. Another similar stringed instrument was the *nebel.* David, the shepherd king of Israel, was apparently able to play both of these instruments. In fact, David often used such instruments to soothe the nerves of King Saul (1 Samuel 16:16,23).

Percussion instruments included the *meziltaim,* akin to modern cymbals (1 Chronicles 25:1; Nehemiah 12:27), and the *menaanim,* a wooden frame in which were suspended a series of disks that would rattle when shaken. *Castanets* were pieces of pottery containing pellets (2 Samuel 6:5). *Tambourines* were also quite common (1 Samuel 10:5; 2 Samuel 6:5). *Gongs* were sometimes used at weddings and other happy occasions (1 Corinthians 13:1). *Timbrels* were instruments beaten by the hand and were associated with processions and merrymaking (Genesis 31:27).

These various instruments were often used in producing music as a part of worship in the temple (1 Chronicles 25). It is well known that many of the psalms were originally designed for musical accompaniment. Psalm 4 was to be accompanied "with stringed instruments" (Psalm 4, title). Psalm 5 was to be accompanied with "flutes" (Psalm 5, title). Psalm 6 was to be accompanied "with stringed instruments" (Psalm 6, title).

Scripture tells us that "David and all the house of Israel played music before the LORD on all kinds of instruments of fir wood, on harps, on stringed instruments, on tambourines, on sistrums, and on cymbals" (2 Samuel 6:5 NKJV). David affirmed, "I will play music before the LORD" (2 Samuel 6:21 NKJV). We are told that "four thousand praised the LORD with musical instruments, 'which I made,' said David, 'for giving praise'" (1 Chronicles 23:5 NKJV). The Levites were stationed "in the temple of the LORD with cymbals, harps, and lyres in the way prescribed by David" (2 Chronicles 29:25). The psalmist proclaims, "I will praise you with the harp, O God, my God" (Psalm 43:4). Indeed, "Praise him with the sounding of the trumpet; praise him with the harp and lyre, praise him with the tambourine and dancing, praise him with the strings and flutes, praise him with the clash of cymbals, praise him with resounding cymbals" (Psalm 150:3-5). Instrumental music and singing continued to be common after the Israelites returned from exile (Ezra 3:10-11; Nehemiah 12:27-47).

Many Christians today believe that because musical instruments were used so predominantly in Old Testament worship, including in temple worship, then certainly God's people in New Testament times—many of them Jewish converts to Christianity—can follow this same pattern. *Not a single verse in the New Testament prohibits this.*

In the New Testament, the apostle Paul says Christians ought to "speak to one another with psalms, hymns and spiritual songs. Sing and make music in your heart to the Lord" (Ephesians 5:19). Paul further exhorts, "Let the word of Christ dwell in you richly as you teach and admonish one another with all wisdom, and as you sing psalms, hymns and spiritual songs with gratitude in your hearts to God" (Colossians 3:16; see also Matthew 26:30; Acts 16:25; James 5:13). While musical instruments are not mentioned, neither are they forbidden. And because omission does not mean exclusion, there is no reason musical instruments should not be used as we sing songs and hymns in praise to God.

Besides, Revelation 5:8 indicates that harps will be used in heaven in worship of God. Hence, if musical instruments were used in *past* worship of God in Old Testament times and will be used in *future* worship of God in heaven, there is no good reason such instruments should be prohibited from our worship of God in the *present*.

The Debate over Traditional Music versus Contemporary Music

Another controversy related to music is whether only traditional hymns should be sung in worship services, or contemporary music is also acceptable. Some churches have opted for traditional hymns alone, others utilize only contemporary Christian songs, while others use a hybrid approach, seeking to combine the best of both worlds. Yet other churches offer their members two kinds of services each week, with one incorporating traditional music and the other contemporary music.

Arguments offered in favor of using traditional music include:

1. The lyrics in hymns are typically richer, more poetic, and are generally more doctrinally oriented than contemporary songs.
2. Many hymns were written by spiritual giants of the past—including men such as Martin Luther and Charles Wesley—and this rich heritage of music ought to be passed on to each new generation of Christians.
3. Because many churchgoers are accustomed to hymns, churches that introduce contemporary music risk losing some of their longtime attenders.
4. Contemporary music is sometimes on the loud side (utilizing full bands), and some people may feel the volume detracts from the worship.
5. To some people, contemporary music is too showy—too performance oriented—and thus detracts from true worship of the Lord.

Among arguments offered in favor of contemporary music are:

1. Because most unchurched people have never sung a hymn in their lives, it makes sense to include music in the service that they can more easily relate to.
2. Martin Luther put Christian words to some of the popular bar songs of his day, and therefore his music was the "contemporary music" of his day. Hence, contemporary music should be allowed in our day.
3. Some of today's contemporary artists are actually writing

hymns, so there should be no objection to using them in worship services.

4. Because many in church listen to Christian radio, which frequently features contemporary music, it makes sense to include songs in the service that most people are already familiar with.
5. Some of today's praise choruses have been specifically designed to be conducive to worship, and therefore ought to be used in church services.

The debate goes on!

The Danger of Extremes Regarding the Use of Musical Instruments

The primary danger of extremes regarding the use of musical instruments in worship relates to divisions in the body of Christ over a nonessential doctrine. Whenever a church says *its* view on music is the only acceptable view, and it makes this issue a test of fellowship, then that church has taken an extreme position that ultimately damages the body of Christ. This should not be.

Areas of Agreement Regarding Hymns and Worship Songs

Despite the divergence of opinions that exists among Christians on the matter of musical instruments in worship services, churches without exception can agree with the following three foundational points: 1) Worship should be a part of our church services; 2) singing hymns and spiritual songs should be a central part of this worship; and 3) the message conveyed by the music is more important than the mode by which it is expressed. Hence, sound theology is more important than the sounds made by instruments. Beyond these points, we must agree to disagree in an agreeable way regarding the use of musical instruments in church services. The same should be our policy regarding traditional versus contemporary music. After all, even traditional music was once contemporary.

Let us not forget the second part of the dictum we have repeated throughout this book, which says, In nonessentials, *liberty*. Because the issues discussed in this chapter are nonessentials, let us choose to show liberty to brothers and sisters who hold to a different view rather than accuse them of being unbiblical in their worship. There are some matters worth dividing the body of Christ over, but music is not one of them.

26

The Nature of Spiritual Gifts

GOD GAVE SPIRITUAL GIFTS to Christians in the church so they could accomplish both the church's internal mission (edifying believers) and external mission (evangelizing).[1] Spiritual gifts are mentioned in several New Testament books—Romans 12:3-8 mentions the gifts of prophecy, teaching, exhortation, leading, serving, giving, and mercy. First Corinthians 12:8-10,28-30 mentions apostles, prophets, teachers, miracles, healings, helps, administration, tongues, interpretation, faith, the word of knowledge, the word of wisdom, and discernment. And Ephesians 4:11 mentions apostles, prophets, evangelists, pastors, and teachers.

While some gifts, such as pastoring and evangelizing, are not controversial, a number of intramural debates have emerged among Christians on other gifts—especially what are called the "sign gifts." Among the questions raised in these debates are as follows: Are there prophets today who predict the future, like the prophets of old? Is speaking in tongues for today? If so, is tongues an intelligible language, or some kind of private language? Is the gift of healing for today?

Some denominations have split over such debates. Others have actually emerged anew and have adopted belief in virtually all the spiritual gifts mentioned in the New Testament as part of their doctrinal statement. These debates entered the mainstream of Christendom as the Pentecostal movement emerged following the Azusa Street revival in the early 1900s. Let's consider the details.

The History of Disagreement

Pentecostalism is a twentieth-century movement that takes its name from the Holy Spirit's working on the Day of Pentecost in Acts 2. Proponents of the movement believe the same phenomena depicted in Acts—that is, a baptism of the Holy Spirit accompanied by the gift of speaking in tongues—should be normative in the church today.

The Pentecostal movement has its roots in the Holiness movement, which emphasized a "second blessing" or "second work of grace," called *entire sanctification*. In this theology, a believer first gets saved—that is, he is first justified and born again. Following this, the believer experiences a period of growth in which he progressively becomes holier. This ultimately culminates in a second work of grace, whereby the Holy Spirit cleanses the person's heart of original sin, literally eradicating all inbred sin, and then imparts His indwelling presence to the person, empowering him to live the Christian life in perfection. This, Holiness proponents claimed, is the baptism of the Holy Spirit. It allegedly happens instantaneously as the believer presents himself as a living sacrifice to God with an attitude of full consecration. Pentecostals took this doctrine of the second blessing or second work of grace and related it specifically to empowerment by the Holy Spirit, which is evidenced by the person speaking in tongues.

Modern Pentecostalism began in Topeka, Kansas, in 1901. In January of that year, a young woman named Agnes Ozman—a student at Bethel Bible College—allegedly spoke in tongues while at the church of Holiness minister and evangelist Charles Fox Parham (1873–1929).

The movement soon spread from Kansas to Houston, Texas, where Parham opened a Pentecostal school. An African-American Holiness minister named William J. Seymour (1870–1922) attended the school and, after studying the apostle Paul's epistles, became convinced that Parham's views regarding the believer and the Holy Spirit were correct. Parham and Seymour agreed that there are three basic works of grace in the life of the believer: 1) salvation, 2) sanctification, and 3) empowerment. This empowerment is from the Holy Spirit, and is manifest by supernatural manifestations such as speaking in tongues. Seymour insisted that the gift of tongues was the true test of being filled with the Spirit.

Seymour then went to California, where the famous Azusa Street

Revival broke out in Los Angeles from 1906 to 1909. This revival, led by Seymour, received some unexpected publicity. Seymour had warned the people in California that if they did not repent and turn to God, God would judge them. One week later, a powerful earthquake hit San Francisco, and suddenly Pentecostalism was thrust into the news media spotlight. Thousands of people from around the United States traveled to Azusa Street, then carried the Pentecostal message back to their communities.

Out of the Azusa Street Revival emerged a number of different Pentecostal church groups—including the Pentecostal Holiness Church, the Church of God in Christ, the Church of God (Cleveland, Tennessee), the Apostolic Faith (Portland, Oregon), the Assemblies of God, the International Church of the Foursquare Gospel, and the Full Gospel Business Men's Fellowship. One reason various new denominations emerged from this revival was that those who spoke in tongues were no longer welcome in traditional (non-Pentecostal) churches.

In the 1960s and 1970s, the Pentecostal experience started to penetrate some mainline churches and crossed denominational lines. Such churches experienced what became known as the Charismatic Renewal movement. By 1980, Pentecostalism had penetrated Catholic churches in over 100 countries around the world.

Meanwhile, a number of Charismatic subgroups emerged—including the Word Faith movement, the Kansas City Prophets movement, the Five-fold Ministry movement, the Kingdom Now movement, the Latter-Rain movement, the Signs and Wonders movement, and others—all of which emphasize all manner of supernatural phenomena rooted in the work of the Holy Spirit. Today it is common to hear about multitudes speaking in tongues, prophets prophesying, and healers healing.

The intramural debate that has emerged among Christians over the issue of spiritual gifts can be broken down into three basic categories: 1) the view that *all* the spiritual gifts in the Bible still exist today; 2) the view that *none* of the spiritual gifts still exist today; and 3) the view that *some* of the spiritual gifts still exist today.

The Different Views

1. *The View that All the Spiritual Gifts Still Exist Today.* Many Christians,

known as Charismatics, believe all the spiritual gifts listed in the New Testament are still in use today. Multitudes speak in tongues during Charismatic church services, and it is claimed that people are regularly healed and experience various miracles. Some have gone so far as to claim people are being raised from the dead.[2] Such miraculous events ought to be normative for today, we are told.

Among the arguments suggested in defense of this view are:

- Jesus is the same yesterday, today, and forever (Hebrews 13:8), and because He doesn't change, there has been no change in His gift of tongues to believers.
- There is no indication in the pages of the New Testament that any of the spiritual gifts have passed away.
- The New Testament books were written for believers of all time periods, and because tongues are found throughout the New Testament, there is no reason they shouldn't be experienced today.
- Many people today possess the gift of speaking in tongues, and this living proof cannot be denied.

In response, cessationists—those who believe the sign gifts have *ceased*—reject those arguments point by point. They say:

- While Jesus does not change, His plan and purpose for people in different times *does* change (for example, no more animal sacrifices for today), and hence this constitutes no argument for tongues.
- First Corinthians 13:8 indicates that tongues would, at some point, cease *of their own accord*—as indicated by the middle voice in the Greek for the word "cease." Many Christians believe this "ceasing," which involved the other revelatory gifts, took place during the time of the New Testament apostles.
- It is true that the New Testament was written for all

believers, and that it mentions speaking in tongues. However, while all the Bible is *for* us, not all of the Bible is specifically *to* us. What the New Testament reveals about tongues may be *descriptive,* not *prescriptive.* That is, the New Testament *describes* the presence of tongues in the early church and its purpose in the early church, but it does not *prescribe* that tongues are for all people of all times throughout church history. Tongues were considered a sign-gift of the apostles, and because all the apostles passed away in the first century (note the requirement in Acts 1:22 that an apostle had to be an eyewitness of Christ's resurrection), it would seem that the sign-gift of tongues passed away along with them.

- While many today claim to speak in tongues, experience should never be used to interpret the Bible, but rather the Bible should be used to interpret experience. The danger of not testing experiences against the Bible is evident in the fact that pagan religions and cults regularly feature speaking in tongues.

2. *The View that None of the Spiritual Gifts Still Exist Today.* There are other Christians who believe that none of the spiritual gifts mentioned in the New Testament are for today.[3] Among the arguments suggested in favor of this view are:

- Because God gave different lists of gifts to different churches (Romans 12; 1 Corinthians 12; Ephesians 4), God apparently never intended for the *cumulative total* of these gifts to be available to *every* church.
- The New Testament doesn't instruct believers, as individuals, to search for or discover spiritual gifts, but only the church body *as a whole* is to "eagerly desire the greater gifts" (the Greek is plural in 1 Corinthians 12:31).
- Scripture reveals there is a more excellent way than

emphasizing the gifts of the Spirit, and that is to make love the priority (1 Corinthians 13:13).

- When church leaders were appointed in the New Testament churches, the apostle Paul said nothing about selecting men based upon their spiritual gifts. Rather, he focused on their overall spiritual maturity. (We will soon see that some of the arguments of the cessationist position contradict the "no gifts for today" position.)

3. *The View that Some of the Spiritual Gifts Still Exist Today.* A third view is that some of the spiritual gifts are for today, while others (the sign gifts) have passed away. Those who hold to this position are called *cessationists,* for they believe certain gifts have ceased. Among the arguments suggested in favor of this position are:

- The sign gifts (such as tongues and healing) were needed only to help establish the church, not continue it once it was established.
- The sign gifts were divinely engineered to miraculously confirm the revelational message of the apostles (Acts 2:22; 3:3-11; 5:15-16; 9:36-42; 20:6-12), and once that message was completed, there was no need for further confirmation (see Hebrews 2:3-4).
- The New Testament apostles were unique, for they had to be eyewitnesses of the resurrected Christ (Acts 1:22; 1 Corinthians 9:1; 15:7-8). Because these unique apostles passed away in the first century, the miraculous sign gifts that confirmed them passed away as well.
- There is significant New Testament evidence that *only* the apostles received and could give these sign gifts to others (see Acts 8:18; 10:44-46; 19:6; Romans 1:11; 2 Timothy 1:6).[4] This being the case, the sign gifts would have ceased once the apostles ceased.
- Unlike the modern form of speaking in tongues, which

is essentially gibberish, the speaking in tongues in New Testament times involved real languages, for they were understandable by those who heard those languages (Acts 2:5-11; see also 11:15-16).[5]

- Unlike the modern form of speaking in tongues—in which people are asked to repeat certain letters, words, or phrases in order to "prime the pump" (such as saying, "Hallelujah" over and over again, faster and faster)—the New Testament form of speaking in tongues was not *taught* or *verbally induced,* but simply occurred *supernaturally.*
- The spiritual gift of healing must have passed away, for even the apostles, late in their work of ministry, were unable to heal (1 Timothy 5:23; 2 Timothy 4:20), and their healings were considered a past event by the time of Hebrews 2:3-4.
- The gift of healing in New Testament times involved *instant* cures, *fully successful* cures, and cures *that lasted.* No one today possesses such a gift.
- The gift of prophetic foreknowledge must have passed away, for the church was built on the *foundation* of the apostles and prophets (in New Testament times) (Ephesians 2:20). Once the foundation was built, it did not need rebuilding. Rather, we are to build *upon* the foundation. A second foundation is out of the question.

The Track Record of Biblical Prophets

There are no Christians today who can match the track record of the biblical prophets, who were 100 percent accurate in their predictions. Some people in recent years, however, have argued for the fallibility of New Testament prophets—a view that serves to excuse fallible prophecies among modern-day Christians who claim to have the gift of prophecy. They argue, for example, that some New Testament prophets never said,

"Thus saith the Lord" like the Old Testament prophets, and allegedly, this allows for the possibility of errors among New Testament prophets. Such an argument fails to recognize that not even all the Old Testament prophets said, "Thus saith the Lord" before their pronouncements (see, for example, 2 Samuel 23:2 and Amos 7:1; 8:1). Besides, Scripture indicates that the same Holy Spirit who spoke through the Old Testament prophets (2 Samuel 23:2) spoke through the New Testament prophets (Acts 21:11).

It is also sometimes argued that New Testament believers were urged to judge or weigh what was being offered as prophecy, thus implying that a New Testament prophet could be in error (1 Corinthians 14:29). Contrary to this view, the reason this instruction was given was to guard against false prophets pretending to set forth prophecies from God. The idea is that if a prophecy comes from a true prophet of God, it will be in line with what previous prophets of God have revealed (because God doesn't contradict Himself). If a prophet tries to pawn off some revelation that contradicts previous prophets, it is clear that such a person is a false prophet (see Deuteronomy 13:1-5 and 18:14-22). Understood in this way, then, the weighing of prophetic statements cannot be taken to imply that New Testament prophets made mistakes.

That New Testament prophets were on the same level of infallibility as the Old Testament prophets seems clear from the following :

- New Testament prophets are portrayed in Scripture as being in continuity with their Old Testament predecessors (see Malachi 3:1; Matthew 11:11; Revelation 22:7).
- The New Testament prophets were placed alongside the apostles as the foundation of the church (Ephesians 2:20), and because the apostles' revelations were divinely authoritative and infallible (1 Corinthians 14:37), we theologically infer that the New Testament prophets were likewise authoritative and infallible.
- The New Testament prophets received revelations from

God, and were hence just as infallible as Old Testament prophets who received revelations from God.

- The New Testament prophets gave bona fide predictive prophecies (Acts 11:28; 21:11), just as the Old Testament prophets did (see Deuteronomy 18:22).

The Danger of Extremes Regarding the Spiritual Gifts

As is true regarding other nonessential doctrines we have examined, there are dangers related to extreme views on spiritual gifts. One such danger relates to the minority viewpoint that there are no spiritual gifts for today. Inasmuch as Scripture indicates that spiritual gifts are bestowed by God so the church can accomplish its internal mission (the edifying of believers) as well as its external mission (evangelism), to say there are no spiritual gifts serves to rob the church of the truth that God has provided divine resources for the accomplishment of its tasks. Such a view clearly does not reflect the New Testament teaching.

Another danger is the claim that the baptism of the Holy Spirit, as evidenced by speaking in tongues, is necessary for salvation.[6] This view clearly goes against the consistent New Testament emphasis that salvation is by grace alone through faith alone (see, for example, Ephesians 2:8-9). Moreover, even in New Testament times, not all the Corinthian Christians spoke in tongues (1 Corinthians 14:5), even though all had been baptized by the Spirit (12:13). It is highly revealing that a number of passages in the book of Acts speak of people being baptized or filled with the Holy Spirit, yet do not mention speaking in tongues (see Acts 2:37-41; 4:31; 6:3-6; 7:55; 11:24; 13:52).

Another abuse comes from those who claim to have the gift of healing. We draw a distinction between the *gift* of healing and the *fact* of healing: We both believe God can and does heal today, but we also believe that the *gift* of healing passed away in the first century. No one today has the healing power of the first-century New Testament apostles. Tragically, some people who visit a so-called divine healer today not only come away from the experience not healed, but are told that the reason they weren't healed is because of their lack of faith. Or, they are told there is sin in their lives, or perhaps a demon is in them. Such teachings can wreak havoc with the spiritual lives of biblically ignorant Christians.

Yet another possible danger involves what has been called the pendulum effect. Some people overreact to an extreme teaching by swinging to the opposite extreme. More specifically, some people respond to extreme teachings about the Holy Spirit and spiritual gifts by swinging to the opposite extreme of virtual noninvolvement with the Holy Spirit and spiritual gifts. This is both tragic and unbalanced, for a Christian cannot have a healthy spiritual life without the Holy Spirit's help.

Still another possible danger is that some Christians may be tempted to pay more attention to the *gifts* than the *Giver* of the gifts. People can become so fixated on the sensational aspects of the things of the Spirit that they fail to keep their eyes fixed on Jesus, the author and finisher of their faith (Hebrews 12:2).

Areas of Agreement on the Spiritual Gifts

Aside from those who follow the minority view that there are no spiritual gifts today, Christians can agree on a number of things related to the spiritual gifts. We can all agree that:

- A proper relationship with the Holy Spirit is central to Christian spirituality.
- Every Christian has a spiritual gift or gifts, selected for him by the Holy Spirit (1 Corinthians 12:11).
- Whatever spiritual gift one has, it should be used to bring edification to the church or help facilitate evangelism of the lost.
- While many Christians (the authors included) believe the gifts of healing and miracles have passed away, all Christians can agree that this does not mean healings and miracles are a thing of the past. God *can* and *does* heal and perform miracles today.
- While most Christians agree there are no apostles today in the *unique* sense of the original 12 who performed the

signs of the apostles (2 Corinthians 12:12), there are still apostles in the looser sense of the word: "one who is sent" (that is, a missionary—1 Thessalonians 2:6).

- While most Christians agree that there are today no prophets in the sense of *foretellers* (of the future and of truths not known), all can agree that there are prophets in the looser sense of *forthtellers* who proclaim the Word of God (truths *already* known—see 1 Corinthians 14:3-4).
- The gifts of pastoring and teaching are portrayed in the New Testament as central, for by such gifts the flock of God in the local church is protected and fed (Acts 20:28; Ephesians 4:11).

Where debates remain on the gifts of the Holy Spirit, we urge Christians to agree to disagree in an agreeable way, following the wisdom of the words "In nonessentials, *liberty*." After all, the *fruit* of the Spirit—which is love (Galatians 5:22)—is more important than the *gifts* of the Spirit. Undoubtedly that is why Paul placed the great love chapter (1 Corinthians 13) between two chapters on the gifts of the Spirit (1 Corinthians 12 and 14) and said, "I will show you the most excellent way" (1 Corinthians 12:31). Indeed, all these gifts will one day pass away, but love will abide forever (1 Corinthians 13:8,13).

27

The Day of Worship

ALL CHRISTIANS OF ALL denominations believe there should be a day each week on which God is worshipped and honored. But Christians are divided over whether that day should be the first day of the week (Sunday) or the seventh day (Saturday). Some who worship on the seventh day have claimed that those who worship on the first are violating one of the Ten Commandments, which states, "Remember the Sabbath day by keeping it holy" (Exodus 20:8).

Strong opinions exist on this issue. We must ever remind ourselves, however, that the day on which we worship does not involve a fundamental of the faith. It is not an essential doctrine (see chapters 2–17). The line "In nonessentials, *liberty*" applies to this issue.

The History of Disagreement

The Hebrew word for *Sabbath* means "cessation." The Sabbath was instituted as a holy day and a day of rest for both man and animals (Exodus 20:8-11). This day was to commemorate God's rest after His work of creation (Genesis 2:2). God set the pattern for living—working six days, and resting on the seventh (Saturday). The Sabbath thus finds its origin in the creation account.

At Mount Sinai, the Sabbath—already in existence—formally became a part of the Jewish law and a sign of God's covenant relationship with Israel (Exodus 20:8-11). Keeping the Sabbath was a sign that showed submission to God, and honoring it brought great blessing (Isaiah 58:13). By contrast, to break the Sabbath law was to rebel against God, and this was a sin that warranted the death penalty (see Exodus 31:14). God provided detailed instructions for Sabbath observance in Leviticus 25, Numbers 15:32-36, and Deuteronomy 5:12-15.

Some may find it odd that Sabbath observance is commanded in the Ten Commandments, for the Sabbath was *already* known among God's people. However, an examination of the fourth commandment (which says, "*Remember* the Sabbath") suggests that though the concept of the Sabbath was already known to the Israelites, it now needed formal statement and clarification. Such clarification would have been necessary because the Israelites were probably not allowed to observe the Sabbath during their time in Egypt.

By the time of Jesus, Jewish legalists had added all kinds of new rules and regulations for properly keeping the Sabbath. The Sabbath thus became a burden instead of a blessing. These legalistic Jews put their own laws in place of divine law (see Matthew 15:9), and Jesus stood against such legalism.

Most Christians believe that during New Testament times, the day of worship changed from Saturday to Sunday, the Lord's day. We will talk about the reasons for this transition a bit later, but at this point, let's note that the primary reason for this was that Jesus rose from the dead on a Sunday. Indeed, the resurrection took place "after the Sabbath [Saturday], at dawn on the first day [Sunday] of the week" (Matthew 28:1, inserts added). Hence, during New Testament times, believers began to worship on Sunday instead of Saturday (Acts 20:7; 1 Corinthians 16).

Church history reveals that by the beginning of the second century, worship on the first day, Sunday, was a near-universal practice. The patristic writers (early church fathers) generally cited the resurrection of Christ as the primary reason for celebrating on this day. The Epistle of Barnabas (c. A.D. 70–100) likewise said, "Wherefore, also, we keep the eighth day [Sunday] with joyfulness, the day also on which Jesus rose again from the dead. And when He had manifested Himself, He ascended into the heavens."[1] Ignatius (A.D. 35–107) spoke of "no longer observing the Sabbath, but living in the observance of the Lord's Day."[2] Justin Martyr said, "Sunday is the day on which we all hold our common assembly, because," among other reasons, "Jesus Christ our Savior on the same day rose from the dead."[3] Clement of Alexandria (A.D. 150–211), Tertullian (A.D. 155–230), and Cyprian (d. A.D. 258) all worshipped on the first day of the week.

During the fourth century, Sunday worship became "official" when ecclesiastical and civil legislation was enacted prohibiting work on Sunday (with certain exceptions). Constantine decreed in A.D. 321,

> On the venerable day of the Sun let the magistrates and people residing in cities rest, and let all workshops be closed. In the country, however, persons engaged in agriculture may freely and lawfully continue their pursuits because it often happens that another day is not suitable for grain-sowing or vine planting; lest by neglecting the proper moment for such operations the bounty of heaven should be lost.[4]

One should be careful to note that it was not Constantine who changed the day of worship from Saturday to Sunday (as some try to claim), but rather he "made official" what Christians had already been practicing for some two-and-a-half centuries. Most Christians since this time have continued to worship on Sunday, though there have been some Christian groups around the world that have continued or, in some cases, revived Sabbath-day worship.[5]

During the Protestant Reformation (A.D. 1517–1648), a renewed vigor emerged for worshipping on Sunday, with an emphasis on rest and a focus on spiritual concerns, especially among the Puritans of England and Scotland. This was largely in response to the general laxness among many people for Sunday observance during that time. We thus read in the *Westminster Confession of Faith* (A.D. 1646) that God "hath particularly appointed one day in seven, for a Sabbath, to be kept holy unto him: which, from the beginning of the world to the resurrection of Christ, was the last day of the week; and, from the resurrection of Christ, was changed into the first day of the week, which, in Scripture, is called the Lord's day, and is to be continued to the end of the world, as the Christian Sabbath." The Confession affirms:

> This Sabbath is then kept holy unto the Lord, when men, after a due preparing of their hearts, and ordering of their

> common affairs beforehand, do not only observe a holy rest, all the day, from their own works, words, and thoughts about their worldly employments and recreations, but also are taken up, the whole time, in the public and private exercises of his worship, and in the duties of necessity and mercy.[6]

Still, there remains those who continue to believe that the seventh day is the God-ordained day of worship for all times. In modern history, it is primarily Seventh-day Adventist denominations and messianic Jews who continue to worship on Saturday. For illustration purposes, let us briefly consider Seventh-day Adventism.

Seventh-day Adventism

Seventh-day Adventism is a denomination (some call it a cult) that emerged out of the Millerite movement. William Miller (A.D. 1782–1849) believed the second coming of Christ would occur in 1844. Though Christ did not come (followers call this the "Great Disappointment"), many nevertheless remained Adventists because they believed the second coming was still imminent. Unlike Miller, who (through convoluted reasoning) interpreted Daniel 8:14 to mean that the second coming would occur in 1844, Seventh-day Adventists interpreted the verse to mean that Christ cleansed the heavenly sanctuary and began a heavenly judgment—the "investigative judgment"—in 1844 that was to end *prior* to the second coming. This judgment allegedly reveals to heavenly intelligences who among the dead are asleep in Christ and who among the living are abiding in Christ. *These alone* are said to belong to God's kingdom.

This group formally emerged in 1845 with a small group of believers in New England led by founder Ellen G. White and some of her associates. They chose the name *Seventh-day* because they believe the Old Testament Sabbath, Saturday, is the proper day of worship and rest. They believe that observing the Sabbath is the proper way to await the soon advent of the coming Lord.

The following reasons are offered in support of this position:

- God made the Sabbath at creation for *all* people (Genesis 2:2-3; Exodus 2:11).

- The fourth of the Ten Commandments requires worship on the seventh day—Saturday (Exodus 20:8-11). The Ten Commandments are *unchangeable* laws, and therefore Sabbath worship is for today. It is both a day of rest and a memorial of God's work of creation.
- Christ Himself observed the Sabbath (Mark 1:21) and is the Lord of the Sabbath (Mark 2:28).
- The apostle Paul, during New Testament times, preached on the Sabbath (Acts 17:2).
- Gentiles in the New Testament worshipped on the Sabbath (Acts 13:42-44).
- Matthew, Mark, and Luke, writing *after* the resurrection, spoke of the Sabbath as an existing institution (Matthew 24:20; Mark 16:1; Luke 23:56).

For these and other reasons, say the Seventh-day Adventists, the day of worship should be the Sabbath, or Saturday.

Churches that Worship on the Lord's Day (Sunday)

The great majority of churches across all denominations, since the first century, have chosen to worship on the Lord's day, or Sunday. There are a number of reasons for this.

First, the basis for the command to observe the Sabbath, as stated in Exodus 20:11, is that God rested on the seventh day after six days of work, and that God blessed the seventh day and sanctified it. The Sabbath day was instituted as a day of rest and worship. The people of God were to follow God's example in His pattern of work and rest. However, as Jesus said when He corrected the distorted view of the Pharisees, "The Sabbath was made for man, not man for the Sabbath" (Mark 2:27). Jesus' point was that the Sabbath was instituted not to enslave people, but to benefit them. The spirit of Sabbath observance is continued in the New Testament observance of rest and worship on the first day of the week (Acts 20:7; 1 Corinthians 16:2).

Second, it must be remembered that, according to Colossians 2:17, the Sabbath was "a shadow of the things that were to come; the reality, however, is found in Christ." The Sabbath observance was associated with redemption in Deuteronomy 5:15, where Moses stated, "Remember that you were slaves in Egypt and that the LORD your God brought you out of there with a mighty hand and an outstretched arm. Therefore the LORD your God has commanded you to observe the Sabbath day." The Sabbath was a shadow of the redemption that would be provided in Christ. It symbolized a rest from our works and an entrance into the rest of God, which was provided by Christ's finished work on the cross. A transition from worshipping on the Sabbath day to the Lord's day therefore makes good sense.

Finally, although the moral principles expressed in the Commandments are reaffirmed in the New Testament, the command to set Saturday apart as a day of rest and worship is the only commandment not repeated. There are very good reasons for this:

- New Testament believers are not under the Old Testament law (Romans 6:14; Galatians 3:24-25; Colossians 2:16), and the Sabbath commandment is a part of that law.
- The apostle Paul indicated that one's choice to observe special days is a matter of personal conscience (Romans 14:5), and no one should cast judgment on anyone else regarding this issue.
- Jesus arose from the dead and appeared to some of His followers on a Sunday (Matthew 28:1).
- Jesus made additional postresurrection appearances on subsequent Sundays (John 20:26).
- John had his apocalyptic vision on a Sunday (Revelation 1:10).
- The descent of the Holy Spirit took place on a Sunday (Acts 2:1).
- The early church was given the pattern of Sunday worship, and this they continued to do regularly (Acts 20:7; 1 Corinthians 16:2).

- Significantly, no rules of Sabbath observance were imposed upon Gentile believers by the Jerusalem Council—meaning that Sabbath observance was not considered to be among the "necessary things" the Gentile believers had to concern themselves with (Acts 15:28-29).
- Paul indicated that a required observance of a special day as a divine obligation goes against the gospel of grace that he communicated to the Galatians (see Galatians 4:9-10).
- Paul gave instructions to the Corinthian church about taking a special relief offering on the first day of the week (Sunday) for the Christians in Jerusalem (1 Corinthians 16:1-2). He likely stipulated "first day of every week" because he knew that they met for worship on that day.

It is for these and other reasons that most Christians worship on Sunday rather than on the Jewish Sabbath.

The Danger of Extremes Regarding the Day of Worship

Like other nonessential doctrines, divergent views on the day of worship are not immune to extremes. One extreme is that one can easily fall into the mentality of paying more attention to the actual *day* of worship than the *worship* that is supposed to take place on that day. An extreme on the side of Sunday worshipers is that, because they are not under the law, they may wrongly undervalue the importance of regular church attendance on Sundays to worship God (see Hebrews 10:25). An extreme on the side of Saturday worshipers involves accusing Christians who worship on Sunday of being commandment-breakers who are out of God's will.

We must not forget that worship involves reverencing God, adoring Him, praising Him, venerating Him, and paying homage to Him—not just externally (by rituals and singing songs), but in our hearts as well (Isaiah 29:13; see also 1 Samuel 15:22-23). Whether this takes place on a Saturday or a Sunday, believers should not harshly judge other brethren who worship on a different day.

While worship is most commonly expressed via songs, hymns, and rituals, wherein adoration and praise are expressed to God, Scripture also teaches that we worship God when we give ourselves totally over to Him on a day-to-day basis. This is taught in Romans 12:1: "I beseech you therefore, brethren, by the mercies of God, that you present your bodies a living sacrifice, holy, acceptable to God, which is your reasonable service" (NKJV). Offering one's body to God is an act of giving God *all* that we are. It is an act of unconditional surrender to His purposes and will in our lives. Scripture calls this a spiritual act of worship on our part. How can we claim to be obedient to this verse if we are judgmental and choose to show *no liberty* and *no charity* to other brothers and sisters in Christ who worship on a different day than we do? Let us remember that the day on which we worship is not a fundamental of the Faith.

Areas of Agreement Regarding the Day of Worship

There are a number of areas on which all Christians can agree on regarding the day of worship: 1) We can all agree that there should *be* a weekly day of worship; 2) we can all agree that this day should honor the Lord; 3) we can all agree that this day should involve an observance of rest and worship; 4) we can all agree that to ignore setting apart one day a week goes against the will of God; 5) we can all agree that God desires this day to be a blessing to man; and 6) we can all mutually recognize—or at least we *should* mutually recognize—that both sides of the debate are seeking to be biblical in their view, and therefore, each side should show respect to the other.

All this being the case, we urge our brethren on both sides of the debate to allow these unifying factors to motivate a spirit of liberty and charity to all who bear the name *Christian*. Let's take the boxing gloves off our hands on the matter of whether we should worship on Saturday or Sunday, and instead raise our hands in praise to the risen Lord—whether we do so on a Saturday or a Sunday. The simple fact is that the particular day of worship is neither a test for orthodoxy nor of fellowship, regardless of how strongly we may prefer one day over another.

28

The Order of Second-Coming Events

WHEN IT COMES TO END-TIME EVENTS, Christians have all kinds of intramural debates. For example: Should Bible prophecy be interpreted literally or allegorically? Should the church be distinguished from Israel? Does the rapture occur before, in the middle of, in the latter part of, or after the Tribulation? Is the millennial kingdom a literal 1000-year period during which Christ physically rules on earth, or is it a spiritual kingdom on earth that exists in the now? Do the prophecies in the book of Revelation and Christ's Olivet Discourse (Matthew 24–25) refer to the prophetic future, or were they fulfilled in A.D. 70 when Rome overran Jerusalem?

The sheer volume of disagreements on these matters means we must be highly selective in this chapter, providing only a representative sampling of arguments presented by respective Christians on these issues.[1] We begin with the fundamental issue of hermeneutics.

The Various Issues Under Debate

Hermeneutics and the Biblical Covenants

A primary debate among Christians in relation to end-time events relates to whether one should use a literal or an allegorical approach when interpreting Bible prophecy. While both sides claim to subscribe to the historical-grammatical method of Bible interpretation (see chapter 17), classical dispensationalists believe that schools of thought that use an allegorical approach to biblical prophecy distort the true historical-grammatical method, as will become clear below.

The Classical Covenant View

In this view, a strict literal interpretation of prophetic Scripture is rejected. Jesus is viewed as the fulfillment of Old Testament promises made to Israel—including the land promises (the Abrahamic covenant, Genesis 13:14-17) and the throne promises (the Davidic covenant, 2 Samuel 7:12-16). The New Testament church is viewed as spiritual Israel, a continuation of Old Testament ethnic Israel. Hence, there will be no literal fulfillment of land promises (or other Old Testament prophecies) to Israel.

Dispensationalists view this position as practicing more eisegesis (reading a meaning *into* the text) than exegesis (deriving the meaning *out of* the text). They charge that this position is not consistent in using the historical-grammatical method, but rather incorporates allegory in prophetic portions of Scripture.

The Modified Covenantal View

While this view also rejects a strict literal interpretation of biblical prophecy, it also modifies things by allowing for a future literal fulfillment of land and throne promises made to Israel. There will allegedly be an *initial* spiritual fulfillment of these promises in the church, but the future will provide a more fully realized and literal fulfillment in which both Israel and the church share.

Again, dispensationalists respond that this view is built upon a faulty and inconsistent hermeneutic that ultimately allegorizes Old Testament promises made strictly to Israel. This view also fails to recognize the church's status as a new creation of God (2 Corinthians 5:17).

Progressive Dispensationalism

Progressive dispensationalism's openness to allegorism in interpreting Bible prophecy is evident in that it rejects that there is a fixed objective meaning of the biblical text. Rather, it holds that there are many meanings in a biblical text, and that we ought to seek a deeper understanding than the author's expressed meaning. This view also suggests there will be a literal fulfillment of the Abrahamic, Davidic, and New covenants in ethnic Israel, but also claims there is a present inaugural fulfillment of these covenants in the church.

Classical dispensationalists respond by asserting: 1) Those who approach prophecy in such an allegorical way are inconsistent, for they approach the rest of Scripture in a literal fashion; 2) there are no objective criteria by which one can determine the alleged *correct* allegorical truth; and 3) their approach goes against the precedent set by prophecies of Christ's first coming, all of which were fulfilled quite literally—including Christ being born of a virgin (Isaiah 7:14), in Bethlehem (Micah 5:2), from the line of Abraham (Genesis 15:1-6) and David (2 Samuel 7:12-16).

Traditional Dispensationalism versus Revised Dispensationalism

Both traditional dispensationalism and revised dispensationalism use a literal hermeneutic in interpreting Bible prophecy, and thus both believe in a national fulfillment of the Abrahamic covenant for Israel. Traditional dispensationalists, however, hold that there are *two* new covenants: one for Israel (yet to be fulfilled) and one for the church (presently being fulfilled). As well, Israel and the church are viewed as two separate peoples with different destinies: one in heaven (the church) and the other on earth (Israel).

Revised dispensationalism, by contrast, holds there is only one new covenant, which, while having a later literal fulfillment in national Israel, has a present application to the church. And even though revised dispensationalists see distinctives between Israel and the church, both are viewed as collectively composing one overall people of God who share in the spiritual redemption wrought by Christ.

The Distinction Between the Church and Israel

On the one hand, there are similarities between Israel and the church. For example: 1) Both are part of the people of God; 2) both are part of God's spiritual kingdom; and 3) both participate in the spiritual blessings of both the Abrahamic and New covenants.

Beyond this, however, there are notable distinctions, including: 1) While the roots of Israel predate Moses, the church began on the Day of Pentecost (Acts 1:5; 2:1-4; 1 Corinthians 12:13); 2) while Israel is an earthly political entity (Exodus 19:5-6), the universal church is the invisible, spiritual body of Christ (Ephesians 1:3); 3) while Israel was composed of Jews, the church is composed of both Jews and Gentiles; and 4) one becomes a Jew by physical birth, whereas one becomes a member of the church via a spiritual birth (John 3:3).

In contrast to such distinctions, covenantalists hold that the New Testament church is spiritual Israel, a continuation of Old Testament ethnic Israel. Dispensationalists respond that such a view is wrong for the following reasons: 1) A consistent use of the historical-grammatical method demands that the unconditional land and throne promises be literally fulfilled *in Israel* (Genesis 13:1-7; 2 Samuel 7:12-16); 2) John the Baptist offered a literal kingdom to national Israel (Matthew 3:2), as did Jesus (Matthew 19:28) and Peter (Acts 3:19-21); 3) the apostle Paul was clear that national Israel will be restored before Christ returns (Romans 11:1-2,29).

The Rapture

Most Christians believe the Tribulation will occur during a definite period of time at the end of the age, and that it will be characterized by great travail (Matthew 24:29-35). It will be of such severity that no period in history, past or future, will equal it (Matthew 24:21). It is called the time of Jacob's trouble, for it is a judgment on Messiah-rejecting Israel (Jeremiah 30:7; Daniel 12:1-4). The nations will also be judged for their sin and rejection of Christ (Isaiah 26:21; Revelation 6:15-17). Scripture says the Tribulation will last seven years (Daniel 9:24,27).

The rapture is that event in which the dead in Christ will be resurrected and Christians who are still alive on Earth will be instantly translated into their resurrection bodies—and both groups will be caught up to meet Christ in the air (John 14:1-3; 1 Corinthians 15:51-54; 1 Thessalonians 4:13-17). Christians debate between five primary views on this event:

The Partial Rapture View

This view, expressed in the writings of Witness Lee (1905–1997) of the Local Church movement, is based on the parable of the ten virgins, which depicts five virgins who are prepared and five who are unprepared (Matthew 25:1-13). This passage is interpreted to mean that only faithful and watchful Christians will be raptured. Unfaithful Christians will be "left behind" to suffer through the Tribulation. Pretribulationists, however, say that this verse has nothing to do with the rapture. The unprepared virgins apparently refer to people alive during the Tribulation period who are unprepared for Christ's second coming (seven years *after* the rapture). Besides, Scripture indicates that if one is a believer, one is saved and hence will participate in the rapture. Moreover, the Spirit's baptism places *all* believers in Christ's body (1 Corinthians 12:13), and therefore, *all* believers will be raptured (1 Thessalonians 4:16-17).

The Posttribulational View

This view, expressed in the writings of George Eldon Ladd and Robert Gundry (among others), states that Christ will rapture the church *after* the Tribulation at the second coming of Christ. This means the church will go through the time of judgment prophesied in the book of Revelation, but believers will allegedly be "kept through" Satan's wrath during the Tribulation (Revelation 3:10). Pretribulationists respond that Revelation 3:10 indicates believers will be saved "out of" (Greek: *ek*) the actual time of the Tribulation.

Posttribulationists argue that Revelation 20:4-6 proves that all believers will be resurrected at the end of the Tribulation. Pretribulationists respond, however, that in context, only those believers who died *during* the Tribulation will be resurrected at this time (Revelation 20:4). Believers who are alive on Earth *prior* to the Tribulation will be resurrected earlier at the rapture (1 Thessalonians 4:13-17).

Posttribulationists rebut that saints are mentioned as being on Earth during the Tribulation, and this must therefore mean the rapture will not have occurred yet. Pretribulationists grant that there will be saints on

Earth during the Tribulation period (for example, see Revelation 6:9-11). But these people apparently *become* Christians sometime *after* the rapture.

Posttribulationists counter by citing Matthew 24:37-40. In this passage, set in the context of the second coming, we are told that "two men will be in the field; one will be taken and the other left." Pretribulationists respond that the context indicates that those who are taken are taken not in the rapture but *in judgment, to be punished* (see Luke 17:37).

Support for posttribulationism is bolstered by the claim that pretribulationism emerged late in church history, finding its origin in John Nelson Darby (A.D. 1800–1882), who allegedly learned of it from Edward Irving (1792–1834). Thus, the majority of Christians throughout church history have known nothing of this "novel" view. Pretribulationists reply that the argument from church history involves the fallacy of chronological snobbery, wrongly arguing that truth is somehow determined by time. The fact is, some in the early church held to false doctrines, such as the doctrine of baptismal regeneration. So, just because a doctrine is early does not mean it is correct. Conversely, just because a doctrine arrives on the scene late does not mean it is incorrect. Many believe that with the process of doctrinal development through the centuries, it makes sense that eschatology would become a focal point of discussion later in church history. Besides, many throughout church history—as early as the first century—have held to the doctrine of the *imminent* return of Christ, a key feature of the pretribulational view.

The Midtribulational View

Midtribulationism—the view that Christ will rapture the church in the middle of the Tribulation period—has been taught by such proponents as Gleason Archer (A.D. 1916–2004), J. Oliver Buswell (1895–1977), and Merrill Tenney (1904–1985). The two witnesses of Revelation 11, who are caught up to heaven, are believed to be representative of the church. Pretribulationists, however, say that there is virtually no indication in the context of Revelation 11 that these witnesses represent the church.

Proponents of the midtribulation view argue that the church will be delivered from God's *wrath* (1 Thessalonians 5:9), which will be poured out during the second half of the Tribulation, but not from the *tribulation* that occurs in the first half. Pretribulationists point out, however, that because the entire Tribulation period is characterized by wrath (Zephaniah 1:15,18; 1 Thessalonians 1:10; Revelation 6:17; 14:7,10; 19:2), it makes more sense to say the church is delivered from the entire seven-year period (Revelation 3:10).

Proponents also argue that because the rapture occurs at the last trumpet (1 Thessalonians 4:16-17), and because the seventh trumpet sounds in the middle of the Tribulation (Revelation 11:15-19), then the rapture must occur during the middle of the Tribulation. Pretribulationists reply that the seventh trumpet sounds at the *end* of the Tribulation (see Revelation 11:15). Besides, the seventh trumpet is unrelated to the rapture. Rather, it deals with judgment.

The Pre-Wrath View

The pre-wrath view, represented by Robert van Kampen and Marvin Rosenthal, argues that the rapture will occur toward the end of the Tribulation before the great wrath of God falls. It is argued that the Bible indicates the church will not experience the wrath of God (2 Thessalonians 1:5-10). Since the word "wrath" does not appear in Revelation until *after* the sixth seal, this must mean God's wrath will not be poured out until the seventh seal (Revelation 6:12–8:1). Hence, the rapture must take place between the sixth and seventh seals.

Pretribulationists say there are a number of problems with this view, not the least of which is that God's wrath is poured out on the earth *prior* to the seventh seal (Zephaniah 1:15,18; 1 Thessalonians 1:10; Revelation 6:17; 14:7,10; 19:2). Scripture pictures the seven seals as sequential, all coming from the same ultimate source—God (Revelation 6; 8). This sequence features divine judgments that increase in intensity as each successive seal is opened. Both humans and warfare are seen to be instruments of God's wrath during the first six seals. Even the unsaved who experience this wrath will recognize it as the "wrath of the Lamb" (Revelation 6:15-16), who Himself opens the seals that cause the respective judgments (see Revelation 6:1,3,5,7,9,12; 8:1).

The Pretribulational View

This view holds that Christ will rapture the entire church before any part of the Tribulation begins. In support of this position, Revelation 3:10 indicates that believers will be kept from the actual hour of testing that is coming on the whole world. Further, no Old Testament passage on the Tribulation mentions the church (for example, Deuteronomy 4:29-30; Jeremiah 30:4-11; Daniel 8:24-27; 12:1-2), just as no New Testament passage on the Tribulation mentions the church (for example, Matthew 13:30,39-42,48-50; 24:15-31; 1 Thessalonians 1:9-10; 5:4-9; 2 Thessalonians 2:1-11; Revelation 4–18). In the book of Revelation, the word "church" or "churches" is used 19 times in the first three chapters, but in the section dealing with the Tribulation—chapters 4 through 18—not a single mention is made of the church. The church is then mentioned again in the context of the second coming in chapter 19.

Scripture asserts that the church is not appointed to wrath (Romans 5:9; 1 Thessalonians 1:9-10; 5:9). This means the church cannot go through the wrathful Tribulation period (Zephaniah 1:15,18; 1 Thessalonians 1:10; Revelation 6:17; 14:7,10; 19:2).

It is suggested that a pretribulational rapture best explains the sudden apostasy that comes upon the world by the removal of the restrainer, who is apparently the Holy Spirit (2 Thessalonians 2:3-7). The Holy Spirit indwells all believers (John 14:16; 1 Corinthians 3:17), and He will essentially be "removed" from the Earth when the church is raptured, thus making possible the fast eruption of apostasy.

Pretribulationists argue that the rapture involves Christ coming *for* His saints *in the air* prior to the Tribulation, whereas at the second coming He will come *with* His saints *to the earth* to reign for a 1000 years (Revelation 19; 20:1-6). The fact that Christ comes *with* His holy ones (redeemed believers) at the second coming presumes they've been previously raptured. (He cannot come *with* them until He has first come *for* them.) This rapture is a signless and imminent event, and could happen any moment.

All throughout Scripture God is seen protecting His people before judgment falls (see 2 Peter 2:5-9). Noah and his family were in the ark before the judgment of the flood. Lot was taken out of Sodom before judgment was poured out on Sodom and Gomorrah. The firstborn among the Hebrews in Egypt were sheltered by the blood of the Passover lamb before judgment fell. The spies were safely out of Jericho and Rahab was secured before judgment fell on Jericho. So, too, pretribulationists believe the church will be secured safely (via the rapture) before judgment falls during the Tribulation period.

The Millennial Kingdom

The millennial kingdom is another topic greatly debated among Christians. The debate is largely rooted in the hermeneutical approach people take when interpreting the prophetic texts in Scripture. Those who take an allegorical approach will generally uphold amillennialism or postmillennialism. Those who take a literal approach will embrace premillennialism.

Premillennialism

Premillennialism teaches that following the second coming, Christ will institute a kingdom of perfect peace and righteousness on earth that will last for 1000 years. Two forms of premillennialism have emerged: Dispensational premillennialism, championed by scholar John F. Walvoord (A.D. 1910–2002) among others, draws a distinction between the church and Israel, and holds that the Millennium will be a time of the fulfillment of unconditional promises made to Israel. Historic premillennialism, espoused by George Eldon Ladd (1911–1982) among others, more generally rests its case on a literal interpretation of Revelation 20:1-6.

Among the biblical arguments offered in favor of premillennialism are that this view 1) naturally emerges from a literal hermeneutic (see chapter 17); 2) best explains the unconditional land promises made to Abraham and his descendants, which are yet to be fulfilled (Genesis 13:14-18); 3) makes the best sense of the unconditional Davidic covenant in regard to the throne promise (2 Samuel 7:12-16); 4) is most compatible with numerous Old Testament predictions about the coming messianic age; 5) is consistent with the Old Testament ending with an expectation of the messianic kingdom (for example, Isaiah 9:6; 16:5; Malachi 3:1); 6) best explains the scriptural teaching that Jesus and the apostles would reign on thrones in Jerusalem (Matthew 19:28); and 7) is most consistent with the apostle Paul's promise that Israel will one day be restored (Romans 9:3-4; 11:1).

Many throughout church history have held to premillennialism, including church fathers Justin Martyr (A.D. 100–165), Clement of Alexandria (150–215), and Tertullian (155–225). Augustine (A.D. 354–430), early in his theological career, held to this view. Other theological luminaries who held to this view include John Nelson Darby (1800–1882), Griffith Thomas (1861–1924), Lewis Sperry Chafer (1871–1952), and James Montgomery Boice (1938–2000).

Amillennialism

Amillennialism, which takes a more spiritualized approach to interpreting biblical prophecy, teaches that when Christ comes, eternity will begin with no prior, literal 1000-year reign on earth. *Amillennial* literally means "no millennium." Instead of believing in a literal rule of Christ on earth, amillennialists generally interpret prophetic verses related to the reign of Christ metaphorically and say they refer to Christ's present (spiritual) rule from heaven. Old Testament predictions made to Israel are viewed as being fulfilled in the New Testament church.

Among arguments suggested in favor of amillennialism are 1) the Abrahamic and Davidic covenants were conditional, and hence do not require a future fulfillment because the conditions were not met; 2) prophecy should be interpreted symbolically, for apocalyptic literature is highly symbolic in nature; 3) Israel and the church are not two distinct entities, but rather are one people of God united by the covenant of grace; 4) this view is most compatible with the idea that the Old Testament is fulfilled in the New Testament; and 5) the New Testament contains many examples that demonstrate that Old Testament prophecies are fulfilled in the church (for example, Jeremiah 31:31; Hebrews 8:8-13).

This view was held by the later Augustine, as well as by Reformers Martin Luther (1483–1546) and John Calvin (1509–1564). Most Puritans were amillennial, as are most Roman Catholics. Famous proponents of the view in more recent history include Oswald Allis (1880–1973), Louis Berkhof (1873–1957), and Anthony Hoekema (1913–1988).

Postmillennialism

The postmillennial view, which also takes a more spiritual approach to interpreting biblical prophecy, teaches that through the church's progressive influence, the world will be Christianized before Christ returns. According to this view, the Millennium will basically involve 1000 years of peace and prosperity that *precedes* Christ's physical return. Primary proponents of this view include A. A. Hodge (1823–1886), B. B. Warfield (1851–1921), A. H. Strong (1836–1921), Loraine Boettner (1932–2000), and R. J. Rushdooney (1916–2001).

Among the arguments suggested in favor of postmillennialism are 1) a universal proclamation of the gospel is promised in Scripture (Matthew 28:18-20); 2) people from all nations will come to salvation (Revelation 7:9-10); 3) Christ's throne is in heaven, and it is from *this* throne—not a throne on Earth—that He rules (see Psalm 9:4,7; 47:2); 4) Jesus' parable of the mustard seed indicates there will be a continual advance of Christianity in the world (Matthew 13:31-32); and 5) it is claimed that world conditions are improving morally, socially, and spiritually—all due to the church's influence.

Of course, many today would challenge the last point given above. It hardly seems that the world is getting better. Moreover, this claim contradicts clear biblical passages that predict an apostasy in the end times prior to Christ's return (Matthew 24:3-14; Luke 18:8; 1 Timothy 4:1-5; 2 Timothy 3:1-7).

Preterism

The word *preterism* derives from the Latin word *preter*, which means "past." According to preterists, the prophecies in the book of Revelation (especially chapters 6–18) and Matthew 24–25 (Christ's Olivet Discourse) were already fulfilled in the past.

There are two forms of preterism: *moderate* (partial) preterism, and *extreme* (full) preterism. Moderate preterism is represented by modern writers such as R. C. Sproul, Hank Hanegraaff, and Gary DeMar. While they believe the literal resurrection and second coming are yet future, they say the other prophecies in Revelation and Matthew 24–25 were already fulfilled when Jerusalem fell to Rome in A.D. 70. Extreme or full preterism goes so far as to say that *all* New Testament predictions were fulfilled in the past, including those about the resurrection of believers and Christ's second coming. This latter view is heretical, denying two of the fundamentals of the Faith: the physical resurrection of believers and a literal second coming.

There is much current debate. For example, preterists point to Matthew 24:34, where Jesus asserted: "This generation will certainly not pass away until all these things have happened." This verse allegedly proves the prophecies in Scripture would *soon* be fulfilled. Contrary to this view, many evangelical Christians believe Christ was simply saying that the generation that is alive at the time such events as the abomination of desolation (verse 15), the Great Tribulation (verse 21), and the sign of the Son of Man in heaven (verse 30) begin to come to pass will *still* be alive when these prophetic judgments are completed. Other evangelicals believe the word "generation" in Matthew 24:34 is to be taken in its secondary meaning of "race." Jesus' statement could mean that the Jewish race would not pass away until these things are fulfilled. Either way, it is argued, the verse does not support preterism.

Preterists also argue from Matthew 16:28 that Jesus said some of His followers "standing" there would not taste death until they saw Him return, "coming in his kingdom." Contrary to the preterist view, many evangelicals believe that when Jesus said this, He had in mind the transfiguration, which happened precisely one week later (Matthew 17:1-13). The transfiguration served as a preview of the kingdom, in which the divine Messiah would appear in glory. Moreover, against the idea that Matthew 16:28 refers to A.D. 70 is the pivotal fact that some of the disciples "standing" there were *no longer alive* by A.D. 70 (all but John had been martyred by then). Still further, there are no records of astronomical events occurring in A.D. 70, such as the stars falling from heaven and the heavens being shaken (Matthew 24:29)—signs that Jesus promised would occur in the last days. And in A.D. 70, Jesus did not return "on the clouds of the sky, with power and great glory" (Matthew 24:30).

Preterists also point to verses that indicate that Jesus will come "quickly" (Revelation 22:12,20 NKJV), and that the events of which the book of Revelation speaks will be fulfilled "shortly" (1:1; 22:6 NKJV).

Futurists point out, however, that the word "quickly" often carries the meaning "swiftly, speedily, at a rapid rate." Thus the term could simply indicate that *when* the predicted events first start to occur, they will progress swiftly, in rapid succession. Likewise, the word translated "shortly" can simply mean "suddenly," not necessarily soon.

A favorite argument among preterists is that the book of Revelation was written prior to A.D. 70, and hence the book must have been fulfilled in A.D. 70 when Rome overran Jerusalem. But futurists point out that some of the earliest church fathers confirmed a late date for the book of Revelation, including Irenaeus (who knew Polycarp, John's disciple), who claimed the book was written at the close of the reign of Domitian (which took place from A.D. 81–96). Victorinus confirmed this date in the third century, as did Eusebius (A.D. 263–340). Hence, because the book was written *after* A.D. 70, it could hardly have been referring to events that would be fulfilled *in* A.D. 70. Against preterism, futurists note that key events described in the book of Revelation simply did not occur in A.D. 70. For example, in A.D. 70 "a third of mankind" was not killed, as predicted in Revelation 9:18. Two hundred million soldiers from the East have never invaded Israel, as predicted in Revelation 9:13-15. Nor has "every living thing in the sea died," as predicted in Revelation 16:3. In order to explain these texts, preterists must resort to allegorical interpretations, for these events did not happen literally.

The Danger of Extremes Regarding the Order of Second-Coming Events

One danger relates to hermeneutics. As noted earlier, premillennialism utilizes a literal hermeneutic when interpreting biblical prophecy, while amillennialism and postmillennialism utilize a spiritualized hermeneutic. The literal method is a hermeneutical essential (chapter 17). Without such a method, we could not know any of the doctrinal essentials. In view of this, it is sobering to ponder that while premillennialists—because of their literal approach to Scripture—are less likely to slip into liberal theology or false views on these essential doctrines, those who allegorize prophecy seem naturally more prone to this danger.

Another danger relates to the issue of date-setting. Christians can be excited about the coming of the Lord, but they should never attempt to set dates for His return. We suggest there are at least eight reasons Christians should not set dates:

- Over the past 2000 years, the track record of those who have attempted to predict the time of the rapture or second coming has been 100 percent wrong.
- Those who succumb to believing date-setters may end up making harmful decisions for their lives (like delaying a college education, or not saving money for the future).
- Christians who succumb to date-setting may end up damaging their faith in the Bible when their expectations are not fulfilled.
- When one loses confidence in the prophetic portions of Scripture, biblical prophecy ceases to be a motivation to holiness in daily life (Titus 2:12-14).
- Christians who succumb to date-setting may damage the faith of new or immature believers when the predicted events fail to materialize.
- Date-setting soothsayers tend to be sensationalistic, and sensationalism is unbefitting to a Christian. Christ calls His followers to live soberly and alertly as they await His coming (Mark 13:32-37).
- Humanists enjoy scorning Christians who have put stock in end-time predictions—especially when specific dates have been attached to specific events. Why give ammunition to the enemies of Christianity?
- The precise timing of end-time events is in God's hands, and we haven't been given the details (Acts 1:7).

Yet another danger is that hurtful divisions could emerge within the body of Christ that lead to public controversy. A recent example involves a well-known author of pretribulational fiction books, who, when another author who holds to a form of preterism wrote a fiction book published by the *same publisher,* said he felt "betrayed" by the publisher for publishing such "nonsense."[2] Some time later, the preterist author wrote a highly inflammatory book that mischaracterized pretribulationism, blasting it as "blasphemous," and associated dispensationalism with the "cultic fringe" like Mormonism.[3] Where is the liberty and charity in such actions?

There are certainly other examples we could point to, but the above is sufficient to demonstrate the damage that can be done by taking an extreme view on the nonessential issue of the order of end-time events.

Areas of Agreement Regarding the Order of Second-Coming Events

Despite the many differences we have discussed in this chapter, there are still many areas of agreement we can point to, and these agreements ought to serve as a basis of unity in the midst of our diversity on these issues:

- All agree that God is sovereignly in charge of the precise timing of end-time events.
- Aside from extreme or full preterism, all the views believe there will be a physical second coming of Christ.
- All the views believe there will be a future resurrection from the dead.
- All believe there will be a future judgment.
- All believe there will be an eternal state in which believers will live eternally with God.
- All agree that one beneficial aspect of studying biblical prophecy is that it motivates one to holiness in life.

The truth is, issues such as the timing of the rapture are not worth fighting over. In the long haul—after we've been with Christ for countless ages in heaven—the question of whether the rapture happened before or after the Tribulation period will truly seem inconsequential. All this is an intramural debate. So let's show some liberty to brothers and sisters who hold to a different view!

29

The Role of Women

ONE OF THE MORE heated debates that has emerged within the Christian church over the past half century relates to the role of women in the church. Much of the debate hinges on the question of whether women may take leadership roles, becoming ordained as elders, ministers, or pastors in the church, with ecclesiastical authority over men. Some churches—those open to what some call *evangelical feminism*—say yes. Others—those who hold to the traditional view (hereafter *traditionalists*)—say no. Let's briefly consider both sides of the debate. (Please note that because of space considerations, we will necessarily provide only a sampling of representative arguments on both sides.)

The History of Disagreement

The woman is "in all things inferior to the man," said first-century Jewish historian Flavius Josephus.[1] Rabbi Judah, a contemporary of Josephus, said "a man must pronounce three blessings each day: 'Blessed be the Lord who did not make me a heathen; blessed be he who did not make me a woman; blessed be he who did not make me an uneducated person.'"[2]

Jewish rabbis in the first century were encouraged not to teach or even to speak with women. Jewish wisdom literature tells us that "he that talks much with womankind brings evil upon himself and neglects the study of the Law and at the last will inherit Gehenna [hell]."[3] One reason for such avoidance of women was the belief that they could lead men astray: "From garments cometh a moth and from a woman the iniquities of a man" (Ecclesiasticus 42:13). Indeed, men were often viewed as intrinsically better than women, for "better is the iniquity of a man than a woman doing a good turn" (Ecclesiasticus 42:14).

In view of this low status of women, it is not surprising that they enjoyed few legal rights in ancient Jewish society. Women were not even allowed to give evidence in a court of law, except in special circumstances. Moreover, according to the rabbinic school that followed Rabbi Hillel, a man could legally divorce his wife for merely burning his dinner.

It was in this oppressive context that Christianity was born. Many people—both men and women—have hailed Jesus as a feminist because of His defense and even elevation of women in a male-chauvinist society. Moreover, the apostle Paul's statement in Galatians 3:28—"There is neither Jew nor Greek, slave nor free, male nor female, for you are all one in Christ Jesus"—has been called the Magna Carta of humanity. Because of the Christian's standing in Christ, some evangelical feminists argue, the subordination of women that was (allegedly) caused by the Fall (Genesis 3) has been replaced with total equality of the sexes in Christ. Any apparent biblical teaching of the need for female submission today, they say, is based on misinterpretations by male scholars.

To some the word *feminism* represents liberation and long-awaited justice; to others, divisiveness. Emotions have sometimes run feverishly high in the debate over gender roles, and this debate has made its way into the theological mainstream. Today, women are being ordained as ministers in some Christian denominations; Bibles are being published using "inclusive language"; and those who take a politically incorrect stand against either of these may find themselves on the receiving end of some rather harsh criticism.

Overview of Evangelical Feminism

An objective examination of church history clearly reveals the substantial impact various women have made through the centuries for the cause of Christ (see Mary Hammack's book *Dictionary of Women in Church History* [Chicago: Moody, 1984]). Be that as it may, church history also reveals that leadership roles, pastorates, and positions of ecclesiastical authority have been the near-exclusive domain of men, at least until recent times. Historically, the first widely publicized book on the role of women in the church that hinted at the formulation of a specific feminist theology was published in 1968: *The Church and the Second Sex,* by Mary Daly (New York: Harper & Row, 1968). Following the publication of this book, the market became virtually flooded with books and articles on feminist theology, all of which challenged the idea that female subordination was ordained by God.

In 1975, a conference of evangelical feminists was held in Washington, D.C., that attracted 360 participants from across the United States. The conference formally endorsed the Equal Rights Amendment and established the Evangelical Women's Caucus, a grassroots consciousness-raising organization with chapters in many major cities.

Some traditionalists at the time argued that the emergence of evangelical feminism may be an example of the negative influence of trends in the wider culture (in this case, feminism) on contemporary Christianity. However, Christian feminists rejected this assessment: "We did not become feminists and then try to fit our Christianity into feminist ideology. We heralded the feminist movement because we were convinced that the church had strayed from a correct understanding of God's will for women."[4]

Evangelical feminists generally (but not always) hold to conservative views on the Bible and theology, but nevertheless embrace the feminist ideal of abolishing—or, at least, significantly adjusting—gender-based roles in society, church, and home. Most believe the Bible is authoritative and, rightly understood, supports their feminist views. Far too often, they say, the church has centered on biblical imagery that represents God as "Father" while ignoring the Scriptures that typify God as "Mother." The Lord, for example, is portrayed as a nursing mother (Isaiah 49:15), a midwife (Psalm 22:9-10), and a female homemaker (Psalm 123:2). The church thus needs to adjust its outlook, they say.

Jesus Was a Feminist

Many have hailed Jesus as being a feminist in a first-century, male-chauvinist society. Reasons cited include:

- In the account of Martha and Mary (Luke 10:38-42),

Mary—instead of helping Martha with domestic duties—took the "male" role of sitting at Jesus' feet and listening to His teaching, which may be interpreted to mean that "women should prefer studying theology over a preoccupation with domestic chores."[5]

- "Jesus commissioned women to be the first witnesses of His resurrection and sent them to teach the male disciples that He was risen."[6]
- Evangelical feminists discount the fact that Jesus chose 12 Jewish men to be disciples. "If Jesus' choice of twelve male [*Jewish*] disciples signifies that females should not be leaders in the church, then, consistently, his choice also signifies that Gentiles should not be leaders in the church."[7] Because Gentiles *are* allowed to be leaders in the church, the same should be true for women.

Female Subordination: A Result of the Curse

Evangelical feminists argue that male headship and female subordination in the marital relationship is a part of the curse. They point to Genesis 3:16, where God pronounced judgment against the woman: "I will greatly multiply your sorrow and your conception; in pain you shall bring forth children; your desire shall be for your husband, and he shall rule over you" (NKJV).

It is thus suggested that "only after Adam and Eve have substituted their will for God's will does the specter of male supremacy and female subordination enter the picture."[8] Thus, "it is proper to regard both male dominance and death as being antithetical to God's original intent in creation. Both are the result of sin, itself instigated by Satan. Their origin is satanic."[9]

The good news, we are told, is that in Christ "the law of the Spirit of life set me free from the law of sin and death" (Romans 8:2). So, "theologically speaking, the death of Christ released humanity from the curse brought about by sin. Woman is no longer to be subjugated under male headship."[10]

Equal in Christ

In Galatians 3:28 the apostle Paul affirmed, "There is neither Jew nor Greek, slave nor free, male nor female, for you are all one in Christ Jesus." Evangelical feminists argue that Paul was not speaking about the equality of men and women in their spiritual standing before God, but of the practical outworking of that standing *in society*. Hence, in view of Galatians 3:28, "all social distinctions between men and women should [be] erased in the church."[11]

Mutual Submission

Ephesians 5:21-24 instructs men and women to submit "to one another out of reverence for Christ. Wives, submit to your own husbands as to the Lord. For the husband is the head of the wife as Christ is the head of the church. Now as the church submits to Christ, so also wives should submit to their husbands in everything."

Evangelical feminists generally make verse 21—which calls for husbands and wives to "submit to one another"—the governing verse of the entire passage. Because of what Christ accomplished at the cross, the male domination brought about by the Fall has been annulled, and now there is to be mutual submission.

Ephesians 5:22-24—which calls for wives to submit *to their husbands*—is more problematic for evangelical feminists. Many claim that a hierarchical model of male/female roles may have been appropriate for a New Testament culture, but such a model is no longer binding on twentieth-century Christians. We are told that "passages which are theological and doctrinal in content [should be] used to interpret those where the writer is dealing with practical local cultural problems."[12] Thus, Ephesians 5:22-24 must give way to Galatians 3:28.

Others say that while Paul taught a hierarchical model of male/female relations in Ephesians, this was based on his rabbinic training, and he was wrong. We are thus told that passages that teach a hierarchical model should be seen as "distorted by the human instrument."[13]

Still others deal with these verses by arguing that the word "head" has nothing to do with the exercise of authority but rather refers to *source*, a meaning supported by two pieces of ancient literature: Herodotus 4.91

and Orphic Fragments 21a.[14] This is in keeping with the Genesis account, for the woman has her source in man. Hence, "there is nothing in the fifth chapter of Ephesians that would even remotely indicate" that wives are responsible to submit to their husbands.[15] Contrary to such a view, however, exhaustive linguistic studies have uncovered *no clear instances* of the meaning "source" for the Greek word in question.[16]

Silence in the Church

In 1 Corinthians 14:34-35, the apostle Paul instructed, "Let your women keep silent in the churches, for they are not permitted to speak; but they are to be submissive, as the law also says. And if they want to learn something, let them ask their own husbands at home; for it is shameful for women to speak in church" (NKJV).

Most Christian feminists say the word "speak" in 1 Corinthians 14:34 refers only to general talking or idle chatter and does not include formal lectures, exhortation, or teaching. Hence, women were prohibited by Paul from chattering or disturbing the meeting, but not from formal public teaching or leading.

As for 1 Timothy 2:11-12—"A woman should learn in quietness and full submission. I do not permit a woman to teach or to have authority over a man; she must be silent"—evangelical feminists generally say Paul was prohibiting women from speaking or teaching because they had not been properly educated. But "because twentieth-century women are better trained and qualified to teach, Paul's directive doesn't apply."[17]

The Evangelical Feminist Approach

From our brief survey above, we may conclude that evangelical feminists sometimes argue their case from the biblical text (for example, Genesis 3:16; Galatians 3:28). Other biblical texts, they say, deal with local cultural situations of the first century and thus must not be seen as normative for modern society (for example, 1 Corinthians 14:33-36; Ephesians 5:21-24; 1 Timothy 2:11-15). Evangelical feminists thus conclude there is no good reason women cannot become ordained as elders, ministers, or pastors and hold positions of ecclesiastical authority over men.

Overview of Traditionalism

Female Subordination Is Not a Result of the Fall!

Contrary to evangelical feminists, traditionalists argue that male headship is established in the creation account in Genesis 2—before the Fall took place. Man was created first. The woman was created from Adam's rib *to be his helper* (Genesis 2:18). While both male and female were created in God's image and were accorded personal dignity, God, in the creation narrative, set them in a nonreversible relation to one another—male in loving headship over the female.

Adam's headship is illustrated in that as soon as the woman was created, Adam *named* the woman (Genesis 2:23). In ancient times, to name someone or something implied having authority over the one named (Genesis 17:5; 2 Kings 23:34; Daniel 1:7).

Traditionalists also point out that when God gave instructions about moral responsibility, He gave these instructions *to Adam alone* (Genesis 2:16-17). And after the Fall, God *first summoned Adam,* not Eve, even though she was the one who had led him into sin (Genesis 3:9). In Romans 5:12, Adam was held *solely* responsible for the Fall, even though Eve played a significant role.

One of Adam's failures was his abdication of responsibility for leadership. Instead of obeying God and leading his wife, he disobeyed God and followed his wife. For this reason, God begins His sentence against Adam, "Because you have heeded the voice of your wife..." (Genesis 3:17 NKJV). In the Fall, therefore, God's intended order of authority was reversed. Eve listened to the serpent instead of Adam; Adam listened to Eve instead of God.[18]

Traditionalists thus argue that God's judgment against the woman in Genesis 3:16 cannot be viewed as the source of hierarchical social order. Rather, it points to the reality that with the entrance of sin, the hierarchical order remains (having been established in Genesis 2), but sin's effect will now be experienced *within* that order. Hence, God's statement in Genesis 3:16 was simply a divine description of *what would occur* (male domination and oppression as opposed to loving headship), not a *mandate* that obedient servants of God should attempt to carry out.

Positional Equality in Christ

The apostle Paul said, "There is neither Jew nor Greek, slave nor free, male nor female" in Christ (Galatians 3:28). Traditionalists point out that, contextually, the verses that precede Galatians 3:28 pertain to justification by faith and how a person comes to be included in the blessings promised in the Abrahamic covenant (verses 15-25). "In Galatians 3:26-28, Paul was saying that no kind of person is excluded from *the position* of being a child of Abraham who has faith in Jesus Christ."[19] That Paul was referring solely to one's *position* in Christ in Galatians 3:28 is evident in the words "sons of God" (verse 26), "Abraham's seed," and "heirs according to the promise" (verse 29).

Elimination of gender-based roles is therefore not a legitimate inference from Galatians 3:28. *Positional equality in Christ* (between man and woman) and *functional subordination* (with the man in authority over the woman) are not mutually exclusive concepts in Paul's theology.

Silence in the Church

How do we relate 1 Corinthians 11, where Paul allows for women praying and prophesying in the church, to chapter 14, where Paul commands women to be silent in church? Traditionalists assert that the evangelical feminist argument that Paul in chapter 14 was merely forbidding disorderly chatter does not fit the context. Paul instructed women to remain silent *because they were women*, not because they were engaged in idle chatter or were disorderly. In order to be subordinate, Paul said, women must be silent—just "as the Law says" (1 Corinthians 14:34). Scholars differ as to what passage(s) Paul meant by the term "Law," but that is beside the point. The important factor for traditionalists is that Paul used the word in reference *to Scripture*—whether the Mosaic law (Romans 7:22,25; 1 Corinthians 9:9) or the Old Testament as a whole (Romans 3:10-19; 1 Corinthians 14:21).

Traditionalists thus claim that Paul's appeal to the law shows he was not simply repeating something he learned from rabbinic literature, but was teaching something backed by God's Word. That Paul cites the law shows that his argument for the silence of women in church was theological and universal, not sociological or cultural.

1 Timothy 2:11-14

In this passage, Paul wrote, "A woman should learn in quietness and full submission. And I do not permit a woman to teach or to have authority over a man; she must be silent. For Adam was formed first, then Eve. And Adam was not the one deceived; it was the woman who was deceived and became a sinner." Traditionalists say Paul builds his argument for female subordination on the *order of creation* and the *order of the Fall.* Paul's reasoning goes like this: "Adam was created first as the head; Eve was created second as a 'helper suitable for him,' and she fell first; therefore, women are under some restriction."

The question of how to harmonize 1 Timothy 2:11-15, 1 Corinthians 11:2-16, and 1 Corinthians 14:33-36 has been answered variously by traditionalists. One predominant understanding is that though women are completely equal with men in their standing before God, they are forbidden to be in a functional position of ecclesiastical authority over men, teaching them in a congregational setting. This implies neither the superiority of the male nor the inferiority of the female. Paul's theology simply reflects the creation order established by God in which man was appointed to function as the spiritual head.

Traditionalists emphasize that women are not prohibited, however, from teaching men on an individual basis—as apparently Priscilla, with her husband Aquila, taught Apollos (Acts 18:26). (They say Priscilla was evidently teaching under the headship of Aquila, to whom the authority belonged.) Nor are women forbidden to personally address fellow believers, male and female, to their "strengthening, encouragement and comfort" (1 Corinthians 14:3). Nor are women forbidden to teach women (Titus 2:3-4) or children (2 Timothy 1:5; 3:14), or take part in other fruitful ministries (Philippians 4:3). After all, traditionalists claim that women are just as spiritually gifted as men are for the work of ministry (1 Corinthians 12:4-11).

In short, traditionalists believe women are privileged to serve God in many different ways within the authority structure He designed. J. I. Packer put it this way: "That women are gifted for and called to service in the church is plain, and gifted persons are gifts that the churches must properly value and fully use."[20] However, as Packer also urges, this call to service (according to Scripture) is not to involve women becoming ordained as elders or ministers with ecclesiastical authority over men.

Of course, there are some views that are neither strictly feminist nor traditionalist but are variations on one or the other. But whatever view one embraces, it should be with humility and charity toward those with whom we differ.

A Supplemental Note on the Ordination of Women

One heavily debated issue today relates to the ordination of women. Traditionalists have long believed that only men should be ordained as elders, pastors, or ministers of churches. However, there is a growing body of churches and denominations worldwide who have broken with tradition and are now ordaining women.

Arguments for the ordination of women include:

- It is okay for women to be ordained so long as they are under the authority of the (male) head pastor.
- There is an example in Miriam the prophetess, who helped Moses shepherd the Israelite nation (she was in submission to Moses) (Exodus 15).
- There are other female prophetesses mentioned in Scripture (Luke 2:36-38; Acts 2:17-18; 21:9; 1 Corinthians 11:5), and if women can prophesy, they can participate in any ministry.
- Jesus and the apostles used many gifted women to help care for and bring the lost to salvation, thus allowing them to participate in a pastoral role (Mark 15:41; Luke 8:2; John 4:28-30,39; Acts 18:18,26; Colossians 4:15).
- Priscilla (wife of Aquila) apparently carried out some pastoral functions, including helping train Apollos (Acts 18).
- There is no indication that women are excluded from having the spiritual gift of teaching (Romans 12:7;

1 Corinthians 12:28-29; Ephesians 4:12); therefore, they can participate in ministry.

- Women—like men—are often recognized as "fellow workers" in ministry (Romans 16:3; Philippians 4:2), and therefore ought to be recognized in ordination.

Contrary to this view, the vast majority of churches throughout history have held that only males can be ordained as elders, pastors, or ministers in churches. Arguments offered against the ordination of women include the following:

- All the disciples and apostles were male, thereby establishing a pattern of male leadership (see Matthew 19:28; Revelation 21:14).
- In keeping with this, from Genesis to Revelation we witness a pattern of male leadership among God's people. The occasional appearance of a female prophetess usually occurs in unusual circumstances.
- Among the biblical qualifications for elders is that they must be the husband of one wife (1 Timothy 3:2; Titus 1:6), which clearly excludes women.
- While some Scripture verses indicate that women can have the gift of teaching, this is tempered by other Scripture verses that restrict the function or role of women in the church.
- For example, the apostle Paul said women are not permitted to teach or to have authority over men (1 Timothy 2:11-14).
- Paul stated that women are to keep silent in church and are to be subordinate (1 Corinthians 14:33-36).

Some Christian churches and denominations are persuaded by the first set of arguments, while others are persuaded by the latter. The debate continues. This is not one of the fundamentals of the Faith, so however strongly one feels, one should do so with respect toward those with whom one differs.

The Danger of Extremes Regarding the Role of Women

As with other doctrinal controversies, there are dangers within the extremes. A danger among extremists on both sides of this debate involves the tendency to read preunderstandings (or theological biases) into Scripture. For example, some on the traditionalist side may read the preunderstanding of "male supremacy" into the biblical text. Some on the evangelical feminist side may read cultural explanations into theological portions of the biblical text with a view to establishing their case for being ordained as an elder or minister with ecclesiastical authority over men. The better policy is that of the International Council on Biblical Inerrancy:

> We affirm that any preunderstandings which the interpreter brings to Scripture should be in harmony with scriptural teaching and subject to correction by it. We deny that Scripture should be required to fit alien preunderstandings, inconsistent with itself....To avoid misinterpreting Scripture one must be careful to examine his own presuppositions in the light of Scripture.[21]

A possible danger among extremists on the evangelical feminist side is that because of their strong feelings on the matter, they may have less than optimal respect for the male leadership in churches. Such an attitude would, of course, violate God's ideal (Hebrews 13:17).

Another danger among extremists on the evangelical feminist side involves the possible undermining of the Bible. It is simply not acceptable to say that some teachings on women in Paul's writings are "distorted by the human instrument" (see chapter 16).

A possible danger among extremists on the traditionalist side is the mind-set that *only men* are to be involved in all aspects of Christian ministry. As we have documented, Scripture indicates that women were involved in a number of areas of fruitful ministry in the New Testament church.

Another danger on the traditionalist side is that men—inside *and* outside the church—may overvalue themselves while undervaluing women, all because of misapplications of the passages discussed in this chapter. Such misapplications must be condemned as sinful distortions of God's original design for man and woman.

Yet another possible danger on the traditionalist side is the view that women's ministries are insignificant. According to the apostle Paul, *all* ministries in the body of Christ are significant (1 Corinthians 12:21-23).

Areas of Agreement Regarding the Role of Women

Despite the divergence of opinions that exists among Christians on the matter of the role of women in the church, most churches within Christendom hold to the following in common:

- All Christians can agree that men and women are equally created in the image of God, and both are hence of inestimable worth to God (Genesis 1:26-27).
- All Christians can agree that men and women are equally spiritually gifted (1 Corinthians 12:4-11).
- All Christians can agree that during New Testament times, women were used of God in the work of ministry in varying capacities, whether teaching on an individual basis (Acts 18:26), ministering to other women (Titus 2:3-4), ministering to children (2 Timothy 1:5; 3:14), or other ministries (Philippians 4:3).
- Christians can agree—or at least they *ought* to agree—that women should *at the very least* be permitted involvement in similar ministries in our day.
- Christians can agree that ministries of both men *and* women are significant (1 Corinthians 12:21-23).

Christians will no doubt continue to debate whether women belong in the pulpit. But even in the midst of our strong differences on this issue, let us choose to agree to disagree in an agreeable way, recognizing the wisdom and virtue of showing liberty on the nonessential doctrines of Christianity. Let us not forget that the debate about the role of women in the church does not relate to any of the essentials of the Christian Faith. So, men *and* women, let's keep things in perspective.

Part Three:

In All Things, *Charity*

IN THIS FINAL SECTION we consider the last third of the famous dictum, *In essentials, unity; in nonessentials, liberty; and* ***in all things, charity.*** All too often believers have been uncharitable in the ways they have defended the essentials of the Faith, forgetting to heed the apostle Paul's exhortation to speak the truth in love (Ephesians 4:15). This applies both to those who make majors into minors (see Part One), as well as those who make majors out of minors (see Part Two). While we need conviction without compromise on the fundamental truths of the Faith, we also need conviction with compassion on all truths.

30

Lessons from the Past

LOOKING BACK OVER THE doctrinal unity on the essentials (chapters 1–17) and diversity on the nonessentials (chapters 18–28), there are many lessons to be learned. Five come to mind and are worthy of comment.

Key Lessons for All Christians

1. It Is Better to Be Divided by Truth than to Be United by Error

Ecumenical zeal at the expense of sound doctrine is an unsound practice. When it comes to essential doctrines, it is better to be divided by truth than to be united by error. Or, as someone once put it, "Better a holy discord than a profane concord."

All doctrines divide at some level. So, realistically, some kind of division cannot be avoided. Theism, for example, divides one from atheism. Those who affirm there is a God are clearly in a different category than those who deny there is a God. Likewise, those who affirm Christ is God are in a separate class from those who deny His deity. The same applies to all doctrines. Thus, at this basic level, there is nothing wrong with being divided by doctrine, for it serves to separate the orthodox from the unorthodox. Simple logic demands that those who affirm a particular orthodox doctrine are not in the same category as those who deny that doctrine.

The lesson to be learned from the history of the church, however, is this: *Be sure that the doctrines that divide us are essential ones.* We have exercised great care in Part One of this book to show that there are 16 essential doctrines that comprise the core of Christian orthodoxy. These should be guarded at all cost.

With respect to these, it is better to be divided by these essential truths than to be united on the basis of errors. Compromise on essentials is an *essential error.* One should never allow cracks in the pillars of a building to go unattended. As the psalmist put it, "When the foundations are being destroyed, what can the righteous do?" (Psalm 11:3).

This brings to mind the first letter of the apostle John, which states this:

> Dear children, this is the last hour; and as you have heard that the antichrist is coming, even now many antichrists have come. This is how we know it is the last hour. They went out from us, but they did not really belong to us. For if they had belonged to us, they would have remained with us; but their going showed that none of them belonged to us (1 John 2:18-19).

The heretics John references held to a Gnostic-type view of Christ that denied the true incarnation and denied that He had truly died on the cross. This Gnostic Jesus was said to save people by the knowledge He imparts, not by any saving act at the cross. John thus assured his readers that these heretics were wrong and that what the apostles taught about Jesus was true.

Notice that while these heretics took the initial step in separating from the church, John made it clear that such a separation was necessary. Moreover, John, in his second epistle, exhorts his readers who confront such errors to take the initiative themselves by separating from them.[1] We read:

> Many deceivers, who do not acknowledge Jesus Christ as coming in the flesh, have gone out into the world. Any such person is the deceiver and the antichrist....Anyone who.... does not continue in the teaching of Christ does not have God...If anyone comes to you and does not bring this teaching, *do not take him into your house or welcome him.* Anyone who welcomes him shares in his wicked work (2 John 1:7-11, emphasis added).

So, again, it is better to be divided by truth than to be united by error.

2. There Is No True Unity Without Unity in the Truth

This brings us to another important related lesson: *True unity is not possible without unity in the truth.* Hence, ecumenical zeal should not overrun doctrinal soundness. It is a fantasy to believe there can be true unity without unity in the truth. Any unity not based on truth is not true unity. It is a false unity.

Jesus prayed for true unity when He asked "that all of them may be one" (John 17:21). But only a few verses earlier He affirmed to the Father, "Your word is truth" (verse 17). To put it in its strongest form, one cannot and should not expect unity between God and the devil. Likewise, there can be no true unity between the truth of God and "things taught by demons" (1 Timothy 4:1).

Holding hands for Jesus and singing *Kumbaya* may produce a *feeling* of oneness, but it does not necessarily reflect true unity in the Faith. That comes only from a commitment by all parties concerned to the central truths of the Christian Faith.

An illustration will make the point. Jesus instructed us to worship God "in spirit and in truth" (John 4:24). So, there is no true worship without worship in the truth. Because *worship* means "honor" or "worth-ship," one cannot truly worship God without speaking the truth about Him. Surely parents would not be honored by a child who spoke falsehoods and lies about them. Neither can God be truly worshiped by songs consisting of words that are not doctrinally sound or that speak falsehoods about Him. Likewise, no matter how good one may feel about a so-called worship or spiritual experience, if it is not based on and does not express *truth*, it is not a *true* experience of God. We conclude, then, that there is, in truth, no true unity without unity in the truth.

3. Orthodoxy Should Not be Sacrificed for Unity

Down through the centuries, and particularly in our time, there has been a seemingly irresistible tendency to sacrifice orthodoxy for the sake of unity. This often involves what may be called the common denominator" fallacy. If any given group has, say, three people, and two of them believe X, Y, and Z, and one believes only X and Y, what do they all have in common? Obviously, X and Y. But suppose Z is the deity of Christ.

Should we, for the sake of the unity of the whole group, reduce our doctrinal basis to *only* X and Y, and not make a big deal about Z? While this is an admirable approach when it comes to nonessential doctrines, it is fatal when it comes to essential doctrines. Orthodoxy on essentials should never be sacrificed for unity.

This "common denominator" fallacy has destroyed orthodoxy in Christian institutions from time immemorial. One cannot count the denominations, churches, and other institutions that have "gone liberal" based on what, on the surface, seemed initially to be an admirable goal—namely, to preserve unity. But *at what cost!* Real orthodoxy on essential doctrines should not and must not be sacrificed on the altar of alleged unity.

4. True Unity Does Not Demand Uniformity but Allows Diversity

Not all diversity is bad. What if the world were all one color? What if there were only one kind of flower? What if there were no variety in animal species? What if there were no ethnic diversity? Or what if there were only one kind of food? This would be a very boring world! The same is true when it comes to differences in churches. Given a basic doctrinal commonality on the essential doctrines, there is something to be said for allowing diversity within unity. This is true in many areas and for many reasons.

First, churches often unnecessarily divide over (for example) the type of music employed in their worship services, or even over the instruments used (see chapter 25). Most of this does not involve unorthodox doctrinal content, and is often a matter of taste, not a matter of truth. On this level, diversity can be as good as many flavors of ice cream. The basic kinds are neither good nor bad in themselves, neither true nor false. Likewise, different styles of liturgy need not involve heresy. Indeed, different personalities and nationalities and even age groups are drawn to different forms of worship. Just ask missionaries or anyone who has traveled widely. This kind of diversity provides a richness and variety that brings a wider appeal to Christianity.

Second, even in the realm of truth, not all diversity is heresy (see Romans 14:2-6). Given that humans are finite and fallible, it is understandable that there will be differences of opinion on nonessential doctrines. Although we all have our own opinions on the mode of baptism, for example, no heresy is involved in the amount of water used to baptize. Also, some teachings are not as important, and have briefer coverage in Scripture, and, hence, may not be as clear as others. So, for example, within the overall framework of the essential doctrine of Christ's physical return and reign, there is room for difference of opinion on the details of the precise order of end-time events.

There is no reason that each of us cannot hold to our own views when it comes to nonessentials. There is good reason, however, that none of these nonessential teachings should be made a universal test of orthodoxy or Christian fellowship.

5. *Orthodoxy Should Always Be Expressed with Charity*

A charge sometimes leveled against orthodox Christians relates to their apparent lack of love. We should note, in preface, that this criticism is sometimes based on a false dichotomy between truth and love. Jesus, for example, was doing the loving thing when He rebuked the Jewish religious hypocrites, even though His truthful words were very forceful (Matthew 23). Apart from the moral obligation to keep confidence regarding private conversations and not to engage in gossip about others, even when it involves truth, it is *usually* the loving thing to do to tell the truth. So, there often is no separation between love and truth, because telling the truth is the loving thing to do. And even when the truth hurts, it can be the loving thing to say, as is evident when a doctor informs us that we need an operation to save our life.

Nonetheless, we acknowledge that some Christians, unfortunately, speak the truth in a harsh and unkind manner. Doing so is both unnecessary and unchristian. The Bible urges us to speak the truth in love (Ephesians 4:15). It is not simply *what we believe* that is important, but also *how we behave*. Yes, Jesus emphasized the importance of truth. He said, "You will know the truth, and the truth will set you free" (John 8:32). But He also said that love, not simply truth, is the distinguishing mark of a Christian (John 13:35). One can be right in what he says and wrong in the way he says it. A Christian should strive to be both right and loving.

To be sure, the manner in which one holds truth does not change its truth value. Truth held arrogantly is not false, just as error held humbly is not true. Nonetheless, many will be inclined to the latter, not because *what is said* is true, but because *the way it was said* was more winsome.

Let us not forget that love is to truth what heat is to light. Others are more likely to accept truth when it is presented in a warm way and not simply as the cold facts. In short, we must constantly remember the third part of this book's dictum: In all things, *charity.*

To ignore charity is to risk doing injury to our brothers and sisters in Christ. J. C. Ryle, in his classic book *Holiness,* noted how hurtful words can be among Christians who disagree with each other, and how such hurtful words are actually self-defeating:

> I must enter my protest against the sneering, taunting, contemptuous language which has been frequently used of late.... To say the least, such language is unseemly, and only defeats its own end. A cause which is defended by such language is deservedly suspicious. Truth needs no such weapons. If we cannot agree with men, we need not speak of their views with discourtesy and contempt.[2]

Ryle thus urges: "Let us exercise charity in our judgments of one another," noting that to "exhibit bitterness and coldness" toward those who disagree with us on some matter "is to prove ourselves very ignorant of real holiness."[3]

Theologian J. I. Packer helps us to understand the importance of charitable behavior in the body of Christ by using the metaphor of a family:

> How ought families—siblings, specifically brothers and sisters—to behave? Well, you are not going to deny that siblings ought to act like and look like parts of a family. If brothers and sisters never meet together, never speak to each other, appear to be entirely indifferent to each other—that is an unnatural and scandalous state. That would be true of any human family. I put it to you without fear of contradiction: the same is true of the family of God.[4]

Packer's point is that "divisions in the church which prevent the family from acting like one family and the body from functioning like one body... are unnatural; unnatural to the point of being shameful."[5] The better way is the way of charity.

Perhaps the most shameful example of a lack of charity in church history relates to the famous East-West split. Following the A.D. 1054 split between Rome and the Eastern church (over the nonessential issue of whether the Holy Spirit proceeds from the Father alone, or from the Father and the Son), a strong wedge was driven between the two groups by the stronger Western sector. The rape and pillage of the Byzantine capital of Constantinople by Roman Catholic crusades is a blight on Christendom. It was followed by this lamentable statement from the Grand Duke Lucas Motaras: "I would rather see the Moslem turban in the midst of the city than the Latin Mitre [liturgical headdress]."[6] Such words and actions should never be named among Christians.

The Proper Balance

Sadly, the history of the church is filled with people who have polarized toward extremes on various issues. Many have made nonessentials into essentials, and others have made essentials into nonessentials. Numerous examples of these types of mistakes have been provided in the previous chapters.

On the one hand, there is the extreme of *compromise on basic conviction*. On the other hand is the extreme of *conviction without compassion*. We suggest that the proper balance should be *conviction without compromise* when it comes to the essential doctrines of Christianity, and *conviction with compassion* on the nonessentials. This is the theme of our next and final chapter.

31

Loving in the Present

IN ESSENTIALS, *UNITY*; in nonessentials, *liberty*; and in all things, *charity*.

It is hard to improve on either the economy of these words or the profundity of these thoughts. In Part One of this book (chapters 1–17) we demonstrated the necessity of standing firm on the 16 essential doctrines of the Christian Faith. This, we contend, is a necessary commitment on which there can be no compromise. In Part Two (chapters 18–29) we demonstrated the dangers and unnecessary divisions in Christendom over violating the admonishment in nonessentials, *liberty*. In this last chapter of Part Three, our aim is to emphasize the all-pervading and too-often-absent principle of love.

The apostle Paul struck the perfect balance when he exhorted the Ephesians about the importance of "speaking the truth in love" (Ephesians 4:15). Fallen humans are, unfortunately, creatures of extreme. On the one hand, some on the conservative side seek to stand for the truth at all costs—and sometimes fail to exercise love as they do so. On the other hand, many on the liberal side often sacrifice orthodoxy for the sake of unity and charity. The wisdom of Scripture dictates that both are extremes, and we are urged to pursue "the most excellent way" (1 Corinthians 12:31).

The Unity of Love and Truth

Love and truth are not opposed to each other. They are both attributes of God. "God is love" (1 John 4:16) and He is a "God of truth" (Psalm 31:5), just as His "word is truth" (John 17:17). So, whatever conflict we experience between love and truth is on the human side, not the divine side. When God utters truth, no matter how much it hurts, it is communicated in love, for in communicating truth, He seeks our highest well-being. We must therefore accept it and defend it. It is much like when a doctor says, "You have cancer and need an operation." Communicating this hard truth is the most loving thing a doctor can do; conversely, the most *un*loving thing he could do is to withhold the truth.

This is not to say that our allegiance to both love and truth never come into conflict in this finite, fallen world; they do. It is only to say that there is a way to balance them and thus fulfill the will of God. Speaking the truth in love *is* possible. Indeed, it is a moral imperative.

Love in the Unity of Orthodoxy

The adage *It is better to be divided by truth than to be united by error*—addressed in the previous chapter—is sometimes misstated and overextended. It is misstated when the division is over a conflict on nonessential truths. It is neither right nor necessary to divide over nonessential doctrines. This does not mean it is wrong to *hold* to differing views, for that is part of the liberty granted on nonessentials. There is no reason a variety of views cannot be held within orthodoxy on nonessential matters such as the mode of baptism, the form of liturgy in church, or the precise details on the order of end-time events.

However, one should remember these three things about holding to different points of view on nonessential doctrines: First, it is always possible that we may be wrong and others may be right. Second, even if we are right, we should hold our view in humility (1 Peter 3:15). Third, we should not sever fellowship or cease cooperation with those who hold to contrary views on nonessential matters.

The above-mentioned adage is also sometimes overextended. Again, we must ever keep in mind that the adage applies only to essential matters. It does not apply to all truth. Gossip, for example, often contains truth, but, it can be extremely harmful to others. This is definitely not an example of "speaking the truth in love." Thus, gossip is repeatedly condemned in Scripture. Indeed, it is sometimes listed among the most grievous of sins (Romans 1:29-30).

As well, things spoken in confidence—in which private truths are shared—should be *kept* in confidence. Pastoral counseling is a case in point. If the counselor breaks confidence with the counselee, sharing private truths with other people, then the trust necessary to help the counselee has been broken. And it is unloving to do things that hinder helping such a person. This too, then, is definitely not an example of speaking the truth in love. It is noteworthy that the Bible often condemns talebearing because it is an unloving thing to do. In fact, it produces disunity. The wisest man who ever lived wrote, "Without gossip a quarrel dies down" (Proverbs 26:20). And, "A gossip separates close friends" (Proverbs 16:28). Indeed, when it comes to truths spoken in confidence, it is better to *conceal* them than *reveal* them. The Scriptures declare: "A gossip betrays a confidence, but a trustworthy man keeps a secret" (Proverbs 11:13).

So, then: Yes, it is better to be divided by essential truths than to be united by error. But it is unloving to divide the body of Christ by gossip or by revealing confidential truths. Such activities should never be named among God's people.

It is also unloving to divide the body of Christ because of one's theological hobbyhorse on a nonessential matter. Probably the greatest division in Christendom, over one of the least important doctrinal issues, was the division in A.D. 1054 between Eastern and Western Orthodoxy on whether the Holy Spirit proceeds from the Father and the Son (Western view) or only from the Father (Eastern view). This millennium-long division by the two largest sections of Christendom is a classic example of an unnecessary—and at times very unloving—division over a nonessential doctrine (see chapter 18).

Love in the Division from Heresy

While it is unloving to divide over nonessential truths, it is also unloving to *not* divide over a denial of essential truths. As we learned in chapter 1, essential truths are those necessary for our salvation. Not to divide over these when error is at issue is one of the most unloving things one could do. Not to defend the truths once for all delivered to the saints is like failing to protect a dam, a bridge, or a government building against terrorists. Indeed, a failure to defend essential doctrines against "destructive heresies" (2 Peter 2:1) is eminently *un*loving, and can have eternal consequences.

Much of today's contemporary church labors under the false delusion that unity is more important than orthodoxy. The truth is that once people accept that premise, neither unity *nor* orthodoxy will long survive. Clearly, orthodoxy is sacrificed when one adopts a "unity at all costs" mentality. But unity, too, is sacrificed, for there is no *true* unity without unity in the *truth* (see chapter 30).

False unity can be found in uniformity or union, but neither produces true unity, which demands a harmony of beliefs, attitudes, and goals. Genuine unity, then, is based on orthodoxy. Without a common conviction over that which is true, no true unity exists.

So, one of the most loving things we can do for Christianity is to preserve its essential orthodoxy, for this orthodoxy in truth is the grounds of true unity. Thus, dividing over essential truths is not only loving, it is necessary. No organization can survive as such without preserving its core truths. Even a square-Earth society must monitor its membership and exclude from it any who believe the Earth is round. This is true no matter how many nice round-earthers would like to join, no matter how much this would increase their membership, and no matter how much unity this would produce between the two groups. *Core beliefs are core beliefs,* no matter how great the temptation is to let down the bar and allow persons with opposing beliefs to join. After all, there are round-Earth societies, and round-earthers can join them. The two groups may even desire to carry on dialogue between themselves individually or collectively. And if people change their minds, they may join the other society. But they cannot compromise their core conditions for membership without engaging in a self-destructive activity.

This does not mean that persons of diverse beliefs, theological or not, cannot engage in joint efforts for other causes. There may be, for example, both square- and round-earthers in the Democratic party. It is perfectly permissible for them to join in the common cause of electing a Democratic president. Likewise, there may be round- and square-earther Republicans who can join together in the effort to elect a Republican president. The same is true of orthodox and unorthodox Christians. They can join together on civil, social, or moral causes *without sacrificing their core doctrinal positions*. Doctrinal and ecclesiastic differences by no means exclude cooperation on civil, social, educational, and environmental causes.

All this notwithstanding, there is no justification for sacrificing orthodoxy for unity. For, as noted previously, on essential doctrines, it is better to be divided by truth than to be united by error. However, no matter *how* necessary the division over essential truth is, there is no excuse for not doing it in a loving way. Difficult as it may be to take a stand on the fundamentals of the Faith, tough love in doing so is still love. And one need not be paranoid about the charge that this is unnecessarily dividing the body of Christ. When one defends the very truths that make the body of Christ possible, one is not dividing the body. Rather, one is supporting the grounds on which that body stands. Further, it is not the orthodox but the *un*orthodox who divide the body. It is not those who affirm the essential truths of the Faith that are divisive; it is those who deny the essentials. Let's put the shoe on the right foot. For example, it is not the orthodox who affirm the deity of Christ who are being divisive; it is the Arians and Jehovah's Witnesses who deny this essential truth who are dividing themselves from orthodox Christianity.

So, firm as we must be in defending the essential truths, even if the disagreement divides one group from another, we must still be loving. Here are some things to keep in mind while defending orthodox doctrine in a loving way: First, we should respect the other person, even when disagreeing with his position. Second, we need to respect the other person's *view*, even if we believe it is wrong. Third, it is not only *what* we say but *how we say it* that is important. For love is the mark of a Christian (John 13:35), and it should characterize all of our activity—even the activity of preserving orthodoxy.

Love in Diversity on Nonessentials

Some people, by their very spiritual giftedness, see issues in black and white. To them, grey is as bad as black. The gift of discernment is an admirable gift, and the body of Christ as a whole should thank God for those who have it. But love must be the overriding virtue (1 Corinthians 13:13); it should never be separated from our discernment of truth. The ability to see doctrinal issues in black and white is not bad in itself. But honesty demands that we make a distinction between the essential and the nonessential doctrines. We must also concede that the nonessential doctrines are often not as black and white as we might like to think.

Indeed, even the principle of perspicuity (clearness) of Scripture, so precious to Protestants, does not contend that *all* truths of Scripture are *equally* clear. It contends only that the *main* truths are clear. That is, the main things are the plain things, and the plain things are the main things. As it has been well said, in the quest for orthodoxy we need to remember that the main thing is to keep the main thing the main thing. We not only do not have as much certainty about the nonessential doctrines, but we should not hold to them with the same sense of finality. And the degree of certainty over an issue should not diminish our charity toward those who do not agree with our views. J. I. Packer, speaking of nonessentials, put it this way:

> None of us...whatever his or her own personal convictions, should feel entitled to say with absolute confidence that the Bible excludes the other way. We are in the realm, not of certainties of faith, but of matters of more or less probable opinion. The most we can say is that "I *think* the Bible excludes the other way; I *think* my practice is the one Scripture directs."[1]

Hence, it is loving for us to allow differences of opinion on minor issues. And it is *un*loving to make a major issue out of a minor one. There is a correlation between the importance of the truth and the emphasis that is placed on it. For if one treats a nonessential like an essential and treats a minor doctrine as though it were a major one, then he has unnecessarily divided the body of Christ. Such an activity does not show proper concern for the body, no matter what the intent may have been.

Truth *and* Love

We conclude this chapter as we began it. A more simple, more comprehensive, and more profound truth is hard to find: In essentials, *unity;*

in nonessentials, *liberty;* and in all things, *charity.* To recap, in Part One of this book (chapters 1–17), we demonstrated the necessity of standing firm on the 16 essentials of the Christian Faith. In this area, God demands *conviction without compromise.* In Part Two (chapters 18–29), we demonstrated some of the dangers and divisions that are caused in Christendom over violating the admonishment, in nonessentials, liberty. In this final chapter of Part Three, our aim has been to emphasize the all-pervading and too-often absent principle of love, thus completing the dictum: In all things, charity.

Speaking the truth in love may not be easy, but it is essential. For truth without love is sterile, and love without truth is senile. But defending the truth in love is both essential and fruitful.

Bibliography

Adams, Jay. *Competent to Counsel*. Grand Rapids: Baker, 1970.

Aid to Bible Understanding. New York: Watchtower Bible and Tract Society, 1971.

Althaus, Paul. *The Theology of Martin Luther*. Philadelphia: Fortress Press, 1984.

Anderson, George. *Justification by Faith*. Minneapolis: Augsburg, 1985.

Ankerberg, John. *The Masonic Lodge: What Goes on Behind Closed Doors?* Chattanooga: The John Ankerberg Evangelistic Association, 1986.

Ankerberg, John, and John Weldon. *Encyclopedia of Cults and New Religions*. Eugene: Harvest House, 1999.

Arndt, Stephen, and Mark Jordan. *A Catholic Catechism for Adults*. San Francisco: Ignatius Press, 1987.

Atkinson, James. *Martin Luther*. Grand Rapids: Eerdmans, 1983.

Bainton, R. H. *Here I Stand*. Nashville: Abingdon, 1978.

Baker's Dictionary of Theology. Ed. Everett Harrison. Grand Rapids: Baker Books, 1960.

Barker, Charles. *Bible Truth: What We Believe and Why*. Milwaukee: Milwaukee Bible College, 1956.

Berkhof, Louis. *Manual of Christian Doctrine*. Grand Rapids: Eerdmans, 1983.

Berkhof, Louis. *Systematic Theology*. Grand Rapids: Eerdmans, 1977.

Besant, Annie. *Karma*. London: Theosophical Publishing Society, 1904.

Bilezikian, Gilbert. *Beyond Sex Roles*. Grand Rapids: Baker Books, 1985.

Bock, Darrell. *The Missing Gospels: Unearthing the Truth Behind Alternative Christianities*. Nashville: Nelson, 2006.

Book of Mormon Student Manual. Salt Lake City: Church of Jesus Christ of Latter-day Saints, 1989.

Bowman, Robert. *Understanding Jehovah's Witnesses*. Grand Rapids: Baker Books, 1991.

Brown, Dan. *The Da Vinci Code*. New York: Anchor, 2006.

Brown, Harold O. J. *Heresy*. Grand Rapids: Baker Books, 1984.

Browne, Sylvia, with Lindsay Harrison. *Phenomenon*. New York: Dutton, 2005.

Buswell, James. *A Systematic Theology of the Christian Religion*. Grand Rapids: Zondervan, 1979.

Calvin, John. *Calvin's Commentaries*. Grand Rapids: Baker Books, 1974.

Calvin, John. *Commentary on John's Gospel*. Grand Rapids: Baker, 1949.

Calvin, John. *Institutes of the Christian Religion*. Ed. John T. McNeill; trans. Ford Lewis Battles. Philadelphia: Westminster Press, 1960.

Catechism of the Catholic Church. New York: Doubleday, 1994.

Chemnitz, Martin. *Examination of the Council of Trent*. St. Louis: Concordia, 1971.

Christadelphian Answers. Ed. Frank Jannaway. Houston: Herald Press, 1920.

Clarke, Adam. *Clarke's Commentary*. Nashville: Abingdon Press, 1977.

Coil, Henry Wilson. *Coil's Masonic Encyclopedia*. New York: Macoy Publishing, 1961.

Copeland, Kenneth. *The Incarnation* (audiotape #01-0402). Fort Worth: Kenneth Copeland Ministries, 1985.

Copeland, Kenneth. *What Happened from the Cross to the Throne* (audiotape #02-0017). Fort Worth: Kenneth Copeland Ministries, 1990.

Craig, William Lane, and Walter Sinnott-Armstrong. *God? A Debate Between a Christian and an Atheist*. Oxford: Oxford University Press, 2004.

Creation. Brooklyn: Watchtower Bible and Tract Society, 1927.

Creme, Benjamin. *The Reappearance of the Christ and the Masters of Wisdom*. Los Angeles: Tara Center, 1980.

Denzinger, Henry. *The Sources of Catholic Dogma*. St. Louis: Herder, 1957.

Divine Principle. New York: The Holy Spirit Association for the Unification of World Christianity, 1996.

Doctrine and Covenants. Salt Lake City: The Church of Jesus Christ of Latter-day Saints, 1990.

Douty, Norman. *The Death of Christ*. Irving, TX: Williams and Watrous, 1978.

Eddy, Mary Baker. *Science and Health with Key to the Scriptures*. Boston: The Writings of Mary Baker Eddy, 2000.

Eddy, Mary Baker. *Unity of Good*. Boston: Trustees under the Will of Mary Baker G. Eddy, 1908.

Elgin, Kathleen. *The Unitarians*. New York: David McKay, 1971.

Erickson, Millard. *Christian Theology*. Grand Rapids: Baker, 1985.

Esslemont, J. E. *Baha'u'llah and the New Era: An Introduction to the Baha'i Faith*. Wilmette, IL: Baha'i Publishing Trust, 1980.

Exposition of the Divine Principle. New York: The Holy Spirit Association for the Unification of World Christianity, 1998.

Fillmore, Charles. *The Metaphysical Dictionary*. Lees Summit: Unity, 1962.

From Paradise Lost to Paradise Regained. New York: Watchtower Bible and Tract Society, n.d.

Geisler, N. L. and William Nix. *A General Introduction to the Bible*. Chicago: Moody Press, 1986.

Geisler, Norman. *Chosen But Free: A Balanced View of Election.* Minneapolis: Bethany House, 1999.

Geisler, Norman. *Christian Apologetics.* Grand Rapids: Baker, 1976.

Geisler, Norman. *Explaining Hermeneutics.* Oakland: International Council on Biblical Inerrancy, 1983.

Geisler, Norman. *Systematic Theology: Church and Last Things,* vol. 4. Minneapolis: Bethany House, 2005.

Geisler, Norman. *Systematic Theology: Introduction and Bible,* vol. 1. Minneapolis: Bethany House, 2005.

Geisler, Norman. *Systematic Theology: Sin and Salvation,* vol. 3. Minneapolis: Bethany House, 2004.

Geisler, Norman and Ron Brooks. *When Skeptics Ask.* Wheaton: Victor, 1990.

Geisler, Norman L. and Ralph McKenzie. *Roman Catholics and Evangelicals: Agreements and Differences.* Grand Rapids: Baker Books, 1995.

Geisler, Norman, and Ron Rhodes. *Correcting the Cults.* Grand Rapids: Baker Books, 2004.

Getz, Gene. *Sharpening the Focus of the Church.* Wheaton: Victor, 1984.

Gleanings from the Writings of Baha'u'llah. Trans. Shoghi Effendi. Wilmette: Baha'i Publishing Trust, 1969.

Glueck, Nelson. *Rivers in the Desert.* Philadelphia: Jewish Publications, 1969.

Gomes, Alan. *Unmasking the Cults.* Grand Rapids: Zondervan, 1995.

Gospel Principles. Salt Lake City: Church of Jesus Christ of Latter-day Saints, 1986.

Gundry, Robert. *Soma in Biblical Theology.* Cambridge: Cambridge University Press, 1976.

Habermas, Gary. *The Historical Jesus: Ancient Evidence for the Life of Christ.* Joplin, IL: College Press, 1996.

Hammond, William E. *What Masonry Means.* New York: Macoy, 1952.

Hanegraaff, Hank. *The Apocalypse Code.* Wheaton, IL: Tyndale House, 2007.

Harris, Jack. *Freemasonry: The Invisible Cult in Our Midst.* Chattanooga, IL: Global, 1983.

Harris, Murray. *Easter in Durham.* Dublin: Attic Press, 1986.

Harris, Murray. *From Grave to Glory.* Grand Rapids: Zondervan, 1990.

Harris, Murray. *Raised Immortal.* Grand Rapids: Eerdmans, 1985.

Haywood, H. L. *Great Teachings of Masonry.* Kingsport, TN: Southern Publishers, 1923.

Heline, Corrine. *New Age Bible Interpretation.* Santa Monica, CA: New Age Bible and Philosophy Center, 1961.

Hewett, Philip. *The Unitarian Way.* Toronto: Canadian Unitarian Council, 1985.

Hodge, Charles. *Systematic Theology.* Grand Rapids: Eerdmans, 1952.

Hoekema, Anthony. *Saved by Grace.* Grand Rapids: Eerdmans, 1989.

Holmes, Ernest. *Gateway to Life.* Los Angeles: Science of Mind Publications, n.d.

Holmes, Ernest. *The Philosophy of Jesus.* Los Angeles: Science of Mind, n.d.

Holmes, Ernest. *The Science of Mind.* New York: Dodd, Mead, 1938.

Holmes, Ernest. *What Religious Science Teaches.* Los Angeles: Science of Mind Publications, 1975.

Holmes, Ernest, and Fenwicke Holmes. *The Voice Celestial.* Los Angeles: Science of Mind Publications, 1979.

Howe, E. Margaret. *Women and Church Leadership.* Grand Rapids: Zondervan, 1982.

Hull, Gretchen. *Equal to Serve.* Old Tappan, NJ: Revell, 1987.

Inerrancy and the Church. Ed. John Hannah. Chicago: Moody Press, 1984.

Ironside, Harry. *Wrongly Dividing the Word of Truth.* Neptune, NJ: Loizeaux Brothers, 1938.

Jedin, H. *History of the Council of Trent.* St. Louis: Herder, 1947.

Jesus Under Fire: Modern Scholarship Reinvents the Historical Jesus. Eds. Michael Wilkins and J. P. Moreland. Grand Rapids: Zondervan, 1995.

John Paul II. *Crossing the Threshold of Hope.* New York: Knopf, 1994.

Josephus, Flavius. *Against Apion.* Grand Rapids: Kregel, 1974.

Kassian, Mary. *Women, Creation, and the Fall.* Westchester, IL: Crossway, 1990.

Komoszewski, J. ed., M. James Sawyer, and Daniel B. Wallace. *Reinventing Jesus: What* The Da Vinci Code *and Other Novel Speculations Don't Tell You.* Grand Rapids: Kregel, 2006.

Küng, Hans. *Justification.* New York: Thomas Nelson, 1964.

Ladd, George Eldon. *A Theology of the New Testament.* Grand Rapids: Eerdmans, 1974.

Ladd, George Eldon. *I Believe in the Resurrection of Jesus.* Grand Rapids: Eerdmans, 1975.

Let God Be True. Brooklyn: Watchtower Bible and Tract Society, 1952.

Let Your Name Be Sanctified. Brooklyn: Watchtower Bible and Tract Society, 1961.

Lewis, Gordon, and Bruce Demarest. *Integrative Theology.* Grand Rapids: Zondervan, 1996.

Lightner, Robert. *The Death Christ Died.* Schaumburg, IL: Regular Baptist Press, 1978.

Luther, Martin. *On the Bondage of the Will.* Grand Rapids: Baker Books, 1976.

Luther, Martin. "The Babylonian Captivity of the Church," in *Three Treatises.* Philadelphia: Muhlenberg, 1943.

Machen, J. Gresham. *The Virgin Birth of Christ*. New York: Harper, 1930.

Mackey, Albert G. *A Manual of the Lodge*. New York: Maynard, Merrill, & Co., 1898.

Mackey, Albert G. *Revised Encyclopedia of Freemasonry*. Richmond, VA: Macoy, 1966.

MacLaine, Shirley. *Dancing in the Light*. New York: Bantam, 1985.

Magnani, Duane. *The Watchtower Files*. Minneapolis: Bethany House, 1985.

Martin, Walter. *The Kingdom of the Cults*. Minneapolis: Bethany House, 1985.

McConkie, Bruce. *Mormon Doctrine*. Salt Lake City, UT: Bookcraft, 1971.

McConkie, Bruce. *What the Mormons Think of Christ*. Salt Lake City, UT: Deseret, 1973.

McDonald, H. D. *Theories of Revelation: An Historical Study 1700–1960*. Grand Rapids: Baker Books, 1979.

McDowell, Josh. *Evidence that Demands a Verdict*. San Bernardino, CA: Campus Crusade for Christ, 1972.

McGrath, Alister. *Iustitia Dei: A History of the Christian Doctrine of Justification*. Cambridge: Cambridge University Press, 1986.

McKeever, Bill, and Eric Johnson. *Questions to Ask Your Mormon Friend*. Minneapolis: Bethany House, 1994.

Metzger, Bruce. *Historical and Literary Studies: Pagan, Jewish, and Christian*. Grand Rapids: Eerdmans, 1968.

Miles, Herbert and Fern. *Husband-Wife Equality*. Old Tappan, NJ: Revell, 1978.

Mollenkott, Virginia. *Women, Men, and the Bible*. Nashville, TN: Abingdon, 1977.

Morison, James. *The Extent of the Atonement*. Glasgow, 1882.

Mueller, Theodore. *Christian Dogmatics*. St. Louis: Concordia, 2003.

Nash, Ronald. *The Gospel and the Greeks: Did the New Testament Borrow from Pagan Thought?* Phillipsburg, NJ: Presbyterian and Reformed, 2003.

Neuer, Werner. *Man and Woman in Christian Perspective*. Wheaton, IL: Crossway, 1990.

Ott, Ludwig. *Fundamentals of Catholic Dogma*. Rockford, IL: Tan Books, 1960.

Packer, J. I. *Knowing God*. Downers Grove, IL: InterVarsity, 1979.

Packer, J. I. *Serving the People of God*. Great Britain: Paternoster Press, 1998.

Pentecost, Dwight. *Things to Come*. Grand Rapids: Zondervan, 1965.

Pratt, Orson. *The Seer*. Washington, D.C.: 1853–54.

Prophet, Mark and Elizabeth Clare. *Climb the Highest Mountain*. Los Angeles: Summit University Press, 1974.

Prophet, Mark and Elizabeth Clare. *The Lost Teachings of Jesus*. Livingston, MT: Summit University Press, 1988.

Ramtha, with D. J. Mahr. *Voyage to the New World*. New York: Fawcett, 1987.

Reardon, Bernard M. G. *Religious Thought in the Reformation.* New York: Longman, 1981.

Reasoning from the Scriptures. Brooklyn: Watchtower Bible and Tract Society, 1989.

Rhodes, Ron. *Answering the Objections of Atheists, Agnostics, and Skeptics.* Eugene, OR: Harvest House, 2006.

Rhodes, Ron. *The Challenge of the Cults and New Religions: Their History, Their Doctrine, Our Response.* Grand Rapids: Zondervan, 2001.

Rhodes, Ron. *The Complete Guide to Christian Denominations.* Eugene, OR: Harvest House, 2004.

Rhodes, Ron. *Christ Before the Manger: The Life and Times of the Preincarnate Christ.* Grand Rapids: Baker Book House, 1992.

Rhodes, Ron. *Christianity According to the Bible.* Eugene, OR: Harvest House, 2006.

Rhodes, Ron. *Find It Quick Handbook on Cults and New Religions.* Eugene, OR: Harvest House, 2006.

Rhodes, Ron. *Reasoning from the Scriptures with Catholics.* Eugene, OR: Harvest House, 2004.

Richards, Legrand. *A Marvelous Work and a Wonder.* Salt Lake City, UT: Deseret, 1976.

Roberts, Jane. *Seth Speaks.* New York: Prentice Hall, 1972.

Robinson, David. *The Unitarians and the Universalists.* Westport, CT: Greenwood Press, 1985.

Robinson, John J. *Born in Blood: The Lost Secrets of Freemasonry.* New York: M. Evans & Company, 1989.

Rongstad, James. *The Lodge: How to Respond.* Saint Louis: CPH, 1995.

Ryle, J. C. *Expository Thoughts on the Gospels.* New York: Robert Carter, 1911.

Ryle, J. C. *Holiness.* Moscow, ID: Charles Nolan, 2001.

Ryrie, Charles. *Basic Theology.* Wheaton, IL: Victor, 1986.

Ryrie, Charles. *Dispensationalism Today.* Chicago: Moody Press, 1965.

Scanzoni, Letha and Nancy Hardesty. *All We're Meant to Be.* Waco, TX: Word, 1974.

Schaff, Philip. *History of the Christian Church.* New York: Scribner, 1902.

Schaff, Philip. *The Apostolic Fathers with Justin Martyr and Irenaeus.* Grand Rapids: Eerdmans, 2001.

Schaff, Philip. *The Creeds of Christendom.* Grand Rapids: Baker Books, 1983.

Schaff, Philip. *A Select Library of Nicene and Post-Nicene Fathers of the Christian Church.* Grand Rapids: Eerdmans, 1964.

Schucman, Helen. *A Course in Miracles.* New York: Foundation for Inner Peace, 1992.

Should You Believe in the Trinity? Brooklyn: Watchtower Bible and Tract Society, 1989.

Sias, John. *100 Questions that Non-Members Ask About Unitarian Universalism*. Nashua, NH: Transition Publishing, 1999.

Simple, Peter. *Baha'i Teachings, Light for All Regions*. Wilmette, IL: Baha'i, 1970.

Smeaton, George. *The Apostles' Doctrine of the Atonement*. Grand Rapids: Zondervan, 1957.

Spangler, David. *Cooperation with Spirit*. Middleton, WI: The Lorian Press, 1982.

Spangler, David. *Reflections on the Christ*. Forres, Scotland: Findhorn Publications, 1981.

Spangler, David. *Revelation: The Birth of a New Age*. San Francisco: Rainbow Bridge, 1976.

Spangler, David. *Towards a Planetary Vision*. Forres, Scotland: Findhorn, 1977.

Spencer, Aida. *Beyond the Curse*. Nashville: Thomas Nelson, 1985.

St. Augustine. *The City of God*. New York: Penguin, 2003.

Steiner, Rudolf. *Jesus and Christ*. Spring Valley, NY: Anthroposophic Press, 1976.

Steiner, Rudolf. *The Reappearance of the Christ in the Etheric*. Spring Valley, NY: Anthroposophic Press, 1983.

Studies in the Scriptures. Brooklyn: Watchtower Bible and Tract Society, 1917.

Swenson, Orville. *The Perilous Path of Cultism*. Saskatchewan, Canada: Briercrest Books, 1987.

Teachings of the Prophet Joseph Smith. Ed. Joseph Fielding Smith. Salt Lake City, UT: Deseret Book Company, 1977.

Tennant, Harry. *Christadelphians: What They Believe and Preach*. Birmingham, AL: The Christadelphian, 1986.

The Ante-Nicene Fathers. Ed. Alexander Roberts and James Donaldson. Grand Rapids: Eerdmans, 1985.

The Baha'is: A Profile of the Baha'i Faith and Its Worldwide Community. United Kingdom: Baha'i Publishing Trust, 1994.

The Bible Knowledge Commentary, New Testament. Eds. John Walvoord and Roy Zuck. Wheaton, IL: Victor, 1983.

The Companion Bible. London: Oxford University Press, 1913.

The Gods Have Landed. Ed. James Lewis. New York: State University of New York Press, 1995.

The Greatest Man Who Ever Lived. New York: Watchtower Bible and Tract Society, 1991.

The Holy Bible. Salt Lake City, UT: Church of Jesus Christ of Latter-day Saints, 1990.

The Oxford Dictionary of the Christian Church, 2nd edition. Ed. F.L. Cross. Oxford University Press, 1978.

The Unitarian Universalists Pocket Guide. Boston: Skinner House Books, 1999.

Toon, Peter. *Foundations for Faith*. Westchester, IL: Crossway Books, 1983.

Van Praagh, James. *Talking to Heaven*. New York: Signet, 1997.

Walvoord, John. *Jesus Christ Our Lord*. Chicago: Moody, 1980.

Ware, Timothy. *The Orthodox Church*. New York: Penguin, 1983.

Warfield, B. B. *Perfectionism*. Oxford: Oxford University Press, 1931.

Wesley, John. *A Plain Account of Christian Perfection*. London: Epworth, 1968 reprint.

White, James. *The Forgotten Trinity*. Minneapolis: Bethany, 1998.

Wierwille, Victor. *Jesus Christ Is Not God*. New Knoxville, OH: American Christian, 1975.

Wierwille, Victor. *The Word's Way*. New Knoxville, OH: American Christian, 1971.

Wilmhurst, W. L. *The Masonic Initiation*. London: John M. Watkins, 1957.

Witherington, Ben. *What Have They Done with Jesus?* San Francisco: Harper, 2006.

Woodbridge, John. *Biblical Authority: A Critique of the Roger/McKim Proposal*. Grand Rapids: Zondervan, 1982.

You Can Live Forever in Paradise on Earth. New York: Watchtower Bible and Tract Society, 1989.

Notes

1. An Overview

1. See Thomas Aquinas, *Summa Theologica* 1.1.1.
2. John Calvin, *Institutes of the Christian Religion*, ed. John T. McNeill, trans. Ford Lewis Battles (Philadelphia: Westminster Press, 1960), 1.7.4.
3. See N. L. Geisler, *Systematic Theology: Introduction and Bible*, vol. 1 (Minneapolis: Bethany House, 2002), chapters 17–23; John Hannah, ed., *Inerrancy and the Church* (Chicago: Moody Press, 1984); H.D. McDonald, *Theories of Revelation: An Historical Study 1700–1960* (Grand Rapids: Baker Books, 1979); John Woodbridge, *Biblical Authority: A Critique of the Roger/ McKim Proposal* (Grand Rapids: Zondervan, 1982).
4. See Norman Geisler and Ron Rhodes, *Correcting the Cults* (Grand Rapids: Baker Books, 2004); Ron Rhodes, *The Challenge of the Cults and New Religions: Their History, Their Doctrine, Our Response* (Grand Rapids: Zondervan, 2001).
5. See the articles and reviews in the *Christian Apologetics Journal* (Spring 2005) published by Southern Evangelical Seminary: www.ses.edu.
6. F L. Cross, ed., *The Oxford Dictionary of the Christian Church*, 2nd ed. (Oxford University Press, 1978), p. 1070.
7. Church historian Philip Schaff claims the creed "is a clear and precise summary of the doctrinal decisions of the first four ecumenical Councils between 325 and 451 A.D" (See *The Creeds of Christendom* [Grand Rapids: Baker Books, 1983], 1.37). This would place it after A.D. 451.

2. God's Unity

1. See Ron Rhodes, *Christ Before the Manger: The Life and Times of the Preincarnate Christ* (Eugene, OR: Wipf and Stock, 2002), chapter 5.
2. For more detailed information on such groups, see Norman Geisler and Ron Rhodes, *Correcting the Cults* (Grand Rapids: Baker, 2006); Ron Rhodes, *The Challenge of the Cults and New Religions* (Grand Rapids: Zondervan, 2001); and Ron Rhodes, *Find It Quick Handbook on Cults and New Religions* (Eugene, OR: Harvest House, 2006).
3. See *Reasoning from the Scriptures* (Brooklyn: Watchtower Bible and Tract Society, 1989), p. 213.
4. *Should You Believe in the Trinity?* (Brooklyn: Watchtower Bible and Tract Society, 1989), p. 20.
5. Orson Pratt, *Journal of Discourses*, 2:345.
6. Spencer W. Kimball, *The Ensign*, Nov. 1975, p. 80.
7. Joseph Fielding Smith, ed., *Teachings of the Prophet Joseph Smith* (Salt Lake City, UT: Deseret Book Company, 1977), p. 370.
8. Orson Pratt, *The Seer* (Washington, D.C.: N.P., 1853–54), pp. 37-38.
9. Norman Geisler and Ron Brooks, *When Skeptics Ask* (Wheaton, IL: Victor, 1990), pp. 18-19.
10. Sylvia Browne with Lindsay Harrison, *Phenomenon* (New York: Dutton, 2005), p. 42.

3. God's Tri-unity

1. James White, *The Forgotten Trinity* (Minneapolis: Bethany, 1998), p. 29.
2. "Beliefs," Swedenborg Web site: www.swedenborg.org.
3. "Doctrines to Be Rejected," Christadelphian Web site: www.christadelphian.org.
4. "Our Faith and Beliefs," Christadelphian Web site: www.christadelphian.org.
5. Ernest Holmes, *What Religious Science Teaches* (Los Angeles: Science of Mind Publications, 1975), p. 61.
6. Charles Fillmore, *The Metaphysical Dictionary* (Lee's Summit, MO: Unity, 1962), p. 629.

4. Christ's Deity

1. *Reasoning from the Scriptures* (Brooklyn: Watchtower Bible and Tract Society, 1989), p. 218.
2. *The Watchtower*, December 15, 1984, p. 29.
3. *Let God Be True* (Brooklyn: Watchtower Bible and Tract Society, 1952), p. 33.
4. *Let God Be True*, p. 110.
5. *Reasoning from the Scriptures*, p. 215.
6. Doctrine and Covenants (Salt Lake City, UT: The Church of Jesus Christ of Latter-day Saints, 1990), 93:21-23.
7. Bruce McConkie, *Mormon Doctrine* (Salt Lake City, UT: Bookcraft, 1977), p. 129.
8. "Doctrines to Be Rejected," Christadelphian Web site: www.christadelphian.org.
9. Harry Tennant, *Christadelphians: What They Believe and Preach* (Birmingham, AL: The Christadelphian, 1986), p. 75.
10. "The Word Made Flesh," *The Christadelphian Messenger*, no. 46, p. 3.
11. Sun Myung Moon; cited in Walter Martin, *The Kingdom of the Cults* (Minneapolis: Bethany House, 1985), p. 364.
12. Victor Wierwille, *Jesus Christ Is Not God* (New Knoxville, OH: American Christian, 1975), p. 5.
13. Victor Wierwille, *The Word's Way* (New Knoxville, OH: American Christian, 1971), p. 26.
14. Wierwille, *The Word's Way*, p. 37.
15. James Buswell, *A Systematic Theology of the Christian Religion* (Grand Rapids: Zondervan, 1979), 1:105.
16. Corinne Heline, *New Age Bible Interpretation* (Santa Monica, CA: New Age Bible and Philosophy Center, 1961), p. 251.

5. Christ's Humanity

1. John Walvoord, *Jesus Christ Our Lord* (Chicago: Moody, 1980), p. 111.
2. James Buswell, *A Systematic Theology of the Christian Religion* (Grand Rapids: Zondervan, 1979), 2:51.
3. Adapted from Charles Ryrie, *Basic Theology* (Wheaton, IL: Victor, 1986), p. 253.

4. See http://angdatingdaan.org/about/about_doctrines.htm.
5. J. I. Packer, *Knowing God* (Downers Grove, IL: InterVarsity, 1979), p. 50.
6. Robert Lightner, "Philippians," in *The Bible Knowledge Commentary, New Testament,* eds. John Walvoord and Roy Zuck (Wheaton, IL: Victor, 1983), p. 654.
7. Gayle White, "Extraterrestrial Encounters," *The Atlanta Journal and Constitution,* April 5, 1995, F04.
8. *The Gods Have Landed,* ed. James Lewis (New York: State University of New York Press, 1995), p. 35.
9. *Gospel Principles* (Salt Lake City: The Church of Jesus Christ of Latter-day Saints, 1997), p. 64.

6. Human Depravity

1. David Spangler, *Revelation: The Birth of a New Age* (Middleton, WI: Lorian, 1976), p. 13.
2. Shirley MacLaine, *Dancing in the Light* (New York: Bantam, 1985), p. 362.
3. MacLaine, p. 357.
4. MacLaine, p. 259.
5. Annie Besant, *Karma* (London: Theosophical Publishing Society, 1904), p. 23.
6. Mary Baker Eddy, *Unity of Good* (Boston: Trustees under the Will of Mary Baker G. Eddy, 1908), p. 50.
7. Mary Baker Eddy, *Science and Health with Key to the Scriptures* (Boston: The Writings of Mary Baker Eddy, 2000), p. 26.
8. Eddy, *Science and Health,* p. 11.
9. Eddy, *Science and Health,* p. 166.
10. Eddy, *Science and Health,* p. 176.
11. Eddy, *Science and Health,* p. 239.
12. Ernest Holmes, *The Science of Mind* (New York: Dodd, Mead and Co., 1938), p. 294.
13. Holmes, *The Science of Mind,* p. 388.
14. Ernest Holmes, *What I Believe* (pamphlet) (n.p., n.d.), p. 3.
15. Jane Roberts, *Seth Speaks* (New York: Prentice Hall, 1972), p. 89.
16. Ramtha with D. J. Mahr, *Voyage to the New World* (New York: Fawcett, 1987), pp. 130, 149.
17. Helen Schucman, *A Course in Miracles* (New York: Foundation for Inner Peace, 1992), 1:32-33.
18. James Van Praagh, *Talking to Heaven* (New York: Signet, 1997), pp. 42-43.
19. H. L. Haywood, *Great Teachings of Masonry* (Kingsport, TN: Southern Publishers, 1923), p. 140.
20. Haywood, *Great Teachings of Masonry,* p. 138.
21. L. James Rongstad, *The Lodge* (St. Louis: CPH, 1995), p. 22.
22. Rongstad, *The Lodge,* p. 47.

23. John Sias, *100 Questions that Non-Members Ask About Unitarian Universalism* (Nashua, NH: Transition, 1999), p. 9.

24. Sias, *100 Questions*, p. 10.

25. Sias, *100 Questions*, p. 10.

26. John Ankerberg and John Weldon, *Encyclopedia of Cults and New Religions* (Eugene, OR: Harvest House, 1999), p. 517.

7. Christ's Virgin Birth

1. See J. Gresham Machen, *The Virgin Birth of Christ* (New York: Harper, 1930).

2. *The Babylonian Talmud*, cited in Gary Habermas, *The Historical Jesus* (Joplin, MO: College Press, 1996), p. 203.

3. J. Ed Komoszewski, M. James Sawyer, and Daniel B. Wallace, *Reinventing Jesus* (Grand Rapids: Kregel, 2006), p. 246.

4. Ronald Nash, "Was the New Testament Influenced by Pagan Religions?" Statement DB109, Christian Research Institute, www.equip.org.

5. Bruce Metzger, *Historical and Literary Studies: Pagan, Jewish, and Christian* (Grand Rapids: Eerdmans, 1968), p. 11.

6. John Sias, *100 Questions that Non-Members Ask About Unitarian Universalism* (Nashua, NH: Transition, 1999), p. 6.

7. *The Unitarian Universalist Pocket Guide*, ed. John Buehrens (Boston: Skinner, 1999), p. 7.

8. Sias, *100 Questions*, p. 4.

9. George Beach, *Catechism with an Open Mind* (n.p., 1995), p. 60.

8. Christ's Sinlessness

1. "Religious Beliefs Vary Widely by Denomination," Barna Research Group, at www.barna.org.

2. "The Word Made Flesh," *The Christadelphian Messenger*, no. 46, p. 3.

3. *Christadelphian Answers*, ed. Frank Jannaway (Houston: Herald Press, 1920), p. 25.

4. Harry Tennant, *Christadelphians: What They Believe and Preach* (Birmingham, AL: The Christadelphian, 1986), p. 74.

5. *Christadelphian Answers*, p. 24.

6. *Christadelphian Answers*, p. 24.

7. *Christadelphian Answers*, p. 24.

8. "Our Faith and Beliefs," Christadelphian Web site: www.christadelphian.org.

9. Gordon Lewis and Bruce Demarest, *Integrative Theology* (Grand Rapids: Zondervan, 1996), p. 346.

10. Kenneth Copeland, *The Incarnation* (Fort Worth: Kenneth Copeland Ministries, 1985, audiotape #01-0402), side 1.

11. Kenneth Copeland, "The Price of It All," *Believer's Voice of Victory*, September 1991, p. 3.

12. Kenneth Copeland, *The Incarnation*, side 2.

13. Kenneth Copeland, *What Happened from the Cross to the Throne* (Fort Worth: Kenneth Copeland Ministries, 1990, audiotape #02-0017), side 2.

9. Christ's Atoning Death

1. See Norman Geisler, *Systematic Theology: Sin and Salvation*, vol. 3 (Minneapolis: Bethany House, 2004), chapters 8 and 9.
2. Alister McGrath, *Iustitia Dei: A History of the Christian Doctrine of Justification* (Cambridge: Cambridge University Press, 1986), 2:36.
3. McGrath, *Iustitia Dei*, p. 90.
4. Anselm, *Cur Deus Homo*, I.XII.
5. Anselm, *Cur Deus Homo*, I.XVIII.b.
6. LeGrand Richards, *A Marvelous Work and a Wonder* (Salt Lake City, UT: Deseret, 1958), p. 98.
7. *Gospel Principles* (Salt Lake City, UT: Church of Jesus Christ of Latter-day Saints, 1986), p. 19.
8. "Our Faith and Beliefs," Christadelphian Web site: www.christadelphian.org.
9. Mary Baker Eddy, *Science and Health with Key to the Scriptures* (Boston: Trustees under the Will of Mary Baker G. Eddy, 1934), p. 25.
10. Eddy, *Science and Health*, p. 23.
11. Ernest Holmes and Fenwicke Holmes, *The Voice Celestial* (Los Angeles: Science of Mind Publications, 1979), p. 284.
12. Benjamin Creme, *The Reappearance of the Christ and the Masters of Wisdom* (Los Angeles: Tara Center, 1980), p. 47.
13. Mark and Elizabeth Clare Prophet, *Climb the Highest Mountain* (Los Angeles: Summit University Press, 1974), pp. 279-80.
14. Mark and Elizabeth Clare Prophet, *Climb the Highest Mountain*, p. 443.
15. Rudolf Steiner, *The Reappearance of the Christ in the Etheric* (Spring Valley, NY: Anthroposophic Press, 1983), pp. 127-28.
16. Rudolf Steiner, *Jesus and Christ* (Spring Valley, NY: Anthroposophic Press, 1976), pp. 16-17.

10. The Bodily Resurrection of Christ

1. Robert Gundry, *Soma in Biblical Theology* (Cambridge: Cambridge University Press, 1976).
2. George Eldon Ladd, *I Believe in the Resurrection of Jesus* (Grand Rapids: Eerdmans, 1975), p. 94.
3. Ladd, *I Believe*, p. 127.
4. Ladd, *I Believe*, p. 101.
5. See Murray Harris, *Easter in Durham* (Dublin: Attic Press, 1986), p. 17.
6. Murray Harris, *Raised Immortal* (Grand Rapids: Eerdmans, 1985), p. 54.
7. Harris, *Raised Immortal*, p. 92.

8. See Harris, *Raised Immortal*, p. 58. In a later edition of this book retitled *From Grave to Glory* (Grand Rapids: Zondervan, 1990), Harris changed the word *essential* to *customary* without recanting his earlier view on the essential spiritual nature of Jesus' resurrection body. Until later challenged, he continued to hold that believers' physical bodies never come out of the grave but that they receive nonmaterial resurrection bodies at the moment of death, while their physical bodies rot forever in the grave. Some of his colleagues, such as Wayne Grudem, pronounced this view orthodox, even though Harris later gave it up. See Norman Geisler, *Systematic Theology: Church and Last Things*, vol. 4 (Minneapolis: Bethany House, 2005), p. 270.
9. Millard Erickson, *Christian Theology* (Grand Rapids: Baker, 1991), p. 778.
10. Ronald Nash, "Was the New Testament Influenced by Pagan Religions?" Statement DB109, Christian Research Institute, www.equip.org.
11. William Lane Craig and Walter Sinnott-Armstrong, *God? A Debate Between a Christian and an Atheist* (Oxford: Oxford University Press, 2004), p. 71.
12. *Let Your Name Be Sanctified* (Brooklyn: Watchtower Bible and Tract Society, 1961), p. 266.
13. *Studies in the Scriptures*, vol. 7 (Brooklyn: Watchtower Bible and Tract Society, 1917), p. 57.
14. *Reasoning from the Scriptures* (Brooklyn: Watchtower Bible and Tract Society, 1989), p. 334.
15. Mary Baker Eddy, *Science and Health with Key to the Scriptures* (Boston: Trustees under the Will of Mary Baker G. Eddy, 1934), p. 44.
16. Eddy, *Science and Health*, p. 593.

11. The Necessity of Grace

1. See Henry Denzinger, *Sources of Catholic Dogma* (St. Louis: B. Herder, 1957), no. 801, 811.
2. Council of Trent, session 6, "Decree on Justification," chapter 6.
3. Denzinger, *The Source of Catholic Dogma*, p. 264.
4. *Catechism of the Catholic Church* (New York: Doubleday, 1994), p. 542, emphasis added.
5. John Paul II, *Crossing the Threshold of Hope* (New York: Knopf, 1994), p. 194.
6. The Holy Bible (Salt Lake City, UT: Church of Jesus Christ of Latter-day Saints, 1990), p. 697, emphasis added.
7. Bruce McConkie, *Mormon Doctrine* (Salt Lake City, UT: Bookcraft, 1966), p. 339.
8. Spencer W. Kimball; quoted in *Book of Mormon Student Manual* (Salt Lake City, UT: Church of Jesus Christ of Latter-day Saints, 1989), p. 36.
9. *Gospel Principles* (Salt Lake City, UT: Church of Jesus Christ of Latter-day Saints, 1986), p. 19, insert added.
10. McConkie, *Mormon Doctrine*, p. 339.
11. Duane Magnani, *The Watchtower Files* (Minneapolis: Bethany House, 1985), p. 232.
12. *The Watchtower*, April 1, 1947, p. 204.
13. *The Watchtower*, August 15, 1972, p. 491.
14. *Divine Principle* (New York: The Holy Spirit Association for the Unification of World Christianity, 1996), p. 283.
15. Orville Swenson, *The Perilous Path of Cultism* (Saskatchewan, Canada: Briercrest Books, 1987), p. 222.

16. Ernest Holmes, *The Science of Mind* (New York: Dodd, Mead and Co., 1938), pp. 33-34.
17. Ernest Holmes, *What Religious Science Teaches* (Los Angeles: Science of Mind, 1975), p. 57.
18. Ernest Holmes, "What I Believe" (pamphlet, n.p., n.d.), p. 3.
19. Ernest Holmes, *Gateway to Life* (Los Angeles: Science of Mind, n.d.), p. 19.
20. Ernest Holmes, *The Philosophy of Jesus* (Los Angeles: Science of Mind, n.d.), p. 16.

12. The Necessity of Faith

1. See Norman Geisler, *Systematic Theology: Sin and Salvation* (Minneapolis: Bethany House, 2005), vol. 3, chapter 15.
2. For more on this, see Ron Rhodes, *The Challenge of the Cults and New Religions* (Grand Rapids: Zondervan, 2002).
3. John Sias, *100 Questions that Non-Members Ask About Unitarian Universalists* (Nashua, NH: Transition Publishing, 1999), p. 2
4. Sias, *100 Questions*, p. 7.
5. *The Unitarian Universalists Pocket Guide* (Boston: Skinner House Books, 1999), p. 2, emphasis in original.
6. *The Unitarian Universalists Pocket Guide*, p. 4.
7. Sias, *100 Questions*, p. 2.
8. See Philip Hewett, *The Unitarian Way* (Toronto: Canadian Unitarian Council, 1985), p. 89.
9. Sias, *100 Questions*, p. 2.
10. L. James Rongstad, *The Lodge: How to Respond* (St. Louis: CPH, 1995), p. 22.
11. Rongstad, *The Lodge*, p. 47.
12. Grand Lodge of Texas, *Monitor of the Lodge* (n.c.: Grand Lodge of Texas, 1982), p. 19.
13. W. L. Wilmhurst, *The Masonic Initiation* (London: John M. Watkins, 1957), pp. 27-28.
14. Jack Harris, *Freemasonry: The Invisible Cult in Our Midst* (Chattanooga, TN: Global, 1983), p. 132.
15. Albert Mackey, *Revised Encyclopedia of Freemasonry* (Richmond, VA: Macoy, 1966), 1:269.
16. William E. Hammond, *What Masonry Means* (New York: Macoy, 1952), p. 165.
17. John J. Robinson, *Born in Blood: The Lost Secrets of Freemasonry* (New York: M. Evans & Company, 1989), p. 256.
18. Cited in John Ankerberg, et al., *The Masonic Lodge: What Goes on Behind Closed Doors?* (Chattanooga, TN: The John Ankerberg Evangelistic Association, 1986), p. 35.
19. Albert G. Mackey, *A Manual of the Lodge* (New York: Maynard, Merrill, & Co., 1898), p. 16.
20. Monitor, pp. 156-57; cited in Rongstad, *The Lodge*, p. 33-34.
21. James E. Talmage, *A Study of the Articles of Faith* (Salt Lake City, UT: Deseret, 1988), p. 96.
22. Legrand Richards, *A Marvelous Work and a Wonder* (Salt Lake City, UT: Deseret, 1976), p. 24, emphasis in original.
23. Bruce McConkie, *What the Mormons Think of Christ* (Salt Lake City, UT: Deseret, 1973), pp. 27-39, italics added.

24. Talmage, *A Study*, pp. 97-98.
25. Talmage, *A Study*, p. 433.
26. *You Can Live Forever in Paradise on Earth* (New York: Watchtower Bible and Tract Society, 1989), p. 250.
27. *You Can Live Forever in Paradise on Earth*, pp. 127-30.
28. *Watchtower*, July 1, 1947, p. 204.
29. *Watchtower*, August 15, 1972, p. 492.
30. Mary Baker Eddy, *Science and Health with Key to the Scriptures* (Boston: The Writings of Mary Baker Eddy, 2000), p. 23.
31. Eddy, *Science and Health*, p. 24.
32. Eddy, *Science and Health*, p. 297.
33. Ernest Holmes, *The Science of Mind* (New York: Penguin Putnam, 1998), pp. 156-57.

13. The Bodily Ascension of Christ

1. Irenaeus, *Against Heresies*, XXVI.i; in *The Ante-Nicene Fathers*, eds. Alexander Roberts and James Donaldson, vol.1 (Grand Rapids: Eerdmans, 1985), p. 352, insert added.
2. Irenaeus, *Against Heresies*, III.xi.1.
3. David Spangler, *Reflections on the Christ* (Forres, Scotland: Findhorn Publications, 1981), p. 28.
4. David Spangler, *Revelation: The Birth of a New Age* (San Francisco: Rainbow Bridge, 1976), p. 121.
5. Mary Baker Eddy, *Science and Health with Key to the Scriptures* (Boston: The Writings of Mary Baker Eddy, 2000), pp. 46-47.
6. Charles Taze Russell, *Studies in the Scriptures*, vol. 7, *The Finished Mystery* (New York: Watchtower Bible and Tract Society, 1917), p. 57.
7. *Watchtower*, April 1, 1947, pp. 101-2.
8. *Awake Magazine*, July 22, 1973, p. 4.
9. *From Paradise Lost to Paradise Regained* (New York: Watchtower Bible and Tract Society, n.d.), p. 144, insert added.
10. *You Can Live Forever in Paradise on Earth* (New York: Watchtower Bible and Tract Society, 1982), p. 145.
11. *Aid to Bible Understanding* (New York: Watchtower Bible and Tract Society, 1971), p. 141.
12. *The Greatest Man Who Ever Lived* (New York: Watchtower Bible and Tract Society, 1991), chapter 131.
13. Murray Harris, *From Grave to Glory* (Grand Rapids: Zondervan, 1990), p. 423, insert added, emphasis added.
14. Harris, *From Grave to Glory*, p. 392.
15. Harris, *From Grave to Glory*, p. 405.
16. Millard Erickson, *Christian Theology* (Grand Rapids: Baker Books, 1998), p. 778.

17. See, for example, Ronald Nash, *The Gospel and the Greeks: Did the New Testament Borrow from Pagan Thought?* (Phillipsburg, NJ: Presbyterian and Reformed, 2003); Gary Habermas, *The Historical Jesus: Ancient Evidence for the Life of Christ* (Joplin, MO: College Press, 1996); Darrell Bock, *The Missing Gospels: Unearthing the Truth Behind Alternative Christianities* (Nashville: Nelson, 2006); Ben Witherington, *What Have They Done with Jesus?* (San Francisco: Harper, 2006); J. Ed Komoszewski, M. James Sawyer, and Daniel B. Wallace, *Reinventing Jesus: What* The Da Vinci Code *and Other Novel Speculations Don't Tell You* (Grand Rapids: Kregel, 2006); and *Jesus Under Fire: Modern Scholarship Reinvents the Historical Jesus,* eds. Michael Wilkins and J. P. Moreland (Grand Rapids: Zondervan, 1995).

14. Christ's Priestly Intercession

1. St. Augustine, *The City of God,* 22.5.
2. See Irenaeus, *Against Heresies,* XXVI.i; in *The Ante-Nicene Fathers,* ed. Alexander Roberts and James Donaldson, vol. 1 (Grand Rapids: Eerdmans, 1985), p. 352.
3. David Spangler, *Reflections on the Christ* (Forres, Scotland: Findhorn Publications, 1981), p. 28; David Spangler, *Revelation: The Birth of a New Age* (San Francisco: Rainbow Bridge, 1976), p. 121.
4. Mary Baker Eddy, *Science and Health with Key to the Scriptures* (Boston: The Writings of Mary Baker Eddy, 2000), pp. 46-47.
5. Bruce McConkie, *Mormon Doctrine* (Salt Lake City, UT: Bookcraft, 1973), p. 387.
6. McConkie, *Mormon Doctrine,* pp. 546-47.
7. *Church News,* March 18, 1989, p. 16.
8. Charles Fillmore, *The Metaphysical Dictionary* (Lee's Summit, MO: Unity, 1962), p. 629.
9. Ernest Holmes, *The Science of Mind* (New York: Tarcher, 1998), p. 480.
10. "A Glossary of ECK Terms," Eckankar Web site: www.eckankar.com.
11. Sri Harold Kemp, "Spiritual Exercises of ECK," Eckankar Web site: www.eckankar.com.
12. *Exposition of the Divine Principle* (New York: The Holy Spirit Association for the Unification of World Christianity, 1998), p. 280.
13. *Exposition of the Divine Principle,* p. 170.
14. Victor Paul Wierwille, *Jesus Is Not God* (New York: Devin-Adair, 1975), p. 128.

15. Christ's Bodily Second Coming

1. See Norman Geisler, *Systematic Theology: Church and Last Things,* vol. 4 (Minneapolis: Bethany House, 2005), chapter 3.
2. See Ron Rhodes, *The Challenge of the Cults and New Religions* (Grand Rapids: Zondervan, 2002).
3. *The Baha'is: A Profile of the Baha'i Faith and Its Worldwide Community* (United Kingdom: Baha'i Publishing Trust, 1994), p. 37.
4. J. E. Esslemont, *Baha'u'llah and the New Era: An Introduction to the Baha'i Faith* (Wilmette, IL: Baha'i Publishing Trust, 1980), pp. 46-47. See also *Gleanings from the Writings of Baha'u'llah,* trans. Shoghi Effendi (Wilmette, IL: Baha'i Publishing Trust, 1969), pp. 55-56, 171.

5. John Ankerberg and John Weldon, *Encyclopedia of Cults and New Religions* (Eugene, OR: Harvest House, 1999), p. 66.

6. Peter Simple, *Baha'i Teachings, Light for All Regions* (Wilmette, IL: Baha'i Publishing Trust, 1970), p. 21.

7. Elliot Miller, "Benjamin Creme and the Reappearance of the Christ," *Forward*, 6:1, 3.

8. David Spangler, *Cooperation with Spirit* (Middleton, WI: The Lorian Press, 1982), p. 4.

9. David Spangler, *Towards a Planetary Vision* (Forres, Scotland: Findhorn, 1977), p. 108.

10. David Spangler, *Reflections on the Christ* (Forres, Scotland: Findhorn, 1981), pp. 14-15.

11. *Studies in the Scriptures*, vol. 4 (Brooklyn: Watchtower Bible and Tract Society, 1897), p. 621; *Creation* (Brooklyn: Watchtower Bible and Tract Society, 1927), p. 289; *The Watchtower*, March 1, 1923, p. 67.

12. *Let God Be True* (Brooklyn: Watchtower Bible and Tract Society, 1946), p. 250.

13. *Studies in the Scriptures*, vol. 3 (Brooklyn: Watchtower Bible and Tract Society, 1891), p. 126.

16. The Inspiration of Sripture

1. For a more detailed examination, see N. L. Geisler and William Nix, *A General Introduction to the Bible* (Chicago: Moody Press, 1986); Norman L. Geisler, *Systematic Theology: Introduction and Bible*, vol. 1 (Minneapolis: Bethany House, 2005); Ron Rhodes, *Christianity According to the Bible* (Eugene, OR: Harvest House, 2006), chapter 1; Ron Rhodes, *Answering the Objections of Atheists, Agnostics, and Skeptics* (Eugene, OR: Harvest House, 2006), chapters 8 and 9.

2. Thomas Aquinas, *On Truth*, 14.10-11, emphasis added.

3. See Geisler, *A General Introduction of the Bible*, p. 357.

4. St. Augustine, *The City of God* (New York: Penguin, 2003), 9.5; 10:1; 11.6; 13:2.

5. John Sias, *100 Questions that Non-Members Ask About Unitarian Universalism* (Nashua, NH: Transition Publishing, 1999), p. 4; Kathleen Elgin, *The Unitarians* (New York: David McKay, 1971), p. 82; David Robinson, *The Unitarians and the Universalists* (Westport, CT: Greenwood Press, 1985), pp. 15, 32, 56.

6. Sias, *100 Questions*, p. 4.

7. John Buehrens and Forrest Church, *A Chosen Faith* (Boston: Beacon Press, 1998), p. 127.

8. Donald J. Wiseman, cited in Norman Geisler, *Christian Apologetics* (Grand Rapids: Baker, 1976), p. 322.

9. Nelson Glueck, *Rivers in the Desert* (Philadelphia: Jewish Publications, 1969), p. 31.

10. William Albright; cited in Josh McDowell, *Evidence that Demands a Verdict* (San Bernardino, CA: Campus Crusade for Christ, 1972), p. 68.

11. John Robinson, *Born in Blood* (New York: M. Evans and Company, 1989), p. 255.

12. Henry Wilson Coil, *Coil's Masonic Encyclopedia* (New York: Macoy Publishing, 1961), p. 520.

13. Ernest Holmes, *What Religious Science Teaches* (Los Angeles: Science of Mind, 1975), p. 10.

14. Holmes, *What Religious Science Teaches*, p. 10.

15. James Talmage, *A Study of the Articles of Faith* (Salt Lake City, UT: The Church of Jesus Christ of Latter-day Saints, 1982), p. 236.

16. Orson Pratt, *Divine Authenticity of the Book of Mormon*, p. 47, emphasis added; cited in Bill McKeever and Eric Johnson, *Questions to Ask Your Mormon Friend* (Minneapolis: Bethany House, 1994), p. 47.
17. Bruce McConkie, *Mormon Doctrine* (Salt Lake City, UT: Bookcraft, 1971), p. 383.
18. Joseph Smith, Genesis 40:33, Inspired Version.
19. See Marian Bodine, "Bible Answer Man" column, *Christian Research Newsletter*, May/June 1992, p. 3.
20. Bodine, *Christian Research Newsletter*, p. 3.
21. Robert Bowman, *Understanding Jehovah's Witnesses* (Grand Rapids: Baker Books, 1991), p. 114.
22. Julius Mantey; cited in Erich and Jean Grieshaber, *Expose of Jehovah's Witnesses* (Tyler, TX: Jean Books, 1982), p. 30.
23. Bruce Metzger, "Jehovah's Witnesses and Jesus Christ," *Theology Today*, April 1953.
24. William Barclay, *The Expository Times*, November 1953.
25. Dan Brown, *The Da Vinci Code* (New York: Anchor, 2006), p. 213.
26. Brown, *The Da Vinci Code*, pp. 345, 341.
27. Brown, *The Da Vinci Code*, p. 231.
28. Brown, *The Da Vinci Code*, p. 256.

17. The Literal Interpretation of Scripture

1. See fuller discussion of this in Norman Geisler, *Systematic Theology: Church and Last Things*, vol. 4 (Minneapolis: Bethany House, 2005), chapter 13; Ron Rhodes, *Christianity According to the Bible* (Eugene, OR: Harvest House, 2006), chapter 2.
2. Donald Campbell, "The Interpretation of Types," *Bibliotheca Sacra* (July, 1955), p. 250.
3. See Dwight Pentecost, *Things to Come* (Grand Rapids: Zondervan, 1965), p. 10.
4. Mark and Elizabeth Clare Prophet, *The Lost Teachings of Jesus* 3 (Livingston, MT: Summit University Press, 1988), 273-74.
5. Mark and Elizabeth Clare Prophet, *The Lost Teachings of Jesus* 2 (Livingston, MT: Summit University Press, 1988), p. 254.
6. Prophet, *The Lost Teachings of Jesus* 2, p. 62.
7. David Spangler, *Reflections on the Christ* (Forres, Scotland: Findhorn Publications, 1981), p. 73.
8. Spangler, *Reflections*, p. 73.

18. The Procession of the Holy Spirit

1. F. L. Cross, *The Oxford Dictionary of the Christian Church*, 2d ed. (Oxford: Oxford University Press, 1978), p. 1361.
2. Phillip Schaff, *A Select Library of Nicene and Post-Nicene Fathers of the Christian Church* (Grand Rapids: Eerdmans, 1989), p. 198.

3. Schaff, *A Select Library*, p. 258, from Session 1.
4. Schaff, *A Select Library*, p. 260.
5. Schaff, *A Select Library*, p. 287.
6. Schaff, *A Select Library*, Canon 28.
7. Cited by Schaff, *A Select Library*, p. 288.
8. Schaff, *A Select Library*, p. 345.
9. Schaff, *A Select Library*, p. 353.
10. Schaff, *A Select Library*, p. 340, from Session I.
11. Schaff, *A Select Library*, p. 342, Session XIII.
12. Schaff, *A Select Library*, pp. 347, 350.
13. Schaff, *A Select Library*, p. 533.
14. Schaff, *A Select Library*, p. 533.
15. Schaff, *A Select Library*, p. 533, Session I.
16. Schaff, *A Select Library*, Session III, p. 539, emphasis added.
17. Schaff, *A Select Library*, p. 543.
18. Schaff, *A Select Library*, pp. 544-45.
19. Schaff, *A Select Library*, pp. 546-47.
20. Cross, *The Oxford Dictionary*, pp. 512-13.

19. Forms of Church Government

1. See Heinrich Denzinger, *The Sources of Catholic Dogma* (Fitzwilliam, NH: Loreto, 2 002), 1840.
2. Vatican II (1962–1963), in distinguishing between implicit faith and explicit faith, allowed for salvation of sincere non-Christians and "separated brethren" such as Protestants, emphasis added.
3. The word *cult* is not appropriate because, despite its sacramental system of mediated grace, the Roman Catholic Church has not officially denied any of the 14 essential salvation doctrines of the Faith. Nonetheless, the authoritarian structure of Roman Catholicism is cultlike or cultic.
4. See Ron Rhodes, *The Complete Guide to Christian Denominations* (Eugene, OR: Harvest House, 2004).
5. We do not use the word *cult* here as a pejorative, inflammatory, or injurious word. We use it in a strictly theological sense. More specifically, for the purposes of this book, a cult refers to "a group of people, which claiming to be Christian, embraces a particular doctrinal system taught by an individual leader, group of leaders, or organization, which (system) denies (either explicitly or implicitly) one or more of the central doctrines of the Christian faith as taught in the sixty-six books of the Bible" (Alan Gomes, *Unmasking the Cults* [Grand Rapids: Zondervan, 1995], p. 7).
6. See Norman L. Geisler, *Systematic Theology: Church and Last Things*, vol. 4 (Minneapolis: Bethany House, 2005), Appendix 7.

20. Grace, Faith, and Works

1. F. L. Cross ed., *The Oxford Dictionary of the Christian Church* (Oxford: Oxford University Press, 1978), p. 1058.
2. Augustine, *On True Religion*, 14; in *Augustine: Earlier Writings* (Philadelphia: Westminster Press, 1953).
3. Augustine, *On the Spirit and the Letter*, 57.58. (Unless otherwise noted, this and all books on Augustine are cited from Philip Schaff, ed., *The Ante-Nicene and Post-Nicene Fathers* [Grand Rapids: Eerdmans, 1952]).
4. Augustine, *On the Spirit and the Letter*, p. 60.
5. Augustine, *On the Correction of the Donatist*, 6.24
6. Augustine, *On the Correction of the Donatist*, 6:23-24.
7. Augustine, *Enchiridion*, p. 30 .
8. Augustine, *The City of God*, 14.11.
9. Augustine, *Enchiridion*, p. 31.
10. Augustine, *Enchiridion*, p. 100.
11. Augustine, *Enchiridion*, p. 98.
12. Augustine, *Enchiridion*, p. 99.
13. Augustine, *Sermons on the New Testament*, LXII, 8.
14. Augustine, *On the Grace of Christ*, p. 24.
15. Augustine, *Enchiridion*, p. 103.
16. Augustine, *On Grace and Free Will*, p. 33.
17. Martin Luther, *On the Bondage of the Will* (Grand Rapids: Baker Books, 1976), p. 79.
18. Luther, *On the Bondage*, p. 199.
19. Luther, *On the Bondage*, p. 129.
20. Luther, *On the Bondage*, p. 216.
21. Luther, *On the Bondage*, pp. 216-17.
22. Luther, *On the Bondage*, p. 216.
23. Luther, *On the Bondage*, p. 230.
24. Luther, *On the Bondage*, p. 230.
25. Luther, *On the Bondage*, p. 230-31.
26. John Calvin, *Institutes of the Christian Religion* (Grand Rapids: Eerdmans, 1957), Book II, Aphorism, 18 in vol. 2, p. 679.
27. Calvin, Book II, Chapter II, p. 164.
28. Calvin, Book II, Chapter II, p. 228.
29. Calvin, Book II, Chapter II, pp. 228-29.

21. The Extent of Salvation

1. Louis Berkhof, *Systematic Theology* (Grand Rapids: Eerdmans, 1977), p. 394.

2. Berkhof, *Systematic Theology*, p. 395.
3. Charles Hodge, *Systematic Theology*, vol. 2 (Grand Rapids: Eerdmans, 1952), p. 553.
4. Louis Berkhof, *Manual of Christian Doctrine* (Grand Rapids: Eerdmans, 1983), p. 218.
5. Berkhof, *Manual of Christian Doctrine*, p. 217.
6. John Calvin, *Commentary on John's Gospel*, vol. 1 (Grand Rapids: Baker, 1949), p. 64.
7. J. C. Ryle, *Expository Thoughts on the Gospels*, vol. 3 (New York: Robert Carter, 1911), pp. 61-62.
8. Calvin, *Commentary on John's Gospel*, p. 125, insert added.
9. Norman Douty, *The Death of Christ* (Irving, TX: Williams and Watrous, 1978), p. 82.
10. Calvin, *Commentary on John's Gospel*, vol. 1, p. 126.
11. Douty, *The Death of Christ*, p. 49.
12. Lewis Sperry Chafer, "For Whom Did Christ Die?" *Bibliotheca Sacra*, October-December 1980, p. 323.
13. John Calvin, *Calvin's Commentaries*, vol. 3 (Grand Rapids: Baker, 1949), p. 214.
14. Robert Lightner, *The Death Christ Died* (Schaumburg, IL: Regular Baptist Press, 1978), p. 56.
15. Paedagogus, as cited by J. Davenant, *The Death of Christ*, vol. 2 of *On the Colossians*, ed. Allport (London, 1832), p. 319.
16. *Demonstratio Evangelica*, cited in Davenant, *Death of Christ*, p. 374.
17. *On the Incarnation of the Word*, cited in Davenant, *Death of Christ*, p. 374.
18. Catacheses, 13:2, cited by George Smeaton, *The Apostles' Doctrine of the Atonement* (Grand Rapids: Zondervan, 1957), p. 498.
19. Oratoria 2, as cited by Davenant, *Death of Christ*. p. 374.
20. On Psalm 49:7-8, Sermon 4, cited by Smeaton, *The Apostles' Doctrine of Atonement*, p. 499.
21. On Psalm 118, Sermon 8, cited by Davenant, *Death of Christ*, p. 411.
22. Martin Luther, *Commentary on Galatians*, as cited by James Morison, *The Extent of the Atonement* (Glasgow, 1882), pp. 121-25.
23. Melanchthon, "Common-places"; in Davenant, *Death of Christ*, p. 337.
24. A thorough discussion of this issue may be found in Norman Geisler, *Chosen But Free: A Balanced View of Election* (Minneapolis: Bethany House, 1999).
25. Jay Adams, *Competent to Counsel* (Grand Rapids: Baker, 1970), p. 70.
26. Cited in Millard Erickson, *Christian Theology* (Grand Rapids: Baker, 1985), pp. 833–34.

22. The Candidate, Mode, and Efficacy of Baptism

1. See Etherbert Bullinger, "The Mystery," in *The Companion Bible* (London: Oxford University Press, 1913), Appendix 193.
2. Charles Barker, *Bible Truth: What We Believe and Why* (Milwaukee: Milwaukee Bible College, 1956).
3. See Harry Ironside, *Wrongly Dividing the Word of Truth* (Neptune, NJ: Loizeaux Brothers, 1938); and Charles Ryrie, *Dispensationalism Today* (Chicago: Moody Press, 1965).

4. See Norman L. Geisler, *Systematic Theology: Sin and Salvation*, vol. 3 (Minneapolis: Bethany House, 2004), chapter 16.

5. *The Canons and Decrees of the Sacred and Ecumenical Council of Trent* (1545–1561), cited in Heinrich Denzinger, *The Sources of Catholic Dogma* (Fitzwilliam, NH: Loreto, 2002), canon 5, no. 858, 264.

23. The Nature and Function of Communion

1. Ludwig Ott, *Fundamentals of Catholic Dogma* (Rockford, IL: Tan Books, 1960), p. 325.

2. Ott, *Fundamentals*, p. 326.

3. Henry Denzinger, *The Sources of Catholic Dogma* (St. Louis: Herder, 1957), canon 8, no. 851, p. 263.

4. Stephen Arndt and Mark Jordan, *A Catholic Catechism for Adults* (San Francisco: Ignatius Press, 1987) 3.3, p. 265, emphasis in the original.

5. Denzinger, *The Sources of Catholic Dogma*, Canon 4, no. 847, p. 262.

6. Ott, *Fundamentals*, p. 370, insert added.

7. Denzinger, *The Sources of Catholic Dogma*, no. 874, p. 265.

8. Denzinger, "Decree on the Most Holy Eucharist," Canon 4, no. 877, pp. 267-68.

9. Denzinger, "The Council of Trent," Session 13 (Oct. 11, 1551), "Decree on the Most Holy Eucharist," Canon 5, no. 878, p. 268.

10. Denzinger, *The Sources of Catholic Dogma*, Canon 6, no. 888, p. 271.

11. We use the word *most* because this difficulty is also inherent in Lutheran theology with their understanding that, in communion, the physical body and blood of Christ is "contained in" or is "under" the communion elements. Despite "denials of various facets of the Catholic position, Luther insisted upon the concept of *manducation*. There is a real eating of Jesus' body." Millard Erickson, *Christian Theology* (Grand Rapids: Baker Books, 1986), p. 1118.

12. Harold O. J. Brown, *Heresy* (Grand Rapids: Baker Books, 1984), p. 229.

13. Erickson, *Christian Theology*, p. 1121.

14. Roman Catholics and Anglicans have issued a 600-word, five-point statement on common Eucharistic beliefs, including the Eucharist as a sacrifice. See "Catholics, Anglicans Agree" in *The Southern Cross*, Jan. 27, 1994, p. 10.

15. Eastern Orthodoxy agrees with Roman Catholicism on this point.

16. F. L. Cross, ed. *The Oxford Dictionary of the Christian Church* (Oxford: Oxford University Press, 1983), pp. 594-95.

17. Brown, *Heresy*, p. 33.

18. Brown, *Heresy*, p. 33.

19. The Orthodox church *permits* but does not *require* that real presence be understood in terms of transubstantiation, which Roman Catholicism proclaims infallibly as the only proper way to understand it.

20. Martin Luther, "The Babylonian Captivity of the Church," in *Three Treatises* (Philadelphia: Muhlenberg, 1943), p. 140.

21. Luther, "The Babylonian Captivity," p. 140.

22. Luther, "The Babylonian Captivity," p. 140. Some Lutheran theologians are uneasy with the term "consubstantiation." See Skevington Wood, "Consubstantiation," in Everett Harrison, ed., *Baker's Dictionary of Theology* (Grand Rapids: Baker Books, 1960), p. 138. Also see Bernard M. G. Reardon, *Religious Thought in the Reformation* (New York: Longman, 1981), p. 78.

23. Erickson, *Christian Theology*, p. 1117, emphasis added.

24. Theodore Mueller, *Christian Dogmatics* (St. Louis: Concordia, 2003), pp. 509-512, emphasis added; see also *The Augsburg Confession*, Article 10.

25. John Calvin, *Institutes of the Christian Religion*, Book 4, Chapter 17, Section 12; quoted in Erickson, *Christian Theology*, p. 1119

26. Charles Hodge, *Systematic Theology* (Peabody, MA: Hendrickson, 1999), 3.641, emphasis added.

27. Hodge, *Systematic Theology*, 3.637-38.

28. Hodge, *Systematic Theology*, 3.626-27.

29. Hodge, *Systematic Theology*, 3.627.

30. Hodge, *Systematic Theology*, 3.628.

24. The Nature of Sanctification

1. See Norman L. Geisler and Ralph McKenzie, *Roman Catholics and Evangelicals: Agreements and Differences* (Grand Rapids: Baker Books, 1995), chapter 12; Ron Rhodes, *Reasoning from the Scriptures with Catholics* (Eugene, OR: Harvest House, 2004), chapters 8 and 9.

2. Norman. L. Geisler, *Systematic Theology: Sin and Salvation*, vol. 3 (Minneapolis: Bethany House, 2004), pp. 289-90.

3. Peter Toon, *Foundations for Faith* (Westchester, IL: Crossway Books, 1983), p. 58.

4. Toon, *Foundations*, p. 49.

5. James Atkinson, *Martin Luther* (Grand Rapids: Eerdmans, 1983), p. 133.

6. Cited by R. H. Bainton, *Here I Stand* (Nashville: Abingdon, 1978), p. 65.

7. Cited by Paul Althaus, *The Theology of Martin Luther* (Philadelphia: Fortress Press, 1984), p. 237, note 63.

8. Toon, *Foundations*, pp. 58-59.

9. Toon, *Foundations*, p. 72.

10. Toon, *Foundations*, p. 72.

11. Toon, *Foundations*, p. 84.

12. Toon, *Foundations*, p. 81.

13. Toon, *Foundations*, p. 81. For a good treatment of the Council of Trent from a Roman Catholic view, see H. Jedin, *History of the Council of Trent*, English trans. F. C. Eckhoff (St. Louis: B. Herder, 1947). The standard Protestant work is Martin Chemnitz, *Examination of the Council of Trent* (St. Louis: Concordia, 1971).

14. George Anderson, *Justification by Faith* (Minneapolis: Augsburg, 1985), p. 34.

15. A detailed treatment of the sacrament of baptism is beyond the scope of this chapter. There are differences concerning it not only between Roman Catholics and evangelicals, but within the Protestant community as well. It should be noted that Luther had difficulties formulating his understanding of baptism in light of his concept of justification. On Luther and baptism, see Althaus, *The Theology of Martin Luther*, pp. 353-74, and Appendix Five.

16. *The Canons and Decrees of the Sacred and Ecumenical Council of Trent* (1545–1561), cited in Heinrich Denzinger, *The Sources of Catholic Dogma* (Fitzwilliam: Loreto, 2002), p. 811.

17. Trent, in Denzinger, *The Sources of Catholic Dogma*, chapter 8.

18. Ludwig Ott, *Fundamentals of Catholic Dogma* (Rockford, IL: Tan Books, 1974), p. 264.

19. While Protestants sometimes use "reward" of eternal life in the sense of something graciously given by God, they do not believe this reward is based on our works but only on God's grace received through faith alone.

20. Trent, in Denzinger, *The Sources of Catholic Dogma*, chapter 8.

21. Denzinger, *The Sources of Catholic Dogma*, p. 261.

22. See John Calvin, *Institutes of the Christian Religion*, Book III (Philadelphia: Westminster, 1960), pp. 11-14.

23. Anthony Hoekema, *Saved by Grace* (Grand Rapids: Eerdmans, 1989), p. 154.

24. George Eldon Ladd, *A Theology of the New Testament* (Grand Rapids: Eerdmans, 1974), p. 440.

25. Hans Küng, *Justification* (New York: Thomas Nelson, 1964), p. 209, emphasis in the original. For an extended treatment of the Old Testament understandings of these terms and the difficulties inherent in translating from the Hebrew into Greek and Latin, see Alister McGrath. *Iustitia Dei*, vol. 1 (Cambridge: Cambridge University Press, 1986), pp. 4-16.

26. Hoekema, *Saved by Grace*, p. 154.

27. Ladd, *A Theology*, p. 446. This is not to imply that Catholics believe that ethical perfection is received by justification; they do not. They distinguish complete ontological righteousness received at justification with perfect ethical (behavioral) righteousness which is not then received, although a measure of it is since the love of God is shed in our hearts (Romans 5:5).

28. Erickson, *Christian Theology*, p. 956, emphasis in the original.

29. John Wesley, *A Plain Account of Christian Perfection* (London: Epworth, 1968 reprint), pp. 12, 26.

30. Wesley, *A Plain Account*, p. 41.

31. Wesley, *A Plain Account*, p. 33.

32. Wesley, *A Plain Account*, pp. 26-27, emphasis added.

33. Wesley, *A Plain Account*, pp. 27, 25, emphasis added.

34. Wesley, *A Plain Account*, p. 34.

35. Wesley, *A Plain Account*, p. 23.

36. B. B. Warfield, *Perfectionism* (Oxford: Oxford University Press, 1931).

37. Wesley, *A Plain Account*, p. 23.

38. Wesley, *A Plain Account*, p. 24.

39. Wesley, *A Plain Account*, p. 42.

25. The Use of Musical Instruments in Worship

1. John Calvin, *Calvin's Commentaries* (Grand Rapids: Baker Books, 1974), Psalm 33.
2. John Wesley, cited in *Clarke's Commentary*, vol. 4 (Nashville: Abingdon Press, 1977), p. 684.
3. "Musical Instruments in Church Services," *Catholic Encyclopedia*, Internet ed., http://www.newadvent.org.

26. The Nature of Spiritual Gifts

1. See Ron Rhodes, *Christianity According to the Bible* (Eugene, OR: Harvest House, 2006), chapter 11.
2. See Norman Geisler, *Systematic Theology: Church and Last Things*, vol. 4 (Minneapolis: Bethany House, 2005), p. 189.
3. See Gene Getz, *Sharpening the Focus of the Church* (Wheaton, IL: Victor, 1984).
4. See Geisler, *Systematic Theology*, vol. 4, pp. 662-63.
5. See Geisler, *Systematic Theology*, vol. 4, pp. 664-70.
6. This is commonly claimed by the Oneness Pentecostals. See Ron Rhodes, *The Challenge of the Cults and New Religions* (Grand Rapids: Zondervan, 2002), chapter 12.

27. The Day of Worship

1. Barnabas, "The Epistle of Barnabas," chapter 15, 1670-1671, insert added.
2. Ignatius, "The Epistle of Ignatius to the Magnesians," in Philip Schaff, *The Apostolic Fathers with Justin Martyr and Irenaeus* (Grand Rapids: Eerdmans, 2001), p. 682.
3. Justin Martyr, "The First Apology of Justin," in Schaff, *The Apostolic Fathers with Justin Martyr and Irenaeus*, chapter 67.
4. Philip Schaff, *History of the Christian Church*, vol. 3 (New York: Scribner, 1902), p. 380, note 1.
5. Roman Catholics generally distinguish between Sunday and the Sabbath, which it follows chronologically every week. In this view, worship of God on Sunday replaces that of the Saturday Sabbath and fulfills the spiritual truth of the Sabbath. Most Protestants, by contrast, generally use the terms *Sunday, Lord's Day*, and *Sabbath* as synonymous terms for the Christian day of worship, though they obviously do not believe Jewish regulations regarding the Sabbath are binding on Christians.
6. *Westminster Confession of Faith*, chapter 21, "Of Religious Worship, and the Sabbath Day," Sections 7-8.

28. The Order of Second-Coming Events

1. A full discussion on these intramural disagreements may be found in Norman Geisler, *Systematic Theology, Church and Last Things*, vol. 4 (Minneapolis: Bethany House, 2005). See also Ron Rhodes, *Christianity According to the Bible* (Eugene, OR: Harvest House, 2006), chapter 14.

2. Tim LaHaye, *Christian Retailing*, January 3, 2005, p. 1.
3. Hank Hanegraaff, *The Apocalypse Code* (Wheaton, IL: Tyndale House, 2007), pp. 44, 63-64.

29. The Role of Women

1. Flavius Josephus, *Against Apion* (Grand Rapids: Kregel, 1974), p. 622.
2. H. L. Strack and P. Billerbeck, cited by Werner Neuer, *Man and Woman in Christian Perspective* (Wheaton, IL: Crossway, 1990), p. 93.
3. M. Aboth 1.5; cited by Neuer, *Men and Women*, p. 93.
4. Quoted in Phyllis Alsdurf, "Evangelical Feminists," *Christianity Today*, July 21, 1978, p. 47.
5. Gretchen Hull, *Equal to Serve* (Old Tappan, NJ: Revell, 1987), p. 115.
6. Virginia Mollenkott, "What Is True Biblical Feminism?" *Christian Life*, September 1977, p. 73.
7. Aida Spencer, *Beyond the Curse* (Nashville: Thomas Nelson, 1985), p. 45, italicized insert added.
8. Mollenkott, "What Is True Biblical Feminism?" p. 72.
9. Gilbert Bilezikian, *Beyond Sex Roles* (Grand Rapids: Baker Books, 1985), p. 56.
10. E. Margaret Howe, *Women and Church Leadership* (Grand Rapids: Zondervan, 1982), p. 139.
11. Letha Scanzoni and Nancy Hardesty, *All We're Meant to Be* (Waco, TX: Word, 1974), p. 72.
12. Scanzoni and Hardesty, *All We're Meant to Be*, pp. 18-19.
13. Virginia Mollenkott, *Women, Men, and the Bible* (Nashville: Abingdon, 1977), p. 104.
14. Grudem, "The Meaning of *Kephale* ('Head')," in Piper and Grudem, *Recovering Biblical Manhood and Womanhood* (Wheaton, IL: Crossway Books, 1990), p. 425.
15. Herbert and Fern Miles, *Husband-Wife Equality* (Old Tappan, NJ: Revell, 1978), p. 31.
16. Grudem, "The Meaning of *Kephale* ('Head')," in Piper and Grudem, *Recovering*, pp. 425-68.
17. Mary Kassian, *Women, Creation, and the Fall* (Westchester, IL: Crossway, 1990), p. 116.
18. G. J. Wenham, "The Ordination of Women" *The Churchman* 92 (1978), p. 316.
19. Wayne House, "Neither Male nor Female in Christ Jesus," *Bibliotheca Sacra*, January-March 1988, p. 54, emphasis added.
20. J. I. Packer, "Let's Stop Making Women Presbyters," *Christianity Today*, February 11, 1991, p. 21.
21. Norman Geisler, *Explaining Hermeneutics* (Oakland: International Council on Biblical Inerrancy, 1983), pp. 14-15.

30. Lessons from the Past

1. J. I. Packer, *Serving the People of God* (Great Britain: Paternoster Press, 1998), p. 25.
2. J. C. Ryle, *Holiness* (Moscow, ID: Charles Nolan, 2001), p. xxiii.
3. Ryle, *Holiness*, p. xv.
4. Packer, *Serving*, p. 23.

5. Packer, *Serving*, p. 23.
6. Timothy Ware, *The Orthodox Church* (New York: Penguin, 1983), p. 81.

31. Loving in the Present

1. J. I. Packer, *Serving the People of God* (Great Britain: Paternoster Press, 1998), p. 27, emphasis in original.